D0081174

FROM STEEL TO SLOTS

ATM

From Steel to Slots

Casino Capitalism in the Postindustrial City

CHLOE E. TAFT

Harvard University Press
Cambridge, Massachusetts, & London, England / 2016

Printed in the United States of America

First printing

Frontispiece: Photo by Chloe E. Taft, with agreement from Sands Casino Bethlehem, 2015.

Library of Congress Cataloging-in-Publication Data

Names: Taft, Chloe E., author.
Title: From steel to slots : casino capitalism in the postindustrial city / Chloe E. Taft.
Description: Cambridge, Massachusetts : Harvard University Press, 2016. | Includes bibliographical references and index.
Identifiers: LCCN 2015038199 | ISBN 9780674660496 (alk. paper : alk. paper)
Subjects: LCSH: Casinos—Pennsylvania—Bethlehem. | Globalization—Pennsylvania—Bethlehem. | Bethlehem (Pa.)—Economic conditions—21st century.
Classification: LCC HV6711 .T34 2016 | DDC 338.4/77950974822—dc23
LC record available at http://lccn.loc.gov/2015038199

To my family

Contents

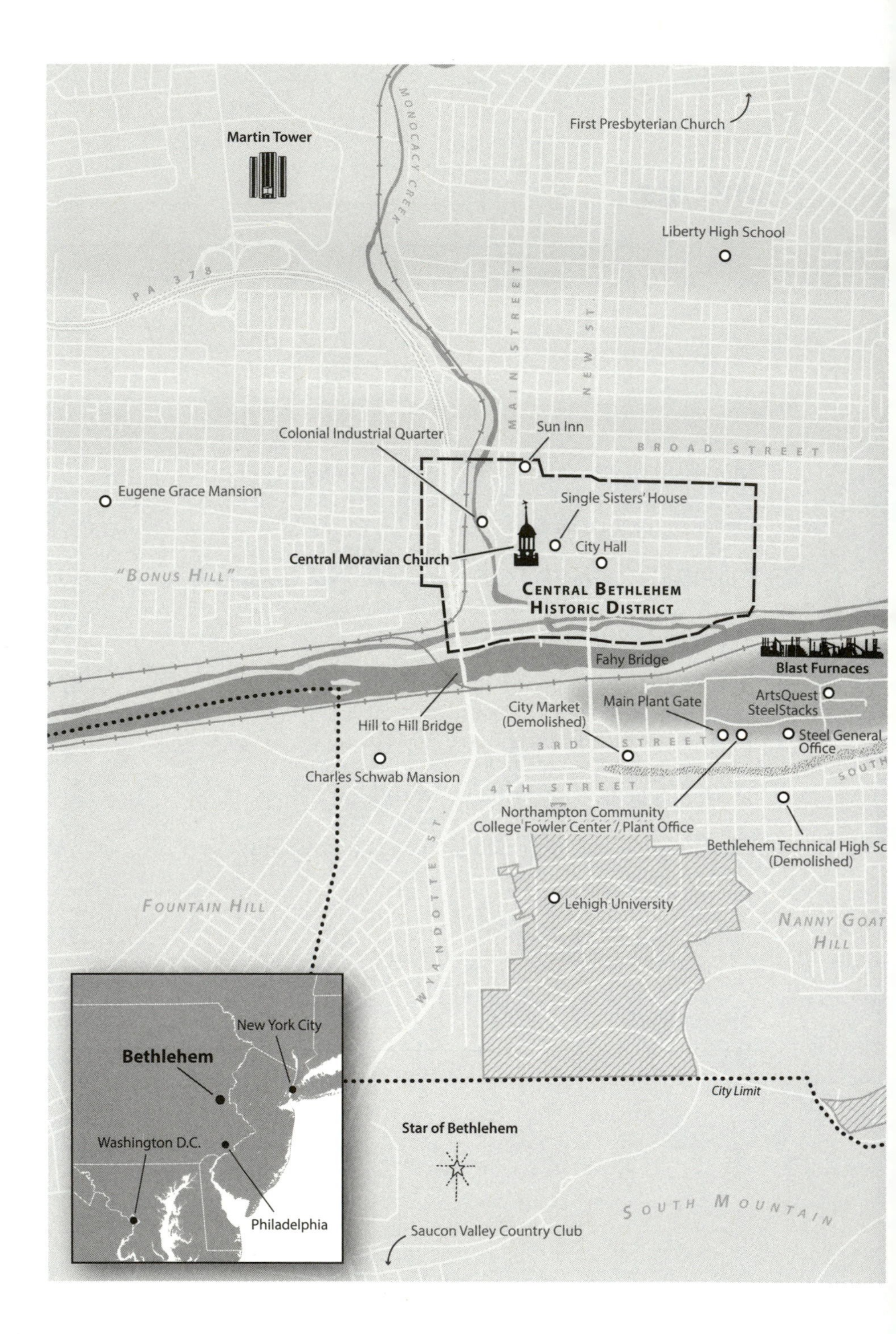
Martin Tower
First Presbyterian Church
Monocacy Creek
Liberty High School
PA 378
Main Street
New St.
Colonial Industrial Quarter
Sun Inn
Broad Street
Eugene Grace Mansion
Single Sisters' House
City Hall
Central Moravian Church
"Bonus Hill"
Central Bethlehem Historic District
Fahy Bridge
Blast Furnaces
ArtsQuest SteelStacks
Main Plant Gate
City Market (Demolished)
Hill to Hill Bridge
Steel General Office
3rd Street
Charles Schwab Mansion
4th Street
Northampton Community College Fowler Center / Plant Office
Bethlehem Technical High Sc
(Demolished)
Wyandotte St.
Fountain Hill
Lehigh University
Nanny Goat Hill
New York City
Bethlehem
Washington D.C.
Philadelphia
City Limit
Star of Bethlehem
South Mountain
Saucon Valley Country Club

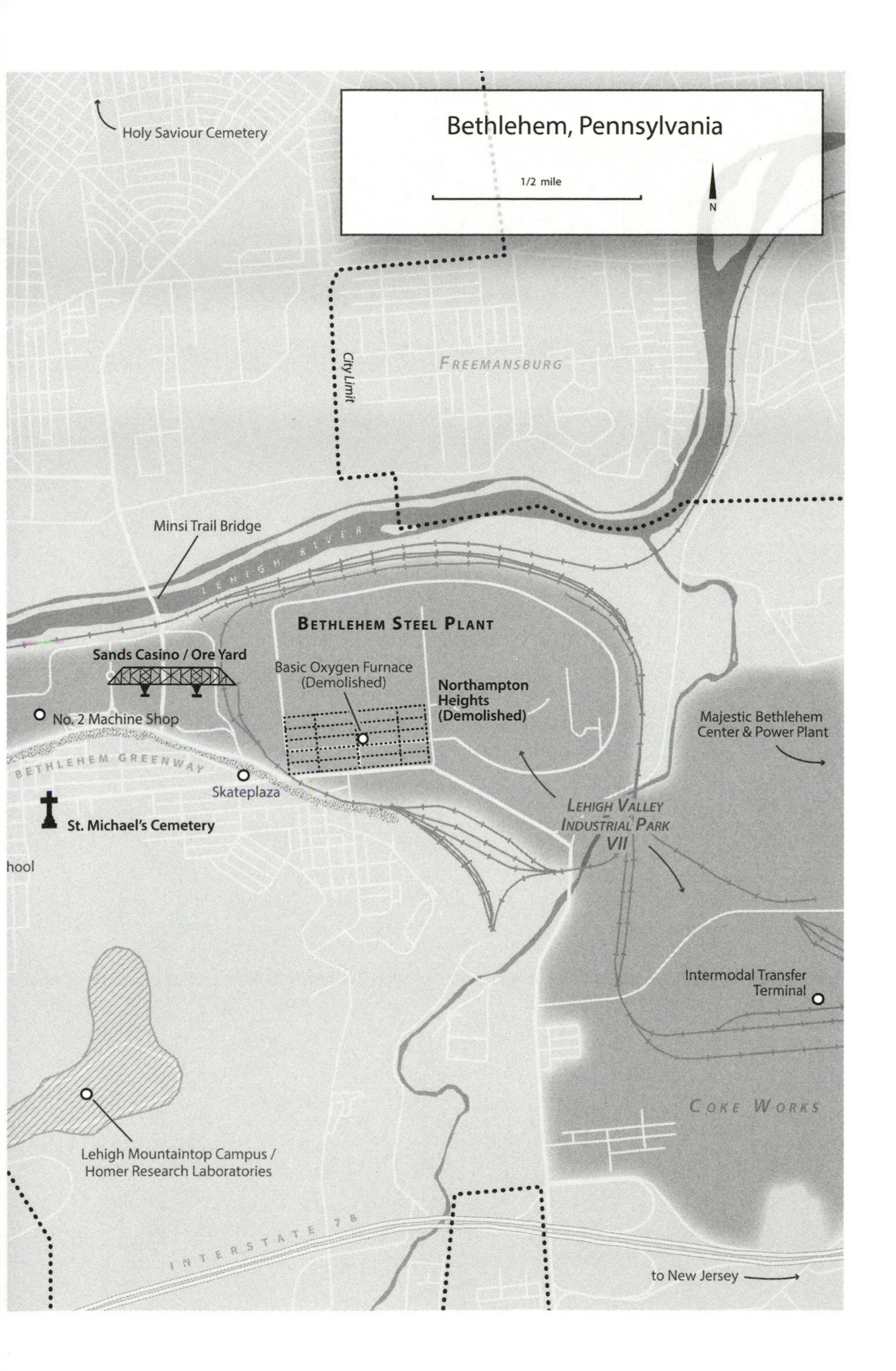

Bethlehem, Pennsylvania
1/2 mile
N
Holy Saviour Cemetery
City Limit
Freemansburg
Minsi Trail Bridge
Lehigh River
Bethlehem Steel Plant
Sands Casino / Ore Yard
Basic Oxygen Furnace
(Demolished)
Northampton
Heights
(Demolished)
No. 2 Machine Shop
Majestic Bethlehem
Center & Power Plant
Bethlehem Greenway
Skateplaza
St. Michael's Cemetery
Lehigh Valley
Industrial Park
VII
hool
Intermodal Transfer
Terminal
Coke Works
Lehigh Mountaintop Campus /
Homer Research Laboratories
Interstate 78
to New Jersey

Introduction

Grand Openings and Closings

BERNIE HOVAN is the go-to guy in Bethlehem, Pennsylvania, for reporters, filmmakers, and ethnographers who want to talk to a former steelworker. He meets their expectations on first impression: a world-worn, hobbling man in his late seventies whose parents immigrated to the United States from Eastern Europe in the early twentieth century to work at one of the largest industrial companies in the world. Bernie has lived on the same block his entire life, down the street from his Slovak Catholic Church and half a mile from the Bethlehem Steel plant's main gate. From his father's first day in 1910 to Bernie's retirement in 1994, his family, including all eight brothers, worked at "the Steel," as it is called locally, for a combined 441 years.

In 1939, when Bernie was a child growing up in the shadow of the mill, eight authors from the Federal Writers' Project came to Bethlehem to compile a guidebook of the region. The North Side of the city had been founded as a religious settlement and was rich in historical structures, but the industrial landscape that dominated the South Side captivated the writers. There, the Bethlehem Steel Corporation, the second largest steelmaker in the world, was beginning to exit the Great Depression by revving up production of wartime munitions. "With its miles of brazen-tongued plants," the authors wrote, "it is a labyrinth of sprawling buildings, towering stacks, gigantic, seething furnaces, and miles of criss-crossed railroad tracks." Thousands of the region's workers "daily answer[ed] the summons of the factory siren."[1] In addition to the plant, this small city west of New York City hosted Bethlehem Steel's corporate headquarters for a global network of factories, shipyards, and mines. Local employment at Bethlehem

Steel peaked at over 31,000 people in 1943, and the corporation as a whole employed nearly 300,000 people that year.[2] It was the sort of bustling city within a city that characterized factory towns across the American urban landscape during the twentieth century.

Even if one was not directly employed at the Steel, for the better part of a century its rhythms and scale dictated the social and cultural order of the Bethlehem community, including where one lived and with whom one interacted. In the early decades of the twentieth century, immigrant families like Bernie's clustered in the dense South Side neighborhoods near the mill, while steel executives and other professionals increasingly settled across the river to the north or in the suburbs. Between 1937 and 1941, Bethlehem Steel and other major American steel manufacturers finally were compelled to recognize the steelworkers' union after decades of confrontations. The former paternalistic system of welfare capitalism—in which keeping labor happy through corporate picnics, employee baseball and soccer teams, and basic benefits was seen as being in the corporation's best interest—slowly evolved into the more formally negotiated and regulated union-management contract.[3]

The concept that labor and capital could prosper together gained traction post–World War II, and in communities across the industrial North, laborers and their families achieved hard-fought assurance of long-term job security and high wages. Indeed, when Bernie began working at the Steel in the 1950s, it seemed that both organized labor and management would continue to mutually benefit from the arrangement. This "social contract" between corporations and their host communities appeared unbreakable across much of the United States. Thousands of people moved firmly into the middle class, and often into new neighborhoods with lawns and garages, in the decades that followed. But like many other former bastions of industrial manufacturing, the Bethlehem plant began a long, slow decline by the 1970s and locked its gates for good in 1998. The corporation, which had once appeared too big to fail, filed for bankruptcy three years later.

Since the closure, Bernie has found himself a local icon of this familiar rise-and-fall narrative of the steel industry, and he is generally happy to oblige. In his booming voice, he recounts to anyone who will listen his cache of carefully rehearsed stories about his work at the plant, complete with practiced pauses and dramatic tear-ups. Bernie's living room is a storehouse of Bethlehem Steel and New York Yankees memorabilia, with five silent, rusting blast furnaces visible from the back porch of his half-a-double house completing the backdrop. Today, not only is the steel factory defunct, but a parish consolidation has stripped his church of its ethnic Slovak heritage. His neighborhood is now majority Latino.

A closer look at the transformations in Bethlehem's social, economic, and physical landscapes, however, suggests there is more to this story. In this book, I explore how locals have variously embraced and grappled with the remaking of their steel town as a postindustrial city. To do so, they must confront the haunting presence of the city's past in the spaces all around them. These are spaces in which legacies of changing economies and visions of forward progress converge and make clear that urban development does not benefit all citizens equally.

My approach to understanding this period of transition is both historical and ethnographic. My research involved time spent in archives, living in Bethlehem, and interviewing dozens of past and present residents, methods on which I elaborate in the Appendix. Those familiar with Bethlehem may recognize some of the people in this book, but not their names. With a few exceptions, the people that I interviewed between 2009 and 2013, including Bernie, are identified in the following pages by pseudonyms to protect their privacy. In most cases, this was their request. My second intent in using pseudonyms was not to take away from rich personal biographies or to deny credit for their perspectives, but to highlight that the voices included in this story reflect worldviews shared by many others. Certain figures are identified by their real names: elected or corporate officials regularly quoted in national and local media such as Bethlehem Steel's former CEO, the local casino president, and the city's mayor; and those whose voices and actions come not from my own interviews or observations, but from the historical record.

In my conversations with Bernie, I caught a first glimpse of the ways in which the Steel's legacy has been used as a tool to refashion a new, collective vision of the future. In many ways, Bernie's willingness to serve as the aging embodiment of a former way of life casts the European immigrant steelworker as what anthropologist Kathryn Dudley calls "the new American primitive," someone left behind by an evolving society. To onlookers, the closing of the industrial plant in Bethlehem—as in so many other cities—seemed to create a perfect mile marker in a collective narrative of progress, requiring that the heyday of the plant's operation and the workers that sustained it be relegated to a past way of life, to obsolescence, in order to move ahead to a new economic model.[4]

In fact, just a mile east of Bernie's home and the Steel's tired blast furnaces stands an exemplar of this "new economy." After Bethlehem Steel's bankruptcy, city leaders placed their chips on the growing gaming industry to attract new jobs and tax revenues.[5] In 2009, an outpost of the Las Vegas Sands Corporation, the largest casino-resort operator in the world, opened amid the crumbling factory buildings. The Sands Casino Bethlehem quickly became one of the most profitable gaming destinations in the state of Pennsylvania and in the Mid-Atlantic region. Now that thousands of flashing slot machines and digital bells have replaced the fire in the blast furnaces and the shift-change whistles of the industrial workplace, the landscape materializes regional, national, and global shifts over the past several decades from an era of manufacturing dominance to an economy based in service, entertainment, and finance.

Taking this evocative landscape as an entry point, I complicate the narrative of economic rebirth and make clear that this forward march is not necessarily a firm break with the past, nor is it inevitable. Rather, new understandings of "the postindustrial" emerge that messily blur past, present, and future. The casino sits on what was formerly a storage area for mountains of iron ore, the raw material used to make steel. Today, Las Vegas Sands has appropriated the yard's twenty-ton ore bridge, originally used to move the material, as the scaffolding for its glowing red sign. The building itself is industrial-themed, new construction dressed up in steel trusses and factory-style roofs. The casino's design team explicitly chose to emphasize the plant's energy "circa 1942," at the peak of the Steel's production and gains in union protections. Orange light fixtures over the slot machines and gambling tables evoke molten steel. Rather than dispense with the past, the design deliberately reincorporates the local landscape and its history into a plan for the community's future. Reactions to the casino make clear, however, that in a community not far removed from the memories of the Steel's operation, the effects of this kind of temporal convergence are not always predictable.

The Bill Weiner Collection

Ore Bridge, Then and Now

The new casino was built on the site of the former Bethlehem Steel ore yards, shown here (top) in a circa 1915 postcard. The High House, which is still standing behind the casino, is visible in the back left of the image. The massive ore bridge that now bears the Sands insignia (bottom) is original to the site. (The Bill Weiner Collection from "Beyond Steel: An Archive of Lehigh Valley Industry and Culture" at Lehigh University; Michael McNett, Las Vegas Sands Corp., 2009.)

We embed social expectations in spaces all around us: in buildings, ruins, vacant lots, and in nature. The postindustrial landscape is laden with contradictory meanings and motivations; structures and their traces act as touchstones for negotiating complex relationships between corporate powers and the communities in which they operate. Where locals still habitually reference "the Steel" that once dominated the South Side of the city, the new casino complex quickly gained the shorthand "the Sands." Through their words, actions, and lived experiences, residents turn spaces of economic transaction into meaningful *places* brimming with cultural associations—both positive and negative—that demand to be reckoned with.[6]

When the Sands opened its doors over Memorial Day weekend in 2009, it set state records for new activity. In just four days, more than 60,000 people wagered almost $61 million at the slot machines and lost a total of $5.4 million.[7] The casino's grand opening ceremony followed two weeks later. It was a symbolic gathering of the governor who had legalized gaming in Pennsylvania five years earlier, the Bethlehem mayor and other local dignitaries, and Las Vegas Sands Corp. executives, with a few hundred invited guests. Anticipating and hoping to manage the weighty implications of opening a casino on the steel company's former ore yard, Las Vegas Sands reinvented the new building's "ribbon cutting" by asking ironworkers to burn through a ceremonial steel chain with a blowtorch instead. After breaking the symbolic shackles of the past, Sands sounded a 620-pound whistle from the S.S. *Normandie*, a French cruise liner whose salvaged whistle had perched atop the plant's now-demolished No. 1 Boiler House for thirty-five years. As the master of ceremonies explained, the whistle was used at the Steel until 1984 "to signify it was time to start work." Now the casino, after its first weeks of economic activity and its promise of community revitalization, was laying claim to the Steel's legacy: Las Vegas Sands was putting Bethlehem back on the payroll. No one mentioned that after the early 1950s the whistle was used only to sound plant emergencies, a reference of warning that might have complicated the intended symbolism of its latest blast.[8]

Bernie was one of three former steelworkers invited to speak at the ceremony. Although he had resisted entreaties from the site's development team to endorse the casino's campaign for a gaming license and a green light from the state a few years earlier, he welcomed the opportunity to participate in the celebration of its success. In many ways he fit into developers' plans for the postindustrial future much like the ore bridge and the whistle—as a relic of a past way of life that could be juxtaposed against new activity. But Bernie's visible pleasure at sharing his stories instead challenged the idea that he was a "primitive" on display.[9]

Concerned about his tendency to let stories run too long for gathered crowds, Bernie chose to memorize his speech ahead of time. "So I stood up, I told them, 'Thank you for inviting me,' and then I went into what I had to memorize," he explained to me two years later. Tapes of the event reveal that Bernie remained seated and nonetheless spoke at length, telling one of his favorite stories about how as a boy he complained that the noise of the blast furnaces kept him awake at night, to his father's prescient scolding that he would cry on the day that they stopped. But as Bernie remembered the ceremony, he was direct and to the point.

> I says, "To the people of the Sands who have given their time to make this possible." And I says, "To the City of Bethlehem that this could be possible. And thanks to Bethlehem Steel, that great steel company, that they can have something like this on their grounds. And to the museum people that are going to be neighbors. And last, but not least, to the Steelworkers' Archives for all of their endeavors, their pursuits, yesterday, today, and tomorrow. If I may say with my eyes full of water and my lips quivering to all of them and you, may the good Lord make smooth the path in their life. God bless you and thank you."[10]

With his speech, Bernie subverted the celebration of Las Vegas Sands to instead emphasize his grief at the plant's closure and his relationship to the Steelworkers' Archives, the organization of retired workers of which he has been a member since its creation in 2001. This opportunity, he told me, was the reason he could openly oppose the casino when it bid for a state license but still support this event. "When I was talking, I kept myself together. I didn't want to break down. I didn't want to. But I did. Inside I did." Bernie's loyalty remained tied to his peers whose smooth path in life, he suggested, was roadblocked by the Steel's closing a decade earlier. From his perspective, the opening of the new casino was more about the continued relevance of what used to be on the site than what has been built for the future.

The ongoing transformation of the landscape in Bethlehem leaves open the possibility of multiple interpretations coexisting in the postindustrial moment. With its casino, Las Vegas Sands architecturally referenced a once-stable past to help make risky investments palatable. To some eyes Bernie's performance as "former steelworker" at the building's celebration illustrated the passing of a way of life, a classic ritual in which one moves from one distinct state to another.[11] But to others the emphasis of his words and his active participation in this characterization called attention to the persistent presence of former steelworkers in the community instead of their displacement. He challenged a perceived lack of social protections in the new economy by invoking memories of a more mutually beneficial relationship between corporations and communities. The Bethlehem Steel site is in this case one of potential, some of which may not represent a clear break with the past. Residents, developers, corporate interests, and politicians locate cultural continuities in and through what planner Kevin Lynch called the "temporal collage" of the urban landscape to both legitimate and contest the destabilizing effects of capital mobility.[12]

By exploring the relationship between past, present, and future as made material in the landscape, I move beyond familiar narratives of factory closures that emphasize economic rupture, social trauma, and barren wastelands. As "deindustrialization" joined the American lexicon with gusto in the 1980s to describe the downsizing, relocation, and closure of U.S. factories, such stories came to define decline in America's so-called Rust Belt, the stretch of country between the Northeast and Midwest in which Bethlehem is situated. Scholars and journalists wrote of the "death" of industrial towns, the "tragedy" of economic decline, and the "shock" and "deluge of plant shutdowns."[13]

To think of deindustrialization as a finite moment or breaking point, however, occludes the diversity of experiences and interpretations of ongoing economic change.[14] In comparison to steel towns such as Youngstown, Ohio, for example, in which three major plants closed within five years of each other, Bethlehem's loss of its lifeblood manufacturer was a longer decline. The fits and starts of the Steel's drawn-out process of disinvestment and downsizing in Bethlehem created a more contradictory and less comprehensible experience of change, not the uniform shock of closure that has been represented in other locales.[15] At the same time, Bethlehem in many ways epitomizes another familiar narrative. Sociologist Daniel Bell declared "the coming of post-industrial society" in 1973 to refer to broad economic shifts underway in the United States that included the growth of the service, health care, education, and technology industries.[16] Today, two regional hospital networks are by far the largest employers in the Lehigh Valley. The utilities, gas products, grocery, and medical technology industries also have local hubs. Lehigh University, Moravian College, and Northampton Community College boast campuses within Bethlehem's city limits, and eight more colleges and universities operate in neighboring cities.

Even as Bethlehem's transformation intersects with well-known trends of industrial decline and postindustrial rebirth, its story is uniquely shaped by local contingencies. Unlike other poster cities for deindustrialization such as Camden, New Jersey, or Flint, Michigan, Bethlehem and the surrounding communities of the Lehigh Valley have fared reasonably well by certain measures of economic health. For example, Bethlehem never lost the swaths of population that so-called "shrinking cities" like Detroit or Buffalo did.[17] While those cities' populations in 2010 represented just 39 percent and 45 percent of their respective postwar peaks, by the same year Bethlehem had regained its peak population of 75,000 from 1960; it never lost more than 7 percent of its residents.[18] Thanks in large part to the casino and other development and adaptive reuse on the former Steel site, the city also has recovered the tax base that it lost with the plant's closure, and those tax revenues continue to grow.

Many other Rust Belt community studies have focused primarily on the immediate effects of factory closures on unemployed union industrial workers. But if one zooms out enough, in Bethlehem one finds a relatively healthy community extending far beyond the plant gates. With the diversification of its economy, Bethlehem's poverty and unemployment rates rank among the lowest of similarly sized former manufacturing towns in the region. Its home values and median household incomes rank among the highest.[19] Many area residents commute to work in nearby New York and New Jersey but live in the Lehigh Valley to take advantage of lower property taxes and costs of living. They delight in Bethlehem's small-town feel and picturesque downtown. The city has emerged as a cultural hub in the region, with a robust schedule of community festivals and events, from intimate documentary film screenings to an annual music festival each August that regularly attracts more than one million people.

But to paint Bethlehem as a picture of postindustrial success again elides the more variegated reality. As others have noted in communities ravaged by capital disinvestment and restructuring, economic recovery affects populations unevenly. Developers' profit motives, it turns out, are often at odds with collective needs, and not all citizens reap the same benefits that boosters of revitalization widely promise.[20] Another look at the casino's opening ceremony affirms that Bethlehem is no exception.

A Postindustrial Photo Op

After the ceremony concluded, Bernie found himself being ushered back to the stage for photographs. He walked into a snapshot of the city's uneasy transition from an economy based on industrial production to one dominated by capital transactions. The chief celebrant at the event was Sheldon Adelson, the chairman of Las Vegas Sands Corp., who is consistently ranked among the top ten wealthiest people in the United States. Although at the time of the grand opening Adelson was valued at $3.4 billion, having lost $22 billion in twelve months during the global economic recession, his fortune by the time I spoke to Bernie had rebounded to $23 billion and would soon reach $38 billion.[21] "This guy from the Sands, he just come back from Singapore," Bernie recounted. "He's a billionaire working with the Sands people in Nevada. And he's loaded with money. And they just built one [a casino] in Singapore and it's thriving, it's doing excellent business. And he helped to build this one with his money, see."

Bernie's description both humanized Adelson as "this guy" who decided to "help" out a city in need by building a casino, and distanced him as a jet-setting billionaire relative to Bernie's lifetime residence on a single block and his attenuated monthly pension. The contradiction was amplified when Bernie talked to Adelson as they organized the photo ops. "Him and I are talking while they're setting up everything. And we're talking just like I'm talking to you. He asked me how old I was, what I did in the steel company." Bernie discovered they were born the same year, 1933, both the sons of poor European immigrants. Bernie dropped out of high school; Adelson dropped out of college. Despite this play at brotherhood, however, the two men's life trajectories have diverged in significant ways.

Bernie labored forty-three years as a rigger, a skilled but physically demanding craft that often required working in the elements or at heights with extremely large and heavy equipment. His jobs included rebuilding furnaces, disassembling old buildings, lifting presses, and fixing machinery. After a lifetime of grueling demands, today Bernie stands with difficulty and needs a cane to maneuver. His body is a testament to the serious strains of industrial labor, trade-offs that are often forgotten when we romanticize the economic heyday of the American working class. Adelson's mobility is also limited, by a nerve condition called peripheral neuropathy, but in other ways the years have been less harsh. Adelson's career took him through the worlds of finance and technology, where he seeded his self-made fortune by developing the premier trade show for the computer industry in 1979. He purchased the Sands Hotel & Casino in Las Vegas, the Rat Pack's old haunt, in 1988, ultimately imploding the landmark building in 1996 to make way for The Venetian. He has been at work extending his casino empire around the globe ever since, particularly in Asia, where he reaps the vast majority of his profits. After Adelson took Las Vegas Sands Corp. public in 2004, he was reported to earn roughly a million dollars an hour.[22]

"I was on all of the pictures that they were taking," Bernie told me with a smile. "And his wife and her mother and her sister, they're all around me and giving me hugs." Bernie's excitement recounting the attention he received was palpable, though it is hard to ignore the underlying economic interests that were performed on the stage that day. To be the recipient of hugs from the Adelson family may play at erasing class differences, but it ultimately relegates Bernie to a grandfatherly role in which the symbolic patriarch of Bethlehem's industrial lineage has ceded control to the next generation of entertainment-industry tycoons. Typified as unionized steelworker and capitalist to most observers, the two men readily embodied and enacted distinct roles that seemed to fit the basic narrative of factory decline and postindustrial revitalization.

Adelson's participation in this ritual of economic progress and promise, however, was nearly as complicated as Bernie's. He was not well received as a figurehead of prosperity in Bethlehem. During his speech at the ceremony he remarked, "In Hebrew, Bethlehem means 'the house of bread.' And what do you need to make bread? Dough. That's what we intend to make here."[23] In a community that prided itself for most of the twentieth century on making durable steel goods for a locally headquartered corporation, Adelson plays the role of absentee capitalist well. His part in the drama reflects the disjuncture that scholars have noted between community and capital in the wake of deindustrialization.[24] With the increasing mobility of global capital, they argue, multinational corporations no longer invest in local places, preferring to jump ship when more favorable labor, environmental, or tax terms present themselves. At the root is a tension between individual profit interests and social commitments.

This tenuous relationship between private capital and public good is a defining feature of urban planning in the postindustrial American city. In contrast to Germany's Ruhr Valley, for example, where an infusion of state resources has transformed former industrial sites into vibrant heritage parks, cities in the United States have faced a steep decline in public funding since the 1970s. Most twenty-first-century investments in urban revitalization in the United States instead take the form of public-private partnerships, where cities and states offer tax abatements and other incentives to attract a range of private development projects, from office towers and warehouses to condominiums and stadiums.[25]

Within this context, former industrial regions across the country are turning to legalized gambling and the construction of new casinos to generate jobs and tax revenues. But what happens when casino corporations are asked to lead economic development well beyond the gambling floor, when they in effect become urban planners? Government bodies that look to gambling to address fiscal crises tout the casino model's ability to spark additional community investments and new tax income for public infrastructure. Host cities seek interventions in more direct ways as well. Casino corporations often pay to improve traffic flows by designing new interchanges. They beautify public spaces near their entrances, and they contract with local suppliers and construction crews. Critics, however, voice concerns about casinos' service-sector wages, negative social consequences, and the failures of earlier models to sustain equitable urban revitalization. Residents of Atlantic City, for example, continue to face extreme poverty levels and have gone decades at a time without a grocery store. Parallel tensions arise in locales dependent on development projects such as prisons or hydraulic fracturing ("fracking") that likewise are led by industries that profit from the competitive extraction of communities' capital, resources, or people.[26] All of these plans for corporate-led revitalization reshape local landscapes in materially, economically, and culturally profound ways.

The unequal costs and benefits of redevelopment in these cases generally compound along lines of class, race, and ethnicity. American cities have long histories of spatial division and uneven distribution of resources. From the massive federal urban renewal projects following World War II to the intensifying impacts of gentrification since the 1970s, rehabilitating urban centers and neighborhoods often means removing the least powerful residents—whether by mandate or as an aftereffect of increased real-estate prices—in order to reclaim spaces for more "desirable" and profitable uses.[27] Urban patterns are shaped in ways that are at once more subtle and intractable as well. Poor residents of color, for example, generally bear the brunt of exposure to industrial pollution, other toxic developments like landfills, and the negative health effects that result.[28] Over the course of the twentieth century, exclusive racial covenants, neighborhood redlining to deny home mortgages to minorities, and the subsidized relocation of factories and white, male-headed households to the suburbs all protected dominant populations' real-estate values and bolstered industry profits at the expense of those most in need. Indeed, racial, ethnic, and class segregation have been enforced and entrenched in so many ways over the past century that wide disparities in access to employment, home equity, and effective schools are a defining feature of the American city today.[29]

Even as Bethlehem's white collar professionals link into and benefit from regional economic growth, encouraging statistics about the city's overall health mask the fact that poverty rates on the South Side have risen. An inflow of migrants and immigrants from Puerto Rico, the Dominican Republic, and other parts of Latin America since World War II has changed the demographic makeup of former steelworker neighborhoods like Bernie's. Many newer Latino residents have moved to the Lehigh Valley from New York as they struggle to find affordable housing and adequate employment in an economy that prioritizes advanced degrees and a command of the English language. Meanwhile, Las Vegas Sands' business plan for the Bethlehem casino—one that has proven to be highly profitable—relies on busing in thousands of gamblers each day from New York's Chinatowns. Many of the Asian bus riders are unemployed or underemployed; they seek windfalls at the baccarat tables or smaller gains by reselling free-play vouchers. Asian casino employees hired to cater to this clientele have found homes in the same South Side neighborhoods as other immigrant groups. Instead of recognizing common histories and interests in regaining the social protections that characterized the heyday of the steel industry, the longtime white residents, Latino immigrants, and new Asian visitors and dealers clash as they struggle to stake out a place in the divided postindustrial city. In an economic and political climate where corporate influence over urban planning and urban life is a given, residents must look for ways to assert expectations for more inclusive community benefits and accountability.

Casino Capitalism, Market-places, and the Uses of History

In many ways, the casino industry offers the perfect entrée to explore the multifaceted meanings and uneven experiences of postindustrialism, much in the same way that steelmaking had come to stand in for American manufacturing as a whole. The flip side of the economic restructuring that fed deindustrialization is the thriving but dangerously volatile finance economy that it ushered in. As political economy scholars have argued, both trends were impacted by so-called neoliberal reforms that gained traction in the 1970s with their business-friendly approaches to regulation, the globalization of profit interests, and the decimation of social protections for workers and the places in which corporations operate. Susan Strange coined the term "casino capitalism" in 1986 to characterize the wild speculation underpinning the global financial markets that increasingly signal and prop up economic growth.[30]

Despite the purported placeless quality of this "new economy," events like Sands Bethlehem's opening ceremony show how the "casino" form of capitalism is institutionalized locally through public policy, corporate agendas, and the built environment itself. Casinos, which have proliferated worldwide in recent decades, metaphorically encapsulate how an economic culture in which high-stakes gambles are rewarded has remade the relationship between capital and community. In place of the postwar social safety net and its culture of collective stability is an assumption that aligning with global profit structures by embracing flexibility, mobility, and short-term opportunities carries the most promise for individual advancement. Much as gambling seeks to erase past failures with dreams of future jackpots, neoliberal capitalism is fundamentally forward looking.

In places like Bethlehem, where people, capital, and policies have long crossed fixed boundaries, the casino acts as an anchor for understanding how global market trends relate to local lived experiences. As community members strive each day to bring liquid capital and its potential social benefits back down to the ground, they use the in-between space of the postindustrial landscape to interpret and address ongoing preservation and redevelopment initiatives, neoliberal economic policies, and shifting demographic patterns.

In this book, I locate a network of market-*places* on the former Bethlehem Steel site and the surrounding neighborhoods through which people give abstract economic actions historical, material, and cultural significance. Whether in the distinction of where residents hang colored as opposed to white Christmas lights to attract tourists, developers' efforts to historicize a former Bethlehem Steel office tower as a landmark of corporate greed, or cultural tensions over casino day trippers' uses of park space, the social construction of place in Bethlehem regularly connects local experiences and legacies to global contexts and transactions. The layered meanings, values, and interests attached to these sites signal the ways in which terms like community and capital, moral and economic, preservation and development, and local and global are not so much contradictory as they are continuously co-produced.

As with the casino's opening ceremony, I argue in particular that the postindustrial landscape muddies distinctions between past and present. History becomes the primary cultural tool used to make sense of, or "place," economic change. It also acts as a political weapon.[31] The choices made to tie the Sands Casino's design to the Steel's industrial legacy, for example, reflect the unsettled balance of power between those who demand that a former way of life be commemorated, and those who employ that same history to validate risky, new-economy investments. The postindustrial landscape is not a blank slate, but a rich resource of past associations and memories that are regularly mined for political, economic, and social purposes. In stressing the fluidity and overlap of these meanings and uses, the concept of the market-place uncovers opportunities for developers and global financiers to realign profit motives with the desires of local communities.

Importantly, although development agendas with an eye on new futures add urgency to efforts to protect the past, asserting place-based values to regain a sense of control amid economic transitions is not unique to the postindustrial era. Local actors have invoked the past and exploited memories to both interpret and shape the risk-based landscapes of global capitalism since the city's founding in 1741 by the Moravians. This band of persecuted Eastern European communitarians developed Bethlehem as its primary North American missionary outpost. The Moravians found a market in the nineteenth century for their handcrafted wares among outsiders who saw the "quaint" religious settlement as being set apart from the industrial revolution. Later, as the town expanded to include non-Moravians, the rapidly growing Bethlehem Steel Company and the Catholic Church cooperated to recruit immigrant labor to work at the plant across the river and build churches that commemorated Old World identities. I explore Bethlehem's framing as a heritage tourism destination called "Christmas City, U.S.A." during the Great Depression and look at the convergence of historic preservation and urban renewal efforts to boost the city's economy during the 1950s and 1960s. In the aftermath of Bethlehem Steel's failed plans in the 1990s to turn the plant site into a "festival marketplace" that would honor the company's legacy, more recent Latino and Asian arrivals attach new memories and hopes to the former steelworker neighborhoods.

Other postindustrial towns that might once have bulldozed closed factories in a raze-and-forget strategy to replace rusting traces with shiny new futures have likewise turned to the archive and to adaptive reuse. Industrial landscapes are incorporated into calculated efforts to attract new urban residents with loft-style apartments or to capitalize on heritage tourism.[32] What is clear in this study of Bethlehem is that there are more than economic implications to these approaches. Like the ore bridge marking the entrance to the Sands Casino, the layered histories in the postindustrial landscape offer scaffolding with which a diverse range of citizens regularly build narratives and rituals that grapple with corporate agendas and modify cultural expectations that sustain forward-looking approaches to redevelopment. Memories of a time when high wages, social protections, and community commitments defined urban corporate presence are persistent. They shape interpretations of the postindustrial landscape in ways that create opportunities to push back on free-market logics and profit-driven business decisions that privilege individual aspirations at the expense of collective needs.

The experience in Bethlehem also reveals, however, that the barriers to more equitable urban development in postindustrial America loom large. Notions of collectivity continue to splinter under deep-rooted class and ethnic tensions, and social protections remain, for many, elusive. While Bethlehem and its casino cannot stand in for all communities given the particularities of corporate histories, demographics, and geographies, this site elucidates broad trends impacting market-places across the country that are attempting to reconcile legacies of capital disinvestment with new promises for revitalization. Postindustrial cities share certain commonalities, the primary one being that most redevelopment projects will have uneven effects. At the same time, local contexts are particular, and the many impacts of economic transitions are unpredictable and ongoing. This leaves us with a dynamic understanding of postindustrialism as an active process of negotiation rather than an inevitable end stage of market evolution.

Valuing the close relationship between the landscape and the everyday experiences of "casino capitalism" offers an opportunity to imagine interventions that go beyond superficial rehabilitation of built structures to address the social infrastructures that underlie them and the inequalities that threaten their durability. In this postindustrial space of potential, the landscape and built environment become narrative and ritual resources to bring divergent cultures into contact, resulting in new understandings of shared situations. In Bethlehem, as we will see, this process is far from complete. But recognizing how residents, politicians, corporations, and developers employ history as a tool for both legitimating neoliberal investment schemes and resisting their control is a first step in guiding redevelopment in American cities toward more inclusive and equitable outcomes in the twenty-first century.

1

Order in the Landscape

DAVID AND MARILYN LAMBERT live on the north side of the Lehigh River, just west of downtown Bethlehem in a modest home next door to their daughter. They moved to Bethlehem in 1956 when David took a professorship at Lehigh University. On his first interview for the position, the man whom he would replace took him on a tour of the city's South Side where the university and the steel plant are situated. David, now in his eighties, chuckled as he recalled his first impressions of the smoke, the blackened snow, and the tightly clustered double houses on the hilly streets rising from the plant's main gate. "I told Marilyn when I got back, I said, 'It's a good job, it's a good university and so on. But it's a terrible town!'" After much debate over this predicament, David accepted the position and took his wife with him on a second visit that May. This time, "we came in the north part of the town, which I hadn't seen." Across the river from the Steel, the North Side is the site of the city's original Moravian founding, still evident in the preserved stone buildings, the cream stucco Central Moravian Church, and the neatly kept homes. "Marilyn thought I had been kidding her all this time!"

The Lamberts pointed out for my benefit what has been obvious to Bethlehem natives and visitors since the eighteenth century. The Lehigh River not only splits the city geographically. A cultural and historical rift is embedded in the city's landscape and the meanings residents attach to its two sides. The division, which has ongoing implications for urban development in the city, was first institutionalized with the Moravians' arrival in 1741, when they founded Bethlehem as a religious communitarian settlement. Through the Moravians' influence, the heavy industry that evolved into the steel plant in the following century was kept separate, relegated to the opposite bank. Over the course of the nineteenth and twentieth centuries, this industrial divide became one of class and ethnicity as well. New immigrants and steelworkers who settled near the plant were perceived by wealthier and more established North Siders to be inferior.

But a 1,800-acre plant in the heart of the South Side could not be ignored. As the Steel gained economic and political clout during the twentieth century, the corporation increasingly shaped the city's social and cultural landscapes in addition to the physical terrain. The company's involvement in city planning and development projects ordered the built environment, while clearly defined workplace structures added a predictability to local employment that could be both stifling and appreciated for its stability. Separate neighborhoods, schools, and social clubs—often built with the Steel's money—put wealthy executives and blue-collar workers in their appropriate places. Particularly after the union gains and enhanced corporate profitability that followed World War II, many employees, from those on the shop floor to white-collar professionals in the offices, planned their lives around the social and economic benefits that came with a career at Bethlehem Steel. Even if short-term volatility in the industry meant frequent layoffs, the goal of secure retirement remained attainable.

Bethlehem Steel's long and slow decline beginning in the 1970s, however, undermined many of the social protections and economic guarantees that workers and residents had come to expect. The corporation ultimately shut down local operations in the 1990s and filed for bankruptcy in 2001. Through this process the Steel abandoned its pension and health care obligations, leaving workers and their families angry and betrayed. As the Steel's management prepared to close the Bethlehem plant, it nonetheless invested in preserving the corporation's legacy through a plan to convert the central parcel of the plant into a heritage tourism and entertainment destination. Rather than walk away from the plant and mark it as a site of postindustrial rupture, as corporations that razed factories in many other manufacturing towns did, Bethlehem Steel, local developers, and city politicians looked for opportunities to tie the industrial landscape to a different economic future. Many residents in the postindustrial city likewise seek ways to move on in a less stable and predictable climate by drawing on memories of a time when social expectations could literally be mapped out and corporate presence in the community, if not always positive, was constant.

Economic development agendas have remained a driving force in ordering, and disordering, community life and expectations since the Moravians first arrived. What the Lamberts saw in the dirty snow of the steelworker neighborhoods and their pleasant surprise at the North Side's stone buildings was the outcome of decades of economic and political decisions made visible and durable. In this landscape in which geographic, social, and cultural divisions have for centuries split the city, competing visions of Bethlehem's postindustrial community and who it should include have remained difficult to reconcile.

A History of Division

The Moravians founded Bethlehem in 1741 as their church's first permanent North American outpost from which to evangelize Native Americans and other European settlers. Also called the Unity of Brethren, this Protestant sect traces its origins to the fifteenth century in what is now the Czech Republic. After being persecuted and driven into exile, the Moravian Church was revived in eastern Germany under Count Nikolaus Ludwig von Zinzendorf in 1727 and quickly extended its reach throughout the Atlantic world. The renewed faith emphasized fellowship and a "religion of the heart" focused on emotional, and almost mystical, surrender to Christ rather than theological particularities. Moravians' fervent evangelism was a function of their ecumenism—a belief that true Christians existed among all peoples.[1] In time, the Moravians became known for their devotion to education and music as well.

Zinzendorf christened the Pennsylvania settlement with the name Bethlehem during a visit on Christmas Eve 1741, affirming the town's spiritual origins and purpose. But from the beginning, Bethlehem's mission also was economic. The town initially organized as a communitarian settlement where residents contributed to a common "Oeconomy" based around artisanal work and trade. Residents did not receive wages, but rather pooled their labor and resources to advance the local community and its missionary outreach, as well as that of the church headquarters in Germany.[2] By 1758 the Moravians had erected more than seventy buildings in Bethlehem and maintained dozens of Church-owned industries, including pottery, carpentry, and hat-making shops, as well as a black smithy, tannery, gristmill, and house for boiling soap.[3]

The Moravians were careful town planners. While many of the group's industrial works were located near Monocacy Creek, which branched north from the Lehigh River, community buildings were clustered up the hill around a central square. Residents lived in buildings organized by age, gender, and marital status, or "choirs." All unmarried women, for example, lived and worked together in the Single Sisters' House. As with most of the original buildings that remain standing and in use today, the choir houses were constructed in native limestone with brick accents and a strictly symmetrical design.[4] After its completion in 1806, Central Moravian Church with its intricate belfry became Bethlehem's dominant landmark. The church was designed to hold 1,500 congregants, even though the settlement was home to less than 600 people at the time.[5]

Bethlehem's unique communal economy and choir systems dissolved within a generation, and the community allowed for private enterprise and family living. The settlement and the church's farmland across the river to the south nonetheless remained closed to non-Moravian ownership or leases. Visitors, however, were welcome. Outsiders noted that the North Side community appeared to be set apart from the rapidly changing world around it. A tourist from Philadelphia remarked in 1790 on the quaint regularity of the Moravians' stone buildings. "There is an air of dignified simplicity remarkably exemplified through these several structures," she wrote. "The greatest order and unanimity is preserved in Bethlehem."[6]

By 1844 the settlement had a population of about 1,000, with numbers growing in the surrounding area. That year, the church began to allow non-Moravians to lease buildings and land, and South Side farms were sold, largely to pay off debt.[7] The Moravians took care, however, to maintain a distinction between their traditional way of life and the noise and dirt of the factories that soon dominated the other bank.[8] During the pervasive industrialization of the nineteenth century, visitors' nostalgic renderings of North Bethlehem intensified, increasingly painting the Moravian settlement as a cherished relic of the past. In 1881, a book describing the rise of manufacturing in the Lehigh Valley elaborated on this then-established distinction:

North Bethlehem

In this 1798 view looking north across the river at the Moravian settlement (top), the South Side is mostly forest and farmland. The stone masonry architecture of the original Moravian buildings, which still stand in Bethlehem's North Side downtown and have remained in continuous use, include the Bell House (1746) and Single Sisters' House (1744) shown here in 1937 (bottom). (Isaac Weld, *Travels Through the States of North America*, vol. 2, 1800, Beinecke Rare Book and Manuscript Library, Yale University; Ian McLaughlin, 1937, Historic American Buildings Survey, Library of Congress.)

> The traveler who arrives after nighfall [*sic*] will be startled by the angry tongues of furnace flame, shooting athwart the sky. He will catch momentary glimpses of active groups of half-naked men through the arched walls of the iron and steel works, and note the sickly hue of sulphurous fires at the zinc works beyond. . . . It is fortunate, however, that these great industries and railroad depot, together with a prosaic borough of workmen's houses are placed altogether upon the southern side of the river, leaving the old town opposite undisturbed in the possession of its richness of antiquated Moravian landmarks.[9]

Primary among these South Side industries was the Saucona Iron Company, founded in 1857. Easy access to the anthracite coalmines in the Lehigh Valley, coupled with the boom in railroad transport, helped the enterprise grow into the Bethlehem Iron Company and later, in 1899, into the Bethlehem Steel Company.

As in other industrial towns in the United States, the needs of the Bethlehem plant—as well as cement mills, quarries, mines, cigar factories, and silk mills in the region—brought thousands of immigrants, mostly from Southern and Eastern Europe, into the community during these formative decades. The population of South Bethlehem, where almost all of the new workers settled, increased nearly sixfold between 1870 and 1910, from 3,500 people to close to 20,000, 58 percent of whom were either foreign-born or children of immigrants.[10] The 1924 Johnson-Reed Act effectively ended the influx, but its impacts were lasting, and the area gained a reputation as being overtaken by foreign customs and vice. In 1927 the city's mayor declared: "Over 95 per cent of the crimes committed here take place on the South Side. It is there we have a preponderance of foreigners. In fact there are no less than forty-eight nationalities represented among the labor element on [*sic*] this city. It is among them that practically all the law violations occur." Meanwhile, other outsiders fueled the fire. Throughout the 1920s, weekend excursionists from New York City and New Jersey headed to the South Side for prohibited liquor, women, and gambling.[11]

As the operations and smoke of the steel plant reinforced perceptions of noise and grime then associated with foreigners, higher-ranking employees and executives at the Steel distanced themselves from the working-class neighborhoods. Charles Schwab, who became president of Bethlehem Steel

South Bethlehem

This 1935 photograph shows the close proximity of steelworkers' housing to the plant down the hill, as well as its density. The smoke-filled sky contrasts with North Side images of the leafy Moravian settlement. (Walker Evans, "Bethlehem Houses and Steel Mill," 1935, FSA/OWI Collection, Library of Congress.)

and incorporated the company in 1904, bought a mansion in Fountain Hill, a separate South Side borough west of the plant. Schwab had previously led the Carnegie Steel Company through its transition to the U.S. Steel Corporation, the nation's largest steel manufacturer. He then helped turn Bethlehem Steel into the next biggest company, largely based on his plan to produce a new type of structural beam for use in building skyscrapers. Between 1910 and 1915 Bethlehem Steel Corporation's employment doubled to 22,000 people.[12]

Schwab passed the presidency on to his protégé Eugene Grace in 1916. Grace had started at the plant as a crane operator and would head the company for the next thirty years. Rather than settle in Fountain Hill, in 1923 Grace bought a house that he expanded to twenty-three rooms in West Bethlehem, on the north side of the river by the old Moravian settlement. Grace and six other senior officers lived within a few blocks of each other on what became known as Bonus Hill—an allusion to their generous pay. The side streets housed aspiring junior executives, professionals, and businessmen.[13] The Steel Corporation had played an integral role in consolidating the separate boroughs of Bethlehem, South Bethlehem, and West Bethlehem into one city in 1917, in part because it hoped to maintain influence over local politics by offsetting South Side immigrant votes with those of wealthier and more business-friendly residents across the river.[14] Even after the Steel helped construct the Hill to Hill Bridge to physically link the two sides of the river in 1924, class distinctions between North and South persisted.

"See, Chloe, everybody in South Bethlehem wanted to get out of South Bethlehem," George Dias explained to me at the kitchen table of his sprawling Spanish deco North Side home. George, a soft-spoken man now in his mid-seventies, grew up above his family's furniture store on Third Street, directly across from the Steel's main gate. George's father had immigrated to Bethlehem from Spain in 1920. Though he founded his successful business soon after, he made money during Prohibition running liquor to New York and at least once found himself in the South Side jail down the street. George's mother, the daughter of Hungarian immigrants, grew up on Atlantic Street in an area known as Nanny Goat Hill. There, immigrants from Hungary, Poland, and Slovakia kept animals and gardens on the slopes of South Mountain. Some of the land technically belonged to Bethlehem Steel, but it was effectively treated as commons. During the winters, George and other neighborhood children went sledding down the narrow city streets past the groceries and bars that anchored every street corner. Each night, George went out with a pail and picked up lumps of coal that had jostled loose from the trains that meandered through the neighborhood, cutting just behind the furniture store. He took them home to fuel the kitchen stove. The city market, a hub of activity in the South Side's downtown business corridor, was a couple of blocks away, near chicken shops where women heated fifty-gallon drums of boiling water, dunked the birds in, and picked the feathers off. Pedestrians crossed to the other side of the street to avoid the stench.

The dirt and the smells and the noise of the steel mill beating all day and all night at the center of South Bethlehem were harder to evade. As long as the steel mill was in operation, and especially before state and federal environmental standards went into effect in the late 1960s and 1970s, residents grew accustomed to a persistent film of iron-rich red dirt that settled across the town.[15] Daily routines revolved around the shift-change whistles at seven in the morning, three in the afternoon, and eleven at night. As the whistles kept time in the masculine world of the dirt's production, women's lives were typically ordered by the rituals of removing it from their homes and sidewalks. They carefully gauged when to hang the laundry out between blasts from the furnace to keep from re-soiling the wash. Steelworkers changed out of their dirty work clothes in the welfare rooms at the plant and left them in buckets that swung on a chain and pulley system overhead. When they brought the clothes home, their wives washed them separately to contain the grime. South Side immigrants' efforts to keep their houses clean reflected a pride in owning property in America for the first time, an opportunity many had been denied in Eastern Europe.[16] In the classic words of anthropologist Mary Douglas, when understood as part of a cultural system, "dirt is essentially disorder," or "matter out of place." Eliminating it through cleaning was not only a practical exercise of hygiene. It was also a symbolic effort to order social and moral worlds, a purification ritual that drew clear boundaries.[17]

Like the executives on Bonus Hill, wealthier residents strove equally hard to keep the taint of the mill from their homes, often by choosing to live across the river closer to the neatly arranged Moravian downtown or in the suburbs beyond. Betty Bramson moved to Bethlehem with her husband Robert, a salesman for the Steel, in 1962. They settled on the North Side, where they still live, three miles from the plant. Like other white-collar residents, they sought some separation from the steel mill and the crowded working-class neighborhoods, but sometimes geographical distance wasn't enough:

BB: I couldn't believe when I moved down here, Chloe. I had grown up in Springfield [Massachusetts]. Well, while we had industry up there, [it was] certainly nothing like Bethlehem Steel. And you could dust your house once a week. Coming down here with those blast furnaces running, you had to dust every day.

CT: Even in this house? Wow.

BB: Because it would, the air would just cause the particulates to float all over the place. And I said to Robert, "I've never lived in such a dirty place." Because that's what it was. And I could see why the women on the South Side went out and swept their walks every day. They were immaculately clean, the women on the South Side. And even wash down the streets. I know I got used to washing my driveway and my garage. Every Saturday I would wash my garage, if you can believe it, and the driveway. And people used to kid me, "Well, you could eat in Betty's garage!"

Betty's work exemplifies the ritual that counteracts disorder in Douglas's anthropological framework. And yet, dirt in Bethlehem plays a more complicated role. In many ways the dust materialized the paradox of capitalist production—the ongoing process of devastation and reinvention that economist Joseph Schumpeter called "creative destruction."[18] While the Steel was in operation, the excesses and waste of the blast furnaces may have been contaminants to be swept away, but they simultaneously signified the community's economic health. On the South Side, it was said that one could gauge the amount of overtime pay workers were earning by how much red dirt accumulated on the windowsills.[19] "My mom used to say that the dust never bothered her," recalled a former resident. "She called it 'pay dirt.' No dust, no paycheck."

From a North Side perspective, it was not just the South Side mill that was dirty and unrefined, but also much of the population that lived in its shadow. As he prepared to graduate from junior high in 1950, George Dias looked forward to attending the Vocational Tech high school with his friends on Fourth Street, just a few blocks from his family's furniture store and the plant. Many of the technical school students would be fed directly into blue-collar jobs at the Steel. By contrast, the city's only traditional public high school at the time (built in 1922 with the help of Bethlehem Steel's continued investments in the city's infrastructure) was located across the river. Noting the economic and cultural divide between the two, George recalled matter-of-factly, "I was afraid to go to Liberty High School because it was on the North Side." That spring the guidance counselor, who doubled as a wrestling coach, nonetheless reordered George's future.

> He grabbed me by the shirt and he said, "You're going to Liberty." And I said, "I don't want to go to Liberty. I'll be out of place. I'm from the South Side. I have a Spanish background." That was a lot of prejudice against foreign-born kids. Not foreign-born, but first generation. So I didn't want to do that. I figured, who needs that? I'll just go take cabinetmaking in South Bethlehem at Vo-Tech and that was it.

For a boy who lived each day in the divided geography of the town, where until the 1950s he had to pay a penny toll to even walk across the bridge to the North Side to watch the high school football games, the ultimate decision to attend Liberty turned George's social world on its head. "You see, in my mind, and I'm going to be very honest with you, South Bethlehem was worn-out sneakers, holes in your pants, and very poorly dressed at times," George explained. "Where North Side, [was] what we classified as the cake-eaters. The cake-eaters wore white buck shoes, V-neck sweaters, very, very high in academic standings compared to South Bethlehem kids. So it was always threatening to me to consider going to Liberty." George, now neatly dressed in a tucked-in polo shirt and khakis, smiled as he told me by senior year he was voted "Most Fun to Be With." Having already expounded during our interview on the need for every American to visit Ellis Island, where with months of research he was able to locate his father's immigration records, George effectively turned his teenage commute across the Lehigh River into his own assimilation story, in many ways reaffirming the divisions he overcame.

While certain of these community divisions had been instituted by the Moravians' practices, by the twentieth century, class distinctions could be linked directly to the Steel's controlling presence in the city, economically, politically, and socially. The levels of dirt on one's windowsills reflected not only the pay-dirt paradox of the Steel's simultaneous wealth and filth. The dirt also symbolized the ways in which the widespread benefits the company conferred upon Bethlehem were inextricably linked to the domineering influence it held over the city. In the words of one former resident whose father was a Steel executive, "Bethlehem had its own order. . . . Bethlehem Steel was sort of the god, the reference point we all took for stability and predictability and, to some extent, cultural value." For residents and workers, this was a god that demanded awe and respect as an economic engine and a builder and defender of America at the same time that many employees worked in dirty, dangerous, and difficult conditions or bristled under the strict social demands of their executive positions.

In addition to affecting residents' daily sensory experiences and their choices of where they lived or went to school, the Steel ordered Bethlehem's cultural landscape in several other ways. The community had two distinct social clubs, for example. Steel elite founded the Saucon Valley Country Club, located in the suburbs over South Mountain, in 1920 as a social home for executives and high-earning professionals. Although one did not have to be a Steel employee to join Saucon Valley, it was effectively a satellite branch of the corporation, which routinely donated materials and labor to maintain the property and its three golf courses. Members' dues often were deducted straight from Bethlehem Steel paychecks. Employees of a certain rank faced intense social pressure to join so they could hobnob with the rest of the upper stratum.[20] The company built another golf club, the Bethlehem Steel Club, in 1947 closer to the mill for its foremen, supervisors, superintendents, and plant managers.[21] Lower-ranked union workers were excluded from both clubs, either explicitly or as a result of high membership fees.

When company president Eugene Grace fancied a golf game, local police literally stopped traffic to clear his way to Saucon Valley's championship courses, where a system of bells on each hole would alert members that they needed to cut their rounds short. Locals regularly offered me anecdotes about Grace's golf outings as a shorthand description of the Steel's executive culture. Several people told me of an occasion where Grace found his shot to the green obstructed by a tree, complained to the caddy, and by the next day was pleased to see the tree had been cut down.[22] Whether or not such local legends are true, residents' understandings of social order in Bethlehem, including perceptions of class hierarchies and the insularity of the Steel's executive echelon, continue to be linked to and elicited by the landscape around them.[23]

The Steel had vast landholdings in the Lehigh Valley and a strong influence on city and regional planning as well. The 1,800 acres of the former plant span four and a half miles along the Lehigh River from the middle of the South Side business district all the way east to the interstate at the city's edge—roughly 15 percent of the land in Bethlehem. The corporation owned thousands of acres more in the surrounding area, employing an in-house real estate department to manage it all. When the Steel's operations were still healthy in the early 1970s, Bethlehem Steel paid 29 percent of the city's real-estate taxes.[24] The Steel continued to invest heavily in the infrastructure of the city, with postwar projects that included giving money and steel for the new city hall in 1967. The Steel also contributed generously to Lehigh University (and its engineering program), St. Luke's Hospital, and many other local institutions that would remain anchors in the Valley even after the plant closed.[25]

Foreshadowing the mixed reactions to the Las Vegas Sands Corp.'s local involvement with the casino decades later, some observers felt the Steel's community service to be rather heavy-handed. Many were convinced that the interstate highway extensions that city officials supported passing near the plant and into New Jersey, for example, were essentially designed to provide a more accessible and gradually graded road for the Steel's trucks. Area residents impacted by the plans fought one route for over fifteen years until construction on this last "missing link" in the interstate finally began in 1984.[26] As one affected resident recalled of the Steel's interest, "By the time they got it built they really didn't need it." Other developers and businesses, however, picked up the advantages of the artery after the plant closed. Today, as we will see, I-78 is a prime asset for importing gamblers from New York and New Jersey.

Whether one benefited or not from Bethlehem Steel's influence, the ways in which the corporation shaped both the geographic and social divisions within the city contributed to a local understanding of order rooted in the community's landscape and built environment—from the smokestacks to the golf courses. This Steel-inflected lay of the land provided a map to daily life and community interactions. For most of the twentieth century, workers and residents retained a sense that they operated within a clear set of paths and boundaries. These signposts set expectations for the fiscal and social benefits of living in a company town as well as the trade-offs that careers at the Steel Company required. As global economic reforms, widespread deindustrialization, and shareholder priorities began to chip away at previously secure local frameworks, however, many area residents saw the social order in Bethlehem splinter anew.

There Were Big Cracks

Although Bethlehem Steel prospered during and after World War II, it was already becoming clear by the late 1950s that the city needed to diversify its economy. In 1957 the Steel accounted for 54 percent of all salaries and wages earned by Bethlehem residents and represented the only industrial expansion within the city.[27] In response, a group of local businessmen from the Chamber of Commerce's Economic Development Committee formed Lehigh Valley Industrial Park, Inc. in May 1959. With an eye on empty land in northwest Bethlehem, the organization hoped to attract more varied employers to the area. That summer, union steelworkers went on strike nationwide over whether industry management could arbitrarily change work practices and conditions. There had been a flurry of strikes at Bethlehem Steel since the late 1930s, but the strike of 1959 would be the longest major work stoppage at the company. It lasted 116 days, affecting every local business that relied on Steel wages or contracts. Ultimately, the federal government intervened, and steelworkers secured most of the contract assurances for which they had fought.[28] As the Steel's revenues fell in the aftermath, executives faced blame for mismanagement. They in turn pointed fingers at the union, saying that many domestic steel buyers had switched to less expensive foreign and nonunion companies to fill orders during the strike. The causes of decline are not mutually exclusive, but the strike undeniably fueled fears in the city of an untenable Steel-centric future.[29]

Like much of the domestic steel industry, the Bethlehem Steel Corporation struggled to maintain its profitability through the latter half of the twentieth century. While market leader U.S. Steel diversified with its purchase of Marathon Oil in 1982 and smaller firms shut down relatively abruptly in the 1970s and 1980s, Bethlehem cut its workforce and closed its older plants over a period of decades. The Bethlehem Steel Corporation's Lackawanna, New York, and Johnstown, Pennsylvania, plants shut down most operations in 1983 and 1992, respectively. Then in 1995, after unsuccessful attempts at a sale, the company closed the "hot end" of its namesake plant, effectively ceasing to make Bethlehem Steel in Bethlehem. Three years later the plant's coke works stopped operations as well, and the last 800 local steelworkers lost their jobs.[30] Although its remaining plants in nearby Steelton, Pennsylvania, Burns Harbor, Indiana, and Sparrows Point near Baltimore, Maryland, continued to operate profitably, huge "legacy costs" for retirees' pensions and health care and increased foreign and domestic competition, among other factors, weighed on the company. In 2001, Bethlehem Steel declared bankruptcy, and two years later the corporation officially dissolved.

As I sat down in Arnold Strong's South Side office in 2011, he apologized in advance for frequently checking his computer screen to "take care of some business" during our interview. Bethlehem Steel's bankruptcy was a precedent-setting case in which the court allowed the company to shed its retiree benefit commitments in favor of shareholder value. Arnold, a former rigger who worked on construction and repair projects throughout the plant, has since looked to online stock trading to supplement his shrunken income. When the federal Pension Benefit Guarantee Corporation (PBGC) took responsibility for Bethlehem Steel's 95,000 pensioners in 2001, the company's plan was severely underfunded, with only $3.5 billion in assets to cover $7.8 billion in liabilities. PBGC picked up $4.3 billion in obligations, the largest rescue the government had assumed to that point. But under PBGC, individual benefits were capped based on retirement age, resulting in a reduced monthly check for most former employees, particularly those with high earnings and those who took early retirement.[31] For Arnold it meant his monthly pension decreased from $1,800 to $1,100.

The bigger blow of the bankruptcy by most accounts, however, was the loss of health coverage in 2003. Until that point, retirees maintained full employer-provided health benefits for themselves and their families, including vision, dental, and prescription coverage. But like the pensions, health benefits for former employees were shed in bankruptcy as $3 billion in "legacy costs." The law that created PBGC to protect employee pensions had no such safety net for corporate-financed health care, leaving many retirees responsible for the full cost. While many steelworkers could foresee the closure of the Bethlehem plant, the corporation's bankruptcy and seeming overnight loss of retirement benefits was a shock for which few were prepared.[32]

Similar crisis moments that signal a sudden loss of economic stability for blue-collar employees, in particular, define most popular accounts and understandings of American deindustrialization. But the case in Bethlehem is less clear cut and more far reaching. The impact on the entire community was drawn out through the company's long process of closure. Although some former workers maintain that they never saw the shutdown coming, many recount telling signs of trouble going back at least thirty years. One might assume only the higher-ups had fair warning, having seen the financial statements and experienced Bethlehem's legendary executive excesses, including frequent golf outings, company-provided custom work on their homes, or crystal and china lunches of Black Angus raised specially on the grounds of the Saucon Valley Country Club.[33] Union workers, however—especially those with jobs that took them throughout the plant, like the riggers—were equally if not more aware of the company's systematic disinvestment, particularly its failure to update the plant's machinery and technology at opportune times. Arnold said that when he started working in the beam yard in 1973, the senior men told him to get out, that the place was tired, old, and going down. "And I would look around and I would see 2,000 other guys working in this department, and there were like 13,000-some people in the plant at that time. And the Steel had been there all my life and I thought, 'It's been there for my father, for my grandfather, and for all these other people. And it's too huge. I mean, there's just too many people here for this thing to go belly up,'" he said. "I just thought these old guys were trying to pull my leg and get my goat."

As a young worker Arnold also assumed that, because the plant's modern basic oxygen furnace (BOF) had just been completed in 1968, the company would have a lasting presence. But a recurrent theme in conversations around town is that the BOF was outdated as soon as it was built. Bethlehem Steel was the last of the major steel companies to build a BOF, an exponentially more efficient technology adopted by other American companies and foreign competitors a decade earlier.[34] Bethlehem was also late to the game for continuous casting, a new method of pouring steel that eliminated the need to make ingots first. Bethlehem's engineers were involved in developing the technology, but its Homer Research Laboratories abandoned the project in 1969, and it was refined by competitors instead. Bethlehem did not complete its first continuous caster until 1975 at its new Burns Harbor plant, updating two other plants in the 1980s.[35] By the time the Steel promised a continuous caster to its plant in Bethlehem in 1993 and even began to sink the foundations, the writing was on the wall. Construction was never completed.

Besides disinvestment in technology, former workers point to other signs of the plant's eventual closure: this plant was landlocked, making the transfer of raw materials expensive; the union and management were increasingly at odds; and the federal government failed to institute tariffs that would protect American steel from foreign manufacturers "dumping" subsidized, lower-priced products. Other factors included: competition from domestic mini-mills that lowered costs by using nonunion labor and scrap steel as raw material; lagging demand for structural steel and displacement of other steel products by aluminum and plastics; and Bethlehem's closed corporate culture that left it isolated from changing market realities.[36]

And yet, despite these retrospective claims of foresight, a deep mistrust continues to permeate many steelworkers' accounts of the Steel's closing. The promise of a pension, health care, steady work, and high wages had led most employees to the company in the first place, but the corporate order that defined the community and premised thousands of careers in the end proved unreliable. As we talked about the plant's demise, Arnold launched into soliloquy, as if this topic is in constant percolation in his mind, his thoughts waiting to spill out. He eloquently captured the widespread sense of betrayal among postwar steelworkers in Bethlehem, addressing the phantom company and life partner that was supposed to take care of him:

> You work your whole life and you struggle and you slave and you think, "There's a light at the end of the tunnel. I'm going to get a pension. I'm going to get benefits. I'm going to be taken care of. And all the work that I did is going to pay off." Not so. Didn't happen. There were big cracks. A lot of us fell through.
>
> You thought all along, "Okay, we're going to get it. Oh, we're going to make it. And if we don't make it, all right, so we have to go to another [Bethlehem Steel] plant. We'll get that time in someplace else and we'll get that pension." And it's like you spend twenty-some years at a place, twenty-five years, and you're looking at actually, okay, I can see just over that next rise. It's kind of like a misplaced lover who loves

> somebody, who keeps leading them on, and never fully committing. "Oh yes, just come on, I'll give you this. Come on, come with me and all you have to do is this. Here's one more hoop I want you to jump through, and then we're going to be lovers and we're going to live forever together and it will be wonderful. And oh, just one more hoop. I mean, yeah, I'm going to take a week's vacation from you, and I'm going to take two more paid holidays. And yes, I might modernize the Bethlehem plant, just stay with me. Come on, come on."
>
> And it's like you feel like, "Wow, I'm really being led on here. Why didn't I leave back in the seventies when these guys said, 'Get the hell out, kid'?" But you know you weren't smart enough, there's other reasons. You got suckered in. You're in, you got the ring in your nose, you need the job, you need the paycheck, you need the security, you're looking forward to that pension. There's a little light at the end of the tunnel, and then everything's going to be rosy. And not so.

The cracks that Arnold and his coworkers fell through severed the ideal once held not only in Bethlehem but throughout the United States of the social contract between corporation and employee—the expectation that labor, big business, and local communities would mutually benefit from industrial profits. The social contract seemed to reach its apogee postwar in the formal union contract. After a series of violent strikes, Bethlehem steelworkers gained union recognition in 1941 via the Steel Workers Organizing Committee—soon to be the United Steelworkers of America (USW). Workers would be rewarded with good wages, and the corporation would benefit from labor's stability and morale. In addition to raising pay and providing benefits, union contracts codified work rules and grievance procedures that added predictability to the workplace.[37] In comparing the corporation to a lover, it is clear that to Arnold the contract was understood beyond the terms on paper. It was an understanding of the company's social commitment to its workforce. Moreover, it was a commitment to the community where the plant was located, which reaped the rewards of a financially sound population and corporate investment in social services and infrastructure.

But by the early 1970s, amid the steel industry's national decline, the relationship was strained, with each side increasingly wary of the other's intentions. As Arnold's description of the emasculating "misplaced lover" suggested, workers came to feel that their own commitment to the social contract was not being reciprocated. Management, for its part, approached each USW contract negotiation with the conviction that union demands were undercutting the corporation's mutually beneficial profitability. A new program implemented at Bethlehem Steel in 1985 called Partners for Progress (PFP) responded to the heightening tension with an attempt to boost morale and cut costs through labor-management cooperation. More than 150 teams of managers and workers at the Steel collaborated on everything from rearranging train schedules in the beam yard to avoid bottlenecks to deciding where to place vending machines. The program held promise for some but was openly mocked by others. A satirical newsletter from the Boiler House during this period cut through the rhetoric of cooperation with its announcement that Partners for Progress would "promote good will and physical well being among employees and foremen" by sponsoring a karate class in the lunchroom, and penalties for vandalism would now include forced attendance at PFP meetings. In 1989, the union withdrew from the program during contract negotiations, stating that the company had failed to keep up its end of the bargain to modernize the plant and ensure job security.[38] As former steelworker Chuck Sabel said of the union viewpoint, "I also had PFP put to me a different way: People 'Blanking' People."[39]

Indeed, the imagined partnership had never been entirely stable from either perspective. Management believed union steelworkers' demands were selfish and shortsighted barriers to the "rational" cost-cutting necessary to keep the company profitable. For labor, even after major contract gains in the 1940s and 1950s, work at the Steel was characterized by dangerous conditions and frequent layoffs in response to fluctuations in steel demand. Numerous steelworkers told me about workplace fatalities as well as serious injuries and scars that mark their own past encounters with molten metal, explosions, and fast-moving beams. Arnold was laid off three times in his career, for between two months and two years. During these downtimes, he worked birthday parties as Claude the Clown and delivered balloons to make ends meet. Other workers treated layoffs as extended vacations. Still, through the 1990s there was often an expectation that these workers would be rehired before their year of unemployment benefits was up, adding a measure of predictability to the fickle market.

Meanwhile, racial and ethnic minorities struggled to reap the rewards of the social contract, which for decades did not equally protect their interests. Unlike many other northern steel towns, Bethlehem never attracted a large African American workforce. Locals suggest this was by corporate design to avoid racial unrest.[40] The company began actively recruiting Latino steelworkers, however, in the 1920s. They were disproportionately assigned to work in the plant's coke works, where huge ovens convert coal into fuel for the blast furnaces. It was the dirtiest, hottest, and most noxious part of the plant. Latino workers also were routinely denied transfers and promotions. Not until the 1970s did the Bethlehem Steel Corporation agree to establish training programs and tests so Latino workers could prove they were qualified to move up the work ladder. Finally, in 1974 the nine largest U.S. steelmakers entered into a consent decree with the federal government that enforced protections and routes for advancement for all racial minorities and women within the industry.[41]

Still, while work at the steel mill may have been characterized by high risks—bodily and socially—the reward for these gambles was real and, for most, achievable. Barry Bluestone and Bennett Harrison defined deindustrialization in their seminal work as the collapse of the social contract, this partnership between labor and management, and the security and predictability that it represented.[42] Through a process of economic restructuring, the worker was replaced by the shareholder in the company's attentions, and shareholders proved to be fussy and demanding partners in need of constant appeasement and assurance. Like Bethlehem Steel's closure, these transitions happened over a period of decades. As early as 1961, Bethlehem Steel CEO Arthur B. Homer, who had recently ranked as the highest-paid CEO in the United States, acknowledged a perceived shift when he defended laissez-faire market logics in a public speech. "Many people today seem to believe that this essential prime mover of our economy [the steel industry] works only for the benefit of investors and management; that profits are dollars which are being withheld from employes [*sic*] and customers," he said. But, employing a corporate logic that would continue to surface in the decades to come, he countered that "security and progress depend on profits" and company earnings benefit both steel users and steelworkers by ensuring continued output and employment.[43]

The tension intensified, however, with technological advances and the rollout in the 1980s of neoliberal trade and economic policies that catered to corporate interests. Since then, companies have decimated their labor forces through automation and moved abroad or to other states. These corporate strategies reduce labor costs, take advantage of tax incentives, and avoid environmental regulations, decisions aimed primarily at boosting shareholder value by improving the bottom line. Workers, meanwhile, increasingly make concessions, hoping to keep corporations profitable in order to protect their jobs, in essence tipping the balance of the social contract toward capital needs.[44]

As scholars like Bluestone and Harrison began to point out in the 1980s, deindustrialization as such has real and often devastating consequences for the workers and communities left behind. For many it is traumatic, characterized by the sudden evaporation of a way of life and foundation of community. The trauma of deindustrialization is experienced both at individual and family levels, through unemployment, divorce, and health consequences such as high blood pressure, depression, alcoholism, and suicide. At the community level, cities see more crime, decreased tax revenues and charitable donations, and the loss of their consumer bases.[45]

The impact of economic disinvestment is coupled with intense feelings of betrayal, of the kind that Arnold and others in Bethlehem outline, as "the light at the end of the tunnel" goes dark. Economists link the postwar heyday of the social contract to what they call the Great Compression. During the 1940s, working-class earnings increased to close the gap with the upper classes, and the effect endured in the following decades.[46] For Arnold, this meant a house and money to go on vacation. Other Bethlehem steelworkers emphasized the ability to get easy credit, allow their wives to stay at home, or afford to send their children to college, an opportunity that many of them never had. But whereas that dream used to represent a comfortable and predictable future, Arnold explained that today, "that American Dream changes. It changes pretty much on a monthly basis now the way things are going." With the Steel's closing and bankruptcy, the unsettling of once-sound plans for a particular lifestyle and secure retirement fundamentally challenged the worldviews of those who had carefully organized their lives and their families around such designs. As pensions shrunk, benefits vanished, and union protections became irrelevant, "The resources that you thought you had all of a sudden are drying up and disappearing, and you still got to play the game," Arnold said. "So there goes the whole game plan."

Moreover, while many workers could direct their anger at the Bethlehem Steel Corporation after it closed the local plant in 1995, the company's dissolution in bankruptcy and the multiple, successive redistributions of its assets to other entities made it an elusive target for blame in the years that followed. Back in his office, Arnold continued his soliloquy, addressing this specter of corporate control more directly:

> You keep thinking that, "It's gonna work. This place is too big, it's too strong. Steel is a primary industry. It's a basic need of an economy and a country." And then when you look around and the government says, "Oh yeah, we're going to bring in steel from Japan and Germany and China and"—Wait, wait a second! "We'll give you a little TRA [Trade Readjustment Allowance] fair trade money for being laid off when there's steel being brought in." Wait, wait! "There's jobs that we can send to Mexico." Wait, that math doesn't—what are you doing? That's mine. That could be my job. Even though I didn't really want it, it's a job.
>
> Well then here come the foreign cars, and then here comes these trade agreements, and here comes deficits and here comes all this crap. And it's like, what? This is not what we signed on for. Had we known this, we would have planned a different course. But you don't know it. And even if you do find out about it, it's usually too late. You can't start fresh. I mean, when I got laid off, I was like forty-nine years old, and then I started looking for a job. It's like, who's going to hire somebody that's forty-nine years old, that got used up and ground up in the steel company and had to do all that heavy work? And now, now my back's always sore, my legs aren't working that well. Where am I going to go?

In the 1990s, before the bankruptcy, many workers from Bethlehem relocated to the corporation's four other U.S. plants in hopes of maintaining employment and achieving their pension requirements. Some continued to commute back to their families in Bethlehem on weekends while they shared apartments with other steelworkers in Maryland or New York during the week. They still worked for the same corporation, but despite their efforts to match capital's mobility with their own, these workers had become outsiders decoupled from their home plants.

Ted Bodnar was among those who refused a transfer. As he explained, "I worked until November 17, 1995. I could've went to Burns Harbor [Indiana]. They asked me twice. And I go, 'I ain't going.' Because I ain't going there with more false promises or more ideas about cutting costs. And then the simplest, easiest way to get rid of me is to say, 'Hey, the guy from Pennsylvania, although he's really good and he's talented, let's get rid of him because this will keep the locals all happy!' No. I ain't playing that game." Ted was a nonunion supervisor, but as the USW increasingly made concessions to management in the 1980s and 1990s, union workers who relocated likewise lost their plant seniority—a set of protections gained through labor negotiations that had added predictability to layoffs. They knew they would be the first to be let go when union representatives at other Bethlehem Steel plants tried to protect the jobs of local workers. Yet, if they refused a transfer, in the eyes of the company they were rejecting meaningful employment and risked losing their pensions.[47]

Jefferson Cowie argues in his study of electronics manufacturer RCA Corporation that community-based competition for jobs of the sort Ted outlined precludes trans-plant cooperation among labor.[48] Unlike RCA, Bethlehem Steel did not move any plants to Mexico, choosing instead to reduce its holdings, but Arnold's invocation of runaway factories broaden his objections—ideologically if not practically—to embody an imagined shared experience of displacement among American workers writ large. The federal government created the Trade Readjustment Allowance program in 1962, and expanded it in 1974, to support U.S. workers who lose their jobs as a result of foreign trade. Designed as a balance to the negative consequences of free trade agreements, TRA provides extended benefits and funds for job searches, relocation, and training. For example, laid-off workers who enroll in Northampton Community College's Casino Training School, now housed in the former plant office building in Bethlehem, are eligible for TRA assistance toward their course fees.[49]

With only dissolved or vaguely defined entities to blame—whether it's the bankrupt corporation, the government, distant foreign competitors, or the decimated union—achieving Arnold's American Dream of financial security in Bethlehem seems increasingly to be more about luck than anything. As one might discover after a night gambling at the casino that now occupies the former ore yard, any sense of assurance about the positive outcomes of the "game" of capitalism post-Steel is illusory. And yet residents actively try to regain a sense of social order and understanding amid a changing economic landscape. Instead of reflecting a fundamental conflict between local life space and abstract global economies, as Bluestone and Harrison theorize, in Bethlehem the rupture between community and corporation is not so complete. While far-reaching economic changes often are imagined as unavoidable and natural market evolutions, these transitions are structured by specific government policies and corporate decisions. Local communities and their residents regularly respond to, interpret, and shape the impacts of such transitions in their daily lives and immediate surroundings.

Arnold's final layoff came in April 1997, a year before the Bethlehem plant closed its gates for good. He described how toward the end the company combined craft work into one job, so that he was no longer just a rigger, but a carpenter and a pipe fitter as well, all skilled jobs that workers took pride in learning separately through years of training. The increased responsibilities led to only a minimal increase in wages but, as he explained, it was a concession that kept him working. He identified each craft by specialty tool—spud wrench, hammer, pipe wrench—now mingling in a single tool belt. "In fact," he said with a smile, "I have my tools here." Arnold dropped to the floor and began digging under the futon in his office. One by one he pulled the tools out, tossing them toward me with a clang. Finally he found the belt, a sort of satchel worn over one's shoulder that holds them all, and put the tools back in their appropriate places, carefully reordering his pre-1997 world: hammer, shackles, burning wrench, building inspector, chisel, bull pin, spud wrench, adjustable wrench. . . .

This was a world that once had weight behind it. The belt nearly dropped to the floor when he handed it to me. For Arnold, it was a thirty-five-pound souvenir of the betrayed social contract. Asked why he hung onto the tools, he replied, "I thought I might need them." Already in the mid-1980s, the riggers had begun to disassemble areas of the plant that had shut down. Parts of the factory were cannibalized, the scrap steel of the buildings chewed up and thrown to the furnaces to make more steel. Machinery and other assets were shipped to other plants. A carefully constructed life was literally taken apart before Arnold's eyes, sometimes with his help. After I left, Arnold would shove his tools back under the futon, but first he took the reconstructed belt from me and displayed it on a filing cabinet. In a small way, Arnold's efforts to make sense of it all and regain some control over his past point the way to a different future.

Life after Bethlehem

The disordering effects of the Steel's decline and closure, and the contradictory experiences of its local influence, reached far beyond the plant where union laborers spent their shifts. White-collar workers and other residents had similarly built lives around the corporation's perceived stability and the structures—economic, social, cultural, and physical—that marked the local landscape. Jim Schuster, for example, began working at the Steel in the research division testing raw materials in 1957. Four years in, the corporation consolidated its research activities from more than a dozen brick buildings near the plant and other scattered sites to a new, cutting-edge complex on the top of South Mountain. Having quietly acquired and pieced together 1,000 acres of wooded land via negotiations with several hundred owners, the Steel cleared seventy-two acres and spent more than $25 million to build the Homer Research Laboratories at one of the highest points in the Valley. The research center's eight steel-framed buildings, faced with white Indiana limestone, created a beacon to the surrounding area and an apt—if overzealous—symbol of the corporation's local dominance.[50]

The research center also carried a certain prestige for the nearly 1,000 scientists, engineers, and technicians who worked there, distinguishing them spatially and socially from the plant below. The cluster of new buildings, a "city on a hill," boasted the latest and greatest in technology. "Everything was new, sparkling," Jim said. "As far as the steel industry, we were probably top of the line at that point." Attractive receptionists greeted visitors in the lobby. The elevator doors were emblazoned with golden H-beams, the company's logo. The entire parking concourse in front of the main building, reserved only for the vice president of research, was paved in a fanned pattern of stones. (Jim heard it was done by masons

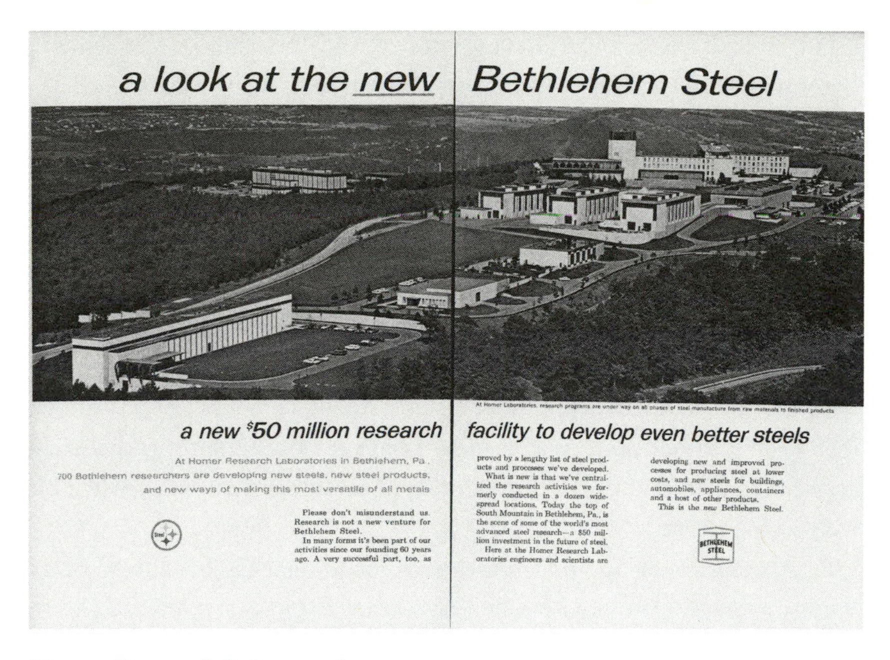

Homer Research Laboratories

This ad from 1966 portrays the gleaming white Homer Labs at the top of South Mountain as "the scene of some of the world's most advanced steel research" and the image of the "*new* Bethlehem Steel." Twenty years later most of the facility would be sold at a loss to Lehigh University. (*Fortune*, January 1966, author's collection.)

flown in from Italy). "I had a dream one time," he told me, "that I went to work, or went into the parking lot out front, and there were weeds growing up through the cracks in the thing. Meaning nobody was there anymore. Talk about a premonition. Talk about something weird. I honestly did. That was several years before I got laid off."

Jim lost his job in 1982 when he was fifty years old. In hindsight, he was in denial even before it happened. He and his wife had gone on a week's vacation that year.

> Well, during the time I was away on vacation, our section manager called all the guys downstairs and after a lot of mumbo jumbo talk said, "When you go back to your rooms, your offices, you will have an envelope on your desk. And the envelope will say one of three things: 1) You have your job in your current situation. 2) You have a job with Bethlehem Steel but we're moving you to somewhere else,

> but you still have a job. 3) You're history." And one of my good friends got nailed on that, and I had heard about it over the weekend. And I never, never, I never put two and two together that I could be one of them.

Although disturbed by the ruthless remove with which his colleagues had been treated, Jim walked into the office on Monday morning refreshed from his vacation and ready to get to work. Like Arnold in the mill, Jim was initially so steeped in the culture of Steel stability that he did not receive the signals all around him that suggested his job was also in danger. By 8:15 two bosses came in and said, "That's it." Jim said it was the worst day of his life to that point, only surpassed seventeen years later when his wife passed away.

Bethlehem Steel, some suggest, was not altogether heartless. Betty Bramson, the Steel salesman's wife who washed her garage clean each week, recounted how the company had an ambulance go up South Mountain to be on hand the morning a friend with a heart condition was laid off from the research department, just in case. "In some ways they were considerate," she said. I heard similar stories about the precautionary ambulance from others. Whether or not the rumor is true, it has stuck as a symbol of the complicated relationship most residents still have with the Steel in their memories. Despite the shock of his job loss, Jim also seemed reluctant to paint the corporation as a callous villain. He described Bethlehem's efforts to set up a center for laid-off workers, providing secretarial help for resumes, phones for job calls, and a psychologist to talk to about it all. Bethlehem was the first major U.S. corporation to develop such a comprehensive program to deal with the emotional impact of permanent layoffs. A sign in one of the "career continuation centers" that had read "Steel is Beautiful" was replaced in the early 1980s with one proclaiming, "There is Life after Bethlehem."[51]

Like many others, Jim took advantage of these resources. Some say the psychological support offered at the career center was akin to counseling after the death of a loved one.[52] Denial, depression, and anger—part of the five stages of grief in Elisabeth Kübler-Ross's familiar model of the emotional impact of personal loss—are particularly evident in many Bethlehem workers' reactions to unemployment. Along with the feelings of corporate betrayal that Arnold described in the trauma of the plant closure, laid-off workers also often experienced profound feelings of guilt.

> I felt almost ashamed that I had lost my job. Psychologically, I was—I, "What did I do? Or what didn't I do?" And I remember one of the psychologists saying, "Don't ever say, 'if only' or 'what if,' because you can't do anything about it. It's water over the dam. So go on." That was good advice. So they took care of it in that regard. In that regard.

Rather than direct his anger at the company, Jim had focused on his own shortcomings, a tendency journalists in the early 1980s dubbed the "why me?" syndrome.[53] Anthropologists documented this reaction among "downwardly mobile" white-collar workers, in particular, where employment status became a measure of self-worth. But many steelworkers likewise refused to go on welfare or food stamps because of the shame associated with job loss.[54]

For workers like Jim, the transition away from steel led to other opportunities. Most white-collar employees had college or graduate degrees and professional networks to draw on. But Jim said that the emotional low that came with the layoff was just as significant as the financial strain on his family. After working odd jobs at a mental hospital, a lumberyard, and a university lab, none of which took full advantage of his skill set, he finally regained a sense of purpose when he was hired as a headhunter for the mining and minerals industry. "I did very well and got my psyche back, my ego got back," he said.

Even though Jim regained his financial and emotional security, the notion that the rug could be pulled out from under him had haunting effects. From the comfort of his living room in 2011, Jim told me about the first time he went back to the research lab, five years after he was let go. In 1986, Lee Iacocca, then chairman of the Chrysler Corporation and a Lehigh University alum, helped the university acquire the Homer Research Laboratories for the bargain price of $18.75 million and convert it to a satellite Mountaintop Campus for its engineering, biology, and education programs. Jim heard that temps were going through the buildings, throwing away all the Bethlehem Steel equipment, and he wanted to see if there was anything he could salvage.

> I remember this like it was yesterday. I walked into some of the labs where we used to work up on the third floor. And all the lights were out. But the computers were still on. And the Bethlehem Steel, I think it was the Bethlehem Steel logo, was on the screen. And it was kind of a greenish, yellowish, fluorescent color, and it kind of shown over the whole laboratory. The lights were out. And on the scales, the weighing devices, were sample dishes that were being weighed, and they had samples in them, like pellets. Iron ore pellets, which are used in the blast furnace to make iron, were still in the individual sample holders. The pans were being weighed on these scales. And it was like the plague came through and—ppffft!—took all the people out. But here was the stuff they were working on. And the notebooks were open!

As he told me the story, Jim literally got goose bumps, the hair on his arms sticking up as his workplace of twenty years transformed into a kind of Pompeii, an archaeological site of a lost civilization, or the post-apocalyptic set of a horror film, one in which the employees play the victims while the corporate H-beam logo casts an oddly persistent glow over the scene. Jim nonetheless insisted again and again that he's moved on. When he took me up to the Mountaintop Campus the next day to show me around, those raw emotions of the 1980s were tempered. "It's all changed," he said. "That would have been 29 years [ago], and so that's a generation plus. So yeah, you have to get over it and move on."

The resilience of most blue-collar Bethlehem workers looking for new jobs and the ongoing diversification of the area's economy likewise helped prevent the extreme levels of unemployment found in other Rust Belt towns.[55] Although Bethlehem's unemployment rate spiked at 9 percent in the early 1990s as the plant shut down, by the end of the decade it was less than 4 percent, only topping 9 percent again with the economic recession in 2009. Unemployment in Bethlehem in the years after the Steel's closure remained just slightly higher than state and national averages, even as most other former industrial cities in the region fared significantly worse.[56]

Still, for some former steelworkers who found employment elsewhere, as school bus drivers, support staff at Lehigh University, or security guards, for instance, the transition from industrial to postindustrial reflected the ongoing clash of cultural systems long ingrained in a city split by class. Chuck Sabel is still raw about his loss of livelihood of thirty-two years and the meaning his work gave him as a scarfer burning off defects on rolled steel. After his last layoff in 1997, Chuck ran into an acquaintance at the grocery store who works at a local bank. The man made an inopportune joke about how, if union workers like Chuck hadn't slept on the night shift or cooked dinner while working the middle shift, they'd probably still have jobs. Statements like these persist more than a decade after the closure among non-Steel employees in town, part of an effort to explain the company's demise by blaming it on excesses of the union contract. For quick-tempered Chuck it was a personal attack on the value of his work identity and, by association, his family and friends.

"Did you ever carry one of your buddies to an ambulance at the bank?" he boomed back red-faced. "You don't know what you're talking about. Because you could have came and worked here just like me. Then you'll get to work every damn holiday. You can rant and rave all you want about double time and a half. You know what it's like driving by your neighbor's swimming pool when he's having a party on July Fourth and you're going to work on middle shift? You ought to think about that once." Chuck stopped the conversation cold, implicitly denying the possibility of finding common ground. In many ways his affirmation of a rift between those who define Bethlehem by its association with the steel company, and those who envision a new, postindustrial identity for the city reflects the latest cultural rift in the community. But memories of the social contract and the ways in which steel manufacturing had ordered life in Bethlehem also infuse daily interactions like Chuck and the banker's with the potential to bring the community's history into visions for the future in a way that goes beyond simple nostalgia. These cultural expectations continue to find expression in the way the landscape is ordered, particularly in its redevelopment.

"They Couldn't Even Make Steel and They Wanted to Control Redevelopment"

Even as it laid off workers through the 1980s and gradually shut down Bethlehem production, the Steel Corporation was hesitant to cut ties completely with the namesake community that it had helped structure over the past century. Rather than lock the gates and walk away, Steel executives believed the oldest section of the plant in the heart of the South Side could be redeveloped as a heritage destination and become a tribute to the corporate legacy. The plans the Steel initiated for the site in the 1990s literally set the foundation, and in many ways the community expectations, for the Las Vegas Sands casino project a decade later.

During the 1970s, 1980s, and 1990s, as American commentators began to regularly invoke the term "deindustrialization" to describe the rash of domestic factory closures, relocations, and downsizings, a number of steel and other industrial towns saw dramatic changes to their landscapes. Cities like Homestead, Pennsylvania, Youngstown, Ohio, and Kenosha, Wisconsin, watched bulldozers quickly follow plant closures to raze all or most of their industrial remains, both in preparation for anticipated new development and in an effort to erase painful memories of economic abandonment. Shopping malls, marinas, and prisons replaced smokestacks and machine shops, or sometimes the empty lots simply stayed empty.[57]

After the Steel Corporation closed its Bethlehem plant, local politicians toured the 1,800-acre site, which had earned the dubious distinction of being the largest industrial brownfield in the country. With the Steel's dissolution in bankruptcy, the site became part of a series of asset transfers that heightened the uncertainty of what would become of the land. A city councilman recalled being told in 2001 that the only way the property could be developed "is if they turned it into a billiard table."[58] Leveling all the remaining industrial buildings would provide maximum flexibility for new construction and offer a clean slate to move on from an outmoded economic and cultural identity. As one resident put it, "You can't sell old steel as progress."

Hank Barnette, the CEO of the Bethlehem Steel Corporation from 1992 to 2000, agrees that razing the plant might have been the most straightforward solution before the bankruptcy. "I cannot tell you how much easier it would have been." But as we talked in the conference room of the law office he maintains in town, he said the historical significance of the headquarters site ultimately led him to a different approach. While many of Bethlehem Steel's top executives left the area, Barnette, now in his early eighties, keeps his primary residence in Bethlehem, just down the street from Eugene Grace's former mansion. By the time Barnette was promoted to CEO after working in the Steel's legal department for twenty-five years, parts of the mill had been long out of use and plans were taking shape to sell or close the rest of the plant. Although the Steel maintained its corporate offices in Bethlehem, the company looked for developers to take the defunct factory land off its hands and bring new use to the burdensome property.

The Steel sold one of its first parcels of unused land to an outside developer, a local producer of shoe inserts, more than a decade before the bankruptcy. The lot sat on the westernmost edge of the plant where a merchant mill, alloy and tool steel mills, and a roll shop had already been closed. But after buying the eleven acres for $200,000 in 1986 and clearing the land, the new owner discovered that the forty-foot foundations the Steel had sunk impeded new construction. When revised plans for a less desirable strip mall surfaced, Bethlehem Steel decided to buy back the land in 1991—for $1.3 million.[59] "We started to have a longer term view," explained Bethlehem Steel's former vice president of public affairs and a key figure in the redevelopment plans.

> Let's get that [land] back, and let's control how the development occurs. . . . If you broke it up into individual lots and then had random development without a master plan for the site, I think it would have been a disaster. So as long as Bethlehem [Steel] controlled the whole thing—you still had to get approval from the city for whatever plans we're using—but then you have a master plan.

As it had for the past century, the Steel wanted hands-on involvement in determining the lay of the land and was willing to spend the money to see its community vision—and the profits predicted from its realization—materialize.

Three years later, in 1994, Steel executives watched the mayor cut a ceremonial ribbon strung between two salvaged beams to open the first successful outside development on the site, a start-up technology center. Its construction was funded by the state, the city, and private investors. The project aligned with the national shift toward leveraging public-private partnerships to fund redevelopment projects after the official end to the federal urban renewal program in 1974. Although the Steel's local influence had begun to fade with its declining employment, the corporation's sometimes paternalistic belief in its unique ability to shape and profit from the city's economic and physical landscapes held strong. Like the casino corporation that followed, the Steel posited that developing inside the former plant gates would help spark new investments in the surrounding community. It was a revision of the social contract in which direct social benefits like pensions were being replaced by the promise of trickle-down advantages from corporate-led plans for economic development.

One of the greatest impediments to this vision, however, was of Bethlehem Steel's own making. The land inside the plant was polluted with over a century's worth of arsenic, lead, and other industrial by-products. Part of the Steel's inability to unload its already-shuttered plants in Lackawanna and Johnstown related to their respective states' environmental regulations that held buyers liable for any future problems. This meant sellers had to restore industrial-use land to greenfield, or virgin, condition. Exercising its corporate clout, Bethlehem Steel lobbied for the Brownfields Act, which ultimately was signed into Pennsylvania state law in 1995 and allowed for remediation specific to intended use, a lower bar for cleaning up land for nonresidential purposes. On the Steel site in South Bethlehem, this required removing 566 tons of contaminated soil and capping other parcels with parking lots, new buildings, walkways, and clean soil.[60]

Meanwhile, the firm enlisted consultants to complete studies of potential uses for the site and hired an outside demolition company to work with Steel employees to begin tearing down many of the empty industrial buildings. This work would clear the way for new construction on portions of the easternmost 1,600 acres.[61] The oldest Steel buildings and the five blast furnaces that marked a 160-acre plot in the center of the South Side between the Fahy and Minsi Trail Bridges, however, were in the meantime spared from demolition. As the most central and oldest parts of the plant, these acres lay at the emotional and symbolic focus of the efforts to transform Bethlehem's post-Steel landscape.

A key piece in the Steel's plan to attract new development involved rezoning the site for more flexible use, rather than retaining its existing heavy industrial designation. For a community increasingly disenchanted with the Steel's drawn-out exit from city affairs, this demand for new zoning led to a series of heated negotiations and lengthy public meetings in the spring of 1996. The Steel initially refused to reveal any plans for the site before the zoning change, and many residents grew wary of continuing to give the corporation what a local reporter called "carte blanche" to dictate city planning. At the same time, they feared alternative scenarios in which the land would lay dormant. "Is the city willing to blindly accept Bethlehem Steel as its surrogate protector of the public interest?" the reporter asked. "I know there was a time when a benevolent Bethlehem Steel pulled all the city's strings, but those days—and for that matter, that Bethlehem Steel—are gone. This is a company whose local ties are fading fast."[62] Others retained hope of attracting new manufacturing and worried that revised zoning would undermine the potential for reindustrialization. A former city official involved in the negotiations pinpointed the public-private tension that emerged: "They couldn't even make steel and they wanted to control redevelopment." As visible evidence of steelmaking's benefit to the community faded, Bethlehem Steel's transition to controlling a postindustrial landscape was not necessarily smooth or self-evident.

Ultimately, the city council granted the broadest flexibility in zoning for the 160 central acres, and late in 1996 Bethlehem Steel hired Robert Barron of Enterprise Development to help negotiate with potential buyers and realize its vision for reusing this parcel in a project it called Bethlehem Works.[63] The Steel's decision to retain Enterprise, which was an offshoot of the Rouse Corporation, confirmed the seriousness of the Steel's interest in real-estate development and in Bethlehem's future. It also signaled the appeal of using the site's heritage toward this end. The Baltimore-based Rouse Corporation's founder, James Rouse, had made his name with the successful redevelopment of Faneuil Hall and Quincy Market in Boston in 1976.[64] Like Baltimore's Harborplace (1980), New York's South Street Seaport (1981), and the scores of likeminded projects that followed across the United States, the Faneuil Hall Marketplace adapted a historic setting—in this case a nineteenth-century market—to postindustrial retail, tourism, and entertainment economies by sanitizing a decrepit area via new shops and restaurants, all in a quaintly cobblestoned setting lined with decorative lampposts.

Rouse's "festival marketplaces" were not the only precedents for so-called "preservation-development" that overlaid new economic enterprise with a historic valence. Rouse was himself inspired by San Francisco's Ghirardelli Square. It had set the stage for industrial adaptive reuse in 1964 by transforming the former chocolate factory's brick buildings into high-end shops, restaurants, and offices, and marked the emergence of preservationist influence on large-scale real-estate investments.[65] Lowell, Massachusetts's textile mills, defunct since the 1950s, likewise became a pioneering national historic park for industrial site interpretation in 1978. In Birmingham, Alabama, a groundswell of citizen support saved the iron-producing Sloss blast furnaces, dormant since 1971, from demolition; in 1981 they became a National Historic Landmark. A museum of industrial history opened on the Sloss site, and the furnaces became a backdrop for concerts and other community events.[66]

While the new zoning agreement reached in Bethlehem had prohibited protecting the Steel site as a historic district in order to give developers maximum leeway with their plans, by the 1990s "tourist city" projects like museums, baseball stadiums, and river walks fed a growing nationwide effort to draw people back to declining downtowns by merging industrial heritage and aesthetics with new entertainment- and service-based economic development.[67] Bethlehem Works hoped to draw public support by comparing its plans to a recent proposal to redevelop the Philadelphia waterfront with an ice rink, amphitheater, cinema, gaming center, and multimedia history presentation.[68] As the Bethlehem mill shut down, steelworkers themselves began imagining potential reuses for the plant site. "We used to joke that it was going to become an amusement park, and there were things that we thought would end up being rides," said Arnold Strong. He and his coworkers laughed about the potential thrill of going up and down in the skip tubs that carried ore to the blast furnaces, or being whisked along conveyors meant for steel beams.[69]

Although the literal reuse of the Steel's machinery for an amusement park may not have been a serious consideration, the emphasis on entertainment certainly was. Initial plans for Bethlehem Works included a multiplex cinema, dozens of restaurants and retail shops, a 260-room hotel and conference center in the old headquarters building, an Olympic-sized swimming facility in the iron foundry, and an ice rink. Special effects on one of the blast furnaces would make it appear as if it were still operating.

A developer from Buffalo announced he would turn the former Carpenter Shop into a themed entertainment center called "The Fundry," complete with mini-golf, laser tag, batting cages, and bowling.[70] Several other developers also showed interest. Local papers regularly announced the latest plans, only to follow weeks or months later with news that the deals had fallen through as the risks and costs of the projects came into focus. Bethlehem Steel spun off a centerpiece of the plan to its own control—the National Museum of Industrial History, proposed for the plant's expansive No. 2 Machine Shop. It promised to highlight both the plant's local history and display large industrial artifacts on loan from the Smithsonian.[71] In each of these plans, developers imagined "history" as a tool for generating profits, and community members saw social value in remembering the Steel's past; but most often these two roles blurred. The calculated balance of preservation and development, and the placement of local memories in regional, national, and global contexts would remain central concerns of all iterations of the redevelopment plan that followed.[72]

Though the profitability of the corporation as a whole suffered through the late 1990s, its government affairs team remained well connected. Executives effectively navigated state and federal funding opportunities and worked with the city to begin laying infrastructure in 2000 through the empty property for the utilities and roadways that private enterprise would require. Typical of urban development projects in these "tourist city" decades, the Steel helped hammer out public-private financing arrangements that would offset the risk of initial investment. In 2000, the city designated the site as a tax increment financing (TIF) district. As a TIF, any increased tax revenues that the property generated from new development over the next twenty years would be reinvested in the site and help pay off its financing.[73]

Then, in 2001, Bethlehem Steel filed for Chapter 11 restructuring. Despite a handful of projects that were completed on the western end of the Bethlehem Works site in the early 2000s, including an ice rink and two more technology centers, development for the most part remained stalled and increasingly uncertain as the Steel's bankruptcy worked through the courts. The in-between state of the site reflected the economic and cultural limbo in which the city found itself, part monument to manufacturing

Forging a Future from a Proud Past
The stage is set for a new opportunity on Bethlehem's South Side. The company that helped build a nation and bring prosperity to Bethlehem is committed to the redevelopment of the South Side. After all, it's been our home for nearly 100 years.
Call to learn about new opportunities.
Bethlehem
BETHLEHEM STEEL
530 East 3rd St., Bethlehem, PA 18015-1390
610-694-2000 www.bethsteel.com

Bethlehem Works

This advertisement from 1999, featuring balloons, picnic tables, and blue skies around the blast furnaces, highlights the heritage-inspired and entertainment-based vision of the Bethlehem Steel Corporation for the reuse of its namesake plant. At this point the plant had closed, but Bethlehem maintained its corporate offices in town as it sought buyers for the land. The casino later adopted similar rhetoric of "Bringing New Life to Old Steel" to promote its project on the Bethlehem Works site. (*Lehigh Valley Images: Bethlehem Area Chamber of Commerce 1999 Membership Directory* [Sinking Spring, PA: West Lawn Graphic Communications, 1999], 25, author's collection.)

and part vision of a postindustrial future. Like the bankrupt corporation itself, both the physical and social structures that once ordered the landscape appeared to be in flux.

The new era, it seemed, was about work of the mind, not the toil of physical labor.[74] Some smaller heavy manufacturing firms in the city continued to operate profitably, including Lehigh Heavy Forge, which had been part of the Steel Corporation. Mirroring trends in other parts of the country, however, Bethlehem's largest employers post-Steel became its hospitals, universities, and later, the casino. In the late 1990s, Bethlehem Steel began preparing the 1,600 acres in the eastern portion of the former steel plant for new life as the Bethlehem Commerce Center. Between a truck-to-rail intermodal transfer station and natural gas power plant that the Steel attracted before the bankruptcy, tenants in two massive new industrial parks on the land thus far include a commercial collection agency, a software developer, an architecture firm, and several large warehouses. On the west end of the plant, where the Alloy and Tool Steel Division mills once stood, are a medical technology start-up and a maker of semiconductor components.

Despite these apparent shifts from manufacturing to warehousing and distribution, from producing heavy materials to precision-based technology, the boundaries that defined the community beginning in the eighteenth century continue to shape the ways in which residents navigate the city's post-Steel terrain. North and South Bethlehem are still distinct spaces with competing claims to Bethlehem's urban identity, and economic development remains implicated in social divisions. When murmurs surfaced in 2004 that legalized casino gambling could jumpstart the fading Bethlehem Works vision of a heritage-based entertainment destination, skeptics raised concerns about whether Bethlehem should welcome another corporate giant, Las Vegas Sands Corp., to the city after the disappointments the Steel left in its wake. Others registered their concern with how a vice-based industry would be able to coexist with the city's spiritual North Side Moravian heritage. The debate over bringing a casino to Bethlehem and the aftermath of its construction both reinvigorated historic boundaries and created new rifts in the city's social and cultural geographies.

Other dividing lines—between past and future, preservation and redevelopment, and local and global interests—have seemed to evaporate in this postindustrial context. Like Bernie Hovan, Arnold Strong opposed the casino when Las Vegas Sands was bidding for a state license to build in Bethlehem. He doesn't see the casino economy as representing long-term stability in the same way that the Steel once did. He worries about service employees' lack of strong benefits and union representation. And yet, as his eyes periodically darted to the online trading screen in his office while we talked, the stock on which his eyes fixated was "LVS"—Las Vegas Sands. Arnold had bought stock in Sands three years earlier in 2008 when the company's credit line dried up in the recession and there were rumors that it too was headed towards bankruptcy. By that point, the company had already begun building on the Steel site, but in a global climate of heightened financial insecurity, its share price had plummeted below $3 a share. Sands temporarily halted construction on its Bethlehem hotel in order to complete the adjacent casino, and CEO Sheldon Adelson said he regretted ever coming to Pennsylvania and building his "house of dough."[75]

In 2011, as Arnold and I discussed the ill fate of the steel company, LVS stock had rebounded to $47 a share. "I saw an opportunity. And yeah, it's a very selfish opportunity. But I took it, because maybe it's my turn to look out for me first," Arnold laughed. "Will it give me what I'm missing on my pension? No. I didn't buy enough. I should have taken my 401(k) and dumped it all on there." Like many Bethlehem residents, Arnold lives each day seeking a way out of the postindustrial contradiction between memories of past corporate commitments to community and the individualistic profit interests that guide future-focused development projects. The chapters that follow examine a series of sites—buildings, neighborhoods, and global market-places—in search of continuities and openings in the landscape through which to reconcile such tensions and find a new way forward.

2

Christmas City and Sin City Simply Do Not Go Together

IN AUGUST 2005, just off Bethlehem's historic Main Street, two costumed gondoliers "with authentic Italian accents" set up a tent at the annual, vaguely German-themed, Musikfest outdoor concert festival. From their landing amid the eighteenth-century Moravian stone buildings, they serenaded thousands of visitors with a pitch to win local support for a proposed multimillion-dollar casino complex a couple miles across town. The gondoliers were representatives of the Las Vegas Sands Corp., the largest real-estate developer and casino operator in the world and a first-time $50,000 Musikfest sponsor.[1] The company, having seen an opportunity to enter the newest U.S. gambling market when Pennsylvania legalized casinos the previous year, had zeroed in on the economic potential of the Bethlehem Steel Corporation's former namesake plant which had been vacant for almost a decade.

The gondoliers reflected Sands' most recognizable brand, The Venetian, the famous casino resort in Las Vegas. Epitomizing the casino business model of themed luxury and escape, aesthetically and temporally distancing visitors from their everyday surroundings, The Venetian had opened in 1999 with an orchestration of white doves, trumpets, and, of course, singing gondoliers. Italian actress Sophia Loren christened one of the motorized gondolas that float down the resort's interior Grand Canal. Beneath a painted ceiling of blue skies and fluffy clouds, visitors pass under a replica Rialto Bridge, through St. Mark's Square, and past the Doge's Palace. In 2007 the corporation would replicate this highly successful model and open a second, much bigger Venetian across the Pacific in Macau, again with gondoliers, Italian landmarks, and a canal three times the length of the one in Vegas.[2]

But in 2005, Jenny Fosco, a Bethlehem activist and historic preservationist, was mortified when she heard about the tent of gondoliers at Musikfest. "So many people were angry. We went in, and they had drawings up, and we were like, 'Are you serious? Why are you fabricating history? This is not like a sand pit in Las Vegas where you're pretending you're Italy. This is real history here! You don't have to fabricate anything!'" Jenny's father worked for more than thirty years in the plant's No. 2 Machine Shop, which upon its construction in 1890 was the largest enclosed industrial building in the world, more than 1,500 feet long. After the Bethlehem Steel Corporation's bankruptcy in 2003 left the future of the local brownfield increasingly uncertain, Jenny actively fought to preserve the industrial buildings, including the Machine Shop, which still claimed the acreage on which Las Vegas Sands had its eye. For Jenny, the tent of gondoliers signaled a total disregard for the Steel site's unique character, an effort to impose a global brand on local heritage. "I seriously think they would have done something stupid like that. I'm sure that's a very successful formula for them that they probably were just thinking: 'That's our brand, The Venetian,'" she told me six years later, an edge of disgust still audible in her voice. "But to their credit, they backed off of that and came back with a very industrial-looking building, which is much better."

The Bethlehem casino's first president, Robert DeSalvio, said his company never intended to build a Venetian in Pennsylvania; Sands merely wanted to display its credentials and "showcase that we can be different things to different audiences." In any case, by the time Las Vegas Sands mobilized its full-blown pitch to Bethlehem's citizens and to the Pennsylvania Gaming Control Board to win a state license to build on the Steel site, its plans for new construction featured exposed brick and beams, gabled roofs, and orange lights meant to evoke the glow of the operating mill. Located on what was once the steel plant's ore yard, its entrance would be spanned by an original ore bridge emblazoned with the red Sands insignia. Supporters emphasized and lauded Sands' verbal commitments to preserve and reuse the majority of the remaining Steel buildings, including the No. 2 Machine Shop. A giant model of planned development for the 124-acre site—the portion of the original 1,800-acre plant in question—was set on display in city hall. The broken windows, gaping roofs, and crumbling walls of the industrial landscape were transformed into clean brick boxes representing a hotel, retail space, an event center, office buildings, and condominiums. A promotional video titled "Bringing New Life to Old Steel"—echoing the Steel's earlier efforts at "Forging a Future from a Proud Past"—promised thousands of new jobs as part of the redevelopment. References to The Venetian brand, at first used synonymously with the company, gradually faded away in the discussions at city council meetings.

But despite these corporate assurances and the mayor's strong support, the community and city council were divided about the prospect of bringing a casino to Bethlehem. The image of gondoliers perched next to eighteenth-century Moravian buildings seeking support for a new casino on the old steel plant grounds goes far to illustrate the complicated role heritage plays in defining community identity as both corporate investors and residents navigate the contested terrain of economic development. Although the casino, which ultimately gained approval in 2006, adopts an industrial theme in an effort to tie Bethlehem's past to its future and ease the transition to a new economy, consumers of urban landscapes do not share a generic nostalgia. They often disagree with developers and with each other over historic interpretations and the future trajectories of urban life.[3] Bethlehem residents, politicians, and developers dispute not only how the Steel should be remembered, but whether it should hold a place in the city's identity at all.

Much of the opposition to the casino as Las Vegas Sands bid for the state license came from community members who preferred to associate Bethlehem not with its South Side steel plant, but with its "quaint" North Side origin as a religious settlement. Since 1937, Bethlehem has drawn on this earlier history to declare itself "Christmas City, U.S.A.," signaled by a giant "Star of Bethlehem" erected atop South Mountain. The city's lighted Christmas landscape, imbued with references to the Moravians' spirituality and North Side order, helped soften Bethlehem's industrial image as it diversified its economy. But as much as Central Moravian Church invokes the regimented predictability of the founders' eighteenth-century settlement, for those left behind by postindustrial transitions, the plant likewise reflects a previous era of security and dependability. Booming steel production and wartime patriotism during the twentieth century fed a civil religion on par with other devotions.

In bringing deep-seated community sentiments to the surface, the local casino debate underscored how the landscape in Bethlehem physically and culturally remains divided and an object of contention for locals who variously interpret which of the city's histories should predominate in future plans. Embedded in this postindustrial landscape are commitments to specific social values that often are excised from the fiscal language that dominates development discussions. While in many ways the promise of new economic investment on the brownfield made the decision to allow Las Vegas Sands to build a casino in Bethlehem a foregone conclusion, the debate and the architectural decisions for its design revealed a unique meeting point between economic development, heritage, and ideas of community morality. The events of 2005 and 2006 made clear that market-based calculations about what is best for a city's future are social constructions as well.

Pennsylvania Takes a Gamble

Sometimes Jacqueline Russo thinks she is cursed. Jacqueline grew up in Las Vegas in the 1960s, where her father was a performer who sang in a quartet on the Strip. A photo of his induction into the Las Vegas Entertainers Hall of Fame hung on the wall of the dining room where we sat with her husband Michael. Jacqueline said she saw firsthand the devastation gambling could wreak when her father brought various down-and-outs home after they had lost all their money on the tables playing craps, roulette, or blackjack. When her father lost his own family's savings through bad investments, she and her mother moved to Atlantic City to live with relatives. Then in 1976, while Jacqueline was in college, New Jersey legalized casinos in Atlantic City. Having thought she left Las Vegas behind, she remembered her astonishment at seeing the new gambling halls go up along the Boardwalk.

Seven years later, she and Michael married and moved to Bethlehem. They bought the townhouse where they still live on the North Side in a neighborhood full of young families. Although Michael had a dental practice on the South Side for several years and interacted regularly with Steel employees, Jacqueline said she felt insulated from the plant's decline and eventual closure. She preferred to associate Bethlehem with its "Christmas

City" Moravian heritage. "Look at this town. It's so cute! There's a church on every corner. I just thought it was just the sweetest place. So I wasn't paying attention to the Steel," she explained. Nonetheless, in Jacqueline's experience, larger economic trends regularly materialize in the spaces she inhabits. "When they started talking about gambling in Pennsylvania, I said, 'Oh, my God.' It really felt like I was being followed."

When I talked to them in 2012, Michael and Jacqueline said that in retrospect Bethlehem's Sands Casino was a done deal as soon as former Pennsylvania Governor Ed Rendell pushed a bill through the state legislature to legalize casino gambling—or "gaming," as it is called in the industry—in 2004. But in 2005, Michael and Jacqueline, along with scores of other area residents, believed that they could convince the city to pass a zoning ordinance that would prevent the Christmas City from becoming host to a state-licensed slots parlor. By many accounts, the city was split almost fifty-fifty on the issue. Proponents said the casino would jumpstart additional economic investment in the city and create new jobs and tax revenues for public infrastructure and services, including education and police. Critics worried about negative social impacts and the failures of other casino-led redevelopment models to effectively revitalize places like Atlantic City.[4] While these concerns are germane to any jurisdiction considering legalized gambling as a form of economic development, Bethlehem's contest played out in 2005 and 2006 in a series of lengthy city council meetings that took an intensely localized shape. At stake were community narratives about Bethlehem's dual histories—Moravian and Steel—as well as the people each heritage represented. Who and what deserved to be remembered, and what role would the casino play in forging, or destroying, that community identity going forward?

Pennsylvania legalized a state lottery in 1971, one of forty-three states (plus Puerto Rico and the District of Columbia) to do so since New Hampshire sparked a renewed fiscal interest in state-sponsored gambling in 1963.[5] Pennsylvania's lottery brings in well over $3 billion annually with nearly a third of sales dedicated to funding programs for the elderly.[6] But facing persistent budget shortfalls, Ed Rendell, Pennsylvania's governor from 2003 to 2011, fixated on casino gambling as an opportunity to offset state deficits even more. Residents of Eastern Pennsylvania already went to Atlantic City to gamble, backers argued, so why not try to keep those revenues at home? Multimillion-dollar state licensing fees plus hefty taxes on gambling revenue could help balance the growing costs of state pensions and universities. While for much of the twentieth century casinos in America were associated in the popular imagination (and often in reality) with organized crime, corruption, and moral depravity, in the last few decades opinions have become more ambivalent. Politicians are well aware that, as with state lotteries, one way to boost casino support is to earmark a portion of revenues for perceived "good causes," thus bridging the distance between so-called rational economic arguments and moral entreaties.[7]

Gaming laws often have domino effects on other states whose legislators see me-too revenue potential. South Dakota jump-started a wave of casino legalization with its 1988 authorization of low-stakes gambling, dedicating a portion of the proceeds to historic preservation and tourism development. Colorado followed suit with a similar law two years later. Iowa was the first state to legalize riverboat casinos in 1989, followed by five more states by 1993. Between 1994 and 2004 the trend shifted toward allowing slots or video lotteries at racetracks, sometimes dubbed "racinos." Proceeds go to a range of public causes, including education, health care, public infrastructure, and economic development. Excluding Native American gaming, which is operated by sovereign tribes and is exempt from state taxes and regulations, by 2015 twenty-four states offered casino gambling at either stand-alone commercial casinos or racetracks.[8]

Still, Michael said that when the Pennsylvania legislature passed its 2004 bill, which authorized racinos and stand-alone slots parlors, most people were taken by surprise.

> Just all of a sudden they decided the lottery isn't cutting it, we need more revenue, and this is the way it's going to happen. We got all these people lined up to just jump in and steal people's money. And we're just going to sock it to the whole community, the whole state. It was underhanded, totally underhanded. We had no warning. All of a sudden gambling was legal. What? It wasn't even a question to any of us!

Michael's distrust of the government's intentions reflects a common perception among casino opponents that gambling is a form of regressive taxation, one that takes money from those least able to afford it or who would otherwise oppose tax increases.[9] But others might dispute his claim that there was no warning. As early as 1977, Pennsylvania state legislators (unsuccessfully) introduced a bill to legalize casinos in the Poconos in response to the new threat of revenue going across the border to New Jersey. Several other bills followed through the 1980s but lost steam when the state's fiscal affairs temporarily improved.[10] Rendell's own interest in legalizing gambling dates to at least 1991 when, as mayor-elect of Philadelphia, he supported state legalization of riverboat casinos. By 1994 casino interests like Bally's and Trump were buying waterfront property in the state just in case.[11] Following a string of failed riverboat bills, a 1999 proposal included legalizing slot machines at the state's four racetracks, but it likewise became mired in opposition.

According to the *Philadelphia Inquirer*, between January 2000 and July 2004 the gaming industry pumped almost $6 million into political campaigns in the state; about $1.7 million went to Rendell. Indeed, legalizing slot machines was part of Rendell's campaign for governor in 2002 and the first bill he introduced after taking office. The efforts languished until July 2004, during which the speed of a new bill's passage—within seventy-two hours of its introduction—accounts for Michael's and most other Bethlehem residents' shock.[12] Opponents were particularly upset that the decision was not put to public vote, a route made available in other states but explicitly denied by the Pennsylvania bill. Most agree such a vote would have prevented the bill's approval.

As passed, the Pennsylvania Gaming Act authorized a state commission to award up to fourteen casino licenses across the state. While the initial law only permitted slot machines, table games (and the possibility of a fifteenth casino) were added in 2010.[13] Unlike in Las Vegas or Atlantic City, only one casino is allowed within each ten-to-twenty-mile radius, creating intentional monopolies that let the state collect large licensing fees and high taxes in exchange for the exclusivity.[14] Indeed, Pennsylvania's tax rates on casinos are significantly higher than in other jurisdictions. Pennsylvania casino operators pay a one-time $50 million licensing fee to the state and an annual minimum $10 million fee to the host locality. Slots revenues are then taxed an additional 55 percent, and table game revenues are taxed 16 percent for the first two years and 14 percent thereafter. By comparison, the tax rate for both slots and table games in New Jersey is 8 percent; in

Nevada it is between 3.5 percent and 6.75 percent. By 2011 Pennsylvania annually collected roughly $1.4 billion in tax revenues from casinos, significantly more than any other state.[15] Portions of the collected revenue in Pennsylvania go to horse racing development, economic and tourism development, police, property tax relief, and municipal and county governments.[16]

Setting the Stage for Community Debate

After Pennsylvania legalized casino gambling in 2004, Bethlehem's mayor and other boosters immediately saw the new possibility of a slots parlor as an answer to the near decade of dust gathering on the Bethlehem Works plan for the Steel site. While the Pennsylvania Gaming Act did not specifically name casino locations, its framers acknowledge that the law was written to make the outcomes of the selection process "extremely predictable." The Lehigh Valley was a shoo-in for a site license from as early as 2003 when state legislators commissioned a report on the revenue potential of slots facilities.[17] Its arterial highway access to New Jersey and New York City places more than 21 million (mostly out-of-state) adults within a market radius.[18] The only question that remained was whether the casino would be placed in Allentown, to Bethlehem's west, or in the Christmas City itself.

Within a few months of the Gaming Act's passage, BethWorks Now, the latest owner of a 124-acre tract in the heart of the South Side that had been part of Bethlehem Steel's previous heritage-entertainment plans, was in conversation with at least four national casino corporations about the possibility of placing a slots parlor on the site of the former ore yard. Meanwhile, Foxwoods, the successful tribal casino resort in Connecticut, explored the far eastern edge of the plant near the highway where the coke works had been. In December 2004, BethWorks Now, made up of a group of New York investors and a local developer, announced a partnership with the Las Vegas Sands Corp. As majority stakeholder in the deal, Sands expressed its intent to follow the original Bethlehem Steel redevelopment plan—only now it would be bankrolled by gambling revenue. Within two months, the newly flush venture (renamed Sands Bethworks) purchased the fifty-acre plot on which Foxwoods had its eye in order to block competition for the state license.[19] Sands Bethworks turned its focus to the only remaining contender, Atzar Corp.'s Tropicana, which was bidding for a site in Allentown, and to gaining local support for its Steel site plans.

Despite the mayor's backing, many members of the community considered the idea of introducing gambling anathema to the small town's identity. "Most people in Bethlehem are under the impression that a casino would 'preserve the history of the Steel Factory,'" one resident wrote to explain the boosters' stance. "I feel that a gambling establishment undermines the entire definition of what the Steel Factory represented," she countered, saying that it would conflict with the local legacy of immigrants' strong work ethics. Other opponents invoked the city's earlier heritage, noting that, "The hard work ethos of Bethlehem Steel which evolved from our self-sufficient Moravian founders is in direct contrast to the get rich quick ethos of gambling."[20]

Invocations of the city's history offered more than a backdrop to the debate. Historical narratives became cultural tools residents and other stakeholders creatively employed to express their moral convictions about economic development and the role of capital in defining community. The various interests in having or preventing a casino in Bethlehem were a complex constellation, but as citizens voiced their opinions, the long-standing divisions between North and South Bethlehem continued to orient local feelings about a new global corporate presence. Efforts to distinguish the Moravians' spiritual founding from the Steel's economic successes—and to delineate which citizens were associated with which heritage—grounded residents' understandings of postindustrial change in their immediate surroundings.

Control over land use thus became a key focus as concerns bubbled in Bethlehem about the potential community impacts of casino-led development. The state Supreme Court ruled in favor of a citizen challenge to a provision in the Gaming Act that would have given the Pennsylvania Gaming Control Board the power to bypass local zoning laws—and any associated community opposition—in its selection of casino sites. But even though the court severed the provision as unconstitutional, the practical limitations to small city governments' abilities to impact state policy decisions became clear as the drama unfolded.[21] Following the court's decision, two members of Bethlehem's city council opposed to gambling—one a Moravian minister—introduced a zoning amendment to specifically prohibit a casino on the Steel site, and the community debate reached a crescendo. Groups calling themselves Concerned Citizens for a Better Bethlehem and Valley Citizens for Casino-Free Development formed to express opposition on moral and social grounds and to push for a voter referendum, even though (as they would later discover) the law did not allow for one. The mayor, like other proponents, continued to echo the developers in his conviction that "the best way, and probably the only way, to achieve our goals and to turn the BethWorks site into a successful multiuse development that preserves and celebrates our history is to use the economic power of legalized gaming as the catalyst for new development."[22] A series of lengthy council meetings commenced, with the debates frequently lasting until midnight and sometimes two o'clock in the morning.

Jacqueline Russo was one of dozens of citizens who regularly spoke at the public forums. Initially these meetings were held in Bethlehem's town hall, a circular building with curved tiers of auditorium seats around a podium that faces the seven-member council. Built in 1967 with a $500,000 gift from Bethlehem Steel, the town hall holds 120 people but rarely sees more than a couple of dozen at its typical biweekly meetings. During the casino debate, the fire chief had to turn people away once it reached capacity. More than 700 people showed up to the meeting for the council's vote on the zoning amendment, by which point they had relocated to a larger space. "Well, it was a circus," Jacqueline said of the typical meeting. "You had to go into the city council building and sign your name if you wanted to speak. Every seat in there was full, and you had to just sit and wait your turn and wait your turn and wait your turn, and God help you if you had any stage fright the minute you got up to the mike. Oh, my gosh."

As political sociologists have noted, the procedures of city government, from following *Robert's Rules of Order* to tight time constraints on public statements, are orchestrated rituals with a heavily performative dimension that Jacqueline's allusion to stage fright invokes. Through this performance, the public enacts ideals of democratic participation in community decisions. Critics, however, suggest this ritual form only allows for dissent within a framework in which the interests of "growth machine" politicians and developers ultimately win out.[23] Many casino opponents eventually resigned themselves to the belief that their influence had been likewise circumscribed. As in the "zoning ritual" through which the Bethlehem Steel Corporation navigated in the 1990s to give maximum flexibility to prospective developers, the inclusion of dissenting voices on the public stage did little to thwart the interests of corporate capital. Nonetheless, these meetings served an important purpose to publicly demonstrate the ways various stakeholders imagined Bethlehem's landscape as a material convergence of the city's history, its moral character, and its economic potential.

Creating the Christmas Landscape

Long before the successes of Enterprise Development and "tourist city" planners across the country, Bethlehem's residents adopted the language of heritage branding to express their desires for the city's future. The Moravians themselves had recognized the potential of their settlement's unique landscape to function as a marketing tool as far back as the colonial period. But during the Great Depression, these efforts took on a renewed urgency. The close link between the Steel Company and the origins of "Christmas City, U.S.A." offers an early example of corporate investment in local heritage. During the casino debate, opponents often invoked the Christmas landscape as a precedent for locally sensitive development that could benefit the bottom line while also supporting a community identity.

Bethlehem's "Christmas City, U.S.A." moniker was the brainchild of the Chamber of Commerce's new president in 1937, Vernon Melhado. He had come to Bethlehem from Jamaica fifteen years earlier after marrying the daughter of a Bethlehem Steel vice president. Himself a Sephardic Jew, Melhado nonetheless saw the potential and had the resources to use Bethlehem's Moravian heritage to bring shoppers to suffering downtown retailers and help offset the lull in steel production. On December 7, 1937, Marion Grace, head of the Chamber of Commerce's Women's Advisory Committee and wife of the Bethlehem Steel Corporation president, stood next to Melhado as she flipped a ceremonial switch to light the landmark "Star of Bethlehem," an eighty-foot wooden structure atop South Mountain, for the first time. The city also illuminated a giant evergreen on the

Hill to Hill Bridge and strung twenty-two blocks of multicolored Christmas lights downtown. Events included a visit from Santa Claus on a sleigh float, community choir performances, and the construction at Central Moravian Church of a large *putz*, the traditional German name for the region's elaborate nativity displays. Throughout the Christmas season the city's newspaper proudly reported that policemen had their hands full directing traffic caused by visitors touring the lights.[24]

In August 1938 Melhado died at age forty-nine of a heart attack while at the North Side home of a prominent Bethlehem widow talking over plans for the second annual Christmas events. As his obituary dramatically put it, "Mr. Melhado literally gave up his life in the interests of this city."[25] The next year, Bethlehem Steel donated a more permanent Star of Bethlehem constructed of galvanized steel and lined with 280 bulbs as a "symbol of righteousness connecting the present Bethlehem with the community that two centuries ago was founded and named by a band of Moravians." At a cost of $4,000, the new star perched atop South Mountain was visible from twenty miles.[26]

Thanks to the war overseas and Bethlehem's role in producing armaments, local Steel employment had rebounded from a Depression-era low of 6,500 in 1933 to 18,200 by 1940. It would peak in 1943 at over 31,000 people.[27] The Star was dimmed as a defense precaution following the attack on Pearl Harbor, but on December 26, 1941, the front page of the paper nonetheless declared it one of the best Christmases since pre-Depression years due to increased employment and bigger payrolls that enabled more gift-giving.[28] As the city's Steel-centric economy gradually became less certain in the following decades, however, Christmas City was again invoked to stabilize the community, in part by reasserting Bethlehem's historic divisions.

In the 1950s Bethlehem embarked on a series of federally funded urban renewal projects that focused to a great extent on "cleaning up" the South Side. As these efforts continued to bring class boundaries between North and South Bethlehem into relief, changes in the city's holiday celebrations had a similar effect. In 1954 the city discontinued its multicolored lighting displays, declaring the associated traffic jams a safety hazard. The usual garish Christmas lighting was replaced with more toned-down, clear white lamps. By the 1960s there was a general municipal agreement that the

North Side would string only white lights, and multicolored lights would be relegated south of the river. The Moravian tradition of placing a candle in every window, which was promoted across the city in the 1940s, soon concentrated in the North Side neighborhoods near the original Moravian settlement.[29] A tour guide in 2000 explained—and one can hear nearly identical language on bus tours of the decorations today—"the white lights decorating the city's north side represent the Moravian heritage brought here by those first settlers, while the multicolored lights that adorn the south side are thought of as representing the ethnic diversity of many more who came from many nations to help make this city great."[30]

The cheery language masks the deeper class divisions that the lighting shift re-inscribed onto Bethlehem's Christmas landscape. The description of Bethlehem's "distinguished" and "tasteful" North Side Christmas displays, implying that they must be in contrast to those on the South Side, still characterizes most accounts. An elderly North Side resident who insists on putting colored lights on the evergreen in her yard even though she lives in the Moravian historic district, told me about a recent scolding from a neighbor who declared, "I think it's terrible that you have all those colored lights. . . . They belong on the South Side with the Puerto Ricans!"—"Puerto Ricans," as we will see, being the most recent racialized shorthand for Bethlehem's poor and ethnic other. Locals often allude to the Moravian legacy to invoke notions of order and regularity in the landscape, reminiscent of those eighteenth-century visitors from nearby urban hubs who admired the founders' neat stone structures.

In 2005 and 2006 many residents similarly appealed to the Christmas City identity to claim Bethlehem's incompatibility with the proposal to construct a casino across the river, a plan they believed would disrupt the material and cultural order they idealized in the Moravian sites. The local newspaper cast the debate as a "battle for Bethlehem's soul."[31] As one resident put it, " 'Christmas City' and 'Sin City' simply do not go together."[32] Proponents argued that it would be immoral to deny citizens the jobs and tax revenue that the casino promised. But many opponents, in particular Moravians and other Christians, were convinced that in addition to compulsive gambling, a casino would usher in corruption, prostitution, alcoholism, crime, bankruptcy, and a range of other vices that threatened to tear families apart and undermine community values.

To support these views, opponents reframed the proposed zoning amendment to explicitly link the community's moral fiber to the aesthetic of the city's lighted landscape. As one Concerned Citizen for a Better Bethlehem told council members, "We urge you to vote for the symbol of the Christmas City, whose light of peace on earth, good will to all, still shines on a daily basis. Don't exchange the Star of Bethlehem for the neon lights surrounding slot machines and beckoning those seeking instant riches." The Star in these arguments was, in the long-standing American religious tradition, employed as a beacon on a hill, defining the city as a chosen place.[33] Resident after resident explained to me the unique "spirit of Bethlehem" that pervades the city, effectively a shorthand for all that is perceived to be pure and good and Moravian in the community. The phrase, though invoked earnestly, also carries the valence of a marketing slogan, affirming the historical relationship in Bethlehem between spiritual identity and economic development. After all, even the eighteenth-century Moravians sold handcrafted souvenirs to tourists keen on seeing the Sisters' House where single women lived.[34]

Karl Fluck, a South Side resident who opposed associating Bethlehem's name with gambling, elaborated on this confluence of heritage, morality, and economic development in his comments to the city council. "The purpose of [a product] maintaining a brand or a trademark is to distinguish and differentiate itself from other products," he explained.

> I respectfully submit that "The Christmas City" is more than merely our brand, it is our heritage and our property right. . . . Our brand, "Christmas City, U.S.A.," does not belong to any one individual, nor can any one individual cede that right to any one entity regardless of their position. Neither the Mayor, the City Council, local legislators, nor the Governor, nor our legislature may trade, sell or otherwise deprive us of the protection of our brand and property right to "Christmas City, U.S.A."[35]

Karl proposed a new understanding of morality not based exclusively on Christian faith. He transformed the notion of property right as a legalistic and deeply American ideal that applies to an individual or corporate entity into a different set of expectations for collective ownership and community participation. In linking heritage and property, he reinterpreted the economic justifications of the state gaming law and adapted free-market ideology to ideals of community benefit. He suggested that the city's heritage is not just a gimmick to sell; it is also a shared moral order embedded in the historical landscape. Ultimately, he questioned the trade-off when future-focused corporate capital usurps the value of accumulated, local experience.

By equating heritage and shared property, however, Karl also elided the complicated reality that various community members interpret and employ Bethlehem's history differently and to sometimes conflicting ends. Margaret Schantz, for example, invoked Bethlehem's Moravian legacy to *support* the plans for a casino, saying, "Thanks to its pious and reverent historical image, Bethlehem is one dull and boring place to live! We really need something up here that will give us a little fun!" As Margaret alluded to, references to the quaint, charming, and peaceful Moravian history can cloak the deep legacy of classed fears that the city's North Side image will be tarnished by outside interests. A South Side community organizer who supported the casino suggested some opponents were driven by "a need to perpetuate the myth of what *they* believe Bethlehem should have been without the Steel's presence."[36]

Michael Russo is among the gambling opponents who elevated the North Side Moravian identity as they imagined a new invasion. He wrote to the state gaming commission:

> Serene at this very moment, our clean Christmas City trembles at the specter of a destabilizing Goliath, the Las Vegas Sands, at our doorstep. . . . Our town's moral fiber was cultivated and nurtured by people of a fervent Moravian faith and community ethic, for a period of 150 years *before* steel ever got planted alongside the Lehigh River. The families of the Steel workers were beneficiaries of that wholesome environment as they settled here.[37]

Michael's religious references to a clean and serene Bethlehem erased the dirt and noise that defined the steel mill since the nineteenth century, much as his wife Jacqueline excised the Steel from her memories of raising her children across the river from the plant and Betty Bramson washed her

North Side garage clean each week. Those who opposed the casino on the basis of the Moravians' spirituality also generally did not note the fact that eighteenth-century Moravian leaders made many important decisions, including marriage pairings, by drawing lots or picking from pieces of paper on which they had written potential answers to a given question. While church elders sometimes described the practice as a "game," this form of spiritual gambling was perceived to reflect God's will rather than chance.[38]

The moral stance from which many casino opponents like Michael speak offers just one angle on the community's complicated relationship to its heritage. As religious studies scholars have argued, there is nothing inherent about a place that makes it sacred, whether it is a church, a Moravian district, or a star on a hill. Rather, sacred space is socially constructed through the various rituals and narratives that shape and define it. Moreover, the sacred regularly blurs with the profane, creating a landscape imbued with shifting and contradictory meanings for its multiple purveyors.[39] For many residents, the Bethlehem Steel plant represents an equally hallowed space and locus of community identity.

Redeeming Old Steel

Art Slesak has lived most of his seventy years on East Fifth Street in a home perched at the base of South Mountain. In the decade since Art retired from teaching high school English, he has worked his way up from neighborhood block watch captain to the appointed chair of the city's South Side Task Force, a conglomeration of organizations, businesses, and individuals with interests in South Bethlehem's development. Art, whose mother and paternal grandparents immigrated to South Bethlehem from Slovakia, was an early supporter of bringing the casino to town and prides himself on his rapport with some of the bigwigs from Las Vegas. When we talked in 2012 he spoke as a battle-worn veteran of the months of intense community debate that preceded the state's licensing decision. He chronicled the various points of contention that piled up over the Las Vegas Sands Corp.'s design plans for the former plant. One of the decisions the company ultimately made was to light the four blast furnaces that line the river in pinks and blues and greens at night rather than tear the rusting structures down. Some people viewed the gesture as a welcome concession to the community's desire to celebrate the Steel heritage. Others saw a smart move to capitalize on the site's tourism potential. But another interpretation emerged from Art's account that illuminates the overlap between social and economic, past and present concerns.

> *AS:* They decided no, we're going to keep them, because it's cheaper to keep them, even though the scrap iron's worth a lot of money. But they lit them up. And if you notice, they're only lit from the south. That's because the North Side didn't want them. They didn't want that light pollution.
>
> *CT:* Oh, I didn't know that.
>
> *AS:* That's—there are people in this town who still think we were wrong in allowing that filthy industry to come here.
>
> *CT:* Meaning the Steel or the casino?

Art facetiously meant the casino, but in this case my confusion over which perceived "filth" he referred to—the smoke of the factory or the moral depravity of gambling—was not a product of my naiveté so much as my increasing awareness of the past's ongoing reverberations in present-day Bethlehem. The city's North and South Sides, and the distinct religious and industrial histories these geographies have come to represent, remain socially, economically, and culturally divided. As with the city's Christmas lighting schemes, the initial decision to illuminate the blast furnaces only on one side and the choices that Las Vegas Sands would make about the casino's industrial-themed architecture highlight how, even in what seem like purely economic decisions, the city's built environment materializes persistent echoes of Bethlehem's competing moral orders and social expectations.

Mary Pongracz, a neighborhood activist who lived near the western edge of the former plant, believed during the debate over the casino license that the star on the hill literally paled in comparison to the promise of honoring the legacy of Bethlehem Steel. "To take this whole thing and concentrate on something the size of that little light over there as opposed to a national museum that's affiliated with the Smithsonian, to the restoration of the four blast furnaces which will not be torn down, we are giving people another reason to come to Bethlehem to see something that is

Blast Furnace Branding

The plant's blast furnaces are a new heritage attraction in Bethlehem and are, like the Star of Bethlehem, lit each night. They provide a dramatic backdrop for Bethlehem's new entertainment district along the Lehigh River, including the Sands Casino and the ArtsQuest SteelStacks concert venue and arts center. A Christmas tree topped with a Moravian star is part of seasonal decorations combining the city's two "brands." (Photo by author, 2011.)

historically . . . viable," she told the city council in 2005. "To me, the preservation of the Bethlehem Steel property is something that every citizen in this town should get up and support."[40]

For many members of the community, particularly those with personal or family ties to the Steel, the Moravian district is not the only consecrated space in Bethlehem. Other everyday landscapes, including the once teeming steel plant, are also sacred spaces through which residents narrate and ritually construct senses of self and community.[41] Richard Hoffer, for example, a former city government employee and community organizer now in his sixties, had three grandparents who worked at the plant. After one grandfather was first crushed by a beam and then died of unrelated cancer in the 1930s, the Steel offered his widow a career as a "charwoman," a cleaning lady responsible for the general office. "They looked out for family that way," he said, and indeed several other people told me of similar scenarios that linked economic survival with corporate ethics.

Richard is also typical in his absorption in the civil religion of steel production that makes the plant such a key battleground over the city's identity.[42] "I really believe that this is hallowed ground," he told me as we talked near the blast furnaces.

> I don't believe that people today much beyond my generation, maybe the next generation, but not much beyond that, really understand what this plant meant to America, to freedom. . . . I don't think people realize how close this country was to not being the America that we have today. Between Nazi Germany and Imperial Japan, the free world was at tremendous risk. And so this plant with the amount of armament that it produced, and other plants like it in America—not just Bethlehem Steel but U.S. Steel and all the other steelmakers—they saved the world. . . . We produced so much of what we used, what the Soviets used, and what the Allies used in Europe, that plants like this should never be allowed to disappear.

The Bethlehem Steel Corporation had been a U.S. defense contractor since the Spanish-American War. In 1918 Woodrow Wilson appointed company president Charles Schwab as director general of the federal Emergency Fleet Corporation, giving him authority over all U.S. shipbuilding for eight months during World War I.[43] During World War II, according to an oft-cited anecdote, Schwab's successor Eugene Grace promised President Roosevelt a ship a day and then exceeded that goal by making a total of 1,085 ships and servicing or converting 37,778 more at the corporation's fifteen shipyards.[44] The Bethlehem plant manufactured armor plates, engine parts, naval guns, and other munitions, finishing them in the High House, a building that goes as deep into the ground as it is tall and now stands just off the casino's parking lot.

Although former steelworkers today have lost their economic and political authority in Bethlehem with the decimation of their pensions, benefits, and unions, through memories like Richard's they tenuously maintain a degree of moral authority over how the plant site should be reused. In 2010, after new construction on the brownfield was well underway, a community leader attempted to change the name of Founders Way, a short street through the plant that Bethlehem Works had decoratively lined with gears a decade earlier as part of its original heritage plan. Employing his own redemptive language of new life for the brownfield, he now asked the city council to rename the street SteelStacks Boulevard, after the new arts center he was building, in order to reflect "the future of our community."[45] The arts center also would be industrial themed, but still the name change rubbed preservationists like Jenny Fosco the wrong way by signaling that the stakeholders with clout in Bethlehem were changing and that private interests might supplant community history. She contacted some former steelworkers and told them, "If you guys are ever going to do anything, you have got to come out to a council meeting in force, as steelworkers, and this is the only way you are going to shame them into not changing that name." They did, and within a month the name change was withdrawn.

Similarly, in 2005 and 2006 as community members made clear that Bethlehem's history was the moral crux—religiously and culturally—on which the casino debate would hinge, Sands increasingly emphasized its plans to incorporate the proposed site's industrial past and the original Bethlehem Works development concepts into its design. By August 2005, while Jenny and others were getting worked up over the absurdity of the Venetian-themed Vegas holdovers in the tent that Sands set up at Bethlehem's annual music festival, Sands was already tailoring its public image to fit the locality. Hundreds of area residents followed the gondoliers' entreaties to watch a short promotional film called "Bringing New Life to Old Steel: A Brighter Future Begins by Respecting the Past," and picked up brochures in which Mary Pongracz, the daughter of a Hungarian immigrant steelworker, was one of six South Side residents featured in their support of bringing jobs and multiuse development to the Steel site.

Some residents believed, as one described in written comments to the Gaming Control Board, that "Bethlehem is the only place where one can put a casino and have it actually *assist* in the preservation of a vital and important piece of American and world history."[46] But even amid agreement that Bethlehem Steel had represented a source of community pride, nostalgias for an earlier era can be variously expressed in relation to plans for urban redevelopment. Casino proponents alternately described the remaining Steel buildings as majestic, worth preserving with gambling funds, and as "a weed patch for sore eyes" or a "rust heap" that the casino could help transform. For other citizens, certain memories of the steel plant were not worth invoking at all. To Joanne Kehley, the daughter of a steelworker who worked his whole life at the plant and then lost his health insurance in the company's bankruptcy, "when he most needed it," the plans for the casino revived parts of the past she would rather forget. "Now people who had worked there would be taken advantage of a second time when they are tempted to gamble their money away," she wrote to the gaming board.[47] The memory of the Steel's embedment in the economic and social fabric of Bethlehem is fresh, and as Joanne makes clear, by inserting itself into that legacy Las Vegas Sands confronts a history much more complex than the superficial theming on which its plans focused.

Still, Michael Russo said he should have known local opponents to the casino didn't stand a chance when he saw how much money Sands was devoting to defeating the zoning change that would block its license approval. Gambling opponents held hand-drawn signs with slogans like "LV=Lehigh Valley, not Las Vegas." Casino supporters, by contrast, "were outfitted to the hilt," he said. "They would come in [to council meetings] with these bright orange t-shirts. And they had these really nice-made signs. We were carrying like handmade placards and makeshift signs, and they had official wooden ones. Oh, my gosh! It was such a setup." Sands orchestrated mass mailings of pre-addressed postcards that adopted steelworkers' legacies for its own needs:

> Dear Mayor Callahan and Bethlehem City Council,
>
> I am writing to ask you to oppose the resolution that will prohibit gambling on the old Bethlehem Steel site. I join with retired and active Steelworkers in support of the Bethlehem Works Now project that will preserve our heritage, create nearly 10,000 jobs, and bring millions of tax dollars to Bethlehem.

According to council members, despite the fact that opponents generally outnumbered supporters at the public meetings, the nearly 3,000 postcards the council received in favor of the casino far exceeded mailings in opposition.[48] Union construction workers, who were promised contracts should the license be granted, likewise came out in force to urge the city council to deny the prohibitive zoning amendment. After nine hours of back-to-back public meetings in September 2005, the seven-member council defeated the anti-casino resolution by one vote. Las Vegas Sands Corp. officially filed its license application with the Pennsylvania Gaming Control Board that December.

Other leaders of community opposition groups agreed with Michael that in retrospect the casino's go-ahead was a foregone conclusion. The head of Valley Citizens for Casino-Free Development said that "seven-eighths of the way through this battle" his Christian-based group was fighting for a public referendum that would let voters decide against a casino, until he realized the state law had been carefully written to deny this opportunity. Citizens for a Better Bethlehem reached a similar conclusion. "I can't point to anything that we were successful on," said David Wickmann, the president at the time of the Moravian Church's Northern Province who led that group. Despite his religious affiliation, Reverend Wickmann made a point not to cast his dissent only as moral opposition. Rather, he framed the issue in the language of finance to speak to developers' interests, stating that "gambling in itself was something that eventually depreciated the community rather than appreciated it."[49] But he said that he gradually "became aware of the fact that this was a done deal, politically a done deal, no matter what we would do, no matter what we would say." At a 2009 public meeting just before Pennsylvania legislators voted to expand the state's casinos from slots-only to include table games, Reverend Wickmann was invited to sit on a panel as the designated voice of community opposition. He again cast the expectations of public debate in explicitly ritual and performative terms, telling residents, "We have gathered for a drama, a huge drama, to say yes to table games. The script has been written, the players are in place, the curtain has opened, and the actors are in position."

From most perspectives, it was the 2004 Gaming Act that ushered in this new script laying out Bethlehem's future. According to former Bethlehem Steel CEO Hank Barnette, the major barrier to developing the Bethlehem Works site in the 1990s came down to an issue of financial risk. The site, he said, was always ideal for a company with deep pockets to transform it from an industrial brownfield into a heritage-entertainment destination. "If we had had this talk in the nineties, 1996, 1997, I would have bet you a Diet Coke that it was probably a company like Disney," he told me.

> But what we found was the companies, and we contacted many of them, they simply would not take the investment risk. Because the payback was too long and the risk uncertain. . . . There was simply not an investor that could awaken the core site. And that did not happen until the Sands came along [following passage of the Gaming Act]. The names of the parties are different than envisaged in the nineties, but what's happening here is essentially the plan that was developed and implemented.

Taking risks has always been a part of successful business development, as it was in Charles Schwab's 1908 decision to borrow $5 million to build a rolling mill in Bethlehem and be the first to mass-produce the structural H-beam. Also called a wide-flange beam, the H-beam defined the age of the skyscraper and made Bethlehem Steel the second largest steelmaker in the world. Schwab told his secretary at the time, "I've thought the whole thing over, and if we are going to go bust, we will go bust big."[50]

Barnette suggested that, in terms of taking risks, the modern casino industry and its affinity to the Steel site reflects the legal and cultural normalization of what were not too long ago judged to be unstable investments. As Barnette put it, the bet that Pennsylvania took on legalizing casinos was in the short term not a gamble at all. Rather, the law injected more certainty into real-estate speculation and development by offering companies like Sands the opportunity to enter a new market with an immediate monopoly on a region's gaming revenue. From the standpoints of investment partner BethWorks Now and local politicians, the Gaming Act promised a capable financial backer and revenues to develop the rest of the Steel site.

Over the next year, Las Vegas Sands continued to support local not-for-profits and community organizations with more than $200,000 in charitable donations.[51] Although this sum was a drop in the bucket for a global corporation with rising profits that had already reached $506 million in 2006, the money plugged holes in the budgets of many small-scale operations in Bethlehem and the Lehigh Valley.[52] Meanwhile, public debates

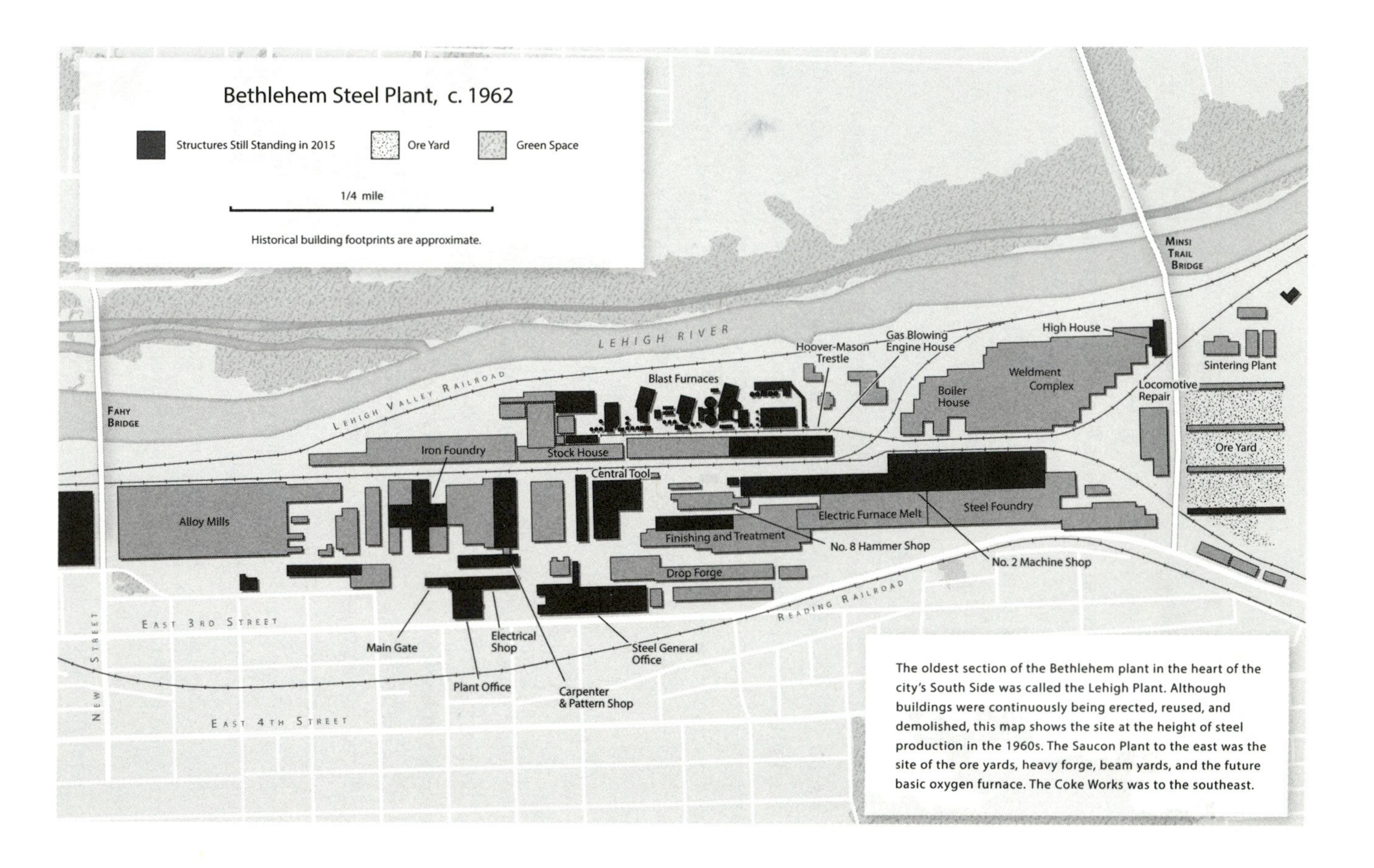

The oldest section of the Bethlehem plant in the heart of the city's South Side was called the Lehigh Plant. Although buildings were continuously being erected, reused, and demolished, this map shows the site at the height of steel production in the 1960s. The Saucon Plant to the east was the site of the ore yards, heavy forge, beam yards, and the future basic oxygen furnace. The Coke Works was to the southeast.

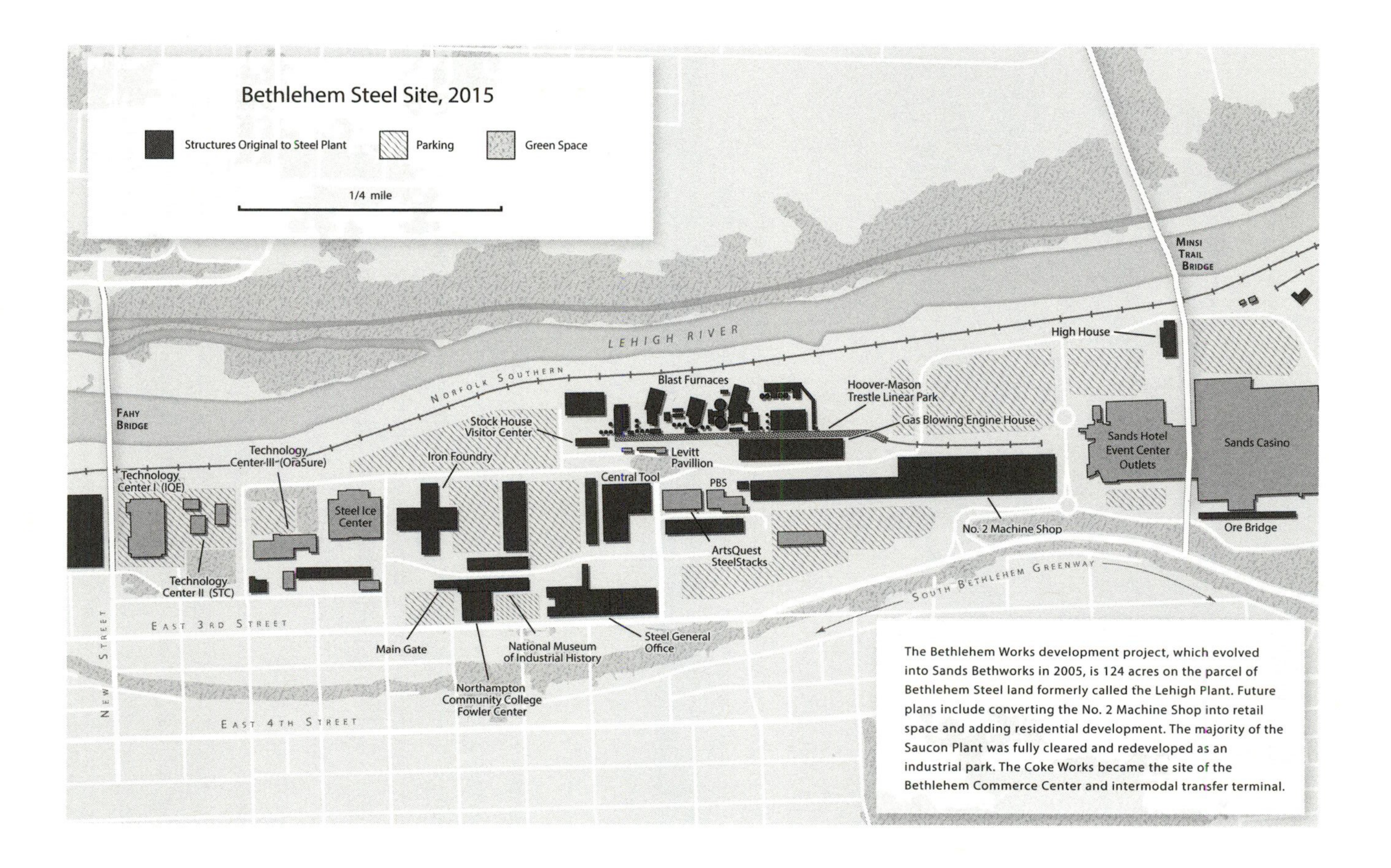
Bethlehem Steel Site, 2015
Structures Original to Steel Plant
Parking
Green Space
1/4 mile
Minsi Trail Bridge
Fahy Bridge
Lehigh River
Norfolk Southern
High House
Blast Furnaces
Hoover-Mason Trestle Linear Park
Gas Blowing Engine House
Stock House Visitor Center
Levitt Pavillion
Sands Hotel Event Center Outlets
Sands Casino
Technology Center III (OraSure)
Iron Foundry
Central Tool
PBS
Technology Center I (IQE)
Steel Ice Center
No. 2 Machine Shop
Ore Bridge
ArtsQuest SteelStacks
Technology Center II (STC)
South Bethlehem Greenway
East 3rd Street
Main Gate
National Museum of Industrial History
Steel General Office
Northampton Community College Fowler Center
East 4th Street
New Street
The Bethlehem Works development project, which evolved into Sands Bethworks in 2005, is 124 acres on the parcel of Bethlehem Steel land formerly called the Lehigh Plant. Future plans include converting the No. 2 Machine Shop into retail space and adding residential development. The majority of the Saucon Plant was fully cleared and redeveloped as an industrial park. The Coke Works became the site of the Bethlehem Commerce Center and intermodal transfer terminal.

The 1913 Electrical Shop

The shop on the left is the future site of the National Museum of Industrial History. Although the museum has faced significant delays in opening, the windows and roof of the shop were replaced in 2009, transforming it from the dilapidated condition of the Pattern and Carpenter Shop next to it. (Photo by author, 2015.)

continued at state hearings and in city council meetings. In an echo of the previous year's events, another city council vote in the fall of 2006 to explicitly confirm that, yes, casinos were allowed in Bethlehem, entailed nine more hours of debate before the affirmation passed. On December 20, 2006, the Pennsylvania Gaming Control Board awarded a license for the Las Vegas Sands Corp. to build in Bethlehem. The board cited as the basis for its choice Las Vegas Sands' financial resources, the potential for strong revenues and job creation, the opportunity for large-scale brownfield reuse, and the company's "respect and homage to the history and heritage of Bethlehem." Residents' moral opposition to the gaming law, it declared, was irrelevant to the decision.[53] Site work on the Steel's former ore yard began within weeks, and by mid-2007 full-scale construction was underway.

Postindustrial Picturesque

As part of its licensing application, Sands had a six- by sixteen-foot architectural model made of its proposal to adapt the Steel's original Bethlehem Works plan and redevelop the rest of the 124-acre site. After it was no longer needed in Harrisburg, Sands put the model, which visually transforms deteriorating industrial structures into neat brick boxes, on display for the public at city hall. Phase One of the "heritage-based" development project involved tearing down ten Steel buildings, including the weldment complex, where armaments were made, the locomotive repair shop, electric furnace melting building, steel foundry, and blast furnace bag house. New construction included the casino and an attached 300-room hotel, retail complex, and event center. While the recession in 2008 threw plans into question, the developers predicted that, over a five-year timeline, additional phases of development would include adaptive reuse of several existing buildings and more industrial-themed new construction. The massive No. 2 Machine Shop next to the casino and hotel, for example, was initially tagged for "Steel Works Lofts," but later became the proposed adaptive reuse site for additional retail stores and a second hotel.

Moving further west, Sands entered agreements to donate land to local not-for-profit ArtsQuest for the new SteelStacks arts center, and to the local PBS television station for a new headquarters. The adjacent stone Stock House, which dates to 1863 and is one of the oldest extant Steel buildings, was turned over to the city for reuse as a visitor center. Sands expected the stalled National Museum of Industrial History, a separate venture now downsized to the 1913 Electrical Shop, to be pushed along by the other development. Next to the museum, the local community college had already set up a South Side branch in the former Bethlehem Steel plant headquarters building. Across the parking lot, the Steel General Office building and former world headquarters, which dates to 1916, was slated for renovation as apartments, part of up to 1,200 lofts the developers initially anticipated for the site.

Preservation-based development schemes thrive on nostalgic allusions. Most visions of a unified past, however, depend on a disjuncture with the blighted present. In other words, for a developer to create a new

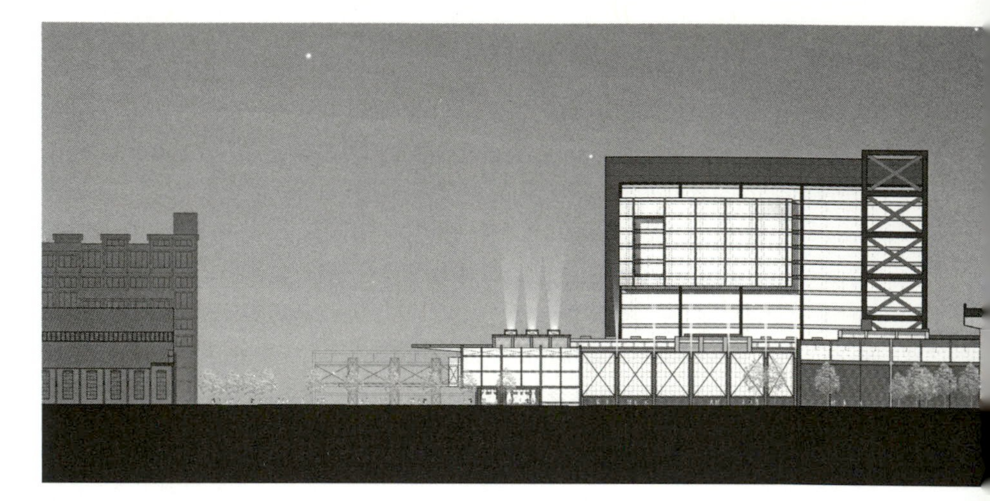

Sands Casino South Elevation

This circa 2007 rendering from RTKL Associates shows the hotel on the left and main entrance of the casino on the right. RTKL chose to depict the building at night, emphasizing the electrical glow meant to mimic the former activity of the steel mill. The tanks on the

era of heritage-themed economic activity, the recent, messier past must be destroyed in favor of representations of a more distant golden age.[54] In Bethlehem, where the city's proud steel heritage and recent decline are temporally condensed within a generation, this type of distancing poses a challenge. While the city hopes it will be a model for brownfield redevelopment in other postindustrial communities, varied interpretations of the casino's architectural design reveal the challenges involved in institutionalizing economic change by historicizing an ongoing cultural presence like the Steel.

The deep symbolism of beginning new construction in 2007 on the defunct Steel site, which sat silent for nearly a decade, was not lost on Las Vegas Sands or its public relations outfit. At the last hearing for the casino license in Harrisburg, a gaming commissioner asked Bill Weidner, the president of Las Vegas Sands at the time, whether his company planned to use American steel for the project. "Is there any left?" Weidner responded to laughs from the panel.[55] Yet in the end, Sands publicly committed to using only domestic steel in its Phase One construction, a good portion of which came from Nucor, where steel from the Bethlehem plant was shipped for recycling after it closed.[56]

roof are purely decorative, as are the crossed steel trusses on the façade. The dark building facing the complex is the vacant No. 2 Machine Shop. (Courtesy of RTKL Associates Inc.)

Unlike Sands' more spectacle-based Las Vegas properties, such as The Venetian, this $743 million first phase of development in Bethlehem attempted to reflect the local history through the vernacular of industrial architecture. Most Bethlehem Steel buildings were designed by the company's in-house engineers from a large archive of stock designs and approved materials. Steel buildings such as shops and mills from the first half of the twentieth century were characterized by red brick walls with structural steel beams and trusses supporting metal saw-tooth roofs.[57] A former steelworker took the casino and hotel's design team—from Las Vegas Sands, global architecture firm RTKL Associates, and interior design firm Walsh Bishop Associates—on tours through the plant to help with the creative process. The architects reportedly pinned over a thousand photos of the Steel site on their studio walls as they in effect used it as their own archive to design new buildings that are recognizably "industrial."[58]

While the Steel's engineers worked with a primarily functional motivation, the casino's design team integrated aesthetic and symbolic concerns. Sands outlined the design concept in early promotional materials:

No. 2 Treatment Shop

This building, constructed in 1888, was used in the heat treatment of armor plate. The large windows and monitor roof are typical of "daylight factory" architecture popular through the early twentieth century. (Joseph E. B. Elliot, 1990, Historic American Engineering Record, Library of Congress.)

> The historical and emotional importance of Bethlehem Steel argues against a Disney-esque interpretation. The design of the casino, hotel, and retail center combines gabled roofs, exposed steel structure, brick, and glass in ways that are compatible with the existing buildings and infuse the project with new energy and excitement now absent from the site. Coordinated dramatic lighting effects in the new building and existing ones will light the site with a glow that will recall the glowing furnaces of the plant circa-1942.[59]

As Weidner explained, "It will be an extraordinarily emotional connection that then can create an added value."[60] But the public debate over Bethlehem's community identity made clear that Sands' decision to link the casino design to the steel mill specifically "circa-1942" is a vision of the Steel's legacy and emotional resonance that can be disputed. Sands' conception

Sands Casino Interior

The industrial theme of the casino's interior is reflected in the exposed steel beams and pipes on the ceiling, the orange color scheme, and the hanging lights that resemble glowing steel ingots. (Photo by author, with agreement from Sands Casino Bethlehem, 2015.)

attempts to usher in a new era of consumer energy divorced from the recent decline of the plant and the feelings of anger and betrayal many Bethlehem residents continue to feel as a result. It grasps for a more distant and favorable nostalgia by focusing instead on the pinnacle of the Steel's wartime production and advancements for union workers. The design overtly taps the pride with which locals reference the company that "built and defended America," helping to win a "good war" that Americans more often celebrate than interrogate.

Although the casino architecture is an amalgamation of industrial elements in the surrounding Steel buildings—it incorporates saw-tooth roofs, steel columns with brick and glass infill, corrugated metal sheathing, and crossed steel trusses—much of the original function of these elements is erased. As the director of design at Las Vegas Sands noted, they were careful "to make sure it doesn't look too large or too bulky."[61] Instead, tower-like structures on the casino and hotel are meant to mimic the smokestack skyline of the steel factory, with the fire in the furnaces and the glow of the steel replaced by electric lights. There are other major differences. Many original Steel buildings are typical of the "daylight factory" style in their use of monitor roofs and lots of windows to let natural light into the workspaces. Though industrial buildings in the early twentieth century often used translucent glass in their windows to soften the glare and better diffuse natural light, some factories placed clear glass in the panes at eye-level to avoid a "prison-like effect."[62] The interior of the new casino, by comparison, entraps visitors and shuts them off from the outside world quite effectively. Like other casinos, there are no windows or clocks on the walls inside the Sands Casino. Owners hope these design strategies will cause customers to lose track of time and prolong their gambling. Indeed, although some monitor windows line the high ceiling of the main casino floor, the lighting at the Sands is distinctly *unnatural*, as one might expect in a space packed with 3,000 neon-flashing slot machines. Overhead, amid exposed beams and ventilation systems, orange rod light fixtures are meant to evoke the glow of molten steel. The windowless design elements, as well as the flat roofs on the parking garage and adjacent retail space, share more similarities with warehouse-style factories typical in America since the 1960s than they do with the Bethlehem Steel of 1942 that the Sands architects referenced in their promotional materials.[63]

Despite some disjuncture between the new construction and the old Bethlehem Steel buildings—both conceptually and materially—the Sands casino complex incorporates two elements original to the site in dramatic fashion to blend past, present, and future. In addition to lighting the four blast furnaces on the river near the center of the development site, the hallmark of the casino structure itself is the massive ore bridge that spans the entrance to the parking garage. As we have already seen, the twenty-ton bridge, now emblazoned with the red Sands branding, is a reminder that the casino was constructed on the Steel's ore yard. As Sands described, "Visitors to the casino will drive under this huge structure and know that they have arrived at a unique destination that combines entertainment, energy, theatrics, and American history."[64] Just as Sands created an "industrial" space in the casino that simultaneously references and denies visitors access to the authentic industrial context outside, the postindustrial picturesque that the ore bridge represents cloaks industrial history with a new consumer-driven and entertainment-based economic model. For a corporation that relies on to-the-minute calculations of shareholder value and customers who dream of future wins regardless of how much money they have already lost, the references to Steel heritage create a bridge, both figurative and literal, to help morally legitimate a postindustrial form of capitalism that in every other sense operates to render the past obsolete.

From a marketing perspective, one might expect that the casino's theme would be designed to appeal to the tourists who come to gamble, shop, and eat at the property. As architects Robert Venturi, Denise Scott Brown, and their colleagues famously said of the Las Vegas Strip, the buildings themselves act as giant signs announcing the entertainment within.[65] Marketing specialists typically select motifs like that of the Sands' Venetian casino resort to transport visitors to an exotic locale, apart from the reality outside.[66] In a way, Sands' circa-1942 industrial theme fulfills a different, and today equally exotic, fantasy—one of stable employment in American manufacturing.

Area residents quickly taught me that Bethlehem's casino design is less straightforward than simple consumer marketing, however. Some visitors to the casino, including former steelworkers, remark on the cleverness of the Sands' orange lighting, the false interior steel support pillars, and some of the Steel blueprints that hang as art on the walls. Some even mistakenly believe that the new structure is a rehabilitated factory building. But many find the industrial experience underwhelming. The high ceilings may give the space an appropriate-to-theme machine shop atmosphere, but some gamblers complain about the noise and cavernous feeling of the space.[67] Others suggest that Sands has not gone far enough to highlight the site's history by displaying Steel artifacts and memorabilia that local steelworker groups have offered to loan.

Jeremy Bergman, a young father with a goatee and pierced ears, commutes an hour each day to deal blackjack and baccarat at the Sands Casino. He applied for the job after being laid off from a small steel plant in Reading. Although he is not old enough to have seen Bethlehem Steel in its heyday, he has several months of first-hand knowledge working in manufacturing. When we talked in a community college classroom in the former Steel office building down the road from the casino, Jeremy humored me with his explanation of the difference:

> *JB:* When you walk into a steel mill, there's a lot of dirt. I mean a lot. Smoke, noise, a lot of movement, machinery. Caution signs everywhere. Earplugs everywhere for you to grab. A lot of heat. A lot of sharp objects. Sometimes fires. That's just from my experience in the little time I worked there. I helped put out a fire three times when I worked there.
>
> *CT:* Whereas, if you walk into the casino, what's missing?
>
> *JB:* There's no machinery. I mean, like if they had a fake crane on the ceiling maybe, or a tow motor, a boom truck, something like that. It'd make it seem more like it. Maybe coils of steel just laying on the side. There's a lot of product laying around in a steel mill. You see a lot of steel, just raw steel.
>
> *CT:* Do you think they could do that here?
>
> *JB:* Oh yeah they could! You would notice the theme then. Because, to tell you the truth, I don't think half the people that walk in even know that there's a theme to it.

Realizing that tourists, for the most part, are not raving about (and may not even notice) the Bethlehem casino's allusions to local history, I became aware through my interviews that the design is intentionally targeted not so much toward destination gamblers as to the local population. A range of constituents repeatedly offered me the phrases, "to pacify the people," "a nice gesture," and "appeasement." If one reads between the lines, casino design is a window into local market politics. As others have argued, a casino's theme is a way to signal compliance with a surrounding community's cultural expectations and gain political acceptance. In California, for example, most Native American casino themes reference the tribes' cultural heritages, but not because marketing departments say the motifs will attract more tourists. The themes aesthetically validate tribal sovereignty in a way that may protect against policymakers and voters challenging the monopoly Native Americans have been granted in the state's gambling market.[68] It is not surprising, then, that during Las Vegas Sands' three-hour final presentation and defense to the Pennsylvania Gaming Control Board in 2006, significant time was devoted to discussing what Sands president Bill Weidner called the "emotional and aesthetic aspects of the project's design" and its "salute" to the city's heritage.[69] For Sands, referencing Bethlehem's industrial past was a way to gain legitimation for its development interests, both locally and from the state licensing board.

While some residents remain bitter about the Las Vegas Sands Corp.'s political maneuvering, most agree that the industrial theme is a better outcome than importing a Vegas-style resort. The Moravian minister who led the community opposition group, elaborated on the power dynamic between Las Vegas Sands and the city that is expressed via the built environment: "There's no question in my mind that [the industrial theming] was a substantial play to open the door to [get into] the community. But on the other hand, that respects the community at least, and if it was a political reason, well, so be it." His references to community respect push local understandings of Las Vegas Sands' business decisions beyond purely financial calculations. Sands' theming strategy not only helped guide its application through the state licensing board, but it also to some extent legitimates and values Bethlehem residents' own sense of community heritage, affirming that the Steel's legacy still holds a meaningful place in national and global economies. As another casino dealer described it, the Sands' theme complies with "the sentiment of the town." It reflects a modification to business models that strive to excise emotion from calculations of profit opportunities rather than recognize the ways in which all market functions are morally vested. Moreover, rather than assume economic shifts are part of universal processes, local understandings of the changing Bethlehem landscape in small ways revise abstract free-market logics. The unique casino theme points to a potential for community benefit and recognition when developers address the particularities and contingencies of place and local history.

Jim Schuster, the former researcher at the Steel, is among those who appreciate the casino's efforts to "blend in," but have not forgotten that Las Vegas Sands still holds the cards in this appeasement strategy. "There's a link to the past, but we're going into the future," he said. "I thought it was very, very benevolent of them to do it that way. And I think it maybe eased the tension, the effrontery of putting that, a casino, in what used to be a steel plant!" His reading of benevolence into the casino design exemplifies the tension between possibilities for local empowerment and feelings of inevitability in the face of postindustrial change. Residents' investments in local heritage landscapes, both the Moravian North Side and the South Side industrial plant, open up spaces to push back on the future-oriented discourse that generally accompanies new development. Beneath Las Vegas Sands' savvy use of history, however, a progress narrative that would render memories of the social contract between corporation and community obsolete remains a powerful frame. Despite Weidner's emphasis on respecting citizens' desires, he affirmed that business decisions are governed by their own ethics. "I want to make sure that we are very clear. I don't want to be disingenuous. We are not social workers," he told the state board. "We want to make money. We are a money-making enterprise [and] we are not ashamed of it. . . . That is our goal."[70]

The Age of the Casino

Coral Lopez moved to Bethlehem in 1997, just as the Steel was shutting down its last operations. Born and raised in Puerto Rico, she had lived in Florida and Texas for a few years before joining her two sisters and aunt in Pennsylvania. A single mother at the time with three young children, Coral found an apartment in a low-rent neighborhood on the South Side. She immediately got involved in community politics, where she heard about plans to redevelop the Steel's brownfield.

> And I kept on telling my sister, it was a year after I was here that I would say, "I'm staying here and I'm going to buy a house." And I was looking for a house in the South Side, and my sisters were both living in the North Side, [and] said, "You're crazy. You don't want to buy a house on the South Side. You're going to waste your money. And that place is just going down the hill. It's just getting worse."

Like previous generations of European immigrants, many Latinos who arrive on the South Side strive to eventually move across the river to North Bethlehem. So when Coral ultimately bought a house in 1999 on East Fifth

Street, a few blocks from the newly vacant ore yard, her oldest sister stopped speaking to her for three months. "She believes she's my mother. She still does. So she was mad at me. She was like, 'You wasted your money. You throw away your money. I can't believe you did that!'"

Today, from its hillside perch, the front porch of Coral's half-a-double house gazes directly out at the blazing red Sands sign. To Coral, who when I spoke with her worked at the recently opened arts center on the Steel site, it is a new beacon of hope for the city and an affirmation of her choice to live on the South Side. "After seeing the darkness and the gray and the sadness of the site that I had from my house . . . for so long," she told me, "then all of a sudden I see life." Coral frequently walks down to the casino to play the slots. She runs into friends there and passes neighbors on the way coming home in their Sands uniforms. While some have criticized the impact on South Side employment, and particularly Latino employment, as being less than promised, Coral has only positive things to say. In fact, Las Vegas Sands asked her to speak on its behalf when it pushed the state to legalize table games in 2010.

In these public forums and in our conversation on her back patio, Coral regularly invoked the casino-led narrative of economic progress and urban reinvention that Las Vegas Sands had promoted with its "Bringing New Life to Old Steel" materials and ritualized through its opening ceremony. It is a narrative shared with other development interests in the city and many local politicians as well. To Coral, any negative reactions to the industrial theme of the casino, like negative reactions to her decision to live on the South Side, reflect a failure to understand a forward-looking economic transition. Coral believes the architectural theming and "industry flavor" of the casino appropriately honor the heritage of the steel company without becoming mired in a past way of life. "When I walk in there and people are telling me, 'Yeah, when they made the I-beam they put it in the water and that's what this fountain is here,' I was like, wow! That is great! And you walk in there and you see all those flashy orange—those are the steel! I'm like wow!" she said. "And then I go in with somebody that worked at the Steel and I'm saying the same thing, and they're like, 'That's not the way it looked!' And I'm like, 'You just ruined my image!'" she laughed. "They're like, 'I never saw any kind of iron piece hanging from the floor.' . . . Well, of course. It's a casino. You don't want to get dirty when you sit in there!"

Coral's interpretation of the Steel theme relies on cleaning up the unpleasant elements of an operating mill to make it enjoyable for today's entertainment-driven uses.[71] Rather than reflect the harsh conditions of work in a factory, the casino theme functions to project a more amenable version of the industrial past. While for Coral it is self-evident that the casino is not actually a steel mill, for those who have worked in a factory her "image" does not jibe with their own experiential knowledge. A thirty-seven-year veteran of the coke works explained the distinction between working his former job at the hot and dirty ovens and playing the slots quite simply: "That's like hell, and this is like heaven."

In Coral's paradigm of the post-Steel landscape, as for many development boosters, this kind of manufacturing-based worldview is fundamentally incompatible with the flexibility and "mind-work" that characterize their visions of the postindustrial economic future.[72] "I'm an artist too so my brain works better in a creative way than not. And not everybody has that. Not everybody has that capacity. And so if you tell some individuals this is going to be *in memory of*, it has to look exactly like, otherwise it's not," she explained. "Individuals that worked at the Steel are in general not people with the creative brain. . . . They are individuals that don't have that vision." Coral's assessment somewhat dismissively cast former steelworkers as being unable to adapt to the heritage-entertainment economy that requires letting go of certain aspects of the past in order to move forward.

Her narrative is a persistent one that informs much of the urban planning literature on postindustrial redevelopment in American cities. It is a story that relies on organizing a community's transition into discrete stages that build upon each other in the name of progress.[73] As the casino debate showed, many residents speak of Bethlehem's history as being divided into two distinct epochs: The Age of the Moravians and The Age of Steel. Javier Parker, a Moravian pastor, was not the only one to suggest that, "What might be synonymous to Bethlehem later on might be the casino. And so that's a new identity. It's unavoidable. That might be the new building that is standing up instead of [the] steel stacks." With his assessment Javier suggested that by adopting the ore bridge as its sign, the Sands has appropriated the Steel ruin as a part of the *casino's* history, thus moving the city narrative forward to a new era, an "unavoidable" result of so-called free-market evolution.

Even casino opponents like Michael and Jacqueline Russo sometimes turn to a similarly naturalized language of development. "You can tell we're sour about it. But at the same time it's working," Michael said three years after the casino's opening. He pointed to the more than 2,000 new jobs plus construction work the casino had already created and the millions of dollars in host fees and taxes it pays the city, county, and state. In 2012, the Federal Reserve Bank of Philadelphia declared Bethlehem "relatively prosperous."[74] Michael typifies the ambivalence toward the Sands and Bethlehem's heritage that many residents feel now that their worst fears about gambling's social ills have thus far failed to materialize. Many North Side opponents are content enough that the casino is at least "over there" on the other side of the river, in what is still perceived as a distinct cultural space. "It's a bitter pill we have to swallow for the economic thriving of the city," Michael explained. To Jacqueline's chagrin, since the casino opened he has become a regular visitor to the slots when he's looking for entertainment. She still refuses to set foot inside.

The community debates over the casino and the various roles history plays in local imaginations nonetheless suggest that the linearity of Coral's model needs to be revised. The Sands' architectural allusions to the city's Steel heritage elicit a hyperawareness and anticipation of how the casino will fit into Bethlehem's economic, social, and historical trajectories. The landscape offers a key site through which residents use a material present to make cultural sense of these interwoven pasts and futures, and in some cases push against politically dominant views of profit-guided development. Here, industrial brownfields are sacred sites, business decisions express moral convictions, and seemingly surface-level metrics of economic growth have far-reaching social consequences. "You have jobs now where there were none. You have a physical facility where you had rust," said one former steelworker. "What are we giving up to have that? There's always a trade-off. And what is the trade-off here? I'm not sure what that is yet." The converging narratives of past and future, rupture and continuity that defined the casino debate permeate Bethlehem's various other cultural landscapes—the landscapes of work, historic preservation, and ethnicity. Economic changes, moral orders, and local histories are experienced and reshaped not only through factory closures or real-estate development, but also in daily life throughout the community.

3

The Postindustrial Factory

LAS VEGAS SANDS CORP. CEO Sheldon Adelson likes to tell how he flitted from job to job as a young man, working his way up from nothing. He sold anti-freeze, advertisements, mortgages. He twice amassed a multimillion-dollar fortune and then lost it before hitting the jackpot with the Vegas-based Comdex computer industry trade convention in 1979. Only then did Adelson re-brand himself as an "entrepreneur," and a highly successful one at that, instead of as a drifter with a short attention span.[1] His vision of the "self-made self" permeates popular job search literature in the postindustrial economy, including *What Color Is Your Parachute?* and *I Could Do Anything if I Only Knew What It Was*, urging readers to "stop waiting for luck and start creating it."[2] Mobility, adaptability, and identifying one's most transferable skills have become prime assets for both employability and job creation in everything from finance to retail.

The casino industry within which Adelson thrives is no exception. The ethos of individual risk-taking is not only central to the excitement that casinos market to their customers. Corporations also instill these postindustrial norms in their employees. While Bethlehem Steel's worksites post–World War II were regimented by union rules, new social structures (or the lack thereof) have ushered in an era of irregular schedules, high turnover, and fragile benefits. Rather than lament their insecurity and vulnerability in service industry positions, however, many employees portray workplace volatility as an advantage. As such, the casino industry is part of a broader realignment of expectations for postindustrial employment. Stability and mobility are not necessarily perceived as distinct workplace paradigms that define the before-and-after of deindustrialization. Rather, as casino employees make sense of their work, stability and mobility begin to resemble and reinforce one another.

The casino industry's arrival in Bethlehem was part of a series of changes that have restructured the economy over the past four decades. As the number of manufacturing jobs has declined precipitously, the global growth of "gaming" as a profitable business reflects the steady rise of the service, entertainment, and finance sectors. When Bethlehem Steel closed its local plant in 1998, casino gambling was still illegal in Pennsylvania. The idea of opening a casino on the site was not yet a feasible consideration. But on a national scale, the climate had been evolving. Before the late 1970s, casinos in Las Vegas were run by small, private, and largely unregulated companies. With the Nevada Corporate Gaming Acts of 1967 and 1969, however, casino corporations took steps into respectable society. The improved transparency and government oversight that came with the decision to allow publicly traded corporations to own casinos increased access to legitimate financing and boosted investor confidence.[3] Harrah's Entertainment became the first "pure casino" company to be traded on the New York Stock Exchange in 1973, and with the legalization of gambling in Atlantic City in 1976, the value of casino stocks jumped. Indeed, as politicians and developers in New Jersey tried to convince voters to support in-state gambling, they touted the risk of this new investment—mostly its potential upside—as being similar to the promise of the stock market. In the flurry of state attempts to legalize casinos in the 1980s—as was the case in Pennsylvania decades later—advocates cast critics' attacks on gaming's immorality as overly emotional and provincial compared to the perceived rationality of fiscal arguments.[4]

The rise of casino stocks also coincided with a broader economic shift toward riskier financial dealings. Critics coined the term "casino capitalism" in 1986 to refer to the post–World War II transformation away from industrial production and toward a less stable economic order based on speculative financial markets. Closely aligned with neoliberal economic reforms that began to accelerate in the 1970s, this "new economy" is marked by flexible labor markets, economic deregulation, and the decentralization of global markets, particularly through advances in information technology. As in a casino full of flashing digital slot machines, profit is no longer based on production of durable goods, but is tied to abstract investments in profit itself. Neoliberal policy shifts emphasize the logic of the idealized "free market," where businesses and investors are unencumbered by government oversight or taxes, as being critical for economic growth. This logic supports the increased privatization of services, the decimation of the welfare state, and the elevation of individual responsibility rather than collective action as guiding principles. The ideal, unfettered mobility of capital on a global scale also promises to make profit less reliant on particular places. In other words, it codifies the dismantling of the social contract.[5]

The new-economy paradigm extends into workplace expectations, amplifying the insecurity that Arnold Strong and other Bethlehem steelworkers found once the plant gates were locked behind them. My conversations across classes in Bethlehem suggested that a worldview based on faith in individual agency, free-market logic, and accepting precarious employment as a natural market condition is broadly adopted.[6] Compared to a planned career at the Steel, the postindustrial expectation is that all work is by definition temporary. Offshoring and job consolidation are routine. Loyalty to a single firm, a hallmark of the postwar period that was reinforced by union seniority rules and benefits, is perceived in the contemporary worldview to be misguided and expectations of job security or social protections to be ignorant. Those who will prosper in this economy, the story goes, will be free agents who embrace mobility, adaptability, and risk. Indeed, the decisions steelworkers made as the Bethlehem plant shut down in the 1990s were by that time understood as high-stakes gambles. Many chose to leave families behind and transfer to other plants, often at the risk of facing another layoff on arrival. Others bet on not being called to transfer while they rode out the wait list on layoff, again hoping to maximize pension returns. For some, a decision to just get out early, cut their losses, and move on, would in retrospect have been the safest bet.[7]

Kevin Engel was among those steelworkers who made a successful transition from the industrial plant to a postindustrial cubicle. Rather than reflect an unbridgeable gap between the "culture of the hands" and the "culture of the mind," Kevin occupies a hybrid culture, making much of the fact that he was able to find another job because he could "talk both languages"—steel plant and office. Kevin began work as an electronics technician at the Steel in 1963, his associate's degree augmented, like most steelwork, by on-the-job training as well as his early interest in computers. He spent the last seventeen years of his Steel career as a union official before he was laid off in 1997. Although he was eligible for his pension, Kevin chose to get certified in computer systems engineering and go on the job market for the first time in thirty-five years. First, he said, he had to develop "the right mindset." "I went to a number of interviews, and as you go to interviews you learn, and you learn how to modify your resume and so forth. And I never put any years on so they didn't know how old I was." In 2000, nearing age sixty, Kevin was hired by a local financial institution and worked there in the information technology department for another decade.

Kevin said the biggest difference between the two jobs was the dress code—from rolling in grease to wearing a tie—and working with mostly women. But he preferred to stress the similarities. "It sounds like I went from steelworker to banker. Because of my working with the union, I worked with people at the senior management level in dealing with grievances. So to move over into the banking industry I dealt with lots of senior management, and I was able to speak their language, and we got along pretty good." Just as he waved off the too-neat narrative (so appealing to an outside ethnographer) that he embodied the transition from manufacturing to finance, Kevin said his job choice had nothing to do with forecasting the future. "I just rolled with the punches. If the Bethlehem Steel in any way would have continued, I would have been here," he said, looking out at the blast furnaces that loom over the arts center where we sat. Indeed, Kevin still identifies most readily as a Steel employee, albeit a highly skilled one, speaking with deference about his ability to work with bankers, never quite losing a trained sense of workplace hierarchy.

Although Kevin landed on his feet with his post-Steel career, in the meantime he worries about his son, who more readily embraces the gamble of modern employment. He was laid off from his high-paying job—in risk management—a few years ago. Kevin thinks his son should have stuck with a lower-paying position instead of hopping from company to company during waves of consolidation, but he knows from his second career that the days of keeping one job for thirty-seven years are over. "The only way to get ahead in a bank, you got to quit and go to another bank," he explained. "The banking industry seems to be a big circle. You keep moving."

While for some, including former industrial workers, this sort of mobility is freeing, it teeters on a fundamentally precarious financial future.

The adaptations that workers make to the loss of the social contract, whether forced by necessity or readily embraced, suggest that the narrative of crisis that has defined deindustrialization primarily as a period of rupture may oversimplify the subsequent lived experience of postindustrialism. On an institutional level, social protections most visible in the form of the union contract have been replaced by emphases on individual risk, a model for which the casino industry seems an apt representative. But culturally, rather than adopt the volatile language of "casino capitalism," dealers and other casino workers continue to actively invoke the language and actions of the industrial workplace in ways that make new economic structures locally legible and suture discontinuities in their postindustrial experiences. By envisioning the casino as a "postindustrial factory," not only in architectural design but also in terms of its labor and production, area residents use the history of the site to make sense of and solidify a tenuous present.

A Long-Term Temporary Solution

Tim Deluca trains casino dealers at the local community college branch just down the street from the Sands in the former Bethlehem Steel plant office building. He likes to emphasize that dealer certification from the college—which involves ten to fourteen weeks of training in two table games—is valid not only in the state of Pennsylvania, but can be transferred anywhere in the world, from a Las Vegas mega-resort to a cruise ship.[8] "As long as you have this trade, you'll always be able to have a job somewhere," he said. "If you're portable and you can travel, you'll always be able to make ends meet here. And I'm a perfect example of that." Tim started his career in 1985 in Atlantic City. In 2003 he left to continue his college education and the following year landed in Las Vegas working for Sands at The Venetian. After several promotions, Tim was laid off in 2008. A year later, when Sands opened the Bethlehem property, Tim's former boss called and offered him a position back east as a shift manager, the first step into executive management. Then in 2010 Tim was laid off again, so he began teaching at Bethlehem's community college for temporary income.

He said he could get back into the industry any time, but he was waiting for the right opportunity. He at one point had his eye on Pennsylvania's eleventh casino that opened in 2012 in nearby Valley Forge, but his fantasy is of the Florida sunshine. If casino gambling is legalized in South Beach (as is periodically discussed by the state's legislature), he said he'd hop on a plane and start over yet again where it's warmer.

As the links between capital and community are reshaped through deindustrialization, relocation is increasingly accepted as a condition of advancement or even employment. Beyond retraining, a primary purpose of federal Trade Readjustment Allowance funds, for example, is to support moving expenses for the unemployed. And yet the social networks, community roots, families, or home mortgages that keep individuals tied to place are easily overlooked when data on jobs and capital are thought of in abstract, impersonal terms.[9] Much as the Sands Casino Bethlehem's opening ceremony and its architectural design blurred narratives of past and future, the casino also is a site through which to explore how residents vacillate between and ultimately fuse the interpretive poles of fixed place and mobile capital in the ways they make sense of and define postindustrial work.

Dealers and slot attendants at the Bethlehem casino range from eighteen years old to post-retirement age. Many of the younger employees have come straight out of associate's degrees, BAs, or aborted college plans. Several dealers I spoke with glowed with the anticipation of being able to use the community college's dealing certificate as a ticket out of the Lehigh Valley. While 89 percent of the dealers trained in 2010 and 2011 were hired full time by the Sands, some have found jobs at other Pennsylvania casinos.[10] When we first talked in 2011, Matt Bednarik, a twenty-three-year-old mixed martial arts aficionado, was three days from starting work at the Sands dealing blackjack and roulette, but already he was thinking of his next move. In what is called "chasing tips" in the industry, he and some friends planned to apply to the new Valley Forge Casino set to open four months later. They believed its novelty would at least temporarily mean bigger crowds, which they translated into more tip income. After a year or two there, maybe the economy would pick up and Matt would finally have the impetus to finish his degree and find a job working with computers, which he said are his real passion. But if not, then Matt thought he'd check out Atlantic City, which at the time was barely hanging on as the second largest gambling jurisdiction in the country and would in 2012 be surpassed in revenue by Pennsylvania.

This notion of the casino industry as what one trainee called "a long-term temporary solution" is a common refrain among dealers in Bethlehem. For many of the younger casino employees, dealing is the latest in a chain of short-term jobs that they were eager to leave for various reasons—the sixty-hour week at the online bookstore warehouse, the part-time, no-benefit work at the big-box home improvement store, the hot and dangerous steel job in Reading.[11] Twenty-three-year-old Nicholas Garcia initially gambled his career choice on a high school suitability exam. "My top three jobs were carpenter in residential construction, law enforcement, military. I went for my first bet," he explained. Nicholas entered an associate's program in construction, but when he couldn't find an internship with a skilled carpenter to complete a four-year degree, he briefly tried his "second bet" in law enforcement before abandoning his college plans. A few months into his new job dealing blackjack and craps, Nicholas still thought about returning to carpentry if the market for new homes recovered.

Dealer Mei Lung, meanwhile, saw working at the casino as the only opportunity to protect her house from foreclosure and stave off bankruptcy in a difficult economic climate. Mei's income as a realtor was decimated by the recession in 2008, a blow exacerbated by her husband's layoff from a nearby pharmaceutical company that outsourced its IT work to India and Argentina. A lawyer in China before she emigrated fifteen years earlier, Mei models the gamble many immigrants make when they leave the social networks of their home countries.[12] While she kept her real estate license active just in case, she was hesitant to imagine a near-term return to financial stability for her family of four. For now, she said, she had no choice but to deal.

Regardless of whether dealers perceive the "long-term temporary solution" of the casino floor as a career progression or a step down, for many an underlying need for work simmers beneath the surface. Amid a regional unemployment rate that four years post-recession still hovered around 9 percent, the full-time, entry-level jobs that dealers sought through the community college training program where I met many of them started pay at roughly $40,000 a year (hourly base rate of $4.75 plus around $15 per hour in tips) and offered benefits after three months of employment. Bartenders and cocktail waitresses could earn twice as much. Many employees also touted the HMO health benefits the casino offered, noting that they required a lower employee contribution than at many other area businesses given Las Vegas Sands Corp.'s scale and bargaining power.

As a reflection of the free-market logic that values mobility, flexibility, and individual responsibility, the Sands Casino in many ways exemplifies broader transitions experienced in the postindustrial workplace. Julia Krause spends three days each week at the casino working as a part-time slots attendant. She weaves between the more than 3,000 slot machines that ring the casino floor, following the periodic cacophony of electronic bells and clanging digital coins to pay out jackpots and hope for tips from the lucky winners. Hired by the Sands at age seventy-five, Julia had been laid off at the Steel in 1992 after spending thirty-two years as a nurse in the plant and corporate dispensaries. Active and seeming much younger than her years, she said she went back to work on opening day in 2009 not simply to supplement her fixed income, but because she loves the excitement of the casino environment. "I almost feel like, oh, my God, this is my home again," she said of returning to the steel plant. Only now, she calls it "the fun house."

Julia often contemplates how expectations for employment have shifted from one industry to the other. She and her husband receive social security and what's left of their Steel pensions and thus are not fully dependent on her Sands' income. Still, her enthusiasm for the new economic model the casino represents was striking. "If everybody had the rules of the casino industry, we'd still have Bethlehem Steel, we'd still have most car industries, and the school district would be in good shape," she told me from the kitchen table of her home in an upscale North Side neighborhood.

To illustrate her point about more efficient fiscal management, she explained how the casino offered employees only one paid holiday each year (Christmas) and gave them a certain number of "flex days" to use as they saw fit, rather than providing designated vacation or sick days. "It's really an interesting concept after working at Bethlehem Steel being an exempt employee, getting eight weeks vacation, getting sick days. If you're out for three months sick [at the Steel] you still get paid. And this whole thing was so new to me, and I found it very interesting." At the pro-labor apogee of the steelworkers' contracts in the early 1980s, union employees had eleven paid holidays in addition to vacation time. Senior steelworkers could earn a thirteen-week sabbatical every fifth year to help compensate for the physically demanding and dangerous work they performed each day.[13] In contrast, the flex days and the "flextime" found at the casino and other postindustrial workplaces simulate the neoliberal deregulation of the marketplace, where an employee is free to determine the most advantageous use of his or her time. And yet, as Julia also noted, many of the employee protections (excessive or not) gained at the Steel through nationwide union negotiations are absent. Her curiosity about the casino's business model is in some ways a luxury compared to those who depend on these jobs for their livelihoods, but her buy-in to employment sans safety net is nonetheless a remarkable example of a widespread shift in postindustrial worker expectations.

When Adelson tore down the old Rat Pack's Sands Casino in Las Vegas and built The Venetian in 1999, he replaced a union casino on the Strip with a nonunion property. The Vegas of the mid-1960s had depended on loans from the Teamsters' pension funds as the major source of development capital when Wall Street was still unwilling to invest.[14] Las Vegas, sometimes called the "Last Detroit" or the "River Rouge of gambling," became a hotbed for union organizing. Indeed, Las Vegas Sands Corp. is one of only two major nonunion casino operators in the city.[15] By the 1990s, Las Vegas Sands had become embroiled in bitter disputes with the Culinary Union, a powerful group representing hotel and restaurant workers. Adelson eventually filed suit against Vegas picketers in 1999, claiming that the sidewalk in front of The Venetian was private property and not protected by the First Amendment. The United States Supreme Court refused to hear the case in 2002, in effect upholding a denial of The Venetian's claim, but appeals related to the case dragged on more than thirteen years later.[16]

This shaky premise to deny free speech endures in deed terms set forth by Las Vegas Sands in Bethlehem. The corporation offered central parcels of land west of the casino to not-for-profit ArtsQuest for the SteelStacks arts center, to the local PBS station for a new office, and to the City of Bethlehem for a performance pavilion and visitor center. The terms of the deal state that this land cannot be used for union organizing or for promoting themes "considered offensive by a reasonable casino operator." Although such clauses are typical of pseudo-public spaces like shopping malls, it was not lost on Bethlehem residents that the land under question is physically part of a former steel plant that hosted bitter labor battles and union gains through much of the twentieth century. Pressure from a small but vocal band of free speech advocates led to assurances from the city that it would not enforce the restrictions. The clause remains, however, in the arts center's agreement, including for outside space billed—perhaps appropriately signaling this broader shift in expectations—as a "21st Century Town Square."[17]

Some residents are wary of ruffling corporate feathers over the clause since Las Vegas Sands has been generous in other ways, including donating the land, and because the in-progress nature of the brownfield development promises more contracts for the union construction crews that built the casino and other complexes on the site. Others fear Bethlehem will again become a "company town," where a high-powered corporation will "get to call the shots on what's best for the public interest."[18] Although Sands holds the economic clout, the relative strengths of citizens' interests in the land remain culturally unsettled.

Meanwhile, as Julia noted, dealers and other employees at the Sands Casino Bethlehem are not unionized, although security guards have moved to organize against Sands' objections. In Las Vegas, the corporation offers wages and medical benefits a nudge above what other casino corporations offer their employees as prophylaxis against collective bargaining.[19] The security guards in Bethlehem are likewise among the highest paid in the state, earning between $12 and $14 an hour in 2015, but they say they want to organize less for the pay than for job stability and a voice in grievance procedures.[20] Union affiliations appear to have limited cachet among Bethlehem dealers, though, when they think about what job security means. Even in Las Vegas, dealers have generally not organized, in part because they fear having to give a cut of their tips to the union. They tend to view themselves as individual entrepreneurs and often move from one property to another.[21] Those dealers who have successfully formed unions at other casinos in recent years, however, have gained vacation, sick leave, and some protections against at-will terminations.[22]

In any case, the service jobs created by the casino industry, including those on the former factory site in Bethlehem, simply do not compare when it comes to the benefits and wages offered by unionized steel mills in the second half of the twentieth century. In contrast to the Steel, where most training took place on the job, at the Sands dealers must pay for their own training before they can be hired, and required licensing fees are deducted from their paychecks.[23] Perhaps the most striking aspect of the casino's employment model is that just as it has in a sense "outsourced" retirement benefits from corporate-contribution pensions to employee-funded accounts, it also has outsourced employees' salaries to the consumers to the extent that dealers make three-quarters of their income from tips.

Like many service jobs, nonunionized casino positions also require one to work varied shifts and lack contract rules to protect from layoffs. Taking this trend of normalized instability to an extreme, Revel Atlantic City, a mega-casino resort that opened in 2012 in neighboring New Jersey, announced that dealers, waiters, and cocktail waitresses would be hired on four- to six-year contracts, requiring those employees to reapply for their own jobs at the end of the term. These conditions were a direct reversal of the seniority rules upheld by union employers of an earlier era like the Steel to add predictability to the workplace. In addition, an unusually large percentage of Revel's initial hires were part-time, meaning they did not receive benefits. The local union called Revel's plan "unconscionable" for undermining employees' abilities to plan long term. Although no other casino had yet to adopt a similar approach, the head of the New Jersey Economic Development Authority seemed unfazed by this harbinger of increased insecurity. "In today's economic climate," she said simply, "people don't have lifetime contracts."[24] The temporary long-term solution of postindustrial work is economically and socially a fundamental break from the nation's manufacturing heyday.

It's All in Gaming

Still, many casino workers have found ways to reconcile their tenuous employment with the idealized vision of entrepreneurial self-achievement that Adelson himself claims. As an adherent to a postindustrial compromise that ultimately naturalizes instability, Rachel Moretti is among those who make sense of economic insecurity by reading opportunity into the cracks. Rachel, now in her late forties, had worked for eighteen years at an off-track betting establishment in New York City before it went bankrupt and she lost her job in 2010. "Of course I was very upset about losing my job, still am," she said. "But I was kind of happy about leaving that behind." Rachel had grown tired of the verbal abuse of patrons who were losing large sums of money, and she saw the layoff as an opportunity to start fresh and build up enough capital to open her own business.[25] After eight months without a job and with bills piling up, however, Rachel said she needed to be realistic. Having worked so long in off-track betting, "I have a very specific kind of skill really. It doesn't really transfer," she said. "I figure let me try this and get my benefits back, turn a little revenue again, but keep my dream alive so I don't have to feel too sad by going back into something I felt like was a bonus I could stop." Much as Matt hopes to one day find a job working with computers, and Nicholas's true passion is carpentry, Rachel had been forced to put her dream of opening an ice cream shop on hold as she sought a job dealing at the Sands.

What's most surprising in this all-too-familiar tale of recession-fueled job loss and dreams deferred is her rereading of the situation as an opportunity rather than a setback. Burying her initial dismay, Rachel performed an interpretive flip, seeing her layoff as freeing and job security as imprisonment:

> The horse racing, it was a very good salary, I had my pension, I had my benefits. So I was really tied in. So I wasn't really able to pursue another dream right then because I wouldn't leave that job. But now I feel like the rug was so ripped out from me, I'm not as afraid anymore to pursue it. So I think that I really want to pursue something else so I don't have to stay with the gambling industry. That's the honest answer. But the truth is I need to turn some revenue, so I figured I have—this is my best shot about getting benefits and a salary.

Having absorbed the ethos of self-created opportunity, economic insecurity became a dream enabler rather than a structural impediment. The increasingly elusive pension and good benefits for which steelworkers and others had fought so long in the industrial workplace are now perceived as traps that hold one back in an ever-changing postindustrial world. And yet, caught between the entrepreneurial framework and the need for financial and personal security, Rachel found that true freedom remains difficult to attain.

The tension between free-market individualism and expectations of the social contract's collective protections continues to shape both corporate structures and employee and public reactions to them. The success of Sands' risk-based business model and reliance on flexible labor in many ways seems exemplary of the freewheeling postindustrial economy. But pure reflections of "casino capitalism" are not easily realized, and even the gaming industry is no exception. Free-market ideals emphasize reducing government oversight and cutting corporate taxes, thus removing the state as a barrier to unrestrained capital growth. As in other jurisdictions worldwide where gambling is legal, however, casinos in Pennsylvania are both highly regulated and heavily taxed. The taxes on gambling profits and the licensing fees that Pennsylvania reaps from casinos have helped offset perennial budget cuts to social services, including police, education, and state pensions. At the same time that it compels the industry to help rebuild social safety nets, the state has effectively levied a new, semi-privatized tax on consumers whose lost wagers at the slots or table games comprise those revenues. Instead of embracing a strictly laissez-faire attitude, the Pennsylvania Gaming Control Board also dictates most casino operating procedures, such as the gaming equipment used, staffing levels, and CPR training for employees. But because of the state's clear interest in the casinos' profitability, many regulations, such as those awarding intentional monopolies and limited licenses, nonetheless directly benefit the gaming corporations. From a business and policy perspective, the state's casinos thus complicate, but ultimately complement, idealized understandings of neoliberal economies as free markets absent state interventions.[26]

Meanwhile, despite the free-market emphasis on unfettered capital mobility, place-based loci of economic activity like the casino floor and the Steel site, and the ways such spaces are imagined and occupied, remain relevant as material and cultural touchstones. The 2012 and 2013 legalization of online gambling in Delaware, Nevada, and New Jersey notwithstanding, the casino industry still depends primarily on physical proximity to consumers and face-to-face interactions that cannot be outsourced. Sands' revenues and hires in Bethlehem skyrocketed in 2010 when Pennsylvania legalized table games and the casino could replace its video blackjack dealers with human ones.[27] Casinos carefully select their locations based on regulatory and demographic advantages that are linked to place. Bethlehem's proximity to New York and New Jersey was integral to its early success.

In the end, though, the entertainment product manufactured in the casino remains essentially about deriving money from money, a fungibility that distances it from other geographic particularities. Such emphases on abstract market transactions invoke conceptions of universal economic orders that to some extent contradict the individualized focus on self-making, personal responsibility, and hard work that self-help books and entrepreneurs like Adelson stress. At the Sands Casino, "luck" is institutionalized in such a way as to bridge this gap between self-controlled decision making and omnipotent forces. Julia picked the time and day of her first shift as a slots attendant, for instance, via a multistep process in which she and her coworkers first selected envelopes that contained different numbers. The numbers determined the order in which they would choose their timeslots. "So they can't say, well they had favorites, or that they did anything. It's all in gaming," she said with a chuckle. She felt lucky she picked high enough to have Mondays off so she could continue to play golf with her women's league. By creating these kinds of internal structures based on individualized luck, the casino industry effectively distances itself from expectations for more interventionist social protections or collective commitments.

While Julia admires what she sees as efficiencies in Sands' policies and operating procedures compared to those at the Steel, their impartiality—both toward employees and players—comes into question when one considers how "luck" is nonetheless created and controlled by the corporate structures in place. For example, casinos closely track individual gamblers—particularly regulars and high rollers—to determine each person's "theoretical win," the amount he or she should walk away with at the end of the day based on average bets, games played, the house's statistical advantage, and a number of other factors. Players whose wins far exceed expectations are not seen as "lucky"; they are rather targeted for extra surveillance or simply asked to leave.

Employees likewise soon learn that regardless of who pulls the lever or rolls the dice, when "it's all in gaming" the odds are generally stacked in favor of the house. Workers are employed "at will," and turnover is relatively high (roughly 20 percent among dealers).[28] In addition to "chasing tips" and moving to other casino properties, dealers face strict firing policies for infractions. Many other dealers find they can't cut it in the casino environment. New dealers are invariably assigned to work at least six months on the late shift, from eleven o'clock at night to seven in the morning. Others grow tired of the cigarette smoke or buckle under the stress of dealing to high rollers and calming irate players who are down on their luck. More senior employees gain some flexibility to determine their schedules and, being a new casino in a new market, there is real opportunity for internal advancement. But as a result, the Sands Casino rarely stopped hiring new dealers in its first five years of table-game operation. While high turnover may undercut the benefits of workforce stability, thanks to a constant stream of new trainees seeking jobs it also helps keep payrolls low.

Even if company gains come at workers' expense, dealers nonetheless frequently associate their own economic stability with the corporation's profitability. Mei worked part-time at a smaller casino in the Poconos before coming to the Sands. In the Poconos, she said, the business seemed less organized, less corporate, and there were fewer players compared to Bethlehem. Indeed, it regularly ranks as one of Pennsylvania's least profitable casinos. In contrast, "Here [at the Sands] they have a lot. They're just very busy. You just feel safe," she said. Her analysis of economic security extended into the built environment. She described the Poconos casino as "like a home" in its scale. Rather than associate its low ceilings and lodge-like porte-cochère with comfort though, she said the impersonal warehouse expanse of the Sands with double the casino floor space was more assuring that it would be a lasting and profitable business.[29]

While Mei measures her financial safety through a local comparison, Nicholas takes a global view. "I wanted something reliable in an emerging industry," he explained, "and the fact that the Sands just introduced table games the previous summer, it seemed like a really great up-and-coming employment opportunity." He was particularly struck by Sands' presence in Asia, where it reaps more than 85 percent of its net revenues from hugely successful mega-resorts in Macau and Singapore. (Bethlehem accounts for less than 4 percent.)[30] Las Vegas Sands Corp.'s market cap (or total value of the company based on its outstanding shares) reached $87 billion in 2014. It is not only the largest gaming company and largest real-estate developer in the world, but it is the largest foreign investor in China ever.[31] "Seeing that was a nice reassurance that even though it's in a different country, it's one big entity that's got a lot of opportunity, and a lot of opportunity for growth. I see it as very stable." Nicholas turns a more cynical interpretation of capital mobility on its head. Rather than associate globalization with an absence of local commitments, he interprets it as a marker of job stability. It is these inverted expectations of the meanings of postindustrial security that lead insiders like Tim Deluca to negate the association of the casino industry and its brand of risk with volatility. "The fact that gambling is the product offered is not a gamble, because you're always going to produce revenue," he said. "Believe it or not, people will always gamble. You build it, they'll come."

A Postindustrial Factory

For area residents, it is clear that Bethlehem's casino physically occupies an economic space that vacillates between past and future, place-based production and mobile capital, often blurring what have been considered distinct cultural categories and interpretive poles. The casino industry is simultaneously stable and volatile, material and abstract in its profit and employment structures. The Sands Casino makes architectural and cultural references to place and community history even as its future-oriented business model is increasingly replicated in other jurisdictions that pass gaming legislation. As the debate over the casino license revealed, some see the casino's local theming as proof of Sands' commitment to the Bethlehem community, while others, like Nicholas, prefer to emphasize the corporation's international reach as evidence of its economic stability. Moreover, some of the contradictions that the casino encapsulates coexist uneasily, such as the frameworks of entrepreneurial self-interest and remnants of social protections. Stakeholders nonetheless interpret these tensions in ways to provide a postindustrial narrative that makes culturally and locally legible the economic transition and social upheaval that the decline of the Steel represented.

Rather than narrate the betrayal and disjuncture that deindustrialization ushered in, casino insider Tim Deluca, for one, likes to stress the continuities between the two economic eras. "You went from one factory, a steel mill, and now you have—what is it, twenty years later—you have another factory. It's the casino," he explained.

> The steel mill produced something. Now the casino offers a product, but they don't produce anything but revenue. So they produce revenue for the casino, they produce revenue for the employees, and they produce revenue for the community, without putting a product out in the street to sell. . . . The tables are your production line, the chips are your assets that you use to facilitate your production, and your dealers are your line workers. And that's the factory.

Amid strong (if exaggerated) local and national sentiments that "America doesn't make anything anymore," Tim's analogy offers a narrative of smooth transition to cleaner forms of production. Like Bethlehem Steel, the Sands Casino Bethlehem reaps profits while providing jobs and benefits for hundreds of area residents and contributing significant tax revenues and charitable gifts to the community. Tim might have added that the Steel's proximity to railroads and ore mines likewise is replaced by the casino factory's highway access to the raw material of gamblers' money in nearby New York and New Jersey. Indeed, here postindustrialism, rather than reflecting rupture with an earlier economic order, instead represents its epitome—production so efficient that the physical product becomes superfluous. Those who have recalibrated their expectations, as many dealers have, to a worldview in line with neoliberal economic reforms embrace that intangibility, which for so many ravaged by deindustrialization remains a source of anxiety and discomfort.

In addition to converting players' money into corporate revenue, Tim's dealer-line workers produce an intangible service for gamblers in the form of entertainment. Walking into the casino factory, one is confronted with an expansive buzzing room washed in an orange glow from the rod-shaped "ingot" lights that hang overhead. Thousands of slot machines flank the sides of the floor, but the most crowded space is the central section of table games. Depending on the time of day and how many visitors have been bussed in from New York's Chinatowns, people may have to line up to get a place at the felt to play blackjack, roulette, craps, poker, or a number of so-called Asian games like baccarat and Pai Gow tiles. Dealers wear uniforms of black pants, orange button-down shirts, and—if they want to make good tips—a smile. "Working the line" at the casino requires not only physical stamina and manual dexterity, but also grueling "emotional labor" as employees carefully manage their feelings to sustain an outward countenance that pleases customers.[32]

More than cater to players, this type of service work occupies a mediating position in a tripartite relationship between management, employee, and customer that vacillates between cooperation and conflict.[33] For dealer Nicholas, the challenge is to perform that balance to meet corporate expectations while simultaneously aligning his own interests with the customers' goals. "My mood is that I'm always hoping for the players to win. Because the more the players win, the more they're going to tip," Nicholas explained. "I sort of have like subtle things that I do to let them know that I'm on their side." When dealing blackjack, where the object of the game is to get cards with values that total more than the dealer's without "busting" or "breaking" by going over twenty-one, he follows a specific operating procedure:

> If the dealer's showing a five, which is probably the best bust card they can have, and the player has like a sixteen and wants to hit, I'm going to be like, "Are you sure about that? Final answer?" . . . And other things, like if the dealer breaks, I always say, "Dealer breaks." But if the dealer has twenty-one [and wins], I switch it up and I say, "The house has twenty-one." Because I want them to know that *the house* has twenty-one; *I* don't have twenty-one. But if I break, that's me breaking for them. . . . So, stuff like that to let them know that I'm pulling for them.

Nicholas said no one trained him in these techniques for strategically adjusting his positionality; it just occurred to him one night when he got three twenty-ones in a row and the players on his table began to grumble. He prefers sitting on the craps table where he sets up and pays bets but is not implicated in the winning or losing numbers the players roll on the dice. Even there, however, he said he pays careful attention to how players like their multicolored plastic chips divided and anticipates when they will want to exchange one denomination for another. He knows who wants to shoot the breeze and who wants to concentrate on the game. This focus on managing player relationships has paid off. Sometimes his regulars throw him tips as they walk by, even if they don't take a seat at his table.

From the casino's perspective, even when Nicholas refers to "the house's" win, the central role dealers play when interfacing with gamblers in the management-employee-customer relationship helps divert players' blame for lost money away from the corporation and its stacked odds. Dealers similarly tend to direct their pay frustrations not at Sands, but at players who don't tip. Still, some of the most striking effects of this postindustrial model of service work that the casino typifies are the surprising continuities with the cultures of work in manufacturing where the management-employee relationship took precedence. For example, sociologist Michael Burawoy famously studied the "games" line workers in the industrial workplace played to combat the monotony of their tasks. Friendly competition among employees, he argued, had the corollary effect of driving up production, ultimately reproducing the conditions within which management constrained them.[34] While Nicholas distances himself from the house on an emotional level when he aligns with players, fiscally his motivation to keep them happy and gambling will benefit not only his tip rate, but also the casino's bottom line.

Nicholas expends a great deal of effort, for instance, coming up with ways to pay out bets on the craps table faster and more efficiently to prove his skills to the players, his coworkers, and his superiors. "There's a lot of camaraderie, a lot of competition," he explained. Craps tables are circled by a supervisor who sits "box" and watches the table, one dealer with a stick to move the dice, and two dealers who set up and pay bets on either side. If there's a winning roll with six people waiting for payouts on each side, Nicholas tries to finish paying his line first and playfully goads the other dealer for being too slow. Speeding up the rate at which he adds to customers' plastic chip assets will hopefully increase his tips, but it also pushes players to more quickly place their next bets. More often than not they will lose money to the house, the ultimate beneficiary of Nicholas's work on the line.

Tim's postindustrial factory analogy has other manifestations beyond the parallels he spells out between assets and line work at the steel plant and on the casino floor. Although dealers regularly tout their entrepreneurial spirit and the flexibility of a casino career, tight surveillance and scripting significantly limit their agency as workers in ways reminiscent of the factory. Steelworkers had to pass through security checkpoints going in and out of the plant. On the job, they operated in strict hierarchies, often with narrowly defined tasks. And yet as other ethnographers of industrial manufacturing have shown, the workplace was not entirely dehumanizing.[35] Steelworkers in Bethlehem acted within these constraints to create free time to cook collective meals in the furnaces or do "government work," a local euphemism for using company supplies for personal, unauthorized projects. Compared to other manufacturing line jobs where work is characterized by its monotony, most steelworkers say they were constantly learning at the plant. Skilled workers in particular saw a variety of tasks throughout their careers and were frequently called on to troubleshoot.

Dealers also display agency in hustling tips, for example, but at least among new dealers in Bethlehem there is a self-conscious awareness that their every move is being scrutinized.[36] Before a dealer can start work, he or she must be licensed by the state, a process that involves a thorough background check and drug testing. The lengthy license application calls for a twenty-year employment history, including explanations of any firings, details of bank account balances and debts, marital history, and money spent supporting dependents, among other questions.[37] Once on the casino floor, dealers must adhere to a tight script as part of the establishment's security measures. As Tim says, it does not take six weeks at the community college training on mock green felt tables to learn to count to twenty-one. The majority of the blackjack course he teaches is rather devoted to learning the particularities of dealing procedures. This includes everything from flipping your palms before each deal to show the ubiquitous security cameras that you aren't hiding any chips, to standing with your body at the appropriate angle to ensure players cannot sneak chips behind your back or change their bets after the first card is dealt. If an angry player yells at you, do not talk back. If a player has a heart attack at your table, do not turn away from your chips to try to save him. Wait for other help to arrive. Stories of dealers who have gone off script and been fired complete the indoctrination.

On Nicholas's first day at the Sands dealing craps, sweat dripped off his brow onto the felt, and his hands shook as he took $100 bets. After a month, Nicholas had yet to waver from his training: "As long as I keep up my end, like coming in to practice and, for instance, just throwing every thought out of my head when the box person tells me to do something, just regurgitating what they tell me to do, and as long as I do what I need to do, I see this really being a good employment solution and good opportunity for advancement." By describing his employment opportunity in this way, as a fixed script, Nicholas undercut the postindustrial narrative of flexibility and self-made success that simultaneously underpins the job's attraction. When I talked to him nine months later, Nicholas had relaxed to some extent, enjoying the improvised banter and personal interactions that accompany the procedures. Rules on the floor nonetheless remain rigid, and he has effectively adopted the culture of surveillance as part of his own routine. Whereas he was once the object of scrutiny, "Now I find that I'm watching the new dealers like a hawk," he said. Nicholas, in his words and actions, situates the line work of the casino floor among locally ingrained expectations for factory work—both its benefits and its trade-offs.

Turning Tim's postindustrial factory analogy around to make gamblers the laborers and producers instead of the casino employees offers another angle from which to understand how people make sense of economic and social transitions. Local gambling opponents suggest the casino is not creating jobs, revenue, and entertainment, but dislocation, debt, and despair. Several dealers told me they see the same people at the casino four or five days a week. "They come every day like a job," Mei said, many "commuting" by bus from out of state.[38] Regulars at table games often gamble during the day shift, when they know more experienced dealers are on the floor. For others, sitting and staring at the digital screen of a slot machine and punching its buttons has a bizarre similarity to postindustrial jobs in finance and other white-collar industries that involve hours at cubby-sized computer stations.[39] Still, the majority of players that work to convert their chip-assets into big bucks at the casino factory have less, not more, to show for it in the end.[40]

Dealers, meanwhile, defend against their own implication in such outcomes. Almost every dealer with whom I spoke was adamant that problem gambling is a matter of personal responsibility, not a condition of the industry. While dealers are more likely to reap tips from gamblers who are winning or who respond to their cheerful banter, they tend to align with the casino corporation's more removed desire to profit when faced with gamblers down on their luck. They regularly portray gambling as a matter of self-control, not unlike conservative "blame-the-victim" attitudes toward other social issues like poverty and drug abuse. Nicholas and other dealers adopt language of choice and self-made opportunity, the same characteristics by which they often define their own work. "It's up to the individual whether they are going to know their limits and they're going to stop and not get in the hole, or they're going to press it up and abuse the opportunity," he said. "It's really not my business. It's their choice and they have to live with it."

Rachel Moretti, on the other hand, is well aware of the negative social underbelly of gambling and the destructive behavior it can foster. Problem gamblers, she said, don't stop until they lose everything. At her previous job in off-track betting, she would purposefully distance herself from her customers to reconcile her own discomfort with this reality and her livelihood benefiting from their losses. "I would kind of treat it as a very social thing," she explained. "I'm going to see you today, and you're going to play, and hopefully you'll win, and then you'll tip me and I'll have a good day." Other dealers likewise spoke of consciously separating their personal lives from the "drama" of the casino floor, while Tim suggested that "convers[ing] with the poor sap blowing his rent money may be all that gets you through your shift." These workplace interactions institutionalize a fissure between consideration of the social effects of gambling and the industry's measures of profitability, much as during the casino licensing debate the state gaming board explicitly elevated economic development rationale over moral arguments. Casino-sponsored hotlines for problem gamblers attempt to reconcile the tension by providing information and support networks for people in trouble. But when the onus is placed on the individual—in everything from dealers' job training to problem gamblers' self-destruction—the collective well-being that the social contract between community and corporation once strived to sustain will never be of primary concern.[41]

Nonetheless, employees and other actors regularly inject their own moral guidelines into their roles in the casino-factory exchange. Rachel, who had wanted to get out of the gambling industry but got drawn back in and applied for a job at the Sands when she needed work, ultimately could not bring herself to take the plunge. "I just felt like it was a job, and I should take it, and it was a good fit. But all along I really didn't want to," she said. After paying $1,300 for training in blackjack and baccarat at the community college, $350 for her state license, and successfully interviewing and auditioning at the Sands, Rachel quit before her first day on the job. "It was just getting louder and louder and louder," she said of the voice in her head. Being on the casino floor during employee orientation brought back visceral memories of working amid the smoke, invectives, and despair that linger around many customers. "I just couldn't do it." She is instead waiting tables while she saves money to go back to school to become a nutritional coach and help people take better care of themselves. She ultimately could not reconcile her workplace desires and sense of social responsibility with employment at the casino.

A Cash Warehouse

For some area residents who remember the manufacturing economy that once flourished on the site where the casino now sits, comparing dealing and gambling to line work is misguided and even insulting. The tension often revolves around the nature of what is being produced. Like many who opposed granting Las Vegas Sands a license to build on the Steel's brownfield, Paul Burton, a Bethlehem steelworker from 1944 until 1983, suggested that although he enjoys playing the slots, the experience at the casino is at odds with the pride he took in his career. Significantly, Paul's investment in his past work, like many other steelworkers', relates directly to the physical product he manufactured:

> *PB:* I could take metal and I could polish it that you could look into it and see your face and take a shave if you thought you needed it.

> You put out a product like that, you've done something. And it wasn't a little bitty thing. The things I worked on were almost as big as this house. . . .
>
> *CT:* Can people that work at the casino have that same pride in their jobs?
>
> *PB:* No. No way. No way.

The reflection of Paul's face, now creased and tired, in the massive parts on which he worked during the Steel's heyday visually captures an industrial era in which one's sense of self was intimately connected to one's job. Paul's self-reflection literally materialized in the products he helped create. Although he appreciates and enjoys the revenue and entertainment Sands produces for the community, the self-creation for which many dealers strive through entrepreneurial postindustrial production is a possibility he ultimately denies. While service work has other advantages, including less arduous physical demands as well as a safer and generally cleaner work environment, the direct comparison of dealing to manufacturing elides the social and economic distinctions that Paul enjoyed as a union member. "Bethlehem, U.S.A." stamps endure on steel beams in structures across the United States, but post-bankruptcy, a portion of the money in Paul's pension checks is irretrievably gone. The contrast between the perceived permanence of the material products Paul polished and the disappearing act of his financial assets lays groundwork to inform a certain skepticism of the fiscal products that the casino churns out.

Perry Buckman, who grew up in Bethlehem but now keeps an eye on his hometown from New York, implicates not only dealers and the corporation in this model of intangible, liquid production, but also gamblers. As he described the casino,

> It's a symbol of a big shell game. Somebody trying to get rich without doing anything. By luck. By *leger de main.* The whole thing—in U.S. manufacturing and definitely in the minds of people running the Steel Company back when I was a kid, you got an honest day's wage for an honest day's work. And if something was U.S. made, it was made honestly and people stood by their product and it was quality. Where's

> the quality to a casino? It's, the whole thing's a sham. It's a big film set. There's lights, glitter, and it's—what's behind? Is that the Wizard of Oz back there? There's no there, there.

Perry's words evoke the well-known description of capitalism's apogee, where "all that is solid melts into air." Rather than turn out house-sized steel parts, the new casino on the plant site reflects what Sheldon Adelson referred to as his Bethlehem "house of dough," a structure built out of digital transactions. In the midst of capitalism's constant creation and destruction, Perry suggests even referents to the site's manufacturing past are only surface deep, leaving one grasping for substance.[42]

In seeking a "there, there," community members like Perry nonetheless invoke ongoing expectations not only that something tangible will be produced and consumed, but that businesses will have solid commitments to the places where they're located. Perry suggests a relationship between profit, place, and production creates an honest, moral system that defined the economic logic of an earlier era. For steelworkers, this "moral universe" often took shape through work rules and procedures codified in postwar union contracts.[43] But just as seniority rules were replaced by at-will employment, gambling by both corporations and individuals essentially values future prospects over past events.

Based on these less tangible and dis-placed conceptions of casino production, the appropriate analogue for the casino may not be a postindustrial factory, but rather a cash warehouse and distribution center. Community boosters and politicians are eager to point out that the "real story" of the redevelopment of the Steel site in Bethlehem is not on the parcel of land in the heart of the South Side where the casino and arts center sit amid the remaining industrial buildings. Rather, they tell us to look at the brownfield's 1,600 acres to the east that were razed and rebuilt beginning in 1999 as an intermodal transfer terminal (to move goods from rail to truck and vice versa) and industrial parks full of warehouses, including two massive distribution centers for Walmart and one for Crayola. Like the casino-factory, the developments have capitalized on the former plant's existing transportation infrastructure while shucking the Steel's legacy of high-wage, unionized labor.[44] Though early expectations of employing 10,000 people on the site remain unfulfilled given these businesses' relatively small workforces, additional warehouses, some more than ten times the size of the Sands Casino, continue to be erected as speculative projects.[45]

Despite its industrial theming, architecturally the open space of the casino floor is itself typical of warehouse design. But rather than house tangible goods like the buildings in the industrial parks, it is a temporary holding ground for money, a cash warehouse. Indeed, the worldwide mobility of the capital that flows through the casino is striking. In 2014 the Sands Casino Bethlehem recorded $470 million in gross revenue.[46] Even as state regulations anchor some of the casino's profits via a high tax rate on revenues and a multimillion-dollar community host fee, many Bethlehem residents claim they can see no tangible evidence of the money.[47] Rather, just as the transportation infrastructure on the east side of the brownfield enables the widespread distribution of goods, the corporate structures in place at the casino clear the way for money that enters the casino to flow back out of the community. As casino critic Michael Russo elaborated,

> There's nothing productive that comes from the Sands. Nothing. It's just a money exchange. People lose it, other people win it. And the guy trucks it over to Vegas. It goes on the express train. So the reality of it all is it's not producing anything. There's nothing to be proud of.

Faced with these accusations, casino supporters rightly point to the roughly 3,000 new jobs created at the casino and its spin-off businesses within five years of opening, the millions of dollars in tax revenues it provides, spillover spending in the local economy, and charitable corporate donations that comprise visible evidence of community benefit.[48] As former casino manager Tim Deluca said, "Even though we don't produce anything per se, we do create a healthy economic environment, which systemically is from the casino." Michael's figurative language of trucks and trains leaving for Las Vegas Sands' Nevada headquarters nonetheless augments understandings of the casino and intermodal transfer terminal's complementary roles in a postindustrial economy built to shuttle assets around rather than make them.

Michael's disappointment in coming to this realization finds echoes throughout the community, particularly from those, like Paul and Perry, used to measuring moral worth by physical evidence of hard work. Justin Wilkins is a structural engineer who became a carpenter after being let go from the Steel during downsizing in the 1970s. "To me, see, all my life I've made stuff. And so I can't understand how you can make a living without making something," he explained. "Where you have a business like that where there's all this cash sloshing around and no physical thing being made, produced, it just seems to me that the opportunities for corruption are rife. But I can't put my finger on it." This inability to "put a finger on it" is a recurring theme in discussions around town. It highlights the sense of volatility and uncertainty experienced with economic transitions, even as successful new-economy businesses like the casino are making large amounts of money.

Some commentators suggest that evidence of high rewards from a high-risk approach to business can legitimate dangerous activities even to those who do not benefit. Gamblers, most of whom will lose money, likewise find assurance of the possibility that they could strike it rich in the bells and flashing lights of others' jackpot winnings.[49] At the same time, Michael and Justin suggest that when the transactions that create corporate profit become increasingly inaccessible and invisible to the layperson, there is a corollary suspicion—warranted or not—of the executives and developers who control the numbers. Given the evident cultural and moral links in Bethlehem and other communities between material production and place, the notion that the potential for accumulation in this model is based not on making anything new, but rather on the dispossession of others' money, aggravates the sense of vulnerability.[50]

Despite the fact that the warehousing or finance industries may offer a more apt analogy for the casino and its nonunion labor structures, the "postindustrial factory" metaphor remains a meaningful tool with which casino workers and area residents make the products of service work locally legible and culturally legitimate their roles in Bethlehem's postindustrial economy. Lack of stability and social protections is not necessarily understood or experienced as distinct from previous ways of life. Local narratives and actions rather challenge dominant understandings of manufacturing and service economies as discrete eras. Amid these blurred temporalities, for example, dealer Nicholas makes and restores furniture in his free time. "Some of the pieces . . . they're just kind of sitting in the basement having no purpose. Just sort of up on the utility shelves just kind of sitting there," he said. Like his dreams of being a skilled carpenter, of participating in an economy that produces tangible goods, they are pushed underground while he pursues the "temporary long-term solution" of being a casino dealer. And yet, like Tim, Nicholas chooses to narrate continuity into his economic environment. Dealing cards and paying out chips, he explained, at least lets him continue to "be working with my hands."

Indeed, the connection runs in his blood. Nicholas's grandfather worked at the Steel for forty years, until the mid-1990s. Like Nicholas and his swing-shift craps crew, he found camaraderie working nights at the plant, working with his hands. Nicholas and his grandfather reflect a generational transmission of connection to the Steel site through their labor. Although Nicholas's grandfather now lives in Florida, he periodically comes back to visit. "When we're driving around town, we have to go across the Minsi Trail Bridge [over the former plant] for something, you can always see, if we're at the red light, him looking around," Nicholas said. "Or if he's riding shotgun you can kind of see like almost a little grin come on his face to see that, all right, they're doing something with it. They put something back there. It's not just like an abandoned disaster."

Las Vegas Sands, the industrial parks, and their most enthusiastic boosters in many ways seek to create a new era of prosperity for Bethlehem by relegating the Steel to the past and signaling the casino and warehouses as its future. Nicholas and his grandfather, however, along with other long-time community residents, represent the tenacious hold and continued relevance of the city's history. The persistence of the past is apparent in the memories of the union's gains for labor security as much as in workers' ready adaptability to corporate structures and surveillance, exemplifying the postindustrial moment as a type of "temporal collage."[51]

Moreover, in Mei Lung's comfort in the Sands' warehouse design and the grin the Steel site provokes in Nicholas's grandfather, the narrative and ritual resources used to make sense of the economic changes that these policies reflect are often located in the landscape itself. Experiencing, grappling with, and assessing postindustrialism through the built environment gives physical expression to new forms of meaning-making. Instead of reinforcing simplified stories of an industrial before and deindustrialized after, or of capital abstractions entirely dissociated from community roots, the "postindustrial factory" metaphor reflects durable expectations of corporate commitments to the communities in which they operate. It should come as no surprise then that there have been prolonged debates over how and whether the industrial structures on the Steel site should be reused. These conflicts shed further light on the ways in which postindustrial communities attempt to reconcile their pasts with their futures by infusing for-profit development with memories of social accountability.

4

A Steel Site in Limbo

IN FEBRUARY 2004, one month after his inauguration as Bethlehem's new mayor, thirty-four-year-old John Callahan traveled to Charleston, South Carolina, for the Mayors' Institute on City Design. The two-and-a-half-day workshop was part of an ongoing partnership developed in 1986 between the National Endowment for the Arts, the American Architectural Foundation, and the United States Conference of Mayors to give mayors training and support in urban planning. "You're supposed to bring kind of a big project in your city that's a challenge for you," he explained to me in his office at Bethlehem's city hall eight and a half years later. Over the couch where he sat across from me hung a black-and-white photo collage of the idled blast furnaces across the river, framed with reclaimed wood. "You can't get one a whole lot more challenging than this," he said with a characteristic grin as he referred to the towering, rusted embodiments of the Steel's demise in the image above him.

At the time of the workshop in 2004, pre-Pennsylvania gaming legislation, the 1,800-acre Bethlehem Steel brownfield was in the hands of the International Steel Group (ISG), a corporation created by billionaire "vulture investor" Wilbur Ross to scoop up distressed steel companies and capitalize on their assets. In many ways, like Sheldon Adelson, Ross became a distant face to associate with financial transactions that detach profit from place. As Callahan described the scenario, the City of Bethlehem had very little contact with Ross, who was based out of Cleveland. "I don't even know hardly who ISG is," he said.

> The one good thing about Steel's ownership is you knew who they were, you knew where they were, you knew how to contact them. And

> you knew, at the very least, that they had a connection to this community because we were, after all, the Bethlehem of Bethlehem Steel, and it was the home plant. And while they had these far-reaching operations around the world, they had a connection to this particular plant that ISG clearly didn't.

The common narrative of deindustrialization is that corporations ultimately follow liquid networks of capital and business-friendly economic policies and regulations. Particularly since the 1970s, these motivations have disrupted reciprocal relationships of the kind Bethlehem Steel once had with the City of Bethlehem, its material infrastructure, and its local supply of labor and raw materials.

Indeed, to ISG, the defunct Bethlehem site was coincidental to its real economic interests in the still-operating assets of the bankrupt steel corporation, particularly the Burns Harbor plant in Indiana that it would sell at a huge profit to leading steelmaker Mittal Steel (now ArcelorMittal) in 2005. The Bethlehem plant "was something that in their mind they sort of wanted to unload, which isn't the best of circumstances if you're the community in which the land lies," Callahan said. "Because, who do they sell it to? What are those people's intentions and willingness to move forward if they don't have that connection to the site, or sense of corporate responsibility of dealing with the site? So, it was a real state of limbo." The "state of limbo" in which the mayor described the brownfield evokes the uncertainty out of which the casino's opening ceremony attempted to craft an escape. City boosters saw an opportunity to mark a transition away from manufacturing and toward a diversified service, entertainment, and distribution economy. It also evokes a space in between local expectations of corporate commitments to the community and broad acceptance that the increasingly mobile, high-level transactions of a global economy value "placed" connections less and less.

Generally, this postindustrial transition is portrayed as a process of inexorable decline and eventual rebirth. But as we've seen, the experience of economic change in Bethlehem has often looked quite different. Local celebrity steelworker Bernie Hovan's speech at the casino's opening ceremony, debates about the casino's architectural design, and experiences of work at the "postindustrial factory" show that residents continue to assert the relevance of Bethlehem's past amid a changing economy. Discussions about whether and how the remaining industrial buildings should be reused and what role historic preservation should play in the city's future—physically, politically, and culturally—further define the Steel site as a space of potential, one that remains open-ended and can blur past and future expectations.[1]

The global economy may be conceptualized as a deterritorialized and impersonal flow of capital, goods, people, services, technology, or ideas, but it is given shape locally in everyday contests over space by individuals with feelings and desires.[2] The incorporation of the Steel's heritage into the overall redevelopment plan for the brownfield can open up this space for local control over the landscape's use and interpretation amid profit-based strategies that more often rely on overwriting traces of the past. In other words, this redevelopment *space* has the potential to remain a *place* that meaningfully relates economic motives to the community's social and cultural needs.

The in-between landscape of "historic renewal," as local leaders termed the convergence of preservation and development in the 1950s, is itself vigorously contested, however. Residents and developers regularly turn to the traces of the manufacturing heyday reflected in the decaying stone and brick structures to—depending on their definitions of progress—either contest or validate today's less secure but more flexible postindustrial economy. The meanings assigned to this local landscape continue to multiply when one steps outside the plant gates and the casino. Three sites—the vestiges of the Northampton Heights neighborhood and the basic oxygen furnace (BOF) in the eastern part of the brownfield; the Steel General Office building at the plant's main entrance; and the Martin Tower world headquarters across the river—act as touchstones for competing narratives about erasure and reuse that disrupt free-market logics and challenge corporate control over planning decisions. Debates about the impacts of urban revitalization often are portrayed as clashes between "emotional" preservationists and "rational" developers. But the distinction is again a false one. Financial transactions—and claims that "the market" is an objective and independent actor—are themselves shaped by personal and cultural values, assumptions, and experiences. The in-limbo postindustrial landscape thus presents an open resource with which to assert that local memories of the past—ones that signaled corporate commitment to people and place—can be complementary to future economic growth. The challenges to realizing this potential remain significant, however, even among "historic renewers." For example, tensions between former steelworkers and professional guides over who has the authority to lead tours of the Steel site reveal competing views of the past's value and relevance.

By the end of the mayoral workshop in 2004, John Callahan was convinced of the economic potential in preserving the Steel heritage, using the blast furnaces along the river as the backdrop. To absentee landlord ISG, the furnaces would be worth more in scrap steel than as standing monuments. But from a local perspective, an adviser told Callahan, "You need to celebrate them. They need to be the central focus of that development. They'll never be built again." Two months later, when Wilbur Ross sold the Bethlehem land to the BethWorks Now investors from New York and New Jersey, the mayor met with the new owners and told them that keeping the blast furnaces was nonnegotiable if they wanted the City's cooperation.

While creating heritage attractions is now a widely accepted development model, the social benefits of remembering a more secure era continue to take a backseat to concerns about revenue potential. Like the former plant itself, Callahan sat "in limbo" in his commitments to meet the needs of both global capital and his local constituency as he attracted and facilitated post-Steel development. On the way out of city hall after our meeting, I passed the mayor's portrait in the entrance hallway. In the richly colored oil painting, Callahan, wearing a tailored suit, stands in front of the rusted blast furnaces.[3] They form the backdrop not only for his postindustrial city, but also for the opportunity to realign the community's economic and social interests in relationship to a new corporate landowner.

Bethlehem's "Historic Renewal"

The branding of "Christmas City, U.S.A." during the Great Depression attests to Bethlehem's deep history of seeing preservation and development as two sides of the same coin. Following World War II, efforts to shape the city's North Side Moravian district remained at the vanguard of national trends as urban renewal legislation and funding fueled a flurry of demolition and rebuilding.[4] Pennsylvania's Urban Redevelopment Law of 1945 set groundwork for the federal Housing Acts of 1949 and 1954 and together gave the City of Bethlehem—and its major employer—new impetus to "improve" its landscape.[5] By 1966, the city reported revitalization plans costing $17.5 million, more than half of which came from federal grants.[6] Clarke & Rapuano, Inc., influential New York planners and landscape architects with close ties to renewal guru Robert Moses, consulted on a foundational report—funded in part by the Steel—for the city's Redevelopment Authority in 1956.[7] Together with the consultants, Bethlehem's city planners applied renewal's clean-slate vision to several of the city's neighborhoods. But unlike many other American cities seeking federal funds for urban renewal between 1949 and 1974, Bethlehem quickly incorporated historic preservation into its development plans as well, a seeming contradiction that foreshadowed trends in urban planning today explicitly linking the two projects.

Clarke & Rapuano's proposals, which for the most part emphasized new construction, made a special case for the Moravian quarter. The firm cited other cities, including Boston, Charleston, and Winston-Salem, as examples of how creating a historic district could boost downtown business.[8] In the 1956 report, the authors drafted city legislation to define a "Historic Bethlehem District" requiring approval of designs, materials, and colors for all new construction or alterations to existing structures within the area.[9] The ordinance passed in 1961, and eleven years later the historic district of eighteenth-century Moravian stone buildings, the stucco Central Moravian Church, the colonial Sun Inn, and nineteenth-century homes and storefronts joined the nascent National Register of Historic Places.[10]

With the help of federal urban renewal grants, ten acres in the district along the Monocacy Creek were cleared in 1963 where the original Moravian industrial works had been overwhelmed by an automobile junkyard. Some of the land was developed for high-rise senior housing, but the city's Redevelopment Authority subsequently leased most of the plot to Historic Bethlehem, Inc. (HBI) for restoration and development as a heritage attraction. This not-for-profit group, buttressed by the support of Steel executive wives and other social and political elites, had formed in 1957 around what it called "historic renewal."[11] As HBI president Frederick

Warnecke explained in 1962, "We expect to see a new Bethlehem built on the old foundations. This will be the finest kind of urban renewal—a kind that conserves the past yet faces the needs of the living present in new and contemporary terms and dreams of a bright future that may well be quite different from either past or present."[12]

It is tempting to narrate a shift during these postwar decades from razing to rehabilitation, a possibility enabled by 1954 Housing Act amendments, but as Warnecke's words suggest, in many respects destruction and preservation played off of and supported each other, particularly when honoring Moravian heritage was invoked as the rationale for both goals.[13] City planners described the downtown area as overcrowded, "defective in design and arrangement," and plagued by "economically and socially undesirable use."[14] A 1961 article in the *New York Herald Tribune* likewise described Bethlehem as being faced with "inner rot. Congestion, grime and obsolescence were all eating away at its core, and where there had once been thriving downtown areas that were a source of pride to citizens, industrial and residential slums were gradually taking over."[15] While similar descriptions nationwide backed plans to tear down old structures and replace them with modern buildings, the same critics lauded Bethlehem's Moravian heritage as a renewal asset, mimicking the language of nineteenth-century visitors who contrasted Moravian purity with the chaos of urbanization.

Late 1950s and early 1960s redevelopment models in Society Hill, Philadelphia, and College Hill, Providence, also emphasized those residential neighborhoods' historic characters as assets, but they were not rehabilitated as heritage tourism sites in themselves. More similar to Bethlehem's "historic renewal" was an effort underway in Portsmouth, New Hampshire, between 1957 and 1965 that involved changing state law to allow the use of urban renewal money to restore the Puddle Dock neighborhood and create the Strawbery Banke outdoor colonial museum.[16] Though Portsmouth promotes itself as the first city to use renewal funds in this way, Bethlehem was right in step. In 1962, the National Association of Housing and Redevelopment Officials featured Bethlehem, alongside Portsmouth and six other small cities, as a model of partnership between "renewers" and preservationists. The professional group's article was quickly adapted and sold as a booklet by the federal Urban Renewal Authority. As the authors wrote, this "happy combination" could "bring the warmth of friendship to renewal

Moravian Colonial Industrial Quarter, 1957 and today

The city used federal urban renewal funds to clear blighted land along the Monocacy Creek in 1963. Non-profit Historic Bethlehem, Inc. then restored the plot's eighteenth- and nineteenth-century buildings: a tannery, waterworks, gristmill, and smithy. (Historic Bethlehem Museum & Sites, Bethlehem, PA; photo by author, 2015.)

from those who may have seen the program only as a harsh destroyer and heartless displacer."[17]

This union, however, was not sealed so readily. Despite Clarke & Rapuano's support of the contained historic district on Bethlehem's North Side, the firm drew up plans in 1969 to revitalize the adjacent Broad Street shopping district by razing buildings on several blocks for the creation of a modern shopping mall, office towers, and a parking garage. A Lehigh professor who actively opposed the plan in the 1970s noted that "the fact that the buildings were modeled in white was significant." Not only did white visually convey the blank slate approach, he said, "You don't actually have to say what the buildings are for to produce a white obelisk supposedly representing progress." Amid those white boxes, the Sun Inn, a historic structure dating to 1758, was to be torn down and replaced by two high-rise office buildings.[18] If preservation was necessary, Clarke & Rapuano suggested that the Inn be relocated closer to the other Moravian buildings so as not to clash with the new construction.[19] Paralleling the concurrent rise and fall of a similar mall development scheme in nearby Lancaster, this Center City plan advanced with limited opposition through the early 1970s, but support waned and the project was halted in 1976 when new investments, tenants for the mall, and other construction failed to materialize.[20] Saved from demolition, the Sun Inn was restored to its original condition on its original site in 1981.

During this period of "historic renewal," local newspapers also reported record numbers of tourists visiting "Christmas City," drawn to the lighted North Side downtown by holiday events almost entirely focused on Bethlehem's Moravian heritage. These included walking tours of the Moravian buildings by guides dressed in period costume, services at Central Moravian Church, and visits to the community *putz* (the elaborate Nativity display).[21] While Christmas City initially used its lighted landscape to attract visitors to downtown retailers, by the 1960s Bethlehem had shifted to selling the "heritage landscape" itself. Such destinations often have popular associations with durability, dependability, and traditional values. Christmas tours of the Moravian buildings in Bethlehem stress the founders' spirituality, work ethic, self-sufficiency, nonmaterialism, and unity.[22] Nonetheless, the drive to bring money to local businesses lies just below the surface. As the director of Historic Bethlehem, Inc. wrote in 1967, "preservation mania" attracts "an ever increasing touring public. And

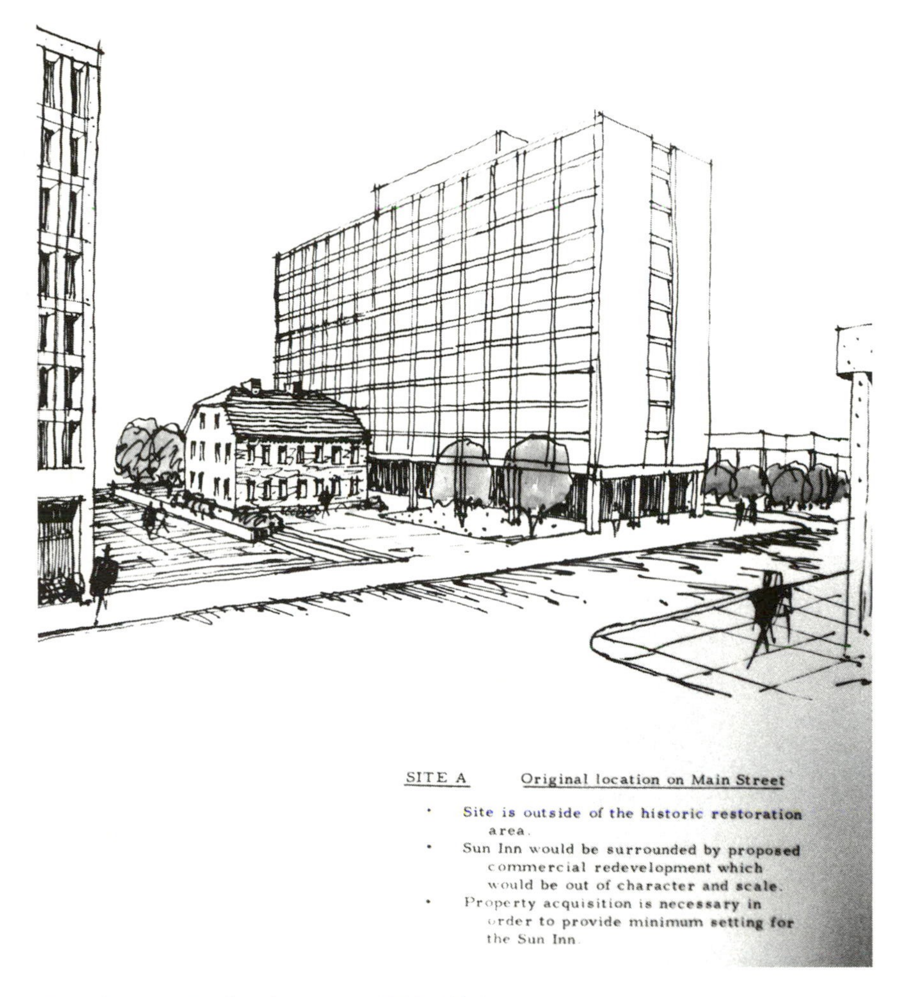

SITE A Original location on Main Street
• Site is outside of the historic restoration area.
• Sun Inn would be surrounded by proposed commercial redevelopment which would be out of character and scale.
• Property acquisition is necessary in order to provide minimum setting for the Sun Inn.

Broad Street Redevelopment, 1969–1976

This 1970 drawing from Clarke & Rapuano suggested moving Main Street's 1758 Sun Inn, a host to George Washington, John Adams, and other colonial notables, because it was "out of character and scale" with plans for new office-tower redevelopment in the North Side's downtown. The new construction on the adjacent block was halted in 1976 before it reached the Inn, which preservationists then successfully restored. (Clarke & Rapuano, Inc., *Sun Inn: An Examination of Four Sites*, 1970, Clarke and Rapuano Records, 1940–1993 (#3074), Division of Rare and Manuscript Collections, Cornell University Library.)

with the tourist comes the tourist dollar."[23] HBI stocked its gift shop extra full during the holiday season with Christmas cards, Moravian cookies, straw stars, putzes, and other festive items.[24]

The culmination of the revitalization efforts that the 1956 report sparked was the Main Street Improvement Project completed in 1978.[25] In contrast to the earlier Broad Street renewal project that emphasized new, modern construction, the Main Street project on the adjacent blocks involved replacing electric streetlights with Victorian-style light fixtures, widening the sidewalks and paving them with brick and stone, planting more trees, and remodeling nineteenth-century storefronts to "historically appropriate" designs.[26] The Steel, growing wary of the slow pace of Broad Street's modernization (and likely fearing it would be called to the rescue), funded a 1976 study by the Urban Land Institute that "strongly urged" going forward with the heritage-based plan instead. "A curious thing has happened on Main Street," the authors wrote. "Formerly the merchants were inclined to be ashamed of the old-fashioned building that extended two, three, four stories above their new shop fronts. Now the situation is reversed, and the fine Victorian architecture has achieved a new prestige." The ULI study concluded that the city should halt demolition and clearance activity on Broad Street, expand its restoration and renovation efforts, and focus on enhancing the tourism potential of its Moravian heritage.[27] In 1981 as the city geared up for another Christmas season and anticipated 30,000 holiday visitors, Columbia University graduate students in a course on "Downtown Revitalization" toured Bethlehem's Main Street as an example of success.[28]

Balancing redevelopment with preservation gained new relevance in Bethlehem amid the Steel's decline. With the closure of the plant, those 1,800 acres on the South Side became newly "historic," and manufacturing joined Moravians as a touchstone for narratives of past stability and order. The practice of incorporating historic preservation and adaptive reuse into redevelopment plans had by the 1980s gained widespread adoption in the United States on the heels of James Rouse's festival marketplace successes. While it was not surprising that Bethlehem Steel had turned to a Rouse affiliate to guide its plans for remaking the plant as a heritage-entertainment destination, by the time the factory closed in the late 1990s, the blueprint of having a single cultural anchor, like a mall, or, as the Steel Corporation imagined, a National Museum of Industrial History, had faded.[29] Instead, a planning philosophy of "creative-placemaking" gained national traction emphasizing more modest and diverse investments in clusters of revitalizing projects.[30] In these decentralized visions, street festivals, art galleries, and heritage attractions exist side-by-side with private sector businesses and mixed-income housing. While the casino in many ways fits with the big-ticket solutions of a previous era, planners and politicians are more apt to explain that Las Vegas Sands Corp. represents a ready source of private investment to drive multiuse development and "placemaking" on the rest of the site.

From Las Vegas Sands' perspective, the extant Steel buildings are valuable insofar as they can support complementary development, whether through their "postindustrial picturesque" appeal to tourists and other private investors, or, as the casino debate illustrated, by appeasing local heritage advocates who stood in opposition to development plans. Since the Sands Bethworks partnership came into ownership in 2004 of the 124 acres and thirty-six buildings at the heart of the site, a third have been torn down to make way for new construction.[31] Remaining plant structures, including the massive No. 2 Machine Shop, are slated for adaptive reuse as retail, residential, and other commercial and cultural spaces. There is one major caveat: the buildings will stay unless they prove impossible to sell or redevelop while standing.

Politicians and developers' emphases on attracting diverse investment are met with diverse community opinions not only about what should be built, but also about what existing structures should be saved. In a post–federal renewal era in which private investment drives urban planning, individuals' perspectives on appropriate redevelopment strategies often parallel their experiences of corporate-led economic change. Residents' varying interpretations of the possibilities for "historic renewal" of the three Steel sites that follow—a neighborhood razed as part of the plant's expansion in the 1960s, and the corporation's two successive world headquarters buildings—illustrate the ways in which the landscape and its histories become not just commodities, but cultural tools used to project future desires.

Corporate Traces and Northampton Heights

Although Las Vegas Sands and its developer partners have replaced Bethlehem Steel as landowners, memories of the Steel's social structures—both its imposing corporate control and the opportunities of the union contract—linger in the material traces on the plant site. The ore bridge on which the Sands hung its sign is a twenty-ton reminder of its obsolete function of moving raw materials for steel production at the same time that it signals the city's entertainment economy future. Such "ruined" objects often take on meanings more compelling than their operational originals because they draw attention to what is missing. They are "nothing made visible," an "absent presence" that can conjure up systems of power that at another time were taken for granted, such as the hegemonic influence of the Steel Corporation on city planning and daily life or the strength of union negotiation.[32] Despite ongoing efforts at physical and cultural erasure, residents continue to occupy and invoke the haunted landscape of the plant to assert this past's relevance and critique its legacy.[33]

Even the corporation itself, though legally disintegrated in bankruptcy, endures in its imprint on the land. Despite common perceptions that bankruptcy means a company has failed and no longer exists, in the business world it is commonly understood as restructuring. Selling its assets through bankruptcy to ISG allowed Bethlehem Steel's remaining plants to continue operating while shedding billions of dollars in pension and health care obligations. Hank Barnette, CEO of the Bethlehem Steel Corporation from 1992 to 2000, pointed out to me that although Bethlehem's structural steel division closed, other local Steel assets survive in new guises. The plant's forging division operates profitably today as Lehigh Heavy Forge, for example, and the railroad that serviced the plant still runs under a different owner to the intermodal rail-to-truck transfer terminal now on the site of the former coke works. Bethlehem's research and IT divisions likewise found new partners and new names. "There is a post-active Bethlehem Steel; there's a post-entity Bethlehem Steel," Barnette said as we talked at the law office he maintains in town. "So many believe that [the Corporation] closed when we closed this division. That was it. This was Bethlehem Steel. And that—in terms of the other businesses, the other divisions, it's simply inaccurate." Zombie-like, the pieces of the Bethlehem Steel Corporation live on in shells of different corporate bodies from which a previous generation's social contract has been excised.

The Steel has long outlived its legal status in other ways as well. Empty plant buildings in Bethlehem continue to evoke comments from some residents about how the union's demands drained the company, while the Martin Tower headquarters on the North Side, with its cruciform design to maximize the number of corner offices, elicits stories of management excess from those who lay the blame on the corporation. Other signs of Bethlehem Steel's demise pervade the surrounding neighborhoods. While many residents in the early twentieth century easily walked to work at the Steel, the proliferation of automobiles by the 1940s created new challenges for worker parking in the dense South Side neighborhoods. Bethlehem Steel tore down blocks of turn-of-the-century residential and commercial buildings in the 1940s, 1950s, and 1960s to make room for employee parking lots.[34] Lots on Third Street near the main gate are contiguous with the plant, but other lots scattered throughout the South Side are haphazard land claims wherever room could be made amid homes and businesses, even if it meant adding only a handful of parking spaces. Although some have been gradually reclaimed for other uses or construction, the number of empty parking lots on the South Side today is striking. "I'm amazed at what it looks like and how *quiet* it is," one former resident in her sixties told me. "There was a time in high school, on the South Side they were tearing down houses and stores. They were tearing those down to provide parking. Now there are all these parking lots, and there is nothing."

The legacy of clearance in the name of economic progress is visible in other areas of South Bethlehem as well. Across the country, postwar urban renewal often veiled agendas to clear cities' poor and ethnically marginal neighborhoods for more "profitable" uses.[35] In addition to addressing the rehabbed Moravian district on the North Side, a 1966 report from the Bethlehem Redevelopment Authority noted that the decline of residential and business districts on the South Side represented one of Bethlehem's most serious problems, comprising five of seven designated redevelopment areas.[36] In the most costly of these projects, the city had declared the entire South Side working-class neighborhood of Northampton Heights "blighted" in 1965. An inspection, performed explicitly to meet requirements for federal renewal funding, found evidence of overcrowding, fire code violations, and lack of hot water, toilets, heat, and electricity.[37] The neighborhood, a twenty-block area just east of where the casino now sits, was one of the most ethnically and racially mixed in Bethlehem. Russian immigrants clustered on Third Street near Mexicans on Columbia Street. Hungarians and other Eastern Europeans were neighbors with Pennsylvania Dutch and much of the city's small African American population. A majority of the Heights' 945 residents were employed at the steel plant that encircled it. But the company expressed interest in the site, purchased (via the Bethlehem Redevelopment Authority) the 280 homes, and by 1968 razed the neighborhood to make way for a new basic oxygen furnace to modernize its steel production.[38]

Many residents appreciated the cash to move out and into nicer homes on the North Side or in the suburbs. In exchange, the Steel promised that updated technology would increase job stability.[39] But Frank Podleiszek, a retired teacher in his late seventies, is among those who dispute the blight designation.[40] As in other communities, the nebulous process of "blighting" was as much a political construct as an empirical condition. Mimicking the favorite renewal metaphors of the time, the district's congressman ominously called the Heights "a symptom of the kind of urban decay which begins in an isolated spot in a city and then spreads, slowly, like a cancer, to adjoining areas and eventually to an entire section of our city."[41] While certain blocks of the neighborhood were falling into disrepair, the majority, Frank claims, comprised well-maintained and respectable housing and businesses. Indeed, less than half of the homes had failed the inspection.

Frank pointed out various establishments on a black-and-white photograph he brought to our interview, an aerial shot of the neighborhood pre-clearance:

> When you got to the Heights, right here on the corner was a hotel, the Sauconia Hotel. And this was Anthracite Street, this was Bessemer, this was Carbon, this was Diamond, and this was Emery. They were all connected with coal or iron or some other, all the names of the streets. And then you had Third Street and Second Street and Front Street. And that's, this is that whole area that was all taken over by Bethlehem Steel. This whole, big area. Now, my house would have been right here.

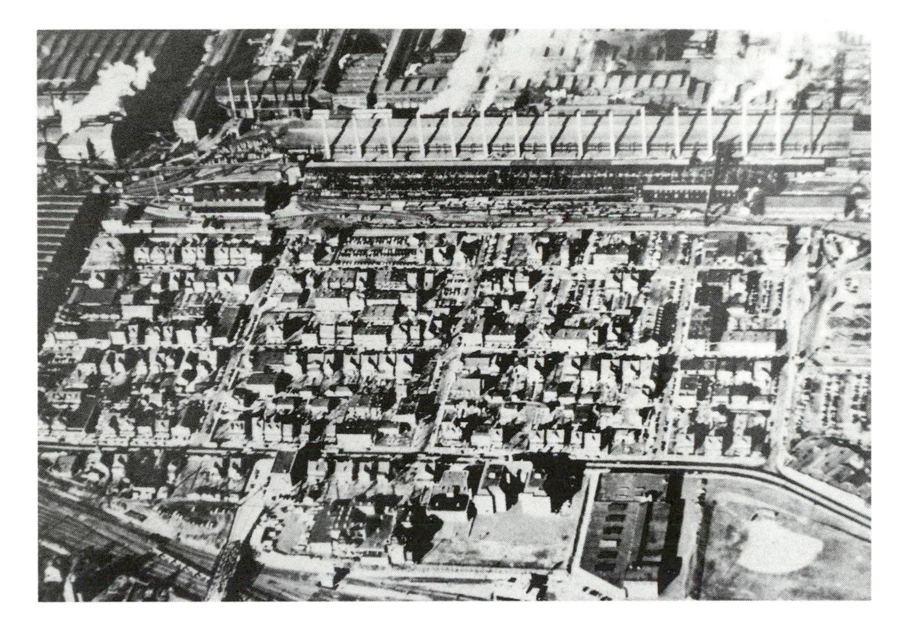

Northampton Heights, c. 1966

Northampton Heights, surrounded by the Bethlehem Steel plant, was one of the city's most ethnically and racially mixed areas. The neighborhood had its own schools, several churches, and stores, bars, and hotels to service steelworkers and their families. (Private collection of Frank Podleiszek.)

Frank described his 1910s three-story brick double on Fourth Street with fondness, recounting how oak pocket doors concealed the parlor for much of December, opening on Christmas morning to reveal a tree and putz. He told me details of stained glass windows, a walk-in closet, and an enclosed back porch as he walked me through the floor plan of the home like a realtor doing a showing of his own childhood. Frank's steelworker father was the son of Slovenian immigrants who purchased the home shortly after it was built. His father refused to leave when it was condemned in the 1960s until after the water and electricity were turned off. "When they were tearing that house down, they had the steel ball to knock it. It just kept bouncing off the wall. The wall would not crumble," Frank said. Implicitly echoing the perceived shift from a secure past to a less stable economic future, he added with a laugh, "They did that to my house now, it would fall apart right away!"[42]

Bethlehem Redevelopment Authority

Bethlehem Redevelopment Authority graphics show plans to raze the entire Northampton Heights neighborhood as part of an urban renewal project. Bethlehem Steel built the new basic oxygen furnace on the site in 1968. After the Steel's closure in 1998, the site was cleared again. It now hosts mostly office buildings and warehouses. (Bethlehem, PA, Redevelopment Authority, *1966 Annual Report*, Bethlehem Area Public Library.)

Frank is not alone in feeling the persistent presence of the neighborhood's erasure. The names of the five cross streets—Anthracite, Bessemer, Carbon, Diamond, Emery—form a mantra that men and women who lived or worked in the area before it vanished repeated to me over and over to invoke an earlier time. Their memory of the five streets, so closely aligned with the Steel Company, draws a map of a period in their lives swept away in the name of economic renewal. Ted Bodnar, a former plant supervisor in his early sixties, is among the bearers of this ritual. One hot summer day, Ted offered to take me on a meandering tour of his life pre-1995, the year he lost his job at the Steel. Ted was raised on the South Side where his Hungarian grandparents settled. First stops on the tour included his childhood home, the old Lehigh University football field where he used to sneak into games, and his grandparents' gravesite at the base of South Mountain.

Midway through this three-hour excursion, he pointed his tired blue minivan east, past the Sands Casino and its giant ore bridge, toward the site of his old office on the far end of the plant. Turning into what has been razed and partially rebuilt as an industrial park, Ted's gestures quickened, and he leaned over the steering wheel to narrate the landscape as we drove.

TB: Now this was the Heights. Over here I know there was a gas station. There were several streets. This is where they—in the term of "urban renewal," they wrecked everything and bulldozed everything. Now that's Lynn Avenue that way. But this way there used to be Anthracite Street, Bessemer, Carbon, Diamond, and Emery Street. I still remember them.

This was Bessemer Street. And we used to also have a plant gate here at one time. But I want to show you one of the last remaining things. Then it went Third Street and Second Street. But as far down—I'll show you—these were all houses here. Okay? But if you look over here—now they ripped everything down and this is where your basic oxygen furnace was.

CT: Where the field is?

TB: Yeah. Where the field is. And right over here we had our mold stripping building, which was built in 1984. We built a new one. They ripped that all down. But I want to show you, right over here you'll get to see. Over here, when the oil embargo came in, we had four or five big oil tanks filled with oil reserves for the plant. This over here is one of the original plant fences. But look-it. That's Anthracite Street. You see the macadam?

CT: Where the gate is?

TB: Yeah. You see where the macadam is? That's one of the original city streets. And this is an original—look at how they used to have the plant fencing. Wrought iron. That's an original plant fence. So now we'd be in the plant again, okay? Now we'd be in the plant. Because they ripped down the Heights. And this was all part of the BOF complex here. I mean, it was massive what they did here.

Ted's recollections jumped seamlessly from decade to decade, mirroring the palimpsestic quality of this layered landscape in his associations. The plant gate evoked a time when thousands of workers entered and left during shift changes, crowding the streets to a standstill. He recalled the giant oil tanks, markers both of Bethlehem Steel's self-sufficiency and of the 1970s energy crisis, a contributing factor to the domestic steel industry's decline. He paralleled the urban renewal clearance of the Heights in the 1960s with the Steel's efforts in the 1980s and 1990s to raze parts of the plant, work that Ted was himself directly involved with. At the same time, in recreating this landscape from bits and pieces of his own past, he implored me to enter a world more complete. His commentary as we drove through this portion of the plant was both an invocation and invitation that attached memory to place in a way that brought past chronology into present experience. Although the emptiness of the space makes it difficult to picture the throngs of people once employed at the plant or the dense neighborhood in its midst, the material remnants that residents like Ted refuse to forget guard against the absolute erasure that new development on the brownfield portends.

As we circled the new buildings that have materialized since the Lehigh Valley Industrial Park bought these 1,000 acres on the east end of the plant from ISG in 2003, Ted elaborated on the collage-like temporality. "What's really ironic is where Northampton Heights was, now they cut streets in again and are putting buildings back," he said. "So in other words, change, it seems to me, always comes back. You know what I mean? Like where they ripped buildings down for parking for the plant, they're putting buildings up again. Well, my problem is, why didn't you just maintain what you had?" This single parcel of land tells a long history of public-private partnerships between the city government and corporate entities including Bethlehem Steel, the Lehigh Valley Industrial Park, and the Las Vegas Sands Corp. Their negotiations over profit potentials and community benefits have structured city planning and city life for over a century. But Ted suggests that the tenuousness of those agreements is revealed in the material traces that linger on the site each time one plan fails and space opens up for redevelopment. Ongoing destruction and rebuilding overwrites what he argues are ultimately constant community needs for order and stability.

Ted's minivan is one testament to that fact that his life post-Steel has been difficult, as he gradually revealed to me that he is many thousands of dollars in debt and has pieced together odd jobs that include helping with high school football practices and driving a bus. The back of his van was brimming with boxes and papers salvaged from a recent fire at his home that left him living in a hotel while he sought to evict tenants from another of his properties. Ted's insistence on showing me everything "original" to the steel plant, including the fence, suggested that these were markers of an earlier order—one that was for him more economically secure—and ultimately a recognition of his now uncertain position in a postindustrial present.

Just beyond the new industrial park buildings, which include an architecture firm, a software developer, and a cold storage warehouse, we came to a dirt road, clearly a path for bulldozers and other land-razing equipment, not for blue minivans. "I hope nobody chases us. But I got to show you this," Ted said as he hit the gas. I had heard that new developers on this parcel of the former plant had kicked explorers like us off their land before. We headed east toward the rail yards, past dump trucks and abandoned train engines until he stopped the car in front of a weatherworn sign that said "Reserved Parking." It marked an open field. "Right here was where I used to park my car," Ted said. "This was my last office. It was right over here. Right where these trees were, there was our office here. Right? And over there, those were piles of ore." Ted got out of the car to look around, taking a moment to orient himself and piece together what this cleared land used to hold, a place, both physical and social, that was clearly designated for him.

Returning to the car, he turned the wheel back toward the main road. "I'm sure we're going to get chased. I'll go, 'Geez, I just made a wrong turn. I'm sorry.'" It struck me that what we were trespassing on was Ted's own life, the twenty-one years he spent working for the Steel. And yet his personal narrative is still shaped by resounding echoes of corporate control over the space and bodies that have marked this worksite as private property from the Steel to today. In other words, Ted's biography—in both its narrative and experiential forms—is inextricably tied to structures of corporate power at the same time that he attempts to rebuild his personal landscape by inviting me into it.

With a grin, Ted looked in the side mirror as we drove away. I asked him how often he comes back to explore the industrial park, and he laughed. "To be honest with you, I looked around on Sunday." That was four days before. "It's just hard—it was a way of life. I mean, you went in there every day." When I called him a couple weeks later, Ted regretted not grabbing a brick from the site of the old office and said he planned to return. Corporate interests may shape the landscape and its users, but Ted also placed and embedded his own critique of their destructive capacity in his desire for a souvenir of the now-fragmented stability reflected in these remains.[43]

As debates over the future of the Steel buildings that remain standing reveal, however, the bricks that scatter the former plant have multiple meanings for their purveyors. Industrial ruins, in occupying what Mayor Callahan called a "state of limbo," offer a unique interpretive flexibility. Extant buildings attest to both the resilience of an earlier economic order and its present obsolescence, to continuity and rupture.[44] Many locals hope to save these relics of the past, but from other perspectives they are waste material signaling a prime opportunity for new development in the plant's crumbled wake. The competing interpretations that Bethlehem stakeholders assign to the Steel site ruins reveal the work the material landscape does to help articulate, shape, and "place" competing value systems and understandings of economic change amid the city's corporate legacies.

The Steel General Office Building: Raze or Remember?

Ted Bodnar sees reminders of his and his community's past in the eastern portion of the plant, but some of the most visible traces—physically, politically, and culturally—are in the 124 central acres on which the original Bethlehem Works redevelopment plan focused in the 1990s. These acres, now in the hands of Sands Bethworks, the partnership between Las Vegas Sands and the New York and New Jersey developers, quickly emerged as the locus of debate about historic preservation and how memories like Ted's could best be saved, interpreted, or monetized via the more than twenty industrial buildings that remain.[45]

Since the 1970s developers have increasingly accepted the political and economic advantages of "historic renewal" or selective preservation. Just as the industrial theming of the casino represented a compromise variously interpreted by different constituencies as respect, appeasement, or opportunism, adaptive reuse can be a crosscutting tool for maintaining local connections to place and history while reimagining structures for profitable use.[46] The built environment and its redevelopment make abstract capitalist processes material both to those with cultural interests and fiscal investments in the landscape.[47] Community debates nonetheless often take shape around a dichotomy of "rational" and "emotional" visions of redevelopment. In Bethlehem, these align with responses to the Steel economy's extinction as either welcome progress or distressing loss. At stake in negotiating the "worth" of memories associated with the Steel Corporation, its workers, and the community is a cultural contest over whose interests should be valued today and whose should be left behind in order to move forward.

The mayor, for example, described community members with investments in the site's history based on their personal and social connections to the plant as sentimental. This cohort, he noted, includes both bitter former steelworkers who want to tear down the buildings out of anger over having lost their pensions and medical benefits in the Steel's bankruptcy—a "Who cares about the history? They didn't care about us," perspective—as well as the other extreme that wants to "save every last artifact, that brick over there" as a monument to a proud history of manufacturing might. In contrast to these "passionate" arguments, the mayor said, are the rational thinkers like himself, those who "were sort of neutral about it. 'Whatever we can save, we can save,'" but "'it's got to make some economic sense.'"

So-called emotional justifications for preservation or appeals from angry steelworkers to "bulldoze the son of a bitch" tend to align with expectations of social commitments from corporate development, while rational arguments emphasize profit motives. But despite the mayor's effort to outline distinct cohorts, residents regularly move between and across these simple groups. Many occupy an indeterminate middle ground as they negotiate the relationship between neoliberal capitalism, the historical landscape, and the open-ended meanings of postindustrialism. As became clear in my conversations, even "rational thought" presupposes an underlying morality—a firm confidence in "the market"—that undercuts claims to purely objective calculation.

Tim Deluca's insistence on the benefits of repeatedly starting anew in his career as a casino dealer and his beliefs about real estate development, for instance, are mutually reinforcing. Tim, who is not originally from Bethlehem, has trouble sympathizing with a preservationist plan that would save the remaining Steel structures because his corporate-friendly perspective on both work and the built environment subscribes to "rational" market logics. Just as he accepts the fact that Sands made business decisions that twice led to his being rendered disposable and laid off, Tim said matter-of-factly, "If you've got a property in Las Vegas that's ten or fifteen years old, they don't refurbish it. They don't dress it up. They blow it up. They implode it." Even before reaching for the dynamite and wrecking ball, many casino properties on the Las Vegas Strip are constantly being made over.[48] Such visions exemplify capitalism's perpetual cycle of "creative destruction" that links the advance of one economic form to the decline and devaluation of another. This formulation makes clear the inescapable instability and insecurity of capitalist systems at the same time that pro-growth thinkers like Tim embrace this approach as a sure-bet justification for clean-slate reinvention.

Emily Dobbins, the head of the casino training school, pointed to Bethlehem Steel's thirteen-story office building near the plant's main entrance as an obvious target for this redevelopment approach. Designed in 1916 by influential Chicago firm Graham, Burnham & Company, and later renovated by famed architects McKim, Mead & White, the building was Bethlehem Steel's corporate world headquarters until the company moved its offices across the river in the 1970s. The structure remained in use as the Steel General Office (SGO) Building for the sales department until the plant closed. Visitors and clients who entered the marble-clad main lobby were greeted by a bevy of attractive young "escorts" or "elevator girls" who led them to the appropriate offices upstairs. A series of hanging limestone reliefs were commissioned to display various aspects of Bethlehem Steel's enterprise in heroic style. A thirty-five-foot mural called "The Story of Steel," completed in the lobby in 1954, centered around two near-naked men pouring molten steel. Four more gray-tone scenes of the city punctuated by the bright orange of hot metal decorated the building's auditorium.[49]

Today, the limestone figures hang unobtrusively in the long hallway that connects the Sands Casino to its hotel, while the four restored murals are near the Sands event center and meeting rooms. Only glimmers of the Steel's past grandeur are visible through the SGO Building's locked glass doors, dirt covering their H-beam insignia. Originally, the SGO Building was slated as the first reuse project on the site, with plans to convert it into a hotel, condominiums, or dorms. But finding a buyer willing to spend the money to renovate has been a challenge. Empty for over a decade, at this point the building is so overtaken by mold that purveyors must don face-masks, not to mention confront the asbestos lurking in the walls.[50]

"That's a sin," Emily said of the building's deterioration. But her concern was not that it hasn't been preserved. Rather, to her it was a sin that the building hadn't been torn down. "They say it's beautiful inside and whatever, but it really needs to be razed." In a startling contradiction of ends and means for those who directly link physical remains to memory, Emily asserted, "You can maintain the reverence of the property and the integrity by tearing it down."

This perspective on the role of history in economic development adapts material traces of the past not as indelible relics, but as accoutrements to forward-looking projects. Tim agreed that reappropriating remnants of the past, like the ore bridge-made-casino sign or the lobby murals, would serve the purpose of thematically connecting the site's industrial history to its future development in a more flexible (and excisable) way that allows room for adaptation going forward. "I'm a capitalist, so I take the emotion out of business," he said. A place, from this perspective, is valuable for its profit potential, not the cultural weight of the community's past that it may drag with it. "All those smelting houses there—pfft! Knock 'em all down. Build condos," Tim suggested. "Bethlehem Steel, you got a lot of emotion tied up in there, and the buildings are historic. But you know what? I'm business. Forget the emotion. Put this [new construction] down there because this is going to produce the revenue. That's how I could best describe a capitalist in this particular scenario."

The line between capitalist and preservationist, however, is not necessarily so clear. Multiple residents with whom I spoke invoked a different historical consciousness to likewise suggest that clean-slate separation from the past is necessary to draw future investment. They argued that Bethlehem would have fared better had it been attacked during World War II. "We went over and bombed the German [steel] plants down to the ground, bombed the Japanese plants. Then we turned around at the end of the war and shipped them all the latest new equipment. And so they got new plants with equipment that was brand new and everything from us," explained one former middle manager at the Steel. While bombed foreign plants were given an opportunity to modernize, he suggested that in Bethlehem the still-standing buildings represent an inertia that was at odds with capital investment and led to a more distressing kind of deterioration.

Self-proclaimed capitalists and advocates of impersonal market logics make a point to excise what could be called "sentimental" considerations from their calculus of economic benefit. These matter-of-fact assertions from residents that their hometown would have fared better had it been destroyed nonetheless invoke lessons from the past in a way that begins to muddy the distinction between capital interests and commitments to preserving place. Debates in Bethlehem about adaptive reuse and heritage-based urban development revise the terms of conflict. Through residents' narratives about and interactions with the built environment, it becomes clear that place-based memories, emotions, and social concerns help shape economic interests rather than repel them.

Although Tim and Emily see the SGO Building as an eyesore in need of demolition to attract outside investment, Richard Hoffer is among the Bethlehem residents who have strong personal attachments to the structure. Richard, now in his early sixties, grew up close to his grandfather who retired in the mid-1960s as head custodian at the office building. "I can remember him taking me in there as a kid at Christmas time. And I want to tell you, there was never a finer looking lobby in corporate America. In my mind's eye I can picture—I mean, it was stainless steel and marble, was decorated with the most beautiful Christmas trees—" Richard's voice cracked, and he paused to collect himself as we sat in the new arts center just down the road.

The Christmas decorations at the Steel are a recurring touchstone in conversations about the company's economic health and its community outreach, as well as the corporate excess that contributed to its undoing. From the first public holiday display in the headquarters lobby in 1949, the ever-changing decorations attracted thousands of visitors. People flocked to see the forty-foot Norway spruce covered with 2,000 white lights erected out front; the fifteen-foot poinsettia trees comprised of 150 individual potted plants that were "replaced regularly so the trees always appear fresh and bright"; or the two angels suspended over the staircase. The twenty-five Douglas firs decorated with cardinals that lined the lobby in 1959 attracted almost 16,000 sightseers.[51]

"I'm sorry for the emotions," Richard apologized after regaining his composure. "My grandfather and I were very close." He recounted childhood memories of a circular room off the lobby ringed with models of ships, buildings, and other structures built with the company's steel. "For a seven-, eight-, nine-, ten-year-old kid, that was cool. That was really cool," he said with a boyish grin. As an adult, Richard had a career in the city government and had another opportunity to tour the SGO Building in the mid-1990s when Bethlehem Steel, exiting the local business, put the structure up for sale. The contrast with his childhood memories shook him. "It was very disappointing to come back and be in that building—let's see, around '96, '97—thirty-plus years after I had last been in it. Because my memories were of the grandeur of the holiday season," he said. "The carpets were torn, the paneling was shabby, paint was peeling off the walls. . . . I actually found it depressing to see how derelict and shabby the building had become on the inside." The decaying building evoked for Richard a wellspring of emotions that blurred the personal, social, and economic. Richard's memories mix a longing both for the security and innocence of childhood and for the corporation's former financial stability when its dominance could be clearly encapsulated and understood via a room full of miniature models.[52] Thus, while the structure today is a practical nightmare, it is laden with cultural value. The embedded opportunity in the remaining Steel structures to recognize and include in market-driven redevelopment the value of what some cast as "irrational" attachments to the past suggests a unique potential in Bethlehem's development landscape.

"Rational Preservation" and Martin Tower

Like Richard, many former steelworkers also have deeply emotional and morally infused connections to the site on which they spent years laboring. For them, preservation of the buildings is a hedge against the contributions they made to their families, city, and nation being lost along with the manufacturing base that supported them. Michael Russo, who worked as a dentist on the South Side during the 1980s and 1990s as the plant shut down, said that in conversations with his steelworker patients, "They were not really positive that their legacy was going to continue. Plain and simple, they thought they were going to be forgotten." Michael remembers tense discussions later when the casino came in and decisions were made about which buildings would remain:

> [The developers] had a map out, and they said, "Well, this building's going to go, that building's going to go, that building, we got to make room for parking, so we got to take down these certain buildings." And don't you know that for every building that they wanted to tear down, there was an argument from the steelworkers. "No, we got to keep that! It's got so many memories!" Down it went. "We got to keep that! It has all these memories!" Down it went.

In an era of economic instability and neoliberal competition, "memories" do not always have obvious value, particularly for developers with no direct connection to Bethlehem's past. Even the corporate-led effort to enshrine Bethlehem Steel via the National Museum of Industrial History failed for years to attract enough capital and, in 2014, still not open, nearly dissolved.[53]

The opportunity for developers to use the city's history to make future plans more legible to locals and gain their support, however, suggests that capitalizing on the built environment as a site of embedded memory and culture can be mutually beneficial for both preservationists and investors. Javier Parker, a Moravian pastor who works in South Bethlehem, indicated that for many people the Steel site acts as a common, if contested, ground for discussing community values and their evolution.[54] When I posited that some people say the industrial buildings are rusted and decaying and should be torn down, Javier responded, "They say that about old people too. They're not torn down. We try to take care of them. . . . If we were to tear down everything that was old, we wouldn't have a history to look forward to." His comparison of buildings to people and phrasing of "a history to look forward to" pointedly captured the intergenerational continuity that the built environment has the ability to evoke via shared social and cultural histories. At the same time, he acknowledged that choices have to be made about what structures should remain and whose stories to preserve.

Even among the stauncher preservationists, whom the mayor described as antiquarians obsessed with saving every last brick and whom Emily and Tim saw as obstructionists, there are wide-ranging opinions on what exactly should be saved. Several industrial veterans, for example, told me that reusing the Steel buildings was a good idea, but that developers kept "the wrong ones." The continuity they sought in preserving the physical remains is directly linked to their function in a former economy and the potential for reindustrialization. Paul Burton, for example, worried that the plant where he spent thirty-nine years of his life had become nothing but "tons of buildings sitting there doing absolutely nothing except rusting." Echoing Tim, he said most of the remaining old buildings are "nothing but junk tin as far as I'm concerned. They're of no value to anyone. That kind of filth should be taken down." Kevin Engel, an electronics technician who worked thirty-four years at the Steel, agreed that the oldest part of the plant that is the focus of preservation and reuse efforts "should have been leveled." According to Kevin, "the real high-tech stuff," the most modern buildings that he believes could have supported new industry, were all to the east of the casino in what was razed for the industrial park.

Like those who say they wish the plant had been bombed during World War II, however, these former steelworkers' association of the buildings with their manufacturing function goes beyond fiscal concerns. To Kevin, their destruction reflects a misguided affirmation of the collective abandonment of manufacturing as a cultural anchor. He finds Founders Way, the road that cuts through the plant to the new arts center, particularly cringe-inducing for this reason. In 2001 the city embedded hundreds of gears and steel beams in the sidewalks and macadam along the street as decorations and crude benches to signal the site's heritage industry potential. "That sort of hurt seeing those things as part of the roadway, barriers along the road. That's what the equipment was reduced to," Kevin said. While working at the plant, "I saw those gears turning. And now they're part of the—they're in the ground, half in the ground." He laughed at the absurdity of a dynamic way of life literally being buried and frozen in place by a vision that depends on memorializing those experiences as part of the past.[55]

To others who calculate economic potential in the extant buildings, preservationists' longing for a former way of life and an ongoing relationship with its material traces reflects nostalgia for a false stability only imagined against an uncertain present. Less appealing aspects of living and working in a steel town, for example, fall away, sometimes through active forgetting. While nostalgia drives many heritage sites' attractiveness to visitors, Mayor Callahan saw it as a potential barrier to development in Bethlehem because it prevented some community members from moving on. At the height of the great debate over whether to allow a casino in Bethlehem, Callahan went to lunch with the president of Moravian College, a staunch gambling opponent. Callahan recounted how, over the meal, the college president confronted him: "If you feel like gambling would be a suitable use for this particular site in your city, is there any use that you would feel would not be okay?" Callahan paused for a minute before responding:

> How about the Steel? How about after all these years of that site being silent—because we know a lot more about pollution and air pollution and asthma and all those things, the traffic and the sound and the noise. How about if I was able to get some company to come back in here and fire up those blast furnaces again and start making steel? Do you realize the opposition that I would have in this community if I got the coke works going again and I got the steel mill going again in our downtown here?

Other residents echo the mayor's concern that the dangerous labor conditions and community shackles to the Steel's corporate structures have been swept under the rug along with the dirt South Side women regularly battled on their stoops. "We often do that with our memories and remember only the good times and sort of filter out the bad," Callahan said. Many of the staunchest preservationists, he claimed, are too young to even remember Bethlehem Steel at its pinnacle.

Though she would disagree, Jenny Fosco, whose father spent his career in the now-crumbling No. 2 Machine Shop, is potentially among this category. In 2003, when she was thirty-five, Jenny formed an organization committed to saving the Steel's physical remains. To her, adaptive reuse of the site had the potential to create a unique district "where people can live, work, and play enveloped by the solidity of America's industrial age."[56] She takes issue with the new SteelStacks arts center and its founding director because, like the casino planners, he pursued new construction with an industrial aesthetic rather than reusing the No. 8 Hammer Shop, an original structure that was on the site. Highlights in the award-winning new design include massive windows overlooking the blast furnaces, exposed concrete and steel infrastructure, and accents of orange paint in the same color used for Bethlehem Steel's beams on the Golden Gate Bridge. "The average fellow in Bethlehem probably tells you it's wonderful what [the director] did there, but I think it's really disgusting," she said after the center opened. "They keep talking about how great—'Oh we kept a beam or something.' Or he has a crane in there. It's like, hello! He knocked down a whole building!" She worries that in two or three generations, "children will not even know the Steel existed." Jenny prefers the approach the city took to restoring the 1863 Stock House as a new visitor center next door.

Beyond suggesting that the built environment can provide social stability and "solidity" in a volatile postindustrial era, however, Jenny strives to make her position persuasive by framing it in economic terms. Much as residents who opposed the casino on religious grounds adopted fiscal arguments to advance their claims, the logic of neoliberalism and its elevation of "the free market" to a moral imperative have influenced discursive choices. Jenny argued on her organization's website that, by pumping new money and investment into the local economy, "the old factory can provide a solid prosperity for local families, much as it has done for the last 150 years," and that rehabilitation would shift investment from new construction materials to creating jobs, and in the end be more cost-effective.[57]

Jenny suggests with this double argument, in which memories hold both social value and profit potential, that the revitalization of the Steel site can be mutually beneficial to preservationists and developers. But she is aware that "preservation" continues to carry a stigma among city boosters keen on securing a new, postindustrial identity. "People hear you're into history or whatever, right away they go . . . 'Oh, you don't want to touch it. You want to put a fence around it,'" she explained. As she gained local notoriety and attention from newspaper reporters, "I kept saying to them, 'Stop

ArtsQuest Center at SteelStacks

ArtsQuest tore down the No. 8 Hammer House, a building it initially planned to reuse, to build the new arts center in 2011. The adjacent Gas Engine Blower House and Central Tool building remain standing but vacant. The blast furnaces, reflected in the new building's windows, provide a backdrop for outdoor concerts and events. (Photo by author, 2015.)

calling me a preservationist!' Because people think you're a crazy building hugger."

The city council passed a municipal historic preservation plan in 2011 that represented a new, though largely toothless, step in documenting Bethlehem's heritage assets and preservation's potential role in economic and community development. As local officials voted on the resolution, one councilwoman indeed sought to assuage developers' fears of crazy building huggers by stressing that "*rational* historic preservationists" would understand that not all buildings can be saved. "We are not turning it into a big museum," she said of the Steel site, emphasizing instead the selectivity of adaptive reuse and its flexibility in meeting developers' needs.[58]

With the casino debate, using fiscal language to make moral arguments against gambling failed to persuade development interests not to move ahead. But, inversely, given the ongoing cultural currency of history in Bethlehem, moral language can be readily accepted when the underlying economic rationale is clear. The local exemplar of this type of "rational preservation" is the listing of Martin Tower, Bethlehem Steel's headquarters since 1972, on the National Register of Historic Places. The twenty-one-story building, the tallest in the Lehigh Valley, sits on the North Side across the river from the plant. It was designed in a cruciform shape with the specific intention of maximizing the number of corner offices for executives. Roughly 1,300 white-collar workers, most of whom had been in the SGO Building, moved to the new tower. An H-beam motif inspired etchings on glass partitions and doors, the shape of the receptionist's desk, and a modern sculpture at the building's entrance. Almost all of the furniture and much of the building's infrastructure were made of steel in celebration of its tenant. The exception was the penthouse, reserved for top executives. Their ornately furnished offices featured walnut paneling, hand-woven carpet, English tapestries depicting the basic oxygen furnace process, and wooden doorknobs inlaid with the company's H-beam logo. The president and chairman had their own marble bathrooms, and two commercial-grade kitchens supported private dining rooms.[59]

Despite some construction setbacks amid growing uncertainty in the domestic steel industry, the tower was positioned in the 1970s as a physical symbol of Bethlehem Steel's corporate dominance and prosperity.[60] At the groundbreaking in 1969, then-chairman Edmund Martin, for whom the tower was named, also offered the building as a sign of the corporation's deep roots in Bethlehem and its commitment to place:

> We have done a lot of thinking about the probable future of the city of Bethlehem and the Lehigh Valley. It looks good to us. In recent years, we have seen the development of a strong community spirit. People are now working together on projects for community betterment with an enthusiasm comparable to that of Bethlehem's founders. This building is, in a sense, our pledge to the community that Bethlehem Steel will do its part to encourage that spirit. In short, it is evidence that we are here to stay.[61]

Much as the Steel had assured residents of Northampton Heights a few years earlier that building the basic oxygen furnace in place of their homes would ensure future employment, new construction continued to represent

Martin Tower

Bethlehem Steel's new corporate world headquarters opened in 1972 on the city's North Side. The red H-beam marks the main entrance to the cruciform skyscraper, which was designed by New York architectural firm Haines Lundberg Waehler to maximize corner offices. Though never realized, plans also existed for a second office tower. Today the building, the tallest in the region, is vacant and in disrepair. Residents disagree about whether it should be torn down. (Photo by author, 2011; Barry Bush, 2007.)

economic stability. Bethlehem Steel would, after all, hit record profits in 1974 before the company's outlook soured. After Martin Tower's dedication, over 21,000 Bethlehem Steel employees, their family members, and other local residents took advantage of open "tour days" to see the building's interior.[62] In his speech, Martin reiterated the connection in Bethlehem between development and preservation through his allusions to the city's Moravian founders. He further positioned himself in the flexible space of "historic renewal" when, in 1972, he became the new president of Historic Bethlehem, Inc.

Nearly four decades later, the abandoned Martin Tower stands as a very different reminder. In contrast to Martin's emphasis on commitment to the city, after the Steel's decline it became a touchstone for stories of the corporation's mismanagement and its disinvestment in place. Some locals disparagingly refer to the oversized skyscraper as "Martin's Last Erection." Empty since 2007, today Martin Tower is marked by hurried graffiti and broken windows. Its co-owners, a Bethlehem developer and a real-estate mogul from New Jersey, are distinct from Sands Bethworks. Although the city altered the corporate campus's zoning to allow residential reuse, the developers' initial plans to adapt the offices into apartments failed to gain sufficient financial backing, and its real-estate value plummeted.[63]

Then, in 2010, the National Park Service surprised many residents by granting Martin Tower tax-friendly National Register status, despite the fact that the building was less than fifty years old, a staple criterion of the designation. The approved application, submitted by the building's owner-developers, states that Martin Tower is nonetheless historically significant because it reflects the reluctance in the 1970s of the Steel's management to adapt its strategies to a changing economy. The building stands as "a symbol of one of America's mightiest industrial concerns as it plunged from the zenith of its power into a steady decline, ultimately leading to failure that resulted in the loss of over one hundred thousand jobs and regional economic hardship." Martin Tower is further described as a reflection of a "corporate culture of extravagance and laissez-faire attitude that flew in the face of a workforce continually being asked to reduce costs in order to make the company more profitable." Going on to note that the lessons of the 1970s are "of particular importance in today's era of failed companies, recession and high unemployment," the application explicitly draws connections between the 2008 economic downturn and the "laissez-faire" neoliberal policies that were just taking hold forty years earlier during the tower's construction.[64]

The description reflects a moral argument that many out-of-work steelworkers and critics of neoliberalism would find compelling. Rather than moving beyond a less-than-rosy past, as the mayor suggested, the wording implies that the active preservation even of negative emotion has a valid role to play in reimagining Bethlehem's as well as the nation's future.[65] At the same time, the application merges the narrative of these policies' betrayal of the American worker with its writers' transparent efforts to secure tax credits that could help ensure profitable future development of the site with minimal attention to historic interpretation. National Register status gives developers a 20 percent tax credit for renovations that maintain a building's "historic" character. For a relatively new structure, this is a vague requirement. Tellingly, the application for Register status made an explicit case for dissociating the other low-rise office buildings on the fifty-three-acre Martin Tower campus in order to exclude them from historic designation. In developers' plans, these buildings surrounding the tower would be razed.[66]

Martin Tower, like many of the Steel buildings, thus materializes competing interests. While some preservationists, including Jenny, agree the tower should be saved for its historic associations to the Steel, many others dispute its symbolic value.[67] Ed Krause worked in Martin Tower as a collection manager in the finance department. He remembers moving into the new, shiny building in the 1970s and the way some people looked down on the departments that had been "left behind" in the South Side offices. But today he claims no positive connection to the structure because of its dismal use value. "That thing is a piece of junk," he told me. "I would like to see them implode it. I don't care what they do with it. I have no sentimental value for Martin Tower."

The range of opinions about the sentimental and economic "values" of Martin Tower, and the regular dissolution of these rigid frameworks, suggest that out of Bethlehem's early interest in "historic renewal," a form of preservation has emerged that can complement neoliberal emphases on rational development. Local sentiment, though powerful, is not a sufficient reason to save outmoded buildings. In the case of Martin Tower, associated memories are valuable to its owners insofar as they can be repurposed for economic advantage via tax credits for redevelopment of the relatively modern structure. The aging SGO Building on the South Side, Bethlehem Steel's headquarters for the majority of its reign, has yet to show similar benefit to Las Vegas Sands and its partners in this fiscal-social calculus. There is no guarantee of more than superficial historic interpretation in a Martin Tower reuse project, and the building may still be torn down if it does not spark new investment. But the potential to include other voices in the spaces of the plant as developers seek community buy-in could nonetheless reassert alternative logics into the future-oriented frame of economic progress.

Interpreting the Steel Site

The interpretive space that "historic renewal" opens amid the Steel ruins, however, is up for grabs. Community groups and individuals committed to preservation disagree over who has the authority to tell the story of Bethlehem Steel and its workers. Should interpreting the former Steel buildings be a way to share subjective experience, or should it be grounded in verifiable facts? As with the casino, there is also a question of intended audience. Are memories being preserved to pass on to future generations in Bethlehem, or to sell the story to outside tourists? The rational-emotional balance that informs development decisions gains new expression in the contest over whether former steelworkers or professional guides and historians should control the narrative embedded in the site.

Particularly since the emergence of social history, public history, and postmodern critiques of top-down narratives in the 1960s and 1970s, interpretive practices at heritage sites increasingly have incorporated a multiplicity of voices and made efforts to disrupt authoritative accounts of the past. While the "man-on-horse" model celebrating the achievements of the white, male elite has a remarkable persistence, it is far more common today for heritage sites to at least nod toward including women's, working-class, and minority histories. So-called house museums that froze time at a particular historical moment or showcased specimens of architectural styles likewise have gradually given way to interest in the entire landscape as a social production in perpetual flux. In the latter approach, the experiences and narratives embedded in the built environment often gain more relevance than the buildings themselves in historical interpretations.[68]

In Bethlehem, the opportunity to tell multiple histories through the Steel site is attractive to a range of parties. The buildings offer a ready anchor for discussing the roles of labor, management, and industry in local, regional, national, and global contexts. They relate to the immigrant experience as well as military history and engineering and technological advances. Heritage sites often serve as a starting point for rituals and narratives about growth and progress, but as Martin Tower's National Register application suggests, the Steel ruins also offer an opportunity to critique the neoliberal policies and economic reorientation that gradually eroded the social safety net. This potential for interpretive multiplicity plays out most visibly in Bethlehem amid the number of small, not-for-profit organizations staking a claim in the area's history. While, in the best case, multivocal history can present a more inclusive picture of a place's past and create a dialogue amid contemporary concerns, bringing all stakeholders to the table presents a significant challenge.[69] As one observing party in Bethlehem noted,

> NMIH [the National Museum of Industrial History] doesn't get along with ArtsQuest, and Historic Bethlehem Partnership, you don't know where their loyalty lies. And everybody in South Bethlehem Historical Society always feels like they're getting stepped on because they're so little. And Steelworkers' Archives, they're disorganized. And nobody can get along. It's like, "That's *our* history. You can't do that." So it's a nightmare.

In 2005 the Lehigh Valley Industrial Heritage Coalition formed to facilitate the cooperation of these and other local groups with an interest in integrating the history of South Bethlehem and the region as a whole into developers' plans. With the help of a team from Rutgers University, the coalition received National Endowment for the Humanities funds as well as grants from the state and city to come up with an interpretive plan for the bankrupt Steel site. Over the next few years, the city, developers, and casino representatives participated alongside local activists and public historians from across the country in the hopes of incorporating Bethlehem's history into the region's economic development in ways that were mutually beneficial to investors and the community.[70] Beyond reusing industrial buildings for retail, office space, or housing, the group focused on heritage tourism as the driving force for revitalization.

But these initial efforts to organize all interested parties into a coalition with a unified vision ultimately petered out. In part, Las Vegas Sands, which is the majority stakeholder in the property and controls the purse strings, had no incentive to participate beyond what it saw as goodwill contributions. Although the Pennsylvania Gaming Control Board had cited Sands' potential to interpret the historic site in its decision to award the casino license, there was no binding preservation agreement, and ultimately the state was content with the creation of new jobs and tax revenues from the property's gambling profits. Meanwhile, some locals viewed the coalition's supporters, academics from New Jersey, as another group of meddling outsiders. As we've seen, history in Bethlehem is no small matter. Control over its use is hard fought for and fast protected.[71] Even attempts like the group's proposals to disrupt top-down narratives simultaneously can ignite holdover suspicions among union steelworkers, for example, of "company" authority. Going back to the mid-1970s, an oral history project funded by Bethlehem Steel and conducted by Lehigh professors and students as part of a local outreach effort raised accusations that the university and the corporation were "stealing" residents' stories; to what end was not clear.[72]

One consequence of this distrust is a parochialism among grassroots groups that ultimately works against common goals of shaping an anti-authoritarian public history. "Now it's this whole adversarial thing. 'You can't play in my sandbox. It's my sandbox,'" explained a former steelworker who has crossed various party lines. "People are not seeing the big picture. . . . Once we're gone, there's no more steelworkers in the Steelworkers' Archives. What's going to keep it going?" The resulting tensions have emerged in discussions about which institutions are the most appropriate repositories for Steel artifacts. The Steelworkers' Archives' collection, which includes clothing, flags, and other worker artifacts, remains uncatalogued and inaccessible in a non-climate-controlled storage facility. In case the Archives runs out of money and dissolves before it secures a venue for public display, which is a reasonable concern, it made plans to add its collection to that of the National Museum of Industrial History.[73] There was no guarantee at the time, however, that NMIH would ever open. The South Bethlehem Historical Society ultimately moved its collection of photographs, postcards, and other memorabilia from an unsecure and uncontrolled location to Lehigh University's academic archives. Historic Bethlehem Partnership, the umbrella organization that succeeded Historic Bethlehem, Inc., meanwhile stepped on some toes when it hosted its first Steel-centric exhibition in 2012 featuring a small collection of artifacts that included executive china from the Homer Research Laboratories and an electric fan from Martin Tower.[74]

One of the most contentious local debates over historical interpretation and ownership, however, concerned who had the authority to give tours of the steel plant. With the opening of the SteelStacks arts center in the spring of 2011, Historic Bethlehem Partnership began collaborating with operator ArtsQuest to lead daily, ticketed tours of the former plant structures in the immediate vicinity. Guides wear work boots, jeans, t-shirts or flannel shirts, and hard hats. With few exceptions, however, these guides are not actually former steelworkers. Since Historic Bethlehem, Inc.'s 1958 founding, Historic Bethlehem's offices and perceived focus have been on the North Side in the Moravian district. Its previous forays into telling the stories of South Bethlehem never garnered as much attention. The organization's "blue-blood" associations, as one resident put it, and the fact that it traces its roots to the support of Steel executives and their wives, further fed steelworkers' union-company distrust of the new venture at the former plant.

"In some ways it's kind of silly," Elaine Couch, the president of Historic Bethlehem, explained to me in an effort to downplay the tension. "There are some people involved in some of the tiny little groups that are very protective, because they're so afraid that we're going to take them over or something." While Historic Bethlehem is not a large operation, it is more established and professionalized compared with the Steelworkers' Archives, for example, which was founded in 2001 and has no paid staff. Elaine, who had several relatives with jobs at the Steel, had attended one of the Archives' monthly meetings before SteelStacks opened to explore the possibility of partnering with them on the new tours. She offered to pay some members to be guides as long as they "follow[ed] my script that I researched and wrote." The steelworkers, sensing they were the best authorities of their own lives, had a different view. "They wanted to be able to point out a building and say, 'I worked there,'" Elaine said. "That's fine, but that's not what people are paying to hear." Instead, the tour script is a more general and ostensibly more appealing narrative tracing the rise and fall of industry and the city's renaissance today.[75]

The Steelworkers' Archives is not without tour experience. Beginning in 2004, its members, almost all of whom are former union workers, periodically led popular trolley tours of the defunct Steel site. The first day of summer tours in 2005, for example, attracted 600 people. Bernie Hovan, the figurehead who participated in the casino's opening ceremony, was among the guides of these excursions. As the trolley entered the otherwise off-limits Steel site and passed the blast furnaces, Central Tool Shop, No. 2 Machine Shop, and ore bridge, he dramatically recounted stories of working as a rigger in the plant.[76] In contrast to Elaine's script, the Archives' historical narrative is a personal and experiential one, the type of bottom-up social history that has gained public history professionals' support.

Bernie's project in transmitting his memories nonetheless rubbed uncomfortably against the constraints of the heritage industry and the Archives' efforts to collect fees at the event. After the first couple tours, two of the younger members in charge of selling tickets to a long line of people came over to Bernie's bus.

> You know what they told me? They says, "Bernie, you're taking too long. It's only an hour. Not an hour and twenty minutes." I went back after I gave the tour, and I went to them two guys that were selling tickets and soda. I asked them nice, "Where do you get that, that you're going to tell me how long to talk on this tour?" Neither one of them said anything, Chloe. Nothing. Did I take still an hour and twenty minutes? Yes.

Bernie's seniority and social capital from the years spent in the steel plant ultimately maintained their value and reaffirmed his authority, particularly within the confines of the Steel site. But the transition that the tours signified from manufacturing to an entertainment economy, with steelworkers acting as service workers, was clearly an uneasy one.

In the end, the potential Elaine saw to incorporate the steelworkers into the new, professionalized tours of the site never took hold, and the Steelworkers' Archives was left out of future discussions.[77] Some suggested that the tour's promoters feared steelworker guides would tell off-color jokes or otherwise offend tourists with their "authenticity." Encounters with real blue-collar workers might also disrupt the script that places Bethlehem's service-industry renaissance in the context of industrial decline.[78] The Archives president at the time, Chuck Sabel, vacillated between claiming the steelworkers voted unanimously not to participate, and saying the other groups "just—whoosh—wrote us off" and "treated us like a bunch of stepchildren." Claims of control over the historical landscape and decisions about how to interpret it reflect both the continued relevance of the Steel's social order and the cultural value that ties to the past hold in Bethlehem as it negotiates its postindustrial identity.

In addition to raising questions of whether steelworkers or trained guides have more authority to tell the story of the steel plant, the dispute over the tours reflected divergent views of what history people are paying to hear. "Their personal experiences are fabulous, and they need to be told, and they need to be documented," Elaine said. "But for the casual tourist that wants to know the story, it doesn't compute." In her view, "A lot of the steelworkers know this plant from their little corner of the world, from what they did. . . . They see it from their perspective." For steelworkers, having a personal, experience-based perspective is exactly the point—as one former rigger said, "they walked the walk and can do the talk."[79] If it is not an entirely generalizable story, it is a useable past. It is how they connect to other steelworkers, their neighbors, and their families as they seek to preserve the local history and their place in it. Elaine, on the other hand, takes a big-picture view aimed at visitors with less familiarity with Bethlehem. She encourages her tour guides to place the Bethlehem plant in the context of the larger corporation and its other factories, shipyards, and mines. She disputes the veracity of some steelworkers' claims that don't seem to add up. "Some of these guys think that Bethlehem Steel was just here. They have a very narrow view and a very narrow focus. . . . What they have told me, some of them, what they think actually happened and what did happen, didn't happen." By denying their subjective memories, the approved tour's approach—in the interest of narrative clarity—in many ways affirms a rational redevelopment model in which preservation is an end-goal for specific profit interests, not a process by which community use-values messily emerge from the open interpretive space.

Elaine acknowledged that the best solution would be to pair steelworkers with her trained guides so that visitors can hear both perspectives but, for the most part, Historic Bethlehem Partnership and the Steelworkers' Archives resigned their efforts at cooperation. A couple years later the steelworkers established their own, separately ticketed tours of the site. When the ArtsQuest/Historic Bethlehem tour first began, however, some Archives members bought tickets, "just to hear the lies they might have been saying." While they found the experience for the most part satisfactory, if sterile, they joked that the tour guide was unable to answer a visitor's question about how many days in a row laborers worked. Capturing the divergent approaches to public history between the two groups, a steelworker exclaimed afterwards, "That's because it wasn't on the script!"

After Ted Bodnar took me on his rambling drive around South Bethlehem and the former plant, he also expressed interest in seeing how his blue minivan excursion compared to the ticketed SteelStacks tour. Despite the uneasy relationship between experiential and professional authority, the social and commodity values of steel heritage, the potential to meld the two visions lies just below the surface. Ted said he hoped to stay under the radar and just observe, but once our hard-hatted guide Terry learned that a "real" steelworker was in our group of fourteen, he awkwardly double-checked almost all of his stories, asking for Ted's opinions. Afterwards, he further legitimated Ted's experiential authority by seeking out his approval of the performance. Terry said he knew that steelworkers had originally been slated to give the tours, and he felt a bit uncomfortable with his own lack of first-hand knowledge. But, highlighting the performativity of all history-telling, he added with a shrug that he also dresses up as an eighteenth-century Moravian to lead tours of the Christmas lights each December and feels perfectly capable even though he's not Moravian either.[80]

Community leader Art Slesak believed the only person with clout in this "little turf war" over history at the time was Robert DeSalvio, the first local president of the casino. "They listen to him because he owns everything." Art also suggested that, despite the Sands' charitable donations and professed commitment to the community, DeSalvio did not have the time or interest to deal with community infighting over preservation. Even with casino executives' initial public commitments to interpreting the site's history, "He's got to answer to Vegas with his numbers, with the money, not with how the neighborhood's doing." "Following the script" in the context of historic renewal means more than elevating documented facts over personal experience. It also means recognizing that economic interests in development trump community connections in the end, as long as the structures of corporate power and the policies that support them remain decisive.

For future-oriented advocates of the casino and clean-slate development like Tim Deluca, their relationship to the Steel site's historical value is shaky or nonexistent. For others, like Ted Bodnar, who associate the Steel landscape with a more predictable and secure past based on manufacturing, the future of those buildings is directly related to their own sense of self and community. But the interpretive resource that the Steel site and its industrial ruins represent also allows for alternative narratives that link community, place, and historical consciousness with economic concerns. The enduring frame of "historic renewal" demonstrates that market-driven development and historic preservation are not necessarily incompatible.

It will be up to various stakeholders, particularly those currently overshadowed by corporate interests, to take advantage of the open spaces, both physical and cultural, that the Steel site provides. The fact that the smoke of festival fireworks at SteelStacks has replaced the smoke of the blast furnaces does not mean all is lost in the transition to an entertainment economy. The people who embed the landscape with memories, experiences, and cultural legibility augment the value of physical structures beyond their bricks and mortar. While many heritage tourism-based projects homogenize place and distance the histories they project from local memory, there is an opportunity in Bethlehem to transmit the social and cultural assets of a past economic order into a more uncertain neoliberal framework. This is the promise of the open-ended limbo of the postindustrial moment.

The challenges to reshaping prevailing logics in this way, however, are substantial. Amid the prospects of using history as a tool for articulating more inclusive and equitable futures, the postindustrial landscape remains plagued by deep-seated cultural and geographic divisions. In the neighborhoods around the former steel plant, where residents continue to negotiate and grapple with shifting relationships between community and corporation, many concerns about the unsettling effects of deindustrialization crystallize around reactions to the post-Steel closure of several South Bethlehem Catholic churches. Not only do the church closures confirm the strong relationship between moral orders and corporate structures, but they also encapsulate on a local level the intertwined trends of economic and social upheaval.

5

Landscapes of Life and Loss

RUTH VLCEK, a small woman with curly white hair and a friendly smile, answered my knock at the door of her suburban townhome wearing an embroidered blouse she bought in Hungary. This was the same blouse she wore to the last mass at St. John Capistrano, the Hungarian Catholic church on Bethlehem's South Side that her immigrant father helped found in 1903 and that she attended for eighty years. She specifically put it on for our interview to tell me about the church's closure.

In June 2008, as part of a broad consolidation, the Roman Catholic Diocese of Allentown, Pennsylvania, announced that it would close forty-five Catholic churches under its purview. Five of the affected churches were national (or ethnic) parishes in South Bethlehem. Built during the turn-of-the-century flood of Southern and Eastern Europeans who came to work at Bethlehem Steel, these churches became centers of religious and social life for native-speakers and their descendants who clustered in the neighborhoods around the plant.

When I talked to Ruth and other former parishioners of the Hungarian, Italian, Polish, Slovenian, and Slovak parishes four years after the diocesan decision, the wounds were still raw. Ruth had found out about her church's impending closure in the Sunday morning paper while she ate breakfast. "To this day it was a blur." She said she found herself at seven-thirty sitting in her car in the church parking lot, more than an hour before mass, unaware of getting dressed or driving the familiar route through South Bethlehem. "I felt like I had to be there," she said.[1] Eventually, "people started coming in for the nine o'clock mass. They were all standing there crying. It was horrible." Ruth wiped away fresh tears as she told me about singing the Hungarian national anthem when they left the church for the last time one month later on July 13. Outside, black crepe paper had been hung across the doors to reflect the funereal atmosphere. Ruth and the other parishioners gathered around the steps to watch the ceremonial locking of the doors, many wailing as the key was turned. Four years later, the memory remained overwhelming for Ruth, and she paused to regroup. "We were all numb," she said. "It was heartbreaking. It really was. It takes a long time to get over that."

After the closures, the five national parishes, located within blocks of each other, were consolidated into Saints Cyril and Methodius, the Slovak church, which the diocese renamed Incarnation of Our Lord to signal its new, nonethnic identity. The bishop defended the closures, citing a shortage of priests and shrinking congregations as parishioners moved away from their old neighborhoods. Indeed, few church members still lived nearby, with most, like Ruth, having moved after World War II to the suburbs or across the river to more prosperous areas. By 2008 the former white ethnic neighborhoods were majority Latino. These new residents kept a sixth parish in South Bethlehem, Holy Infancy, viable as it adapted to host Spanish masses. Even though descendants of the other European church founders continued to commute to masses at their South Side parishes every week, for many years there had been no baptisms or weddings, only funerals.

There is more to the story than statistical explications of demographic shifts, however. These quantifiable transitions are morally infused and experienced. Postindustrial economic and ethnic disenfranchisement are linked here, as the church closures, like the steel plant shutdown, represented for white ethnic parishioners a loss of cultural space in the old neighborhood. Even as many of the former parishioners have benefited from the upward mobility typical of first-, second-, and third-generation Americans in the twentieth century, the church closures reflect the passing of this earlier era of perceived stability and predictability. As with widespread parish closures elsewhere in the United States in recent years, the shutdowns echo certain characteristics of the new economic order signaled by the casino, where mobility and flexibility are valued over durability and connection to place.[2]

Residents' descriptions of the local built environment, in particular, continue to ground abstract concepts of economic, social, and moral displacement. As in the contested space of historic preservation on the Steel site, buildings outside the plant gates thus become touchstones for cultural order. Connecting this built environment to the economic landscape extends understandings of moral ground far beyond the casino floor or sanctuary walls. Neighborhood homes also are regularly invoked as concrete and relatable signs of hard-to-articulate personal experiences. In the same way that common narratives of deindustrialization as a unidirectional decline toward obsolescence deny the continued relevance of the past to community residents, a tale of assimilation as a move to the suburbs that doesn't look back is reductive. South Bethlehem's history informs present experience even for those who no longer live there.

Social tensions embedded in this landscape, however, endure. They reflect an underbelly to the positive opportunities to use local memories to reinsert communal values into profit-based development decisions. Latino migrants and immigrants encounter fundamentally different challenges than their European precursors, as they not only face racial discrimination but also enter a less robust economy for unskilled labor. The perceived decline of the neighborhood as white ethnic steelworkers were pulled to more prosperous neighborhoods and suburbs via postwar union wage gains and federal housing subsidies, among other benefits, is coupled with claims that new Latino immigrants pushed them out. Referencing the change in demographics becomes a way to talk about a sense of lost control without addressing underlying structural inscriptions of racism, unemployment, and frayed social protections.[3] Bethlehem's Latinos, meanwhile, have their own stakes in the South Side neighborhoods as they identify and celebrate diverse roots in the community. But although Latinos now make up one quarter of the city's population—and an even larger proportion in South Bethlehem—they do not necessarily see their needs or cultures reflected in heritage events or other revitalization efforts. Progress-oriented visions of urban development that are being proposed and realized in South Bethlehem and many other communities are often based on rebuilding or renovating housing to meet suburban tract-home aesthetics. They ignore residents' diverse needs by implicitly reinforcing expectations for assimilation to white, middle-class culture. If the South Bethlehem landscape were instead treated as a resource for accommodating incongruous desires, the intent of "community development" could be reimagined as reaching beyond economic measures. Rather than emphasize upward mobility and individual gain—the frameworks upon which common assimilation narratives *and* redevelopment initiatives are built—these neighborhood landscapes of structural and demographic change, and their overlapping histories, can open a space for social dialogue across race and ethnicity about shared anxiety, loss, exclusion, and even hope.[4]

The Parish Boundaries of South Bethlehem

As Bethlehem Steel found its corporate footing at the turn of the twentieth century and began massive growth under company president Charles Schwab, thousands of immigrants, mostly from Southern and Eastern Europe, flocked to the city for jobs. As outlined earlier, the population of South Bethlehem, where almost all of the new workers settled, increased nearly sixfold between 1870 and 1910, from 3,500 people to close to 20,000. Almost 60 percent in 1910 were either foreign-born or children of immigrants.[5] The area gained a reputation as being overtaken by foreign customs and vice. Boarding houses for single men and prostitution dens lined the border of the plant along Second Street, and through the 1920s, liquor, women, and gambling on the South Side drew weekend excursionists from New York City and New Jersey.[6]

But in the early twentieth century, like many other urban industrial communities in the United States, South Bethlehem also was a vibrant center of religious life. By 1926, of Bethlehem's 36,000 churchgoers, more than a third were members of eleven Roman Catholic churches concentrated on the South Side.[7] While most parishes in the Catholic Church are territorial, comprising all Catholics within their boundaries, ethnic groups in cities across the country petitioned for special permission to build churches that catered to their specific nationalities and languages.[8] Along with several ethnic Orthodox, Lutheran, and other Protestant churches, the openings of the South Bethlehem Catholic parishes chronologically reflect the peaks of successive waves of European immigration to the United States. The oldest Catholic parish in Bethlehem is Holy Infancy, founded in 1861 by Irish immigrants, followed in 1888 by the German church Holy Ghost. Three years later, Slovak immigrants founded SS. Cyril and Methodius. The Italian church, Our Lady of Pompeii, was

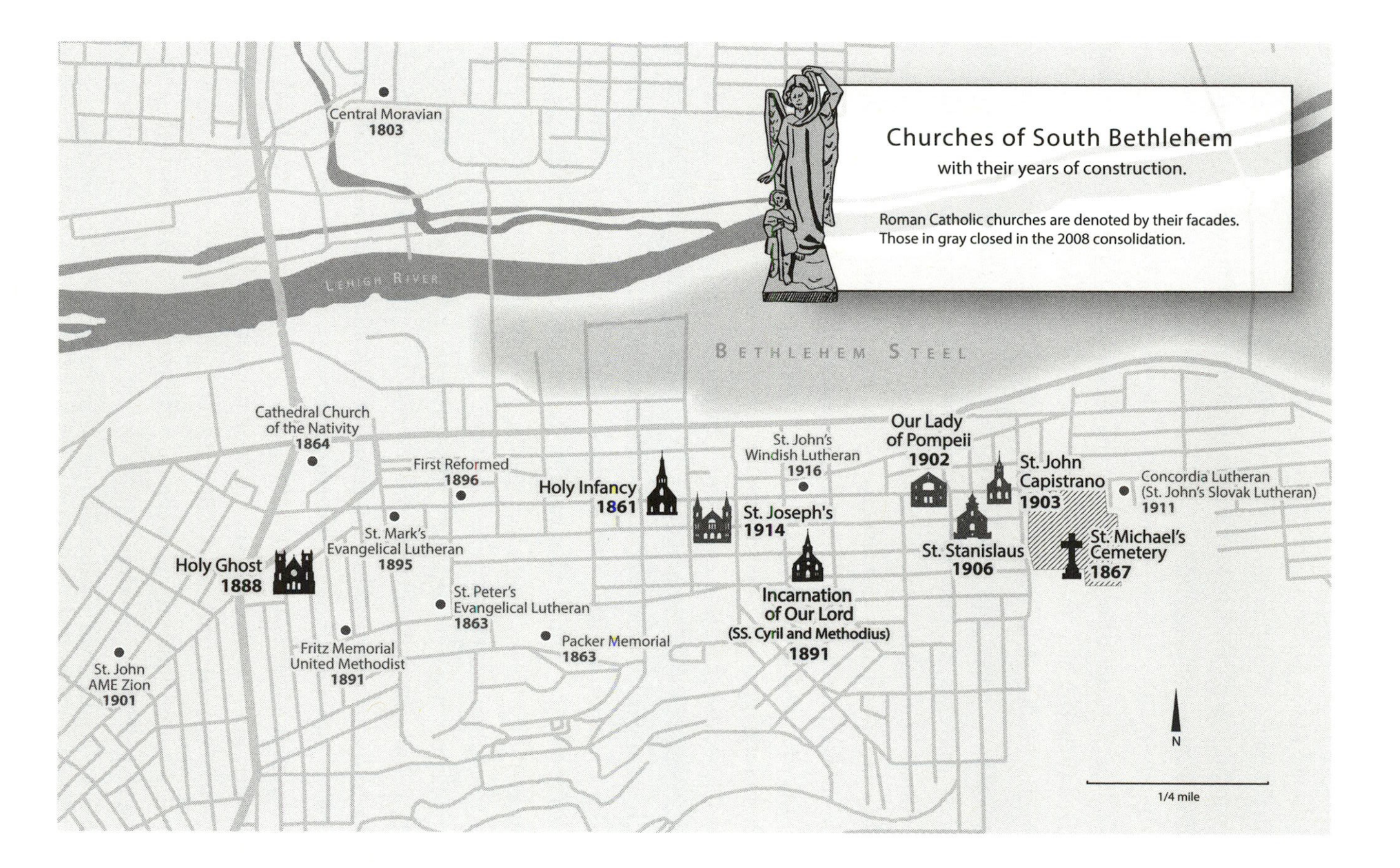
Churches of South Bethlehem
with their years of construction.
Roman Catholic churches are denoted by their facades.
Those in gray closed in the 2008 consolidation.
Central Moravian 1803
Lehigh River
Bethlehem Steel
Cathedral Church of the Nativity 1864
First Reformed 1896
Holy Infancy 1861
St. John's Windish Lutheran 1916
Our Lady of Pompeii 1902
St. John Capistrano 1903
Concordia Lutheran (St. John's Slovak Lutheran) 1911
St. Joseph's 1914
St. Mark's Evangelical Lutheran 1895
Holy Ghost 1888
St. Stanislaus 1906
St. Michael's Cemetery 1867
St. Peter's Evangelical Lutheran 1863
Incarnation of Our Lord (SS. Cyril and Methodius) 1891
Packer Memorial 1863
Fritz Memorial United Methodist 1891
St. John AME Zion 1901
N
1/4 mile

built in 1902, and St. John Capistrano, the Hungarian church, was established in 1903. After initially using St. John Capistrano's space, Polish parishioners built St. Stanislaus three years later. Another group of St. John's parishioners, Windish Slovenians who speak a Hungarian dialect, split to form St. Joseph's Catholic Church in 1914 after temporarily meeting in Holy Infancy's basement.

By the middle decades of the twentieth century, Hungarians comprised the largest of the ethnic groups on the South Side. Ruth Vlcek's father arrived in Bethlehem in 1900 and worked the next forty-five years at the Steel. The church he helped build on Fourth Street, St. John Capistrano, seated 800 people, and membership reached more than 2,500.[9] As in the other churches, St. John's priest came from the European homeland, and homilies and hymns were in the native language of the parishioners. Even the church buildings, constructed by the immigrants, materially reflected ties to native countries. The stained glass windows at St. Joseph's, for example, donated in 1917 by its members, represented various parishes in the Prekmurje region of Slovenia from which its parishioners came—an image of Christ Ascending to represent Church of the Ascension in Beltinci, St. Nicholas for St. Nicholas Church in Murska Sobota, a window for the Croatian parishioners, and a window inscribed *Slovenska Deca*, or Slovenian Children, for the relatives left behind.[10] Over the next century, parishioners thus continued to ritually, narratively, and materially map their ancestral homelands onto the spaces of South Bethlehem, even as they adapted their cultures to a new country.[11]

The parish system ordered Catholics' faith and social habits not only in the churches, but also in the ethnic neighborhoods that surrounded them.[12] Social life in South Bethlehem revolved around the various church societies, picnics, and dinners featuring *halupkis* (stuffed cabbage), spaghetti, stroganoff noodles, *dios torte* (Hungarian nut cake), and other Old World recipes. Many of St. John's events took place in the Hungarian social club across the street, while SS. Cyril and Methodius's Slovaks met at the Sokol hall. Most of the ethnic churches had affiliated K–8 parochial schools for the neighborhood children, taught by nuns from the home country, and youth competed with other churches in a parochial sports league.

Bethlehem's religious landscape also intersected with the broader class divisions that the Steel Corporation defined. The South Side Catholic churches were founded as working-class institutions, and up until their closings most parishioners had direct familial relations to steelworkers. Steel executives, on the other hand, for the most part attended the Episcopal Cathedral Church of the Nativity, founded by Bethlehem's nineteenth-century, American-born elite; Central Moravian Church, in the historic district; or First Presbyterian Church. Eugene Grace, who succeeded Charles Schwab as president of Bethlehem Steel in 1916, even had his own reserved pew at "First Pres," which at the time was located near the North Side downtown. Upper management faced intense pressure to join First Pres and later aid the Steel Corporation in paying to build a massive new Presbyterian church on fifty-two acres further north in 1955. Some recall these donations taking the form of payroll deductions. "If you want to have your husband move up the ladder at Bethlehem Steel, you should join First Pres," a researcher's wife remembers being told. Others compare the relocated church's long driveway to that of the exclusive Saucon Valley Country Club. As one former salesman joked, "instead of hanging a cross in the sanctuary of First Presbyterian Church, there was an I-beam."

Back on the South Side, Bethlehem Steel and the Catholic Church, the two dominant institutions in many of the immigrant laborers' lives, likewise developed close ties. Catholic clergy directly recruited new workers from Europe. According to a former steelworker whose grandparents emigrated from Slovakia at the turn of the century, the priest at SS. Cyril and Methodius explicitly offered Charles Schwab a never-ending supply of workers on condition that the company promise to hire everyone recruited and then take the immigrant workers' church offerings directly out of their paychecks. The Hungarian priest had similar conversations with Schwab to ensure Hungarian jobs were protected during production slowdowns.[13] The Steel is prominently listed as a major donor on plaques denoting the founding benefactors of St. John Capistrano.[14]

Where ethnic parishes ordered the neighborhoods outside the Steel's gates, social divisions by nationality also often determined the department to which one was assigned inside the plant during its early decades. The Irish worked in the open hearth, the Germans in the machine shops, and the Hungarians at the blast furnaces.[15] The newest immigrants found themselves in the least skilled and most physically demanding positions. But just as boundaries between South Bethlehem's ethnic church neighborhoods, all in close proximity to one another, often blurred, workers likewise found common ground on the job.[16] Although the corporation for the most part maintained the upper hand in its relationship with the Catholic Church, using its communication line into the clergy as a way to preempt worker unrest, in 1910 steelworkers at the Bethlehem plant launched a 108-day (ultimately unsuccessful) strike demanding better pay, shorter hours, and safer working conditions. The corporation brought in trains full of replacement workers and summoned the state police, leading to a violent clash that resulted in the shooting death of an unarmed Hungarian laborer at a South Side hotel where organizers congregated. Although most priests had followed corporate instruction to dissuade their parishioners from striking, eight thousand steelworkers marched in the man's funeral procession from his home to St. John Capistrano Church and St. Michael's Catholic Cemetery.[17] It would be decades before the Steel officially recognized the union, but solidarity among workers at the plant began to temper the interethnic divisions that the parishes initially reflected.

The Johnson-Reed Act of 1924 effectively put an end to European immigration to the United States, ensuring that future "ethnic" generations were for the most part American-born. As former St. John's parishioner Ruth explained, when her oldest sister went to the parish school in the 1920s, the nuns taught immigrant children how to speak English. By the time Ruth, seventeen years younger, attended the school, the Hungarian priest taught Hungarian once a week to try to preserve the cultural heritage. Many first- and second-generation Americans fought in World War II, and many others worked on behalf of the war effort at Bethlehem Steel's network of plants. With U.S. and industrial patriotism at an all-time high, the war accelerated the post-1920s emergence in the United States of a shared "whiteness" among previously fractured European ethnic communities.[18] Donald Resnik, the son of Slovenian immigrants, says that before World War II he would not have been welcome at any South Bethlehem Catholic church other than St. Joseph's. Even though Holy Ghost, the German church, was just half a block from where he lived as a child, "I couldn't go in there. If I went in I'd get dirty looks because I was a foreigner." Thomas Bukowksi, however, who is of Polish descent, told me that as a teenager in the 1950s he would sometimes go to Our Lady of Pompeii, the Italian church, instead of St. Stanislaus because the mass was shorter, and young George Dias attended an Italian catechism class with his friends even though he was Spanish-Hungarian and protestant. While each church maintained unique ethnic traditions until it closed, in later decades they developed cooperative relationships, reciprocating at each other's fundraisers, and in one case even sharing a priest. Maintaining the churches' historical ethnic distinctions, even as many congregants intermarried, nonetheless remained important in defining the South Side's moral and cultural geographies apart from parishioners' shared theology.

Meanwhile, after World War II, moving out of South Bethlehem increasingly became a marker of upward mobility and Americanization. Steelworkers, aided by wage gains after the corporation finally recognized the union in 1941, left their South Side row homes within walking distance of the plant for single-family homes with two-car garages on the North Side and in the suburbs. Some South Side houses of worship, like the Greek and Russian Orthodox churches and the local synagogue, moved north in the 1960s, 1970s, and 1980s to follow their congregations. But because of parishes' institutional and doctrinal ties to place, the national Catholic churches remained.[19]

Many older parishioners continued to commute back across the bridge every week for mass at their ethnic churches, but younger generations often joined the territorial parishes in their new neighborhoods. Over the next several decades, as in urban churches across the country, the South Side parishes hemorrhaged members. At St. John Capistrano, for example, parish income shrank nearly 25 percent between 1979 and 1981 alone. Its membership in the mid-1980s had dropped more than 1,000 people to 1,500, and by 2002 numbered less than 800.[20] Meanwhile, four parish schools in South Bethlehem closed because of low enrollment beginning with Our Lady of Pompeii in the 1960s. St. Joseph's school closed in 1977, followed by St. John Capistrano's four years later. After SS. Cyril and Methodius School closed in 2006, the only parish school that remained in South Bethlehem was Holy Infancy, the beneficiary, as we will see, of a more recent wave of Catholic emigration from Latin America.[21]

The Double Shutdown of Plant and Parish

The narrative of European immigrant assimilation, upward mobility, and relocation from urban centers is in many ways a familiar tale in which city churches become one more unavoidable casualty of national demographic trends. When compared with the narrative of Steel decline in Bethlehem, where presumed obsolescence has been complicated by the plant's continued relevance in the present, this notion that the old neighborhood could be entirely left behind comes into question, however. The mixed temporalities elicited by the parallel shutdowns of plant and parish suggests this past has a persistent presence and utility in residents' daily experiences despite the progress-oriented social and economic benefits of moving out of South Bethlehem.

When I began to pose to my informants the idea that the community effect of the church closures in 2008 seemed to me to mirror the closure a decade earlier of the Bethlehem Steel plant, they agreed the comparison was apt. Not only did the decline in Steel revenue and employment disproportionately affect residents and business owners concentrated near the plant, but it also disrupted moral constructs in the community. Religion is often defined among scholars as a world-making endeavor, a set of beliefs that help order and make sense of one's purpose in life and contain threats of chaos.[22] For a century, Bethlehem Steel served a similar role, culturally, socially, and economically. For many former steelworkers, the experiences of working at the mill each day and the oft-invoked connections between the Steel, defending America in its wars, and building structures like the Empire State Building with Bethlehem's iconic H-beam, served to order their worlds and shape their sense of moral worth.[23] Like religious institutions, lived spaces of the city, including Bethlehem's once-teeming steel plant, act as discursive and material building blocks through which residents narrate and construct fear and desire, disappointment in the past, and hope for the future.[24]

When Bethlehem Steel began to downsize in the late 1970s, people described the loss of their social networks at the plant as being torn away from their families. Catholic Church administrator Carl Stepchak's Hungarian grandfather, for example, spent his career as a scarfer grinding off irregularities on steel beams, and all of Carl's aunts and uncles also had jobs at the plant. He told me about his uncle's first trip back to Bethlehem after steel production ceased in 1995. "When he comes home he walks the whole South Side. He goes and looks at all the homes where his classmates lived and all that," Carl explained. "And I'll never forget the first day he came home after the Steel closed, he went down to the chain link fence and cried. And he tapped me on the shoulder, and he says to me, 'Never forget where you came from.'" In many senses, the Steel was like an ancestor that had begotten life and passed away.

Ten years later with the closure of the Catholic churches, the echoes between work and religion reverberated as the loss of the national parishes recalled the plant's earlier demise. "You feel that loss of a member of your family," Julia Krause, a parishioner in her seventies, said through tears, blurring the stories of the Steel and St. John Capistrano:

> Everybody in my family ever worked at Bethlehem Steel. My grandfathers, my father, my uncle. We were all Steel people. So of course when this happened and you see Bethlehem Steel, the buildings going idle, why it's a big shock to you. And you think, boy, it wasn't supposed to happen. It was supposed to be a forever thing and it isn't. And of course the church was really a shock. I just couldn't handle that.

Although most parishioners were aware that their once-healthy religious institutions were suffering financially and that church officials were considering a consolidation, the one month's notice of closure that the diocese offered in 2008 abruptly brought many of them out of denial. As with responses to the Steel's demise, they consistently describe the church closures as funerals. "I mean everybody just sobbed. It was like going to a viewing," Carl said of the last mass. "People still can't get over it, because it was like you lost your mother." Or as former Our Lady of Pompeii parishioner Angela Donatello said, "It was like part of your life that passed away."[25] As the two main social institutions for many European immigrants in the twentieth century—the Steel Company and the Parish—ceased to exist in South Bethlehem, moral, social, and economic scaffoldings that had held up family and personal histories crumbled. The plant gates and church doors were locked behind them.

The role the landscape itself plays in reorienting community identities comes into relief as parishioners discuss the fate of their former churches. Just as Bethlehem residents disagree whether the steel plant buildings should be preserved to honor the proud legacies of steelworkers and industrial production, or torn down to erase the pain of betrayal associated with the corporation's closure and bankruptcy, former parishioners do not all agree on how their old churches should be used. Debates over how to best "move on" reveal the complex interactions between a church's brick-and-mortar presence and Catholic faith's professed transcendence, between the city's established past as an industrial center and less certain visions of its service-economy future.

After the churches closed, most of their interiors were stripped, and the statues, altars, stained glass windows, pews, and other sacred objects were warehoused for sale to other Catholic parishes. As has been the case in dioceses across the United States that have consolidated and closed parishes in recent years, the Catholic Church's official, post-Vatican II position is that the buildings are not themselves sacred; rather, people are the "living stones" of the church, and God can be found anywhere.[26] Many Bethlehem parishioners agree and are critical of those who have yet to join another church. Others say such by-the-book understandings miss the point that, for ethnic communities, the church was about more than belief in God. It was a locus for communing in faith through personal and ancestral connections to the structure itself.[27] "I have a picture of my father building that church. He's up in the scaffolding," Donald Resnik from St. Joseph's, the Slovenian church, told me. "The diocese said the building is not faith. Faith is your faith in God, and the building is incidental. Which is nonsense," he said. "The socialization after mass and everything kept it a cohesive parish and it improved [our] faith. . . . You can't separate your faith from the building." In what some describe as a post-ethnic age—at least for white Europeans—the church had grounded "symbolic" or "voluntary ethnicities" that ceased to be significant markers in other contexts.[28] The diocese, in maintaining that national parishes have outlived their usefulness for new immigrants, further dissociated the parishioners' cultural identities from old neighborhood structures.

Helen Molnar, who in her sixties was a "young" parishioner at her former church, elaborated on this sentiment as she compared St. John Capistrano to her new, much larger parish on the North Side:

> We knew every inch of that church [St. John's]. That's one thing I said about the new church. . . . I mean, we go to mass there every week, but we just go into the sanctuary. We sit there, we go to mass, and then we leave. Where at St. John's we were so involved there. I knew what was in all the closets. We knew what was in the furnace room. . . . We knew where everything was in the kitchen. We knew that whole church inside out, upside down. It was like a home.

With her mental map, Helen captures the overwhelming sense that, for many of the parishioners, not only their histories and their faith, but their very *selves* were a part of the physical structures. They knew every nook and cranny like the backs of their hands. But unlike the Catholic Church's emphasis on the mobility of congregants as "living stones," for the Molnars, relocating to a more prosperous part of town did not mean that this former life could be so easily left behind.

Still other parishioners, echoing steelworkers who can't bear to visit some of the newly rehabbed industrial buildings on the steel plant site, wish the traces of this former self could be erased to let them move on with their lives. Four years after the closures, Julia and Ed Krause had not yet joined another parish. Julia described how she had recently driven by St. John's and noticed that the cross had been taken off the steeple. Through tears she said, with her husband nodding his agreement, "It just breaks your heart every time you go by it. . . . I'd rather see it torn down. I would rather see it torn down."

Regardless of their views on what should be done with the structures, many parishioners agree with Ruth Vlcek that "the cruelest thing was the way they closed the church." The Catholic Church offers some flexibility for last mass procedures but encourages rituals that signify the transition to new parishes.[29] The South Bethlehem parishioners, however, most vividly recall the sense of finality they experienced. After the last blessings on that July Sunday in 2008, recessionals featuring Paschal candles, symbols of Christ reborn, led congregants outside. They watched as the sanctuary doors of their respective churches were ceremonially locked behind them. St. John Capistrano's bereaved parishioners congregated in the basement hall for coffee and cake, many of them seeing each other for the last time. In the anthropological sense, as a textbook ritual, the Church's prescribed procedure for the closure would symbolically resolve uncertainty as it laid out next steps for parishioners by relegating their national parishes to the past and invoking rebirth. But those most involved in the church community suggest that the ritual closing was ineffectual in leading them forward. By dissociating the churches from their ongoing cultural utility and negating their physical rootedness, the diocese denied the value South Bethlehem maintains in parishioners' efforts to "place" the postindustrial present. The institutional failure of the Church, like that of the Steel, to provide the permanence and security its brick and stone buildings promised leaves open a more ambiguous space for alternative structures of meaning to take hold.

In contrast to the official closure, for many parishioners the more meaningful rituals that emerged in this space were personal ones that invoked the long histories of the churches in the community. For example, every day before being dismissed from class at St. John Capistrano's parish school, Ruth and the other children would line up by grade in the recess yard, sing a hymn, and say a prayer to the Guardian Angel, a once-white marble statue turned dark by the layers of protective paint and soot from the nearby steel mill. For Catholic children across the United States in the mid-twentieth century, the figure of the guardian angel, representing constant oversight, protection, and dependability, was central to their faith and upbringing.[30] One of Ruth's greatest fears with the closure was that the statue would be vandalized. She worried about what she called St. John's bad location, implicitly referencing the new concentration of Latino households that surround it. When she heard a soup kitchen might open nearby, "I was so worried with the kind of people that draws to places like that, that something was going to happen to our Guardian Angel." Similar to Richard Hoffer's childhood memories of the Christmas decorations and replica buildings and ships in the corporate headquarters lobby, Ruth's attachment to the Guardian Angel reflects the material memory of a more certain and clearly defined period in her life, a childhood that was morally and socially structured and protected not only by the Steel Corporation, but also by the Church.

And so after the announcement that St. John Capistrano would close, Ruth took it upon herself to organize a Sunday afternoon ceremony that began in the recess yard. The crowd soon outnumbered the five dozen people for whom she had planned. As they processed from the Guardian Angel in the yard to the church sanctuary, Ruth handed each of the last sixty parishioners a carnation she had tipped in blue, the color of the Virgin Mary. Inside, two girls accepted the flowers in front of the statue of the Blessed Mother, which had been draped in a blue and silver satin cloth. The ceremony was an improvisatory blend of the afterschool ritual and the annual May procession they did as children to crown the Virgin Mary. In effect, it was the reenactment of an idealized Catholic childhood amid the reality of adult turbulence and anxiety.[31]

While many viewed the diocesan decision behind locking the doors as a performance of rupture, Ruth's ritual, combining "two very important things in our life," placed the church in a long continuum of personal and community significance. As Ruth said, "We had to do these things in order to slip into whatever was coming."[32] By emphasizing the slippery continuity of time rather than its fissure, she reoriented the closure in her own moral landscape. Residents of neighborhoods cleared by urban renewal, such as the Heights, often hosted reunions to socially reassemble in the present the physical places of their pasts. Ruth similarly continues to meet twice a month with a group of devoted elderly parishioners from St. John's (whom she calls "the girls") for special prayers.

Despite these ritual attempts at continuity and reclaiming a sense of security, the feelings of upheaval among the former South Side residents are pervasive. Even though the bishop gave affected parishioners special permission to continue to travel to South Bethlehem for mass rather than join their territorial parishes, few congregants went to the new Incarnation of Our Lord Church, formerly the Slovak parish. Instead, they dispersed to attend the churches near their homes on the North Side or in the suburbs. Angela Donatello, from Our Lady of Pompeii, described how, "When our church closed, I felt like a refugee," a person literally dis-placed. Some complained that they feel lost in larger parishes where the priests don't know their names. Aging and unwilling to prolong the fight, many resigned to give up the last bit of moral and social claim on Bethlehem's South Side.

A small group of parishioners from St. Joseph's, however, appealed the diocese's decision. In 2011 the Vatican agreed that the church had been closed improperly. It reopened, but only for members' funerals and for St. Joseph's Day each March. Many of the mostly white-haired congregants at the St. Joseph's Day mass that I attended in 2013, some of whom were accompanied by their grown children, had not seen each other since this event the previous year, and the reunion atmosphere was striking. The elaborately painted sanctuary had a distinctly boisterous ambiance not typical of Sunday services. But an hour later as the mass came to a close, the occasion took a bittersweet turn. Former parishioners sung the last hymn, "*Veš O Marija*," a slow and beautiful tune celebrating the Virgin Mary, in Slovenian. For a few minutes, their experience growing up in the South Bethlehem parish was recreated in the present. Several of the elderly women around me dabbed their eyes with tissues, and I was myself moved by the emotion in the air. As we walked out of the church and congregants headed to a banquet lunch, one of the women in front of me remarked, "I still think it's awful what they did to our church. It wasn't right to close it. I'm sorry, but I still think it was wrong." Almost five years after the fact, wounds—like those in the scarred landscape—remained open. After the last of the former parishioners' funerals, no one is assured that memories of the church's impact in the South Bethlehem community will endure.

The continued relevance of the double shutdown to former steelworkers' and parishioners' lives makes it difficult to simply move on. Their surrender to a new cultural paradigm is more deeply layered than the purely economic shift that most references to postindustrialism highlight. Ritually, the ethnic Catholic parishioners and their churches are caught between an imagined past, closely linked to the Steel's operation, in which a childhood sense of security held sway, and an uncertain future where trusted institutions have been dismantled, where Ruth must become the guardian of her Guardian Angel. While some residents find meaningful ways to ritually reconnect their pasts to the present, the challenges to making sense of economic, demographic, and religious changes in a neighborhood that feels increasingly unfamiliar to white European immigrants' descendants continually reinforce social tensions. In contrast to the closed South Side churches that surround it, Holy Infancy retains a vibrant membership and easily escaped the 2008 consolidation. This parish now offers three of its eight weekend masses in Spanish and two in Portuguese. The new Latino population that has kept it viable suggests a cultural transition as much as an economic one.[33]

Some parts of the past—including the racism and classism that have distinguished North Bethlehem from South Bethlehem for more than two centuries—may be better left behind. The church closures nonetheless highlight pervasive feelings of loss and anxiety that could be useful to remember amid the politically dominant narratives of economic progress and harmonious multiculturalism. Within these fissures, the double shutdown of plant and parish offers an opportunity to explore a more contradictory lived experience of postindustrialism that exposes limitations to development-led efforts at community revitalization.

Latino Immigration and Transformations in the Old Neighborhood

The sale in 2011 of Our Lady of Pompeii to Primera Iglesia Bautista Hispana de Bethlehem, a Latino Baptist church, and Holy Infancy's language-segregated masses reflect a new racial and ethnic geography in South Bethlehem that has developed since World War II. Meanwhile, the adaptive reuse of two other churches—St. John Capistrano was sold to a mental health clinic for offices, and St. Stanislaus was transformed into gallery space and affordable housing—point toward some of the most pressing social and economic needs of this community today.

Facing a labor shortage given the new restrictions on European immigration and pressure from native workers to raise wages, in 1923 Bethlehem Steel's management brought in the city's first large group of Mexicans by train from San Antonio.[34] Despite reports of resistance by local steelworkers, as the Mexican consul general in San Antonio understood it, "the Mexican workers were hired to perform jobs of little importance and which are not very desirable to the workers of that region," jobs that "have always been done by immigrants from other countries or men of color."[35] Local lore suggests this also was a strategy to avoid recruiting African Americans to the Bethlehem plant, giving the city a distinct racial legacy compared with many other Northern industrial centers that have large black populations, including other Bethlehem Steel factory sites like those near Buffalo and Baltimore.[36] The company set up a worker colony for the imported Mexicans at the coke works on the east end of the Bethlehem plant. Fees for housing and the four-day voyage north were deducted from the workers' pay. Additional barracks for Mexicans in Northampton Heights offered twenty bunks per room. Of the roughly nine hundred Mexican workers that initially came, most left town within a year. The camp closed in 1939, with only about fifty Mexican families remaining in Bethlehem. Still, beginning in 1929 when the diocese appointed a Spanish-born priest, Holy Infancy, founded as an Irish church, became the permanent home for Spanish, Portuguese, and Mexican Catholics. They initially met in the basement.[37]

A more sustained Latino migration picked up in the late 1940s, mostly from Puerto Rico where there were no citizenship barriers.[38] Bethlehem's Puerto Ricans came predominantly from the rural towns of Corozal and Patillas, which, like the rest of the island, faced high levels of unemployment. Some came directly to work at the Steel or area textile mills and garment factories. Others learned about promising opportunities from friends and relatives in Bethlehem while working various industrial and agricultural jobs in the region. Like the Mexicans before them, Puerto Rican steelworkers were disproportionately assigned to work in the plant's coke works, where huge ovens exuding noxious fumes converted coal into fuel for the blast furnaces. As Latino workers recall, based on the fact that they came from hot countries, "It was understood that we could stand the heat better than some other nationalities."[39] By the 1960s, Puerto Rican steelworkers began meeting with corporate managers and even the Puerto Rican governor to secure equal rights at the plant. As noted earlier, until Bethlehem and other steelmakers signed a consent decree in 1974 over discrimination with the U.S. Department of Justice, Latino workers routinely were denied transfers and promotions in favor of workers with less seniority but whiter complexions.[40]

Outside the plant, Puerto Ricans and other Latinos moved into the neighborhoods the "now-assimilated" Europeans had built a generation or more before. By 1966, just after the Spanish mass was finally moved from Holy Infancy's basement to the sanctuary, the church counted 1,800 members from Puerto Rico.[41] Two years later, the church welcomed four Spanish-speaking nuns from Argentina, and in 1970 the parish school reversed a dwindling enrollment by introducing bilingual kindergarten. The same year, Holy Infancy helped found the Council of Spanish-Speaking Organizations of the Lehigh Valley, a social service center for Latinos.[42] By 1982 Holy Infancy had 6,500 Hispanic members. Bethlehem's Hispanic and Latino population has continued to grow between 40 and 50 percent every decade since.[43]

In postwar decades that emphasized the hierarchical succession model of immigration, in which new arrivals were expected—like the Southern and Eastern European immigrants before them—to assimilate to white cultural standards, South Bethlehem's Puerto Ricans faced heavy scrutiny. Police targeted new arrivals, accustomed to socializing outside, for "loitering." Many were unaware that Puerto Ricans were U.S. citizens. At the time, the Puerto Rican government encouraged emigration to help offset the island's high rates of poverty and unemployment. Latino residents told me how the governor of Puerto Rico invited Bethlehem's mayor and police chief to the island in the early 1950s to resolve cultural misunderstandings. The desired outcome on both ends nonetheless remained assimilation to mainland norms.[44]

Toward this goal, Lehigh County created a "Committee on Puerto Ricans" in 1958 to help the migrants adjust. A newspaper series on "The Puerto Rican" in Bethlehem the same year, designed to educate the broader public, made an earnest attempt to combat documented discrimination by landlords, employers, police, and other residents by showing that Puerto Ricans did not contribute disproportionately to crime in Bethlehem and were capable of owning homes, holding steady jobs, and "fully adjust[ing] to 'our way of life.'" The reporting in the series simultaneously reaffirmed various stereotypes of Puerto Ricans as gamblers, bad drivers, poor students, transients, and male chauvinists.[45] When twenty-five Puerto Rican mayors visited Bethlehem in 1961, a group of Boy Scouts met the visitors outside Holy Infancy Church where they sang both "The Star-Spangled Banner" and the Puerto Rican anthem, "La Borinqueña," before sitting down to a dinner of chicken with Pennsylvania Dutch potato filling. This, the newspaper reported, was the "first evidence of the assimilation [the mayors] so strongly advocate to their migrating countrymen."[46]

These various attempts at cross-cultural understanding emerged in the 1950s and 1960s during a boom time when jobs were plentiful. Ethnic European parishioners, many of whom willingly moved out of the South Side based on their economic gains, nonetheless adopted a racialized language of decline when faced with changing demographics in the blocks around their churches. Such language characterized much of the nationwide discourse on postwar urban transitions.[47] Matching urban renewal concerns about "blight," much of the attention was directed toward housing, which had for earlier European immigrants represented a chief asset. The aforementioned local newspaper series, for example, argued that when Puerto Ricans stop living three men to a room and move their families into nicer homes, "their modern kitchen is a sign that the immigration from Puerto Rico was a success."[48]

For Latino families prosperous enough to eventually follow the white European migration to the North Side, the expectations of cultural assimilation were even more pronounced. Sofia Sanchez, whose father came to Bethlehem from Puerto Rico in the early 1950s and got a job in the coke works, remembers moving when she was nine years old from a small, two-bedroom apartment on the South Side to a single-family house across the river. That was in the late 1960s. "Was it a big deal? It was unheard of!" she said over breakfast more than forty years later at a South Side diner. As in the early twentieth century, perceived threats of infiltration defined a moral geography of Bethlehem's neighborhoods along racial and ethnic lines. "For a long time nobody bothered with us. And it wasn't until later that I learned, oh my God, the neighborhood thought, 'Oh, here goes the neighborhood.'" Sofia laughed as she recalled going to see the new house for the first time with her brother and sister:

> There were so many rooms. It's an old Victorian home. So it had the attic, it had three bedrooms on the next floor, then it had a living room, it had a sun porch, there was a dining room, a kitchen, and a whole yard with a garage. We were like, "Oh my God! We struck it rich! Oh my God! What do we do with all this?" We got a dog, and we got a swing set that was there. My dad fixed it up. It was like, "Wow!" We were like the ones who made it.

Despite the cookie-cutter vision of achievement that Sofia's description of the house reflects, moving to the North Side also marked her first memories of racial discrimination. "I remember moments of realization that we were different, and sometimes it was embarrassing," she said. She recalled carefully watching her white classmates cut their meat at the Catholic high school banquets so she could learn proper etiquette. "It was nerve racking because you knew eyes were on you. . . . I learned to be when I was with the whites I was white, when I was with the Puerto Ricans I was Puerto Rican." Today, Sofia spends most of her time back on the South Side, where she is principal of the public elementary school. It is across from the casino in one of the poorest and most heavily Latino areas of town, the neighborhood where she was born.

The narrative of postwar assimilatory improvement was not universally available to new Latino residents, many of whom faced an increasingly tight labor market for unskilled work by the 1970s.[49] Between 1970 and 1980 the percentage of families in South Bethlehem living in poverty more than doubled from 8.6 percent to 19.8 percent. By 2000 one quarter of these neighborhood families had incomes below the federal poverty level.[50] Meanwhile, the growth in real-estate values in South Bethlehem, where much of the housing stock dates to the early twentieth century, lagged behind the increases in the city as a whole.[51]

Many residents continue to refer to all Spanish speakers in the community as Puerto Rican despite the fact that, in 2013, 27 percent of Bethlehem's Latinos came from other countries, including El Salvador and the Dominican Republic, and the diversity is increasing.[52] Moreover, many Latinos in the community are second- or third-generation migrants who have relocated to the Lehigh Valley from New York and other urban centers within the continental United States. Plenty of residents of European descent, and even many older Latino residents, are quick to blame this diverse group of "Puerto Ricans" for the economic decline of South Bethlehem.[53] But many prefer to describe the shift in terms of the built environment and the landscape itself as a way to give substance to their claims. When the nebulous term "blight" was disproportionately affixed to minority neighborhoods in the 1950s and 1960s, housing issues became euphemisms for racial ones.[54] Today, former South Bethlehem residents likewise often point out that Latinos don't take care of their homes in the same meticulous way their European predecessors did, implicitly diagnosing unbefitting character as a cause of neighborhood decline without acknowledging the neglect of absentee landlords, the collapse of the industrial economy at the plant down the street, and other structural impediments to reinvestment.[55]

A former Steel employee, for example, drove me down Fourth Street where his Hungarian immigrant grandparents used to live:

> Now Chloe, if you noticed, you go from ethnic Hungarians to minorities. See. You see all the ethnic Hungarians, everybody maintained their house. They all had beautiful backyards, manicured backyards. And the big thing was rose bushes. All gone. . . . The immigrants had pride in their workmanship and pride in their home and pride in their gardens and pride in their yards. And it doesn't seem to be that way no more now.

Others complained that the new residents, whose own "ethnicity" does not carry the same positive valence, don't sweep their steps and sidewalks every day like the European immigrant women did. Another former South Side parishioner was more to the point, explaining why in the early 1980s he finally left the home his Hungarian ancestors built across from St. John Capistrano. "We were the last ones in there before the neighborhood went down and we had to move," he said. "Spanish and the minorities came in and took over. . . . It was all ruined. All the neighborhoods were ruined by them." As in other urban centers facing dramatic postwar demographic changes, this language has become familiar, particularly where racial tensions are exacerbated by economic disinvestment.[56]

Beyond selling or leaving their houses, Bethlehem families with white European immigrant roots, I was startled to learn, also have made efforts to dig up ancestors' graves at St. Michael's Catholic Cemetery, now surrounded by Latino neighborhoods, to move them to what they perceive as less-blighted resting places. Reburials are an active form of historic revisionism. They address the concerns of the living by reconstructing the past to culturally resituate the deceased, in this case in an elevated socioeconomic status.[57] The practice reflects an extreme form of realigning the city's moral geography to meet expectations for cultural and economic assimilation.

Holy Infancy, the oldest Catholic church, had founded St. Michael's Cemetery on the slope of South Mountain in 1867, though it became a resting place for Catholics of all ethnicities in the early twentieth century. The hillside location could make a difficult trek for hearses and pallbearers who carried coffins to plots set off with decorative wooden rails and limestone grave markers. A few mausoleums and larger granite stones stand out, denoting wealthier families. Many of the names on the older graves, some of which I could associate with local contacts, are spelled as they were in Europe, before being Americanized upon immigration. By the 1950s, however, St. Michael's was in disrepair, with many families already abandoning the neighborhood and the care of the graves. According to church administrator Carl Stepchak, at one point the front retaining wall fell down and coffins hung out over the sidewalk on Fourth Street. With no perpetual care available, the cemetery became a litter-filled target for vandals armed with cans of spray paint and a penchant for toppling gravestones.[58]

Carl rattled off the names of families that ultimately dug up what was left of their loved ones and reinterred them at the better-maintained Holy Saviour Cemetery. Holy Saviour is located on the wealthier North Side where many immigrant descendants have since relocated. Other reinterment efforts failed with discoveries that wooden coffins had long since disintegrated, or the locations of the graves were lost to the memories of past generations. Carl's Hungarian great-grandfather, for example, was buried in St. Michael's with a wooden marker. "My one uncle only knew where his grave was. And he's dead. So we will never know where he's buried now," he told me. Today the cemetery is overgrown, with many stones falling over or shrinking back into the woods that have reclaimed the upper reaches.

The sense of loss of family history that Carl described is directly linked to and elicited by the landscape around him. The old European Catholic neighborhoods for which St. Michael's Cemetery stands in as a final resting place have in many ways disintegrated with a previous era, along with the moral, social, and economic ties these ethnic communities once held to South Bethlehem. At the same time, efforts to rehabilitate the past by reburying the dead in a more socially elevated position suggest that South Bethlehem's history can be activated to address ongoing preoccupations

St. Michael's Cemetery

Walker Evans (top) photographed St. Michael's Cemetery, looking north and showing the close proximity of the steel plant, while working for the U.S. Office of War Information in 1935. The row homes at the base of the cemetery are typical of the South Bethlehem housing stock that remains today. Shown in 2011 (bottom), the cemetery is maintained primarily by volunteers and is a frequent target of vandals. The cross in the Evans photo is no longer there. (Walker Evans, "Bethlehem graveyard and steel mill. Pennsylvania," 1935, FSA/OWI Photograph Collection, Library of Congress; photo by author, 2011.)

Holy Saviour Cemetery

Statues from each of the five consolidated parishes were relocated to Holy Saviour Catholic Cemetery, founded in 1923 on the North Side. The pedestal for the Guardian Angel, on the far left, bears the inscription: "In Honor of the Parishioners of St. John Capistrano Church Bethlehem." (Photo by author, 2015.)

with changing neighborhood demographics. With St. Michael's for most purposes abandoned, statues from each of the five consolidated Catholic parishes, including the St. John's Guardian Angel that Ruth was so worried about, were likewise moved across the river to Holy Saviour where they stand as memorials to a bygone time.

A Fractured Latino Landscape

Thus far, Latinos have for the most part been left out of the many efforts by Bethlehem's former church parishioners and other white residents at preserving historical continuity. Former South Bethlehem residents often see these more recent immigrants as causes of cultural rupture, despite Latinos' own generational pride and independent claims to the neighborhoods. Even in the face of pervasive on-the-job discrimination and difficult working conditions, the wave of Latino immigrants who arrived in the 1940s and 1950s and their Bethlehem-born children benefited from the high postwar wages that the Steel Company provided. In many cases they bought homes and cars and moved out of the South Side. Oscar Romero, a founding father of Bethlehem's Puerto Rican community who is now nearing ninety, is fond of saying that he was born in Puerto Rico, but Bethlehem is his home: "I feel that this is my town. This is where I make—if I were still living in Puerto Rico, I never could afford what I afford when I live here." Many in Oscar's generation are critical of more recent Latino arrivals who appear less willing to assimilate or do not have similarly stable employment. Elders warn against drug use and mistreatment of women. They emphasize acting "orderly," respecting the law, and learning English.

But for many new immigrants, the promise of upward mobility through hard work that the Steel and the ethnic Catholic churches helped support is no longer a realistic possibility. As a more recent migrant said of the generational divide, "the reality is that there are two Puerto Ricans, two different Puerto Ricans."[59] Ethnic and class distinctions between the two sides of the river persist as well, with today's South Side area around the old churches comprising some of the poorest and most heavily immigrant neighborhoods in Bethlehem. South Bethlehem is 42 percent Latino according to the 2010 U.S. Census, and the percentage continues to grow.[60] Despite reports on Bethlehem's relative economic health as a post-manufacturing small city, authorities acknowledge that many South Bethlehem residents, especially Latinos, have been left behind.[61] Against a national poverty rate of 15 percent, 39 percent of Bethlehem's Latinos are officially poor compared with 12 percent of non-Hispanic whites.[62]

Progress-oriented narratives of assimilation, like many plans for economic development, assume a homogenous vision of neighborhood uplift. They often neglect the bricolage reality of South Bethlehem residents' needs and desires. The shared space of anxiety amid postindustrial transition, however, offers the potential for common ground upon which to build. The loss that European ethnic groups in today's postindustrial moment feel for their communities—and the social, economic, and moral stability they associate with their pasts—is an equally salient absence for the poor and working-class Latino immigrants who have moved into the old neighborhoods and struggle to find their bearings in an increasingly tenuous economic climate.[63]

Several people with whom I spoke pointed to the lack of employment and affordable housing as two of the biggest challenges South Bethlehem residents face. Compared to the Steel era, there are fewer opportunities for unskilled work in the area, and many jobs require fluency in English. According to the 2013 American Community Survey, Hispanics and Latinos in Bethlehem faced 16 percent unemployment compared to 8 percent among non-Hispanic/non-Latino whites.[64] Social services from community organizations and the municipal, state, and federal governments encounter persistent underfunding. Aid is often cut off as soon as a beneficiary gains any kind of work and a leg up, but before two feet are on solid financial ground. This creates a vicious cycle in which many residents repeatedly go on and off of welfare. Sofia Sanchez, the principal of the neighborhood's elementary school, explained, "It kind of pulls you down, will crush you, to the point where there's no movement. . . . It is stagnant."

At the same time that they are financially stagnant, residents constantly move homes and even cities. Sofia sees the trend first hand when students leave her school mid-year. Previously working-class and poor residents might look for jobs and relocate to nearby Allentown or Reading. In a troubled economy, she said, "They're going to Texas, Ohio. Places that they've mentioned I'm like, 'there's Puerto Ricans there?'" This is not the freeing mobility heralded by neoliberal policies. Despite expanding geographic networks, "A lot of them come back, like within a week," Sofia said, noting that her school has learned to hold on to kids' school files rather than throw them away. The extended kin and immigrant networks many Latinos have in Bethlehem often represent their most promising resources.[65]

Beyond high levels of unemployment, this diverse community's needs—cultural, social, and economic—are not necessarily being met by existing efforts to improve housing in the name of postindustrial redevelopment either. "A lot of organizations have come and promised to make Bethlehem's South Side a better place to live, and build up the hype, but then could not understand the people and walked away," said Javier Parker, a Moravian pastor from Nicaragua who ministers to Latinos in donated space at the Windish Lutheran church. "Even as a Latino, I came assuming, thinking, that I'm coming to solve their problems, and I'm coming to be like the savior. I got all this funding, and I'm going to make a ministry, and everybody is going to like it. No." This savior mentality jumpstarts many promising outreach programs to Bethlehem's poor, including ones by the Sands Casino. But as Javier notes, a cultural fissure between mainstream visions of economic progress—often in the form of gentrified housing—and residents' own needs and desires can create barriers not easily overcome.

As an example, Coral Lopez, a Puerto Rican woman in her forties who came to Bethlehem in 1997 and immersed herself in local politics, told me about a small residential renewal project with which she was involved. A local community development program, funded via federal tax incentives for area banks, allocated money to do a "facelift" on a block of homes on Steel Avenue, across from the proposed casino site, in 2005. In order to spend the limited funds most efficiently, the organizers decided that all eleven of the homes would be painted the same color with the same new mailbox and brass numbers. "You know, we're talking about uniformity and making everything look the same and pretty," Coral explained. With a plan in motion, the organization approached the homeowners and told them the facelift would be free, they just needed to sign their permission.

> And the homeowners look at the pictures, look at everything, and they're like, "Hell no! You're not going to paint the house. Hell no, my mailbox is not going to be the same mailbox as my neighbor. Are you crazy?" So all of this was planned without even considering the neighbors! . . . And the neighbors didn't want it. They're like, "No way are you going to paint my house like everybody else's. We like it different."

Coral's tale highlights the trouble with overlaying a uniform vision of progress, a so-called suburban aesthetic that is remarkably homogenous across the United States, on a local neighborhood with unique needs. The plans to paint the houses on Steel Avenue the same color and install matching mailboxes mimicked the look of low-cost tract housing that dominates private redevelopment efforts in struggling urban centers everywhere.[66] In this vision, "multiculturalism" is hailed as a form of market equality that promises opportunity for uplift regardless of race or ethnicity, as long as local communities do not disrupt the market logics of efficiency and profitability that the facelift plan on a small scale reflected.[67]

While the goals of these and similar projects may sound appealing, and the aspirational, middle-class aesthetic is in many cases popular with working-class residents, their implementation often requires displacing local people and cultural structures that have shaped places over time. As one Latino South Side resident said, making the link between aesthetic and economic logic explicit, businesses and homeowners near the defunct plant were encouraged to maintain and paint their buildings at the time, "Because the casinos are coming. It's all about appearances now. . . . Got to make this place look presentable." Emphases on fixing up buildings' façades, many residents are quick to point out, do little to address the underlying frameworks, both physical and social, that are implicated in their decline, just as many worry that a casino economy based on flashing lights and digital transactions may hide the financial desperation and structural inequalities that tenuously hold it up.[68] Without acknowledging and addressing the sense of place and history that residents attach to the neighborhood, no facelift will fully capture this important interconnection between the built environment, economic structures, and perceptions of community vibrancy.

Despite the visible decline in much of South Bethlehem's housing stock, the homeowners on Steel Avenue who rejected the plan for uniform mailboxes are not the only residents who assert cultural claims to the neighborhood and take pride in its buildings. Many Latinos have themselves become landlords, renting their homes to more recent immigrants or Lehigh University students. Others, like Victor Delgado and his wife Anabel, have invested significant capital and sweat equity into their properties. Victor, in his mid-forties, is the son of a Puerto Rican upholsterer who came to Bethlehem before Victor was born and settled next to St. Michael's Cemetery. Now Victor and Anabel live in a half-a-double house a few blocks to the west, where their neighbors include Puerto Ricans, Dominicans, and white Lehigh students. Without denying that there are "little spots here and there" where "people try to make it bad," Victor said the South Side is gradually getting the more positive attention from both the city and other residents that he believes it deserves.

The Delgados' pride in their home and their block signals an investment in community that delves deeper than outside appearances. When municipal services fail to sweep their side street, Victor and his wife take it upon themselves to do the cleaning, a historical echo of the European immigrant women so often referenced with their brooms. Victor, who works in construction, said they live comfortably, but he dreams of a bigger yard and a garage where he can work on his motorcycle and car, amenities that would most likely mean moving across the river. In the meantime, he has built a large wooden deck that takes up the entire back yard of his South Side home. "If I had an option to move, I probably would. But for now I like where we live," he said. Each time Victor suggested to me that he would consider moving, Anabel, who is more comfortable speaking in Spanish, chimed in with a declarative "I love my house." She described the tiki bar and lights that complete the deck and make it the envy of their friends. Victor agreed it is unlikely they will leave the neighborhood. One of his few complaints is that leaves from his neighbor's tree fall onto this prized outdoor space, but the neighbor himself has been a friend for years and watches the house when they're gone. "That's about the best thing in our neighborhood," Victor said of the residents on his block. "We trust each other."

Barriers to cross-cultural cooperation are deeply entrenched, along lines of race, ethnicity, and class. Efforts to stabilize a neighborhood often form in opposition to other groups, even among residents who acknowledge common experiences.[69] The rejection of forced uniformity in South Bethlehem and evidence of commitment and pride in the community, however, suggest local structures of meaning can adapt the blanket logics of economic renewal to residents' diverse cultural needs. The link between the built environment and the moral investments that define homes, blocks, and neighborhoods creates an opportunity for community participation in redevelopment that incorporates the area's various histories as assets instead of excluding them. The complexity of the local landscape offers a rich resource in which to identify collaborative potential amid cultural tensions.

Celebrating Ethnicity: The Challenge of Social and Spatial Inclusion

In addition to discrepancies in employment and housing, the voices of Bethlehem's Latinos are not well included in the dominant narrative of the city's heritage-based cultural rebirth either. Three generations of Puerto Rican presence in the community, including both entrenched labor discrimination and Steel-enabled success stories of upward mobility, are regularly elided by emphases on the community's European immigrant origins. Not only are Latinos rarely represented in the various oral history projects and historical organizations that focus on the Steel, but attempts to host Latino cultural events in the city have attracted mixed responses in and out of ethnic communities. For large segments of the population, the access to community spaces and open interpretations that the heritage landscape offers remains limited.

Bethlehem's Puerto Rican Day parade, an annual event until it was discontinued in 2012 for lack of funds, dates back to the surge in the city's Puerto Rican population in the 1960s. In 1970, when racial tensions in town were at a crisis pitch, Holy Infancy Catholic Church began hosting a carnival for St. John the Baptist Day to honor the patron saint of Puerto Rico. The community event, which began as a small procession from the parish school to the church, grew by 1972 into a more visible procession from the church to city hall where the Puerto Rican flag was ceremonially raised alongside the Stars and Stripes. In 1975 the church-based events expanded when community leaders organized a Puerto Rican Cultural Week. The festivities commenced with a couple hundred people at the flag raising and included a baseball tournament, screenings of Spanish films at the public library, a night of folk dancing, and a big-band "dance rally" and buffet.[70]

A seven-car motorcade representing Puerto Rico's districts led the event's closing parade. Other participants included city officials, Puerto Rican merchants, and weight lifters flanking the newly crowned Puerto Rican Week Queen. One float promoted "bilingual-bicultural education," and stock cars brought up the rear. The largest group represented remained Holy Infancy Church, which sponsored three floats and the participation of its various sodalities, boy scouts, cheerleaders, and its uniformed baseball, basketball, and volleyball teams.[71] Though not technically a national parish, in many ways Holy Infancy had evolved from an Irish church into a new ethnic home supporting the cultural ties and social life of the more recent group of migrant parishioners. The procession from Holy Infancy across the bridge to the seat of municipal government linked the ethnic community to the city as a whole. At the closing ceremony that followed the parade, local Puerto Rican community leader Sergia Montz adopted Bethlehem's immigrant narrative of succession to make Puerto Ricans' growing presence culturally legible to non-Latinos as well as new arrivals: "We have been here in Bethlehem many years. Not as many perhaps as the Moravians—but like them and like those who came after them we want to establish our homes here and improve our lives."[72]

Despite efforts at cultural communion, the divergence in local perceptions, expectations, and experiences of immigrant communities deepened over the next several decades of political and economic reforms as the Latino population continued to grow. Today, the annual Puerto Rican flag raising falls in the same week as the celebration of Slovenian independence, which is occasion for another flag-raising ceremony at city hall. Together they encapsulate the city's striking demographic and cultural shift.

When I first attended the Slovenian flag raising on a Friday morning in June 2011, I was glad I had changed out of shorts and a t-shirt. Many in the crowd of roughly seventy-five people, overwhelmingly elderly, looked as if they were going to church at St. Joseph's. Donald Resnik, dressed in a suit and bow tie, passed out red and blue corsages, the colors of the Slovenian flag, to board members of the ethnic organization that plans the event. I recognized a number of former steelworkers in the audience as well. Several were not themselves Slovenian, but they nonetheless shared the pan-European white ethnic identity that emerged after World War II and a desire to join the banquet lunch that would follow. Rows of folding chairs faced a wooden podium where local officials and Slovenian community leaders gave short speeches. They were followed by a keynote address from the second secretary to the Slovenian ambassador to the United States who happens to be from Bethlehem's Slovenian sister city, Murska Sobota. In an effort to pass their heritage to a new generation notably absent from the event, as they had been from St. Joseph's, the two flag raisers were paired with young children. The ceremony concluded with the singing of

Puerto Rican Day Parade

A float in the 2011 parade passed by Puerto Rican residents of a double house in South Bethlehem before heading across the river to city hall. (Andrew Hida, 2011.)

the national anthem in Slovenian, a language familiar only to about half of the attendees.

The following day I headed back to city hall to watch the end of the Puerto Rican Day parade as it crossed the bridge from the South Side and rounded the corner for another flag-raising ceremony. Just as stock cars had provided the finale for the 1975 parade, decades later a local hot rod club brought up the rear. In contrast to the relatively solemn Slovenian event, which had been accompanied only by an electric keyboard, the hot rod stereos, honking horns, and blasting island music formed a full-on sonic invasion of the Moravian historic district in which city hall sits. No chairs were set up, so attendees, including a large motorcycle club in black leather vests and bandanas, clustered together in the shade to await the bilingual speeches and singing of "La Borinqueña." It was an exuberant celebration with no formal dress code—several people came draped in Puerto Rican flags or wearing Puerto Rican flag t-shirts and bikinis—and a much younger average age than the Slovenian event the morning before.[73] I was one of a handful of non-Latino attendees.

Both ceremonies, in which the raising of a national flag was the central event, ritually connected Bethlehem's ethnic communities to migrant networks. And yet there remains an unresolved tension between the Puerto Rican community's American identity—legally, politically, and culturally—and local perceptions of its outsider status that continues to erupt in ways that celebrating Slovenian identity no long elicits. Even the middle school band left as soon as it finished playing "The Star-Spangled Banner," the apparent end of its official parade commitments, while the rest of the crowd was in the midst of singing the Puerto Rican anthem. Online comments on a news story about the parade, a skewed barometer given the screen of anonymity, nonetheless reflected a startling degree of hostility. Some of the milder responses among calls to use the event as a convenient opportunity to eliminate the congregated Latinos, included the now-expected refrains, "Too bad they don't take pride in the properties they rent!!! Too bad they don't take pride in the US as they do with there [*sic*] cars!!!" and "All I see them do is ruin neighborhoods."[74] From what I could find, no one had posted any anti-Slovenian comments the previous day.

The two ceremonies and the reactions to them highlight the lived distinctions between the descendants of Europeans who, cut off in 1924 from subsequent waves of fellow immigrants, reanimate their pride in country as a bulwark against this national heritage being forgotten, and the ongoing migration of Puerto Ricans amid divisive public opinion and a tense political climate regarding Latino emigration to the United States today.[75] At the same time that immigration reforms in the 1960s led to significant increases in new residents from non-European countries and gave preference to certain skilled workers, neoliberal economic policies restructured and foreclosed many other work opportunities. Cultural institutions in postindustrial cities frequently invoke a blanket ideal of multiculturalism to help resolve the discrepancy. They seek to quell discord between the expectations immigrants face and the opportunities available to them by celebrating ethnic diversity at a safe distance from these structural and political factors.

As part of this trend, the summer of 2011 in Bethlehem also marked the replacement of a community-organized Puerto Rican festival with the ¡Sabor! Latin Festival at the recently opened ArtsQuest SteelStacks arts center across from the blast furnaces. The new event represented an effort to include Latino ethnicities beyond Puerto Ricans, involve this growing community in the "cultural renaissance" planned for the former steel plant, and attract wealthier white patrons seeking a multicultural experience.[76] By the weekend event's second year, ArtsQuest hosted its own Puerto Rican flag raising and series of speeches in addition to a hot rod show, youth dance recitals, and several Latin music performances. Roughly nine thousand people attended.[77]

But despite organizers' earnest efforts at including Bethlehem's Latinos in this vision of the city's future, Adrian Mendoza, the former head of a South Side community outreach group who moved from Puerto Rico in 1994, said the ¡Sabor! Festival falls flat. Like the corporate vision of new housing in the South Side neighborhoods with its cookie-cutter approach to "progress," some have described the arts center's efforts as setting up a "Walmart of culture." "They have good music. But they lose the essence [of] what is the festival about: an ethnic community, or a group culture. ArtsQuest is watering [down] everything," Adrian told me over coffee following the 2012 event. I asked him what he meant by "the essence."

> Who we are. Puerto Ricans. If we do a festival by Puerto Ricans to the Puerto Ricans, it's a Puerto Rican festival. We're going to have our food, we're going to have our music. That they bring there, yes. But I'm paying for a plate of rice and beans and some pork, $9. You go to drink a beer and pay $4 for a beer.

Adrian explained that when the Puerto Rican community hosted its own festival, called Borinquenfest, they owned and ran their own food kiosks. He laughed at the absurdity of ArtsQuest, a predominately white organization, commodifying his culture and reselling it back to him.[78] He suggested his Puerto Rican identity has been recast as profit potential rather than having intrinsic value.

"The place is a beautiful place, no doubt," he said of the new building on the Steel site. "But you don't feel comfortable. You don't feel like you want to yell and scream and have fun. You have to be very quiet, you have to sit down. . . . Because it's an outside place, it's not really our place. We don't build this." The problem with ArtsQuest, he said, isn't the architecture per se. It is by now clear that residents continually adapt Bethlehem's built environment to their own needs. Still, several people commented to me how few Latinos, particularly working-class residents from the South Side, come to ArtsQuest, even with its close proximity and wide range of free programming. "Even though we are there, we don't feel that this is the right place to do our festival. We feel like, not confined, confined is not the word. But we feel intimidated to do things the way that we are normally. We are not the 'proper' people," Adrian said with a self-deprecating laugh.

When Adrian says "we don't build this" to explain Latino disconnect from the ArtsQuest center, and when former ethnic European parishioners suggest that the Catholic Church's view that a building is not sacred is misguided, they are not simply referring to the physical structures. For these communities, the built environment represents a social experience, one that is grounded in place and shaped by the people that inhabit it. Moral judgments are built into and negotiated through the neighborhood landscape. Economic development in South Bethlehem that goes beyond an emphasis on fixing exteriors and building new facilities can address this lived reality. As one resident in his twenties who grew up knowing the negative connotation of being a "South Sider" explained, some of the greatest "progress" in the neighborhood over the past decade is not just about new allotments of economic resources. "Progress to me for the South Side, I can't really define it solely on looks. Because I'd say at least half of it is the sense of interest that comes along with all this aesthetic progress," he said.

Local outreach efforts, including facelifts and ethnic festivals, are positive starting points that signal this ongoing change in attitude and renewed attention to neighborhoods long considered second class. But unidirectional narratives of decline followed by renewal, or of assimilation and uplift, bypass the history of discrimination dating back to the inundation of European factory workers at the turn of the twentieth century, or even to the Moravians' colonial exclusionism. The neighborhood experience of South Bethlehem is rooted in ongoing economic and cultural loss and anxiety about the future. For both the ethnic church parishioners and the new Latino residents, the postindustrial landscape is in many ways one of marginalization. More locally sensitive urban development that acknowledges the link between the economy, the built environment, and community morality could address these fears and inequalities from a common starting point rather than reaffirm the racism and classism they breed. Even among those who recognize a common cultural experience, many more-established residents will remain hesitant to acknowledge the structural changes that have made it difficult for new immigrants to replicate their own past models of success. When coupled with neoliberal policies for economic growth, such as cookie-cutter housing programs that often neglect the diverse and unique needs of local communities, these divisive attitudes block opportunities for addressing the concerns of underprivileged residents.

A new rallying point in the community vision of South Bethlehem's revitalization, meanwhile, threatens to unite these diverse local populations through a different commonality—shared discrimination toward other outsiders. Ethnically diverse Europeans were assured of their collective "whiteness" in opposition to later Latino arrivals. Today, resistance by both white and Latino residents to a new Chinese immigrant population, drawn to South Bethlehem by entertainment and jobs at the Sands Casino, shows that interethnic tensions over economic opportunity and the uneven effects of redevelopment continue to define these working-class neighborhoods. As the casino makes clear the links Bethlehem has to far-reaching networks of capital, people, and policies, the challenges of being a city at once global and uniquely local, future-focused and historically particular, suggest that in the unsettled spaces of postindustrialism, the barriers to demanding social accountability from corporate developers are as great as the openings.

6

What Happens in Bethlehem Depends on Macau

ON APRIL 11, 2012, executives at Las Vegas Sands Corp.'s sprawling new resort in Macau unveiled a sixteen-foot-tall, 5,500-pound bronze and gold statue of the Chinese God of Fortune. The bearded, robed figure sits in a 12,000-square-foot glass atrium, facing the entrance to one of the property's two themed casinos.[1] Sands Cotai Central was the corporation's fourth casino resort to open in Macau since this "special administrative region" was transferred back to China from Portuguese colonial rule in 1999 and the government opened up its gaming industry to foreign investors in 2002. (Casino gambling remains illegal in the rest of China.) While in many ways the God of Fortune statue reflects an effort to cater to local culture, the resort is at heart an exaggerated emblem of global enterprise in a postindustrial age.

Las Vegas Sands was the first foreign company to open a casino in Macau, called Sands Macao, after the government liberalized its gaming regulations. Within two years, in 2006, the region's annual gambling revenue surpassed that of Las Vegas. In 2013, twenty-nine million Macau gamblers—mostly VIPs from Mainland China and Hong Kong who wager sums that dwarf American standards—lost $45 billion at thirty-five casinos, seven times the amount of money that passed through Las Vegas.[2] Although increased Chinese government oversight beginning in 2014 dampened growth, Las Vegas Sands' Macau properties, together with its Marina Bay casino resort in Singapore, by then represented 87 percent of the corporation's worldwide profits (compared to Las Vegas's 10 percent and Bethlehem's 3 percent).[3]

Following the unveiling of the God of Fortune statue at Cotai Central's grand opening, spectators outside listened to the China National Symphony Orchestra Choir as two tightrope walkers, 500 feet above them, crossed a 1,700-foot-long wire. The wire spanned the distance to yet another Sands casino, The Venetian Macao, built in 2007. The high-wire act did more than wow the thousands of patrons who watched from below. It also appropriately commemorated the global landscape of risk in which the casino sits. Like the economy of gambling itself, premised on idealized fluid monetary exchange and speculation, the Cotai Strip where the casinos were built is literally an exercise in creating something out of nothing. Las Vegas Sands made the Strip entirely out of landfill, three million cubic meters of sand that fused together the islands of Coloane and Taipa. Paired with the government's courtship of private investment, this new "integrated city" of casino resorts that has risen from the sea takes corporate control over international urban planning to an extreme. Indeed, the Las Vegas Sands Corp. has trademarked the name "Cotai Strip" for the location it invented.[4] For Sheldon Adelson, the Macau resorts represent a business model that he hopes to export to other untapped global markets.

Meanwhile, more than 8,000 miles away, gamblers stood three deep around a "hot" midi baccarat table at the Sands Casino in Bethlehem. Baccarat is one of the simplest casino table games to play. If a player's cards value closer to nine than the cards in front of the dealer, anyone who has bet on him will win even pay on their gamble, and anyone who has bet against him will lose. Already the most popular table game in Macau, its prevalence at American casinos has increased rapidly in recent years. As in other U.S. casinos, the players at the baccarat table in Bethlehem, besides one curious ethnographer, were all ethnic Chinese.[5]

Many Chinese players believe, or at least play along with the idea, that they can influence the outcome of the game with dramatic gestures and shouts, regardless of the game's fifty-fifty odds. A middle-aged man at the table rubbed two facedown cards against the felt and spun them before he began to slowly bend the long edge back. The high stacks of pink and black-striped chips in front of him represented a wager of at least $2,000, and he drew out the suspenseful performance of peeling back the cards to reflect how much was at stake. By peeking at the edge of the card, he knew it was either a six or a seven—it depended on whether there was a pip (or dot) in the middle. If it was a six, the cards would beat the dealer's hand and win the bet.

The other players, spectators, and I craned to see, but before he revealed the rest of the card, he banged the table with an emphatic call, and the rest of the players (all of whom had bet in accordance) and the dealer (also Asian) took up the chant, "*Cheui! Cheui! Cheui! Cheui!*" The man two seats down made a whooshing sound, and everyone around the table made sweeping motions with their hands. The call was to "blow away" the extra pip that would make the card a seven and lose the bet. After several tense seconds, the player peeled back the rest of the card and displayed a win. There were cheers as he sat back in his chair. The woman on the end of the table marked a grid the casino provides to help players track trends, and the dealer paid out bets and disposed of the now-bent cards. A white man on his way to play blackjack muttered unintelligibly as he negotiated his way through the Chinese crowd, which seemed to pay him no attention.

While the scale of operations in Bethlehem cannot compare to Sands' casinos in Macau and Singapore, for a city whose Chinese residents have never totaled more than 1 percent of its population (and whose Asian residents together make up less than 3 percent), the effect of the local casino's baccarat-heavy marketing strategy is striking.[6] The movements of capital, policies, and people that link Bethlehem to global networks of labor and exchange connect residents to locales far beyond the Lehigh Valley. Through these networks, corporate finance, neoliberal economic regulations, immigration and visa policies, and transportation infrastructures converge in eastern Pennsylvania. In some ways, the casino industry's landscape of risk exemplifies the postindustrial boundlessness imagined by commentators who equate globalization with homogenization and democratization of opportunity.[7] As local heritage activist Jill Archer said in dismay when Sands opened its Bethlehem property, "Suddenly we're just one more place where you can go to the casino." And yet Bethlehem residents' accounts by now make clear that this vision of a "flattened," generic landscape does not match the day-to-day encounters through which they localize understandings of a global economy.

We have seen how experiences of economic change in Bethlehem challenge dichotomies that would distinguish production and service work, "rational" and "emotional" development interests, and economic and cultural displacement, suggesting all reflect ongoing processes within postindustrial transitions. Nor is what is referred to as modern globalization so distinct from local, everyday life. Along with state policies and corporate actions that elevate the notion of a free market and direct capital in specific ways, "the global" takes shape and gains influence via community-level processes of placemaking.[8] Even as for-profit business interests see localities as essentially disposable, easily sold or dismantled once they no longer benefit the bottom line, Bethlehem residents imbue local places with durable social meanings and memories of postwar commitments between corporation and community. Bethlehem and its various landscapes are thus best conceived of as market-*places.* The casino's industrial theming, considered by many locals to be an appeasement strategy on the part of Las Vegas Sands (though not necessarily an unwelcome one), offered one example of how interactions between corporate and community interests play out in architectural design. Latino residents' refusal to accept a homogenous, matching-mailbox aesthetic for their homes likewise showed how local needs and desires can be both shaped and expressed via the built environment. When global economic risk—a free-market abstraction—is spatialized and made material, local residents assert place-based values to push back on the volatility and uneven impacts of corporate profit motives. They see the postindustrial landscape as a last realm of influence to capture liquid capital for their benefit.

Bethlehem's new population of Asian gamblers and casino employees make clear how local experience is connected to—and constitutive of—global flows of capital, regulations, and people. Local reactions reveal both the tensions and congruencies between fixed community and mobile corporate interests. The forces that today create new economic opportunities by dissolving political, regulatory, and cultural boundaries, for example, simultaneously exacerbate postindustrial fears and anxieties. To many longtime residents, the arrival of Chinese (and to a lesser extent Korean) clientele at the Bethlehem casino is a particular reflection of this imagined boundlessness—the global, risk-based transactions in which the casino industry participates.

The landscape again emerges as a resource, and also a weapon, that can be used to grapple with uncertainties. Everyday exercises in elevating local interests over those of capital often take a xenophobic and racialized edge. White and Latino residents' determination to draw spatial boundaries around the casino, public parks, and other community spaces are part of an effort to regain control over the places they associate with memories of a more balanced relationship between corporation and community. At the same time, these actions reflect exclusionary visions of what postindustrial place and the people who populate it should look like. Addressing instead the ways in which an asymmetrical power dynamic between corporations and communities has been institutionalized could temper prevalent perceptions among whites and Latinos that the Chinese themselves represent barriers to adequate wages or competition for jobs. Recognizing the far-reaching networks of which Bethlehem and its market-places are a part offers the potential for incorporating diverse community interests into plans for future development rather than exploiting cultural difference for competitive gain.

A Global City from Steel to Slots

In October 2009 Bethlehem's local newspaper cosponsored a town hall forum to discuss impending changes to state gaming laws and their expected effects on the Lehigh Valley. The casino had been open for five months, and Pennsylvania was on the verge of adding table games to the first-phase legalization of slots to increase revenues statewide. Slot revenue in Bethlehem was already outperforming several other casinos in the state, but Las Vegas Sands had indefinitely stopped construction of the adjacent hotel tower and retail center as the recession threatened to upend the corporation's massive, in-progress global expansion. Credit lines dried up, and Sands also put development projects in Macau on hold as it continued to work to complete its casino resort in Singapore. The corporation's share price had plummeted from a high of $144 in the fall of 2007 to trade as low as $1.38 in early 2009. By the time of the town hall meeting, it had rebounded to the mid-teens and the company staved off bankruptcy thanks to an emergency infusion of $1 billion of CEO Sheldon Adelson's personal cash.

A standing-room-only crowd of anxious Lehigh Valley politicians, business owners, and residents who were awaiting the promised community benefit of the casino's taxes and tourists gathered in a conference room at the South Side branch of the local community college, housed in Bethlehem Steel's former plant office building. During the forum, a panel of city, state, community, and business leaders discussed the future of gaming in Pennsylvania and its local impact so far. Robert LaFleur, a financial analyst, offered to put things in perspective. "Here's an interesting tidbit for you all here," he told the audience of roughly 200 people.

> Part of the success of the restart of the hotel and the table games [in Bethlehem] in many ways is going to result, or is going to come about through global economic forces and the success of Las Vegas Sands and their parent company in securing additional financing in places as far away as China and Macau and Hong Kong. . . . That's just the nature of the global economy that we're all in right now. So you better hope the Hong Kong stock market hangs in there.

Robert's statement was met with quiet laughter, as I and other audience members began to grasp these new, and apparently volatile, ties that linked Bethlehem directly to Asia. To offset heavy debt and resume construction in Macau, Sands had announced an upcoming initial public offering of a spin-off subsidiary, Sands China, on the Hong Kong stock exchange. The flash of its share price on a digital ticker would, the analyst suggested, determine whether the naked steel frame of the hotel down the street from where we sat would take more permanent shape. Global risk, in other words, had taken material form in the local built environment. His comment was striking to those of us used to thinking of Bethlehem as a quintessential American steel town, not an outpost of Asian finance.

Then I looked at the large silver H-beam icon, the corporate emblem of Bethlehem Steel, which still hung on the back wall of the conference room. Of course, Bethlehem has long been a part of global economies. It is a market-*place* shaped both by far-flung economic transactions and local contingencies.[9] Even before Bethlehem Steel was incorporated in 1904, the city served as an international hub for the Moravian Church. At its founding in 1741, Bethlehem was the center of Moravian activity in colonial America and became the headquarters of the Church's Northern Province, which comprises most of North America above the

Mason-Dixon line.[10] Bethlehem's finances had reached even further, tied to church leader Count Zinzendorf in Germany. Missionary work linked the settlement to the transatlantic economy and international lines of credit. The church even invested in a merchant ship in order to make travel across the ocean more cost-effective.[11] Bethlehem felt the consequences when a banker who held a number of church deposits failed in Portugal, and much of the reason the Moravians in Bethlehem abandoned their communal "Oeconomy" in 1762 had to do with financial pressure from church debts abroad.[12]

The Moravian Church's financial connections remain international. Despite staunch opposition from church leaders to bringing a casino to Bethlehem, the president of the Northern Province at the time of the community debate readily acknowledged that the global landscape is less cut and dry. While the Moravian Church in Bethlehem refuses to accept charitable donations from Las Vegas Sands, in Alberta, Canada, where gambling is also legal, some casino revenues are funneled to not-for-profits. The funds the Moravian Church there receives are used primarily to support mission work in Tibet. As one church administrator likes to say of the relationship between the church's expansive spiritual and economic interests, "No margin, no ministry."[13]

Not surprisingly, the Bethlehem Steel Corporation, at one point the third largest industrial company in the world, represented a similarly global institution.[14] As in other cities in the industrial United States, the Steel's active recruitment of immigrant labor had a definitive impact on Bethlehem's social and physical landscapes, as the many national parishes on the South Side made apparent. When restrictions on European immigration in the 1920s led Bethlehem Steel to shift its attention to finding employees south of the border, some locals speculated that the Mexican recruits it brought to Bethlehem were being trained to open new plants planned for Mexico and other Spanish-speaking countries.[15]

It is not hard to imagine why such rumors, though unfounded, seemed reasonable. In addition to vast holdings of plants, mines, shipyards, and other real estate in the United States, Bethlehem Steel's empire extended to South America, Asia, Africa, and beyond. Its interests in Cuban ore mines dated to 1889, and the corporation at various points owned or operated additional mines in Sweden, Chile, Venezuela, Brazil, Mexico, Canada, Liberia, and South Africa.[16] According to a former manager in the finance department, investments in South American mines, and the resulting tax savings, were part of a complex financial strategy by which these savings, off of borrowed money, could be reinvested back in the United States for a higher return. During the 1950s, many of Bethlehem Steel's foreign transactions passed through tax havens Bermuda and the Bahamas.[17] Like many other companies, the corporation registered its fleets of ships in Liberia and Panama to take advantage of minimal regulations and low labor costs. Bethlehem Steel's long practice of treating place as a disposable asset has left traces throughout the archival record. Navigating the three-volume dossier that documents more than 245 companies in the history of the Steel Corporation's holdings through 1970 is as obscuring as it is illuminating. It reveals webs of interconnections and an ongoing worldwide restructuring of subsidiaries as financial incentives and profit opportunities evolved.[18] Like global capitalism itself, this was a landscape in constant flux.

If the history of Bethlehem Steel rightly troubles the notion that "globalization" is a modern phenomenon, it also suggests that the global economy today thrives on new priorities, modes of exchange, and vulnerabilities. The structure of Bethlehem Steel's international operations in many ways bridges what are often thought of as distinct industrial and postindustrial economies—the one involved with creating and transporting tangible goods and raw materials, the other with more elusive, less "grounded" financial products. Over the course of the twentieth century, Bethlehem Steel's chairmen evolved away from steel managers and operators like Eugene Grace, who worked his way up from crane man. They became salesmen in the 1970s and accountants in the 1980s. The latter included Dan Trautlein, the first "outside" CEO who earned his chops at Price Waterhouse & Co. rather than within the Steel. He reportedly told corporate management matter-of-factly, "We are not in the business of making steel. We are in the business of making money."[19] Attorney Hank Barnette took over in the 1990s. By the end of the decade, as Barnette prepared to step down, internal memos confirmed the shift in the business's emphasis. As part of a plan to stay fiscally solvent, the following instructions circulated at a corporate board meeting in 1999:

> Corporate behavior should take into account the responsibilities that a corporation has to all of its key constituents (e.g., customers, employees, communities, creditors, retirees), but the primary focus of any

> "for profit" business should be the long-term maximization of stockholder value. In order to achieve this objective, *all employees should adopt this philosophy as the guiding principle in their decision making and behavior* as it relates to formulating key policies, implementation of policies/strategies/plans and day-to-day execution. (emphasis in original)[20]

The widespread shift in corporate emphasis from production to "shareholder value" during the late twentieth century was central to the dissolution of postwar commitments to those secondary "constituents" listed in the Bethlehem Steel memo.[21] While the uneven effects of global economies are not new, the explicit reprioritization of who should benefit—with employees, communities, and retirees coming out on the losing end—signaled the fulfillment of an idealized escape from the tethers of locality.

Even as corporate management reflected this adaptation to a business climate dependent on strategic calculations to boost share prices rather than on manufacturing ability, labor relations, or community support, the presumed advantages of the finance-driven approach proved difficult to harness. The deliberate disinvestment in many of Bethlehem Steel's production facilities added barriers to profitability. During the third quarter of 1977, Bethlehem Steel shut down parts of its Johnstown, Pennsylvania, and Lackawanna, New York, plants and recorded a $750 million write-off for scrapped equipment and pension and benefit costs for the 12,000 employees it laid off. At the time, the resulting net loss of $477 million was the largest three-month corporate loss in U.S. history.[22] Bethlehem Steel's losses five years later would more than triple this record.[23]

Locals repeatedly offered me variations of two stories, in particular, of pivotal moments in the demise of the company and the domestic steel industry as a whole. Both are premised on perceptions of disrupted balances between local needs and global markets. They identify specific buildings as market-places that materialize the everyday interplay between the two. The first recurring tale is of the shock in 1967 when both Bethlehem Steel and market-leader U.S. Steel were underbid by roughly 30 percent on the multimillion-dollar contract to build the World Trade Center's iconic twin towers in New York. Though initially the New York Port Authority had assumed that these two companies, with their large, integrated plants, were the only viable candidates to fill the massive order, in the end it made more economic sense to split the contract into pieces and award the work to a consortium of fifteen smaller companies from across the country, some of which were nonunion. About half of the steel used was still American-made, including foundational supports that came from nearby Coatesville, Pennsylvania. Some was even fabricated out of steel that initially came from the big two corporations. But Bethlehem residents generally refer with scorn only to the foreign steel imported for the project at reduced cost, particularly from Japan, where the government subsidized production.[24] Some go so far as to suggest that the inferior quality of the foreign steel used was the reason the Twin Towers collapsed in 2001.[25]

The second type of story relates the company's demise to its disengagement with the local built environment. These narratives reference other buildings that were constructed with foreign structural steel despite their immediate proximity to the Bethlehem plant. Lifelong resident Richard Hoffer, for example, told me about a bank his friend built in the 1990s. "To do a competitive bid he had to settle for steel that was made in Korea. It was less expensive to be made in Korea, shipped across the Pacific, warehoused on the West Coast, and then shipped across America. It was less expensive," he told me, replaying his disbelief all over again. In 1992 it likewise was revealed that not all of the steel being used to construct a new South Side hotel, located just blocks from the plant, was from Bethlehem Steel. Protesting steelworkers said much of it was foreign-produced (a claim the hotel partners denied). In fact, some of the steel likely came from Nucor-Yamato, a nonunion, mini-mill partnership with a Japanese firm in Arkansas that also had taken much of Bethlehem's business. Even the fraction of the steel that reportedly had a Bethlehem Steel stamp was shipped in from warehouses across the country, not from down the street.[26] Ted Bodnar, a former plant supervisor, agreed with Richard that "there's no way logically" that this foreign or warehoused steel could be cheaper than the steel produced locally. And yet in pointing out the absurdity of this economic reality, they both acknowledged and affirmed that a new marketplace logic, sustained by specific state policies, trade routes, and corporate profit structures, had taken over.

Since the 1970s, neoliberal economic reforms have ushered in a number of shifts that gradually rewired expectations of how place and capital relate. Despite being the location of the corporate headquarters and namesake plant, Bethlehem was not necessarily at the center of Bethlehem Steel's strategic focus in later years, especially after the Burns Harbor, Indiana, plant, a far more profitable and modern endeavor, opened in 1964. From a management perspective, other hubs of government affairs, finance, international trade, suppliers, and customers took precedence. As Hank Barnette explained, "My focus was on 90 percent of the company elsewhere, and particularly on Washington, DC, and New York, where I spent as much time as I did here in Bethlehem."

Even as Barnette made a point of applauding Bethlehem Steel's decision to maintain its corporate offices in Bethlehem after its production moved elsewhere, he surprised me by saying that where a corporate headquarters is located today is less relevant than before. When I mentioned that ArcelorMittal, the inheritor of Bethlehem's operating steel plants, is a foreign company—based, I later confirmed, in Luxembourg—he did not give me the simple confirmation I expected. ArcelorMittal is a *global* corporation, he said, with division headquarters all over the world. Moreover, although the firm's CEO is an Indian citizen who lives in London, individuals do not own companies. "Once you're a publicly traded company and your stock is available to the world market, companies like a basic manufacturing company often are held by banks, pension funds, things of that sort," he explained. Even if governments see it differently and legally link incorporation to a specific jurisdiction, economically speaking he said that characterizing a corporation as a domestic or foreign entity would depend on the profile of its shareholders. I left with the feeling that, from a corporate perspective, my fixation on place-based headquarters was to some extent naïve and irrelevant in today's global market.[27] Where goods are produced has for a long time not necessarily been based on geographic proximity to their end uses. Barnette similarly suggested that advances in technology, communications, and financing structures mean that dwelling on the location of a corporate headquarters is in many respects a holdover from a bygone era. And yet, not everyone can so easily break with past expectations.

Networks of Risk and Regulation

Casino industry veteran Tim Deluca earlier described the Sands Casino as a "postindustrial factory" in which dealer- and gambler-laborers produce profit. Despite the narrative continuity this analogy provides between manufacturing and service work, many former steelworkers and others expressed discomfort with a company that, like financial institutions, does not make a tangible product. In fact, to a greater extent than other entertainment venues, the business seems to be premised not just on creating an experience but on taking something away. Their concerns revealed cultural tensions in local expectations for capital's geographic attachment. The nearly 3,000 jobs and infrastructure that the casino created in Bethlehem on vacant land, as well as its use of local suppliers, the millions of dollars it pays in taxes and host fees, and its charitable donations, undeniably benefit the local community in ways that echo the Steel's heyday.[28] At the same time, the capital that is produced, critics suggested, can flow out of Bethlehem to Las Vegas via digital transactions even more easily than steel beams could be exported by rail or truck.

In the postindustrial global economy, corporate calculations often determine that market-places are themselves easily transferable. The terms "runaway factory" and "runaway shop" gained cultural currency in the 1970s and 1980s to denote manufacturing plants that relocated to other parts of the country and world seeking lower-wage, nonunion labor and other relaxed regulations. At the 2009 town hall forum about the casino in Bethlehem, the financial analyst Robert LaFleur explained the exchange of capital among Las Vegas Sands' global properties in a way that similarly made place-based regulations seem like dragging anchors on profitability. In terms of the taxes on casino revenues, "every dollar that you [Pennsylvania] get is a dollar that Las Vegas doesn't get, it's a dollar that Macau doesn't get, it's a dollar that Singapore doesn't get," he said. From a corporate perspective, the ideal liquidity of financial assets and their growth potential rub uncomfortably against the reality of laws attached to fixed locations. As a result, corporations nimbly negotiate and attempt to eschew local efforts to pin down their profits, while places—whether cities, states, countries, or other jurisdictions—must constantly adjust their legislated policies and incentives to compete for mobile capital and the associated community benefit it could bring.[29]

Given the political and historical contingencies of a regulatory landscape that steers financial flows in specific directions, there are limits to conceiving of globalization as a de-territorializing process or one that eliminates regulations altogether.[30] And yet, despite geographical variations in economic incentives and barriers, policies offering similar profit advantages to corporations have become in some cases as mobile and ubiquitous as global capital. The expansion of Las Vegas Sands' international casino empire offers a clear example. When the government of Macau liberalized its gaming regulations in 2002, the primary motivation was to attract foreign investors. Given the Macau government's and its gambling economy's not-unfair reputation of corruption and links to organized crime, the opening of borders ostensibly signaled to the global corporate community that Macau was "modernizing."[31] When Singapore legalized casino gaming in 2005, political leaders likewise reasoned that gambling had become so broadly accessible that Singapore needed to join the fray to compete for international money. Gambling would be not only an economic solution, but an entrée into a worldwide neoliberal market culture, a signal that Singapore was willing to adapt and take risks to attract foreign investment.[32]

Casino design itself reflects a certain language of economic reform and development in which the built environment comes to materialize market expectations. The government of Singapore, for example, evaluated casino proposals in large part based on architecture, seeking designs and iconic buildings that would secure Singapore's image as a leading Asian city.[33] Las Vegas Sands won a license to build a casino resort in Singapore in 2006 based on a space-station-like plan for three, fifty-five-story hotel towers connected at the top by a "skypark" platform. Moshe Safdie, the resort's Israeli-Canadian architect, is known for designing the Habitat '67 model community in Montreal, the National Gallery of Canada, and the Yad Vashem Holocaust Museum in Jerusalem, among other international projects. Many of Sands' other casino resorts also build upon proven Western blueprints. Given its success in transplanting The Venetian and its Grand Canal to Asia, for example, the corporation began construction in 2013 of a fifth casino-resort in Macau called The Parisian that features a half-scale replica of the Eiffel Tower.[34]

And yet, Sands' Asian projects also deliberately adapt design elements to their localities, as the golden god of prosperity statue at Cotai Central in Macau suggests. Paul Steelman, a prominent casino architect who in 2004 designed Sands Macao, the company's first Chinese casino, has said that even though Las Vegas Sands already planned to build The Venetian Macao second, it wanted the Sands Macao to be different. "A lot of people probably make the mistake of trying to put Las Vegas wherever they go," Steelman said. But Sands wanted to "show that they were very sympathetic with the market," and tailor the casino to the local demographic. "They didn't want Las Vegas." In addition to highlighting Sands Macao's strict *feng shui* design and red motifs, which are auspicious in Chinese culture, Steelman noted that in studying the local scene it became clear that gambling in Macau was more of a "gladiator sport" than an entertainment activity. As a result, the architects reconfigured the casino floor to be like a stadium. Chinese patrons spent more hours gambling and cared less about secondary activities like dining and shopping, so the emphasis was on quick "fuel stations" like noodle and tea bars directly on the casino floor instead of full-service restaurants on the perimeter like in American casinos.

Thus, rather than see Macau as a site to transplant Western design, Steelman believes the exchange is flowing in the other direction—that Macau is a catalyst for global innovation. "Those projects in Macau are all changing the way casinos are designed throughout the world," he said. "Every single day we're allowed to try new things."[35] Indeed, in 2013 the Malaysian casino corporation Genting Group announced Steelman's firm would design a Chinese-themed casino in Las Vegas.[36] Even in Bethlehem, Sands made plans in 2015 to convert some casino floor space to the "stadium-style" electronic games that are trendy in Macau and Singapore.[37]

Like U.S. states that have legalized gambling, Macau and Singapore's governments also have tailored their economic development policies and regulatory landscapes to ensure local benefits from global casino investments. Most fundamentally, casino revenues are heavily taxed. In Macau, these casino taxes made up 83 percent of the government's budget in 2013. The money has been reinvested in education—including a $1.3 billion campus for the University of Macau—health care, housing, and other forms of social welfare.[38] Against private sector objections, in 2010 the government instituted a "one-for-one" policy by which one local construction worker must be hired for every foreign construction worker hired.[39] Similarly, the Macau casinos are required to hire only local citizens as dealers. The population of the special administrative region, which is just over eleven square miles, had grown to 636,000 people by 2014, but with ongoing gaming expansion and an unemployment rate of just 2 percent, a labor shortage has driven up wages. Dealing in Macau as a result pays significantly better than other local employment opportunities and compared with dealing in the United States.[40]

Las Vegas Sands, for its part, is actively engaged in negotiating with other nations to expand its global gaming reach. It looks to neoliberal market reforms that make economic borders increasingly permeable and enhance corporate leverage over these kinds of citizen protections. Japan, South Korea, Thailand, and Taiwan top the corporation's list of desirable markets, but former Las Vegas Sands Corp. president and chief operating officer Michael Leven said that Vietnam would be a more likely target for opening a new Sands casino, specifically because it offers the least resistance politically.[41] Even if Vietnam were to limit opportunities for its own citizens to gamble, as is the case in Singapore, the increasing mobility and wealth of Chinese citizens in particular makes it and other East Asian markets attractive business prospects.

Meanwhile, in 2012 Sands CEO Sheldon Adelson made headlines with an announcement that he would invest between $20 and $30 billion to build a massive casino resort complex near Madrid, Spain. Dubbed Euro-Vegas by the global media, the plan called for up to six casinos, twelve hotels, nine theaters, a convention center, shopping malls, restaurants, and three golf courses. It promised to generate more than 200,000 jobs in a country with over 25 percent post-recession unemployment. Adelson made no secret of the fact that the area was a prime target precisely because of the country's weak economy. He played Madrid and Barcelona against each other to seek regulatory concessions, including lower tax rates, exceptions to no-smoking laws, lower minimum wages, and relaxed immigration policies to bring in foreign workers. Patrons were expected to flock to Euro-Vegas from Europe, the former Soviet Union, and, of course, Asia upon completion of the first phase in 2017.[42] But when the Spanish government ultimately rejected Sands' demands for concessions in late 2013, Adelson killed the project.[43]

These international forays, which comprise the majority of Las Vegas Sands' business, replicate processes that lead manufacturers to relocate from the United States to more "favorable" business climates, or underpin efforts to gain concessions from domestic workers and governments. As a Las Vegas Sands executive told Art Slesak, the head of the South Bethlehem community development task force, "Every casino is for sale every day." For the right price, investors in the global market readily shed and shuffle properties. In 2013 executive Michael Leven confirmed that the Sands Casino Bethlehem would indeed be sold if a buyer came forward with a strong offer, given that despite better-than-expected earnings, four years after its opening it no longer fit the corporation's global, mega-resort portfolio.[44] Although over-saturation of the mid-Atlantic gaming market and increased competition in neighboring New York and New Jersey loom, for the most part Sands Bethlehem—unlike many Rust Belt factories—remains profitable enough as a regional casino to escape discussion of closure or downsizing even if Las Vegas Sands sheds its local commitments. Meanwhile, where Sands' expansion into the global economy will end remains anyone's guess. "There is room for five to ten Las Vegases," Adelson said in 2012. "There is room for that many of these mega resorts and it still would not saturate the market."[45] A market-place, from this perspective, represents site-specific profit potential to be mined and extracted until it runs out.[46]

Local experiences of this global economy nonetheless point to cracks in the expansion model's framework as many Bethlehem residents question how competitive free-market logics relate to their personal and communal needs, desires, and histories. Sands' decision to indefinitely halt construction on the Bethlehem casino's hotel and retail space in 2009 as a result of the global recession prompted narratives of betrayal echoing residents' disappointment with Bethlehem Steel, the previous major corporation to renege on promises to the community. A front-page headline in a local paper above a photograph of the skeleton structures read "Honeymoon's Over," suggesting that the material landscape had shown the imagined contract between global profits and local needs to be less enduring than expected.[47]

Robert DeSalvio, the local casino president at the time, explained that stopping construction that fall was purely a business decision to devote resources to opening the gambling floor and begin to recoup costs in an uncertain economic climate. "Obviously we answer to our shareholders," he said simply, implying that in the end no other justification was necessary.[48] Although Sands ultimately completed the hotel and shops in 2011, as promised, local awareness that the corporation is willing to sell the

Bethlehem casino for the right price continues to undermine any feelings of security that the finished structures might provide. The anxiety escalated in 2014 when sources revealed that Las Vegas Sands had entered into negotiations with Tropicana Entertainment to unload the property. Although the talks ultimately failed, many residents remain concerned that a new owner would not honor Sands' conciliatory commitment to preserving what is left of the site's industrial history.[49] The factory remnants have taken on a double significance as material markers of tacit agreements between the community and its corporations, first Bethlehem Steel and now Las Vegas Sands. In the meantime, Sands continued to inch forward with a new master plan to develop the remainder of the site, including the No. 2 Machine Shop that still sat vacant more than six years after the casino's opening. When reporters or other citizens periodically asked Sands representatives what accounted for the delay, they were told that the plans were under the purview of corporate headquarters in Las Vegas.[50]

In small ways, individuals and communities interpret and push back on the globalization process in their daily lives. Their acts of resistance take various forms, not all of which are complementary to progress-oriented visions of economic expansion and harmonious living. In Bethlehem, the recognition that one's livelihood may be at the whim of global market fluctuations often comes into focus through the local landscape. Here, the ways in which residents understand abstract forms of financial danger merge with spatialized efforts to protect community boundaries. Reactions to Asian gamblers and casino employees newly venturing into the South Bethlehem community take shape in those tense spaces where local and global structures coalesce.

Culture Clash on the Casino Floor

Not long after it opened, Sands Bethlehem became the highest-grossing casino in Pennsylvania for table games by a significant margin. It solidified a number two position among twelve open casinos in slots and overall revenue. By many accounts the Sands was by 2012 one of the top-performing regional casinos in the country. Bethlehem residents and community stakeholders are well aware that it is not just the global mobility of capital and neoliberal policy reforms that has contributed to Sands' success in Bethlehem. It is also the complementary networks by which people migrate to this market-place. Las Vegas Sands' dominance in the Pennsylvania gaming market is credited in large part to Bethlehem's close proximity to New York City and northern New Jersey, where the corporation has aggressively marketed to the area's sizeable Asian, and in particular Chinese, populations. Bethlehem is only a ninety-minute drive from New York, closer than Atlantic City. While the Sands does not disclose what percentage of its gamblers is Asian, about half of its 22,000 daily patrons, or 4.5 million people each year, come from outside the Lehigh Valley; New York's Chinatowns are the epicenters of this traffic.[51]

Tensions between corporate and local opinions of the "value" of Chinese gamblers further reveal the entanglement of economic, moral, and spatial claims in this global postindustrial landscape. In the "postindustrial factory" of the casino floor, dealers are not the only so-called "line workers." As discussed previously, gamblers are equally apt representatives of the casino's profit-producing labor force. Las Vegas Sands' entrée into Macau was motivated by efforts not only to take advantage of the sheer size of the Chinese market, but also to capitalize on Chinese gambler-workers' perceived high productivity. In some ways the relationship resembles centuries-old models of corporate colonization in which Western businesses have seen benefits in using foreign labor forces, often citing workers' racial or ethnic attributes as justification for their practices.[52] In the casino industry, Chinese patrons are regularly identified as being culturally predisposed to playing games of chance, making them long-duration, high-wager gamblers. The steel industry's practice of assigning Mexican and Puerto Rican workers to the coke works based on their assumed tolerance for high temperatures reflects a history of applying similar logics at home. At the Bethlehem casino, Las Vegas Sands both brings "foreign labor" to the Lehigh Valley and caters to Chinese gamblers' needs in order to ensure continued productivity.

To many Bethlehem residents, however, it is the Chinese gamblers themselves, not the casino's labor structures, that represent an infiltrating force. Locals were surprised to watch, for example, as the casino's industrial theming—a key premise of Las Vegas Sands' successful bid for the state license—gradually morphed away from Steel referents. New décor instead features Asian design elements that signal future profit possibilities rather than fading memories of a manufacturing economy. In the years after its first one hundred tables opened in July 2010, the Sands twice expanded. In May 2011 it added a seventeen-table high rollers' room called Paiza Club, named after a type of Chinese passport given centuries ago to important officials and guests. The room features curvilinear feng shui designs, gold and red motifs (the Chinese colors of wealth and good fortune), and a gold, spiral-shaped glass hanging sculpture that resembles a dragon (also a Chinese symbol of luck).[53] In November 2012 the Pennsylvania Gaming Control Board granted Sands permission to add thirty-one more tables, fourteen of which were designated for midi baccarat, and two for Pai Gow poker, games played overwhelmingly by Asian clientele.[54] On these tables the numbered seats skip from three to five to avoid the number four, which is inauspicious in Chinese tradition. In addition to regularly expanding its offerings of "Asian games"—which along with baccarat and Pai Gow poker include a dice game called Sic Bo and a domino game called Pai Gow tiles—the casino began hosting "Grand Dragon Master" baccarat tournaments and has a popular Chinese restaurant in its adjacent food court. In late 2012 the casino opened an upscale noodle bar called Chopstick, staffed by Chinese-speakers, to add to the casino floor's initial offerings of a Jewish deli, an Irish pub, and celebrity chef Emeril Lagasse's Italian restaurant, burger joint, and steakhouse.

Including U.S.-born citizens, there are more than 4.3 million people in the United States who identify with the Chinese diaspora.[55] Chinese immigration to the United States has steadily increased since American immigration reform in 1965 and China's loosening of emigration restrictions after Mao Zedong's death ended the Cultural Revolution in 1976.[56] Emigration further accelerated from the 1990s on such that roughly 40 percent of the 1.8 million foreign-born Chinese living in the United States in 2010 arrived after 2000. The New York/Northern New Jersey metropolitan region is home to 22.5 percent of this population, the highest concentration in the country.[57] In 2012 the United States, among other countries, further relaxed its visa requirements to specifically attract more visitors from China to help boost the domestic tourism economy.[58] The number of Chinese coming to the United States each year on temporary visas, the majority of which allow six-month stays, more than quintupled between 2003 and 2012 to 2.1 million people.[59]

Amid this institutional and political infrastructure that connects capital, regulatory, and human migrations and feeds Chinese immigrants and

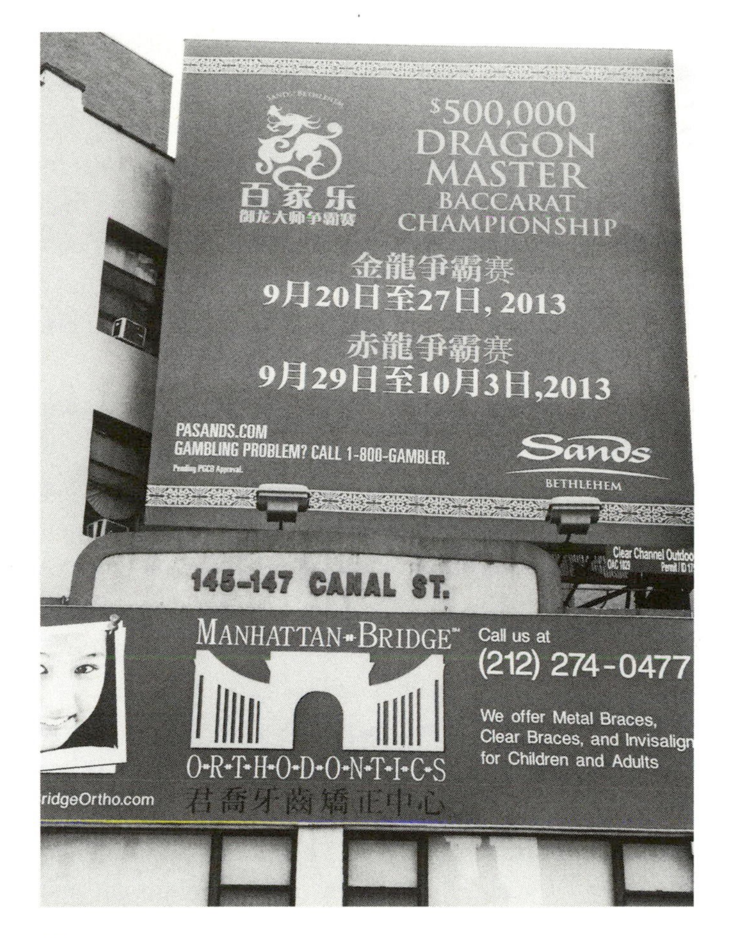

Chinatown

This billboard advertising two baccarat tournaments—"Golden Dragon" and "Red Dragon"—at the Sands Casino in the fall of 2013 was located in the center of New York's Chinatown on Canal Street, near where daily buses bring gamblers to Bethlehem. (Scott Moskowitz, 2013.)

visitors into the U.S. economy, bus lines to the Bethlehem casino represent a regional link. The gamblers at the Sands tables are among the tens of thousands of Chinese New Yorkers who board discount buses in Chinatown each week to casinos in Connecticut, New Jersey, and Pennsylvania.[60] Two of these Chinatown lines, 88 Baccarat and Lucky 9 Enterprise (again featuring auspicious numbers in Chinese culture) each make more than a dozen daily, sold-out trips to the Sands. Of the twenty-nine bus companies with which the Sands had agreements in 2013, 88 Baccarat and Lucky

9 were among the cheapest fares, offering round-trip tickets to the casino for $15, half what the more mainstream bus partner that departs from New York's Port Authority charged. Other lines, including Full House Travel and Golden Mega Express, make dozens of daily trips from New York's "second Chinatowns" in Queens and Brooklyn.[61] With their tickets, patrons receive cards worth $45 in free slots play. Many, particularly non-Asian gamblers, who have sought tickets on the Chinatown buses complain that they are rarely able to secure a seat because regulars buy tickets in advance and make the trip every day.[62]

The money bus patrons and other Chinese players bring to the tables seems to justify Sands' aggressive, ethnic-specific marketing. According to casino management, "Asian-style table games" consistently outperform games like blackjack, roulette, and craps. By August 2011, for example, baccarat represented 45 percent, or $28 million, of the monthly wagers, or "drops," at Sands Bethlehem's tables. The baccarat drop in Bethlehem increased 560 percent year-over-year from August 2010, compared with a 210 percent increase for table games overall.[63]

Casino employees say they see regular bus riders cash out their chips before they head home, as if they are collecting their daily wages. Mei Lung, a dealer who immigrated to the United States from China in the late 1990s, is herself flabbergasted by the activity. "Where is the money coming from?" she asked. "I know how hard my parents saved their money. And they [some Chinese gamblers] play every day. . . . Some people, they do walk away with a lot of money, but most of the players, they lose. So I don't know. They still come every day like a job."

Casino executives believe that Chinese culture has historically encouraged risk-taking and games of chance. At the same time, Chinese immigrants who have been influenced by Confucian traditions often value thrift, hard work, and discipline, seemingly putting them at odds with casino activities. A Korean gambler raised in China referred to his casino "work" taking the bus every day from Flushing, Queens, to Bethlehem as something that forced him to "keep regular hours."[64] This work ethic, both inside and outside of the casino, may be equally a result of economic need and exploitative labor conditions where there is no option but to put in long hours.[65] From this perspective, legal gambling in mainstream casinos represents a step up from Chinatown's low-wage, and

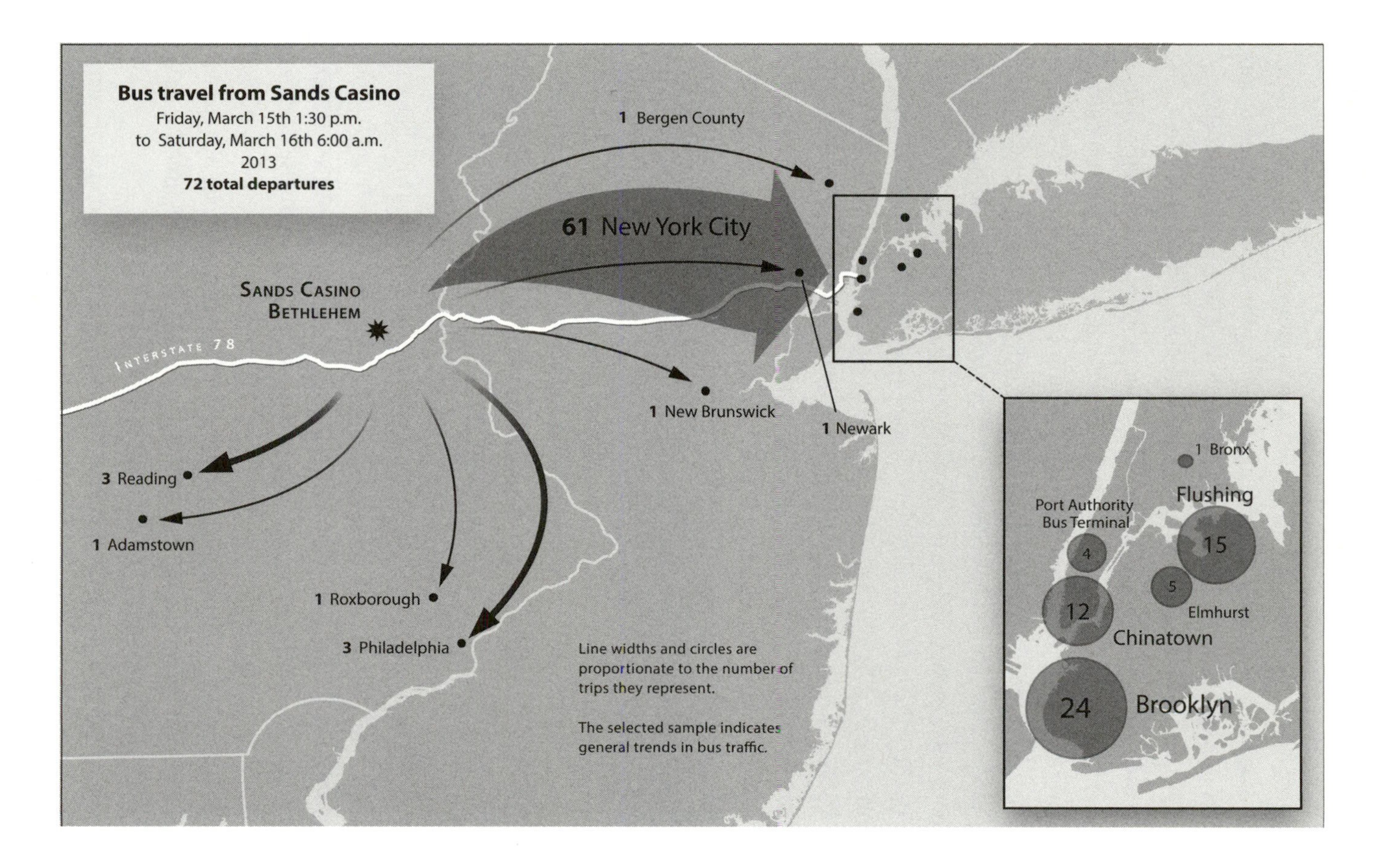
Bus travel from Sands Casino
Friday, March 15th 1:30 p.m.
to Saturday, March 16th 6:00 a.m.
2013
72 total departures
Sands Casino
Bethlehem
Interstate 78
1 Bergen County
61 New York City
1 New Brunswick
1 Newark
3 Reading
1 Adamstown
1 Roxborough
3 Philadelphia
Line widths and circles are proportionate to the number of trips they represent.
The selected sample indicates general trends in bus traffic.
1 Bronx
Flushing
Port Authority
Bus Terminal
4
15
5
12
Elmhurst
Chinatown
24
Brooklyn

sometimes illegal, economies. Daily bus trips to Bethlehem might paradoxically reflect a certain vision of upward mobility that syncs with entrepreneurial logics of self-created opportunity.[66]

The bus network also offers a support structure for immigrants or long-term visitors who do not speak English, have few transferable skills, and lack job opportunities in the mainstream economy.[67] For some riders, going to the casino is not so much work as a social event. Like their white and Latino counterparts, many gamblers are elderly, looking for company and entertainment. They may be recent immigrants who have come to join relatives in the United States and have few other contacts.[68] Many, some say most, of the Chinese bus riders that visit the casino do not gamble. Some pool their money and give it to the best player; others sell the free-play vouchers they get with their bus tickets; and others go simply to get away from the city.[69]

Driving into the Sands parking garage, it is not unusual to see Chinese patrons eating the brown-bag lunches they brought from home on the bottom level. Others regularly practice the slow, fluid movements of tai chi, a Chinese martial art, outside the entrance to the bus waiting room. A patron in his seventies reading a Chinese newspaper in the adjacent outlet mall explained to an interpreter that he had been a businessman in Hunan, China, before following his son to the United States in 2011. He said he comes to the Sands to get out of Flushing, where, "I have nothing to do all day." He enjoys Bethlehem because "the environment is clean, there isn't a lot of pollution, and people are polite."[70] I spoke with a Chinese woman in her forties who told me she was spending every day that week at the casino, from one o'clock to six, because she was on vacation from her job in New York. She and the three friends who came with her on the bus don't gamble, but they enjoy hanging out in the mall. Another group of middle-aged day-trippers spent the afternoon playing a Chinese card game at a picnic table outside the ArtsQuest SteelStacks arts center. Unable to speak English, they responded to my efforts to communicate by repeating my word "casino" and pointing down the road, helpfully directing me to where they mistakenly inferred I wanted to go.

Targeting an Asian clientele has been an undeniable economic success for the Sands, and a few non-Asian dealers told me they particularly enjoy manning the baccarat tables because of how much the players get into the game with their dramatic performances of peeling back cards and blowing away pips. But other casino dealers and gamblers are less enthusiastic. As noted earlier, dealers make three-quarters of their wages from tips, which are pooled among all dealers and divided evenly. "I'm not a big fan of Asian games. Not by any means," one dealer, a young white man, told me.

> I understand that they bring in a lot of revenue to the casino. However, I can't tell you the last time an Asian has tipped me. So, from a dealer standpoint, there's not a whole lot of drive to ensure that the Asians have a good time. . . . If you were to tell me that we're going to close up all the baccarat tables and never deal baccarat again, I'd be like, "Hell yeah!" Because that would mean more blackjack tables, more craps tables, and more tips.

Customer service models that stress being sensitive to Chinese gambling behavior, including the fact that China does not have a tipping culture, often rub against the tripartite relationship in which the dealer brokers the exchange of money from gambler to corporation.[71] Without the potential for tips, some dealers' investments in their work are ultimately undermined. Other complaints include language barriers, crowding tables, and "lack of common courtesy." Another white dealer told me he specifically trained in roulette despite the need for baccarat dealers (hence better chances of being hired) because he did not want to interact with Asian customers.

The casino's intense focus on its corporate relationship to Chinese gamblers—its other workforce—not only leaves certain payroll employees feeling neglected, but it also creates tensions with the majority white and Latino local clientele. Acceptance into the U.S. economy does not guarantee social acceptance.[72] Discrimination and exclusion of Chinese immigrants and residents of Chinese descent in the United States has a long and violent history, notably indoctrinated with the Chinese Exclusion Act of 1882 that specifically barred Chinese entry and their naturalization as citizens here until 1943. Similar to other nineteenth- and twentieth-century immigrant groups, including those in Bethlehem, who came to America looking to better their lives, the Chinese faced discrimination that was in large part economically motivated. White workers tagged "foreigners" as competition for jobs and causes of economic recession.[73]

Some locals' twenty-first-century distaste for Chinese people at the casino is racially inflected in ways that are strikingly similar to that of nativist Americans before them who emphasized Chinese propensity for disorder and disease.[74] One man whose fear of the casino's intrusion into Moravian Bethlehem informed his early opposition to its construction now visits the Sands regularly "for entertainment." He is among the many Bethlehem residents who racialize the Chinese and the spaces they traverse through a discourse of deviant behavior and poor hygiene:

> The Asian people are not the same manners. They're rude. They stand over you. They watch you and they talk loud and they bump you in the chair next to you. They make all the restrooms junky and they don't know how to—I won't say it in front of the recording. They bring in their own food. They are just sloppy. Sloppy and dirty. And they make the casino dirty. So that place would be a much nicer place without them.

In a community historically primed for being wary of ethnic change, the impact of globalization becomes an intensely local experience, one that is frequently expressed through ingrained discrimination. "We thought ordinary suburbanites were going to be drifting over from New Jersey. We weren't told about the New York contingent," the same man explained, using the new local euphemism for the Chinese day-trippers. "So you know, what other surprises have they [the casino] got cooking? It makes you very distrustful." For this man and many other Bethlehem residents, Asian clientele represent their distrust for Las Vegas Sands, a distrust that is accentuated by perceptions of racial difference. They believe that the casino is looking out for outsiders and its bottom line, not locals or its dealers. At root, this is a post-Steel economy that *looks different* than they had imagined.

The paradox of attributing both positive and negative social and economic behaviors to "Chinese culture"—depending on one's perspective of whose interests are being served—is not lost on local casino patrons. On the one hand, a slot attendant, in her distaste for Chinese clientele whom she said lack manners and hygiene, believes cultural explanations are insufficient. "They all blame it on their culture. Well, you're not in China anymore. Somebody should be directing them to what the courtesies are in a casino." She denies an overly simplistic view of Chinese culture to assert another simplification, that there are universal expectations for how one should behave when gambling. Despite the fact that the casino industry has a global reach, it is clear in comparing Bethlehem to Macau—where tipping is not expected, for example—that casino culture is not homogenous. Referencing "culture" to explain clashes on the casino floor falsely fixes understandings and expectations of behaviors and beliefs that are actually in constant motion, negotiation, and adaptation to both local and global contexts.

The thousands of daily visitors to the Sands have many motivations, some of which have nothing to do with gambling. Certain observers might see evidence of exploitation where gamblers are treated as a racialized labor force. To others, the bus riders are independently infiltrating their city. In any case, there is a fundamental tension in the "cultural excuse" used to explain their presence. Both exculpatory and accusatory, it highlights the close relationship between economic and moral infrastructures. The casino industry sees the opportunity for profit as validation of both Chinese culture's unique value and of a marketing strategy that tolerates contentious behavior. Local objections to this economic model, on the other hand, highlight the inability to ignore historically embedded expectations that corporate practices will have community benefits. As such, many residents' sense of moral behavior, right down to their disgust at gamblers spitting on the casino floor, is tied up with their views of the global economy's efficacy in serving their own needs in addition to corporate profit interests.

"You Don't See Chinamen in Bethlehem": Reasserting Boundaries

If the culture clash on the gambling floor is a product of seemingly boundless global flows of people and capital, flows that are supported by neoliberal policies and business practices, it is not surprising that the tensions have spread beyond the casino walls. Concern among both white and Latino Bethlehem residents about "outsiders'" uses of public space suggests a local, place-based reaction to this purported dissolution of boundaries and an effort to reassert control over the landscape. We saw how the homes and churches in the neighborhoods that surround the former steel plant are reference points for postindustrial experiences of loss and anxiety among a diverse range of residents. Even though the tensions between Latino immigrants and residents of European ancestry remain unresolved, these constituencies find common ground in their frustration with the perceived intrusion of Chinese interlopers into the cultural spaces they dually claim.[75]

The offending foreigners in the eyes of local critics include day-trippers who venture out into the community while they wait for their return buses and, to a lesser extent, the increasing number of Asian American dealers who have been hired at the casino to cater to this clientele. Sands has placed job ads in New York's Chinese and Korean newspapers and recruited Asian employees from other casinos. By 2013 the casino's workforce of more than 2,100 had grown to be 20 percent Asian, roughly seven times the concentration of Asian residents in the city as a whole.[76] Many of the new hires moved their families into the low-rent neighborhoods near the casino, those same neighborhoods that marked an entry point for working-class European and Latino arrivals to the city. As community leader Art Slesak, who is of Slovak descent, explained, "That's what this neighborhood was all along. This is where people came. This was the first stop." While the shared immigrant experience does not go unnoticed, the challenge remains among residents in making that historical continuity relevant in a postindustrial economy that links neighborhood change to individual and community disinvestment, displacement, and competition for resources.

Sofia Sanchez has noticed Asians entering and leaving homes on Mechanic Street, near where she lived as a child. "Now I know what everybody else feels like," she said, comparing the situation to her own experience growing up Puerto Rican in a formerly Hungarian neighborhood. "Are they doing what we're doing, what we did? That you bring somebody over and they stay with you until they can get their own place? I haven't figured that out. Unbelievable, the numbers. Unbelievable." The Chinese population in South Bethlehem increased almost 60 percent in the first five years of the casino's operation, to roughly 450 people. That represents the largest Asian-origin group in the neighborhood, but makes up just 2 percent of total residents.[77] While the increased presence of Asian residents since the casino opened is measurable and certain blocks have shown greater shifts, numbers have fluctuated. The transformation—at least as officially counted by the U.S. Census Bureau—is not as drastic as some make it out to be, suggesting either undercounting by officials, overreaction by residents, or both.

Regardless of quantifiable measures of change, the social impact among many more-established residents is indisputable. As one former steelworker, speaking from life experience, simply stated, "You don't see Chinamen in Bethlehem." The new *visibility* of Asians in Bethlehem, regardless of the fact that the South Side's Lehigh University has a long history of hosting Chinese students, is precisely the issue. Sofia made an effort to get to know the parents of the Asian children enrolled in the neighborhood elementary school where she works. By 2012 there were about a dozen families, she said, marking a noticeable uptick from recent years. Other neighbors, however, remained wary. Coral Lopez described conversations among members of her block watch that sound similar to white discourse about Latino immigrants. "Oriental they call it, Chinese, Korean. And so they're like, 'They had a Jersey license plate. They're probably dealing drugs in here now,'" Coral recounted.

Neighborhood watch, in which resident volunteers keep each other and the police posted on suspicious activity on their blocks and patrol the streets at night, captures a link between fear, anxiety, and spatial policing that often emerges amid economic and demographic change. Cultural critic Jane Jacobs famously advocated in the early 1960s for more resident "eyes on the street" to prevent urban crime. The nationwide neighborhood watch movement emerged most cohesively in the early 1970s, a period in which deindustrialization and racial unrest had taken hold of urban centers. Federal programs such as urban renewal and the War on Poverty were losing credibility as neoliberal policies privatized social services and undercut former expectations of state intervention.[78]

Similar to moving a dead relative out of the blighted St. Michael's Catholic Cemetery, finding ways to regain a sense of control over the landscape counters disruptions in one's sense of a recognizable and secure community. Whether through Neighborhood Watch or individual practices, the policing of public space in Bethlehem becomes a mode by which the surveilling community defines place and regulates moral and social boundaries,

No Trespassing

These signs were installed around the perimeter of a technology firm on the west end of the Steel site in 2012. The Chinese translates as: "Private Property, No Trespassing." It is common to see warning signs on Steel-site construction projects posted in Chinese as well. (Photo by author, 2015.)

protecting against unwanted risk and contamination.[79] Social critic Mike Davis has argued that this type of boundary-making is the zeitgeist of urban design in the neoliberal age, particularly as it denies access to an underclass that disrupts the shiny and hopeful aesthetic of urban redevelopment and the image of equal opportunity it projects. Davis explains that the built environment is "full of invisible signs warning off the underclass 'Other.'"[80] Signals might include benches that discourage laying down, hard-to-find building entrances, or a lack of public toilets.

In South Bethlehem, some of these signs are not invisible at all. For many established residents, the potential for disorder is embodied in the most mobile local representatives of global capital and migrations—the casino's Chinese bus riders. On a walk one day in the summer of 2012, I noticed new signs installed outside a technology firm about a mile west of the casino. They marked the building's perimeter, including a large grass lawn, as private property. Most striking was that the red words on the signs were not only in English and Spanish, but also in Chinese. The clear target was the increasing number of nonresident Chinese gamblers who venture outside the casino complex while they wait for their return buses to New York.

The presence of Chinese visitors walking around Bethlehem is new enough that I was even startled by their increased visibility between my two summers of residence in 2011 and 2012. Aware of the problematic tendency to exaggerate ethnic difference, I, like others, nonetheless saw this clientele as distinctly out of place when they congregated on the sidewalks, walked the streets with umbrellas shading against the sun, or sat in bus shelters reading Chinese-language newspapers. My first impression on seeing an increased number of Asian visitors walking down the Third Street business corridor on the South Side, however, was that finally the casino boosters' claims that the Sands would bring tourists into the community had been realized. When I noticed more Chinese tourists congregating on the benches in the shadow of the former steel plant's blast furnaces and Blower House outside the ArtsQuest SteelStacks arts center, it seemed as if developers' expectations—that cultural activities at ArtsQuest would help to disseminate the capital drawn to the casino—were coming true. And yet I soon learned that, in many peoples' eyes, these Asian visitors were the "wrong type" of public for the reinvigorated space and community placemaking they envisioned.[81]

"A lot of local people are sort of a little perturbed about them starting to filter out into the community," one resident explained. Sofia, whose public elementary school is only a few blocks from the casino, struggles daily to draw a protective boundary around the recess yard, for example.

> There have been several times where I had to go outside my school and say, "You can't sleep here." Like they'll sit there for hours. Or they'll sleep there. Or they'll smoke. And I tell them, "No smoking, no smoke." [They say,] "Oh, okay, okay." And then I leave them there,

> but when I see our kids go outside for recess, it makes me nervous to have somebody there, and I go out and tell them, "You can't stay here. The kids are here." And then they leave.

Others complain about transgressive behavior along the Greenway, a public path and park lined with benches that was completed in 2012 in place of the former railroad tracks that traversed the South Side. "I already saw one shoulder-deep in a trash can digging around," a South Bethlehem resident told me. "I like yelled, just playing around, 'What the hell are you doing over there?'" He mimicked how the Asian woman looked up, shrugged, and kept digging. "Like no! Don't do that!" Others report that the increasingly visible visitors sometimes move and use peoples' patio furniture along the Greenway, take vegetables out of residents' gardens, and publicly urinate. Many of the day-trippers are recent immigrants from rural areas of China. Accordingly to police, most offenses are misunderstandings about private property. Other actions, such as reports of taking ducks from the river or washing in public facilities also speak to the fact that many of the visitors are poor. Some actually depend on the daily bus rides for a place to sleep.[82] As on the casino floor, the emphasis on the Chinese visitors' cleanliness, hygiene, and respect for property highlights the perception that the community is being "polluted" by Asian tourists' noncompliance with what residents accept as moral behavior. This framework of contamination and its historical precedents, particularly with anti-Chinese discrimination in the United States, makes clear the relationship between moral, economic, and social decay. Behavioral transgressions like those on the Greenway disrupt ideals of a "healthy" community that is still rebounding from institutional withdrawal, increased poverty, and the dissolution of the social contract.[83]

ArtsQuest representatives said the organization does not have a problem with Asian visitors using the benches and tables outside the SteelStacks arts center—"they're meant for the public"—but they reported issues when the center is closed and public restrooms aren't available.[84] Unlike ArtsQuest's recent efforts to attract and engage the local Latino population with events like the ¡Sabor! Latin Festival, as of 2015 there had been no events at the center specifically targeted at the Asian tourists.[85] According to some observers, ArtsQuest is not interested in promoting celebrations of cultural events like Lunar New Year because Chinese and Korean visitors rarely spend money outside the casino. Getting people to move between the casino and SteelStacks "is ultimately part of the plan," one resident acknowledged. "It's just the Asians go over there and they'll try to get everything comped and for free like they do at the Sands, and it just doesn't work that way." An arts center employee affirmed that if they spent money, "it would probably be a different story," but instead, he said, security guards periodically ask the Asian tourists to move along so as not to "scare off" other visitors.

Public spaces and the publics expected to use them are increasingly linked to opportunities for profit as neoliberal economic policies and public-private development partnerships displace former community understandings of civil liberties and social protections.[86] As the debate over deed prohibitions against labor organizing and free speech on the parcels of land outside the arts center and the city's new visitor center showed, these quasi-public spaces become grounds on which past, place-based models of positive corporate relationships to communities rub uncomfortably against the economic incentives that buttress the casino industry and other private development. Although the parcels of land around the Steel site have deep histories of supporting immigrant and working-class communities, Asian immigrants and tourists are excluded from these unifying narratives. Rather, Chinese gamblers are implicitly linked through local experience to the global restructuring of the manufacturing economy and the social changes that took down Bethlehem Steel and led to community disinvestment and displacement.

One example of the fallout over this association is the belief among some members of the city's large Latino community that they are being sidestepped and pushed out of jobs at the casino. "Somehow the casino trusts the Oriental group to deal with their money more than the Latino," suggested one recent South American immigrant. He speculated that maybe local Latinos, who in 2015 made up only 14 percent of Sands employees—less than two-thirds the number of Asians—have trouble passing the extensive background check that many casino jobs require.[87] Adrian Mendoza, who came to Bethlehem from Puerto Rico in the 1990s, believes the oversight runs deeper. "The problem with economic development of the site, they start building thinking not about the people of the South

Bus Waiting Room

The bus waiting area is located on the bottom level of the casino's parking garage. The room is full at all times of day as many Chinatown bus riders who do not gamble wait hours for their return rides. (Copyright © 2013 Yeong-Ung Yang.)

Side," he said. Adrian pointed to the outlet mall that opened adjacent to the casino in 2012. "You go to the mall that they develop there, they're hiring people bilingual for Mandarin. How is that going to help the people here? I was there. I see the signs in the store." As long as South Side residents face high levels of unemployment, structural crises and inequalities will find expression in other ways, and the Chinese tourists and residents, many of whom like Latinos face economic hardships compounded by ethnic discrimination, provide one outlet for frustrations.

As Adrian suggested, however, discussions about the ways Asians are "ruining" the casino, the neighborhoods, and public places sometimes evolve into a critique of the casino operator itself. Corporate actions, as we've seen, are interpreted as moral choices. Many accuse Las Vegas Sands of turning a blind eye to what they consider Asians' offensive, and in some cases illegal, behavior in the interest of continuing to cash in on their gambling labor and losses. As one local patron said, "They've sold their souls for the few big baccarat players that come in on those buses."[88] From Sands' perspective, one solution to community tensions is a form of containment that responds to locals' desires to define clear spatial boundaries. The Sands doubled the size of its bus waiting area, an uninviting cinderblock enclosure on the first floor of the parking garage, to 175 seats in 2012 and expanded seating at the food court so that day-trippers waiting for their return buses would have less need to leave the casino complex. The strategy suggested that integration and cultural understanding outside the casino walls were beyond the corporation's purview, concern, or realm of possibility, even as the very premise of the casino's business model is to profit from the capital, regulatory, and human mobility that these visitors reflect.

Can You Build a Tolerance for Risk?

In the spaces of the Greenway, the arts center, and the casino's bus terminal, moral, economic, and social threats to community, expressed via accusations of boundaries transgressed and polluted, blend into experiences of vulnerability in a global economy seemingly devoid of local protections. Cultural responses to the uneven effects of the postindustrial economy attempt to bring abstract market terminologies, policies, and technologies into everyday comprehension. Even if casino revenues represent a fungible form of capital to Las Vegas Sands, the postindustrial landscape of which the casino is a part emerges as a resource by which both corporation and community try to anchor the volatility of global profit structures.

One of the most nebulous features of capitalism is and always has been "risk." The ArtsQuest SteelStacks arts center regularly runs a short film in its cinema that focuses on this concept to thematically bridge the city's history from its founding and manufacturing heyday to the post-Steel present.[89] The narrative begins with the arrival of the Moravians on an unpredictable land occupied by Native Americans. Later, Bethlehem Steel president Charles Schwab is characterized as a "risk-taking entrepreneur" who "gambled the entire company's future" in the early twentieth century with his "incredibly risky venture" and decision to invest millions in borrowed money in a new process for making structural steel. The film chalks the decline of the steel industry up to a failure to continue this high-stakes approach to business as the plant became a "dinosaur that couldn't compete" and was constricted by union contracts and a shortsighted management. The narrative thus draws parallels between the Steel's early activity and the postindustrial present, both of which operate absent the interim period's union and other institutional protections.[90] In this telling of the story, risk-taking is unquestioned as the favorable way of doing business.

The term "risk," like other language of economic progress and globalization, carries a universalizing quality that connotes objective analysis and condenses a multiplicity of concerns into a single calculation.[91] The pervasive discourse and generally accepted import of risk-taking in the global economy is, like gambling, fundamentally forward-looking. For corporations like Las Vegas Sands, taking risks in the present—for example, building an island in Macau on which to invest billions of dollars in casino resorts—is a calculated and necessary move to make money in the future.

On the gambler's end, the probable outcome of taking risks is likewise calculable: the casino model guarantees that the majority of players will lose money. But individuals nonetheless understand and interpret risk in a variety of ways that make sense of past experiences. I asked Jeremy Bergman, a young blackjack dealer-in-training who used to enjoy making trips to try his luck in Atlantic City, whether learning the "house" side of the game had changed his outlook on gambling.

> I mean, I'm more wary of it. I'm definitely—I go to gamble with my buddies. It's always been for fun. But now I'm going to make sure I only bring a little bit of money, and if I lose it, I'm done. If I win, I'm gone. There's no high hopes of hitting it big. You're most likely, if you hit big, you're going to think, "All right, I'm lucky." And you'll lose it all.

On a macro level, he agreed that risk-taking is a sure-bet loss for players in this industry. But Jeremy complicated his objective analysis minutes later when he mentioned that his parents go to the Sands Bethlehem every weekend and that his dad not too long ago won a car.

> *CT:* Does he still think he's going to win big again, or does he also realize he got lucky?
>
> *JB:* Well, my mom and dad *are* pretty lucky. But I mean, they still go and try. But they only take a little bit of money with them. They use their free play and—I mean, my mom won $200,000 on the Powerball [lottery] too. . . . So they're lucky.

In contrast to my use of the term "lucky" to denote the arbitrariness of his father's win, Jeremy's matter-of-fact tone reflected a conviction that his parents are intrinsically lucky people (and responsible gamblers) that will not come out on the losing end. Personal relationships with and narratives about the few individuals who win big culturally validate the benefits of taking risks, not just in the casino, but in the broader contexts of economic policies and entrepreneurial undertakings. The upside of risk, however, is in these cases reconceptualized as individualized luck or foresight, rather than the collective gains that the peak years of the steel industry represented for its workers. After all, the benefits now are predicated on others' losses. In this sense the risk economy directly denies the mid-century maxim that a rising tide would lift all boats.[92] Suggesting that those who fail to come out ahead are either irresponsible gamblers or just plain "unlucky" people ultimately legitimates postindustrial economic inequality.

The appeal of neatly encapsulating the postindustrial experience in terms of risk or luck also is at odds with the fundamental uncertainty upon which these notions are premised. As a local financial advisor explained to me, beyond the falsely universalizing implications of risk's positive effects, the "objectivity" of risk-analysis also remains in many ways a farce. Since competition is no longer local—it is rather against people you don't even know exist—"you can't identify all the risk," he said. Moreover, to the economically disadvantaged individual or community, risk generally carries not the potential for gain, but a troubling valence of danger. As the experience with Chinese immigrants and visitors in Bethlehem shows, heightened anxiety and fear—economically, socially, or otherwise—also tend to strengthen cultural and spatial lines of division.[93] By contrast, the continuing relevance of the past in Bethlehem and memories of postwar social protections suggest there are opportunities to rein in the most volatile and inequitable aspects of a global risk culture by re-embedding local expectations for cross-cultural stability and security.

The global and local are, in the end, not oppositional; they refer to the co-construction of economic and social systems at multiple scales. Through its industrial-themed casino, Las Vegas Sands in some ways offers assurance to the Bethlehem community that its past is relevant and its location is important and unique. Its workers adopt the language of the factory to describe their work despite fundamentally weakened social safety nets. In steel and concrete, with orange lights and exposed beams to reference the steel plant that once operated on the site, the casino places and legitimates an otherwise amorphous market, whether it's based on playing the slots or, for shareholders like former steelworker Arnold Strong, playing the stocks. Is Las Vegas Sands then, in effect, able to *build* a tolerance for risk? If so, does it offset or protect in any real way against volatility and danger? Or do structural improvements—in both the physical and institutional senses—reach no deeper than appearances, like the "facelifts" prescribed for the homes on Steel Avenue?

Bethlehem native Perry Buckman earlier noted of the casino that now occupies the Steel site that "the whole thing's a sham. It's a big film set. There's lights, glitter, and it's—what's behind? Is that the Wizard of Oz back there? There's no there, there." For him, a physical structure does little to ground the intangibility of what is produced in a gambling and entertainment economy or to justify the risk. To others, including many historic preservationists or politicians like the mayor, the industrial-theming of the architecture, regardless of whether it was an appeasement tactic, nonetheless opens the door to other investments and reuse projects. There is new potential to actively document the history of the Steel site or attract more economic development that will benefit the community, even if the casino itself is not viable in the long term.

In some ways, making narrative, geographic, and cultural links between Bethlehem Steel and the casino is a futile effort. As Robert DeSalvio, the former Bethlehem casino president said, and many residents echoed, there is no comparison between The Age of the Steel and The Age of the Sands. DeSalvio is not ignorant or dismissive of Bethlehem's local history. But by adopting a narrative of progression, one that relegates the manufacturing economy to the past, he denied certain continuities. The steel heritage of the city, he said,

> was a great platform for us to reinvigorate a site that had gone dormant. But let's face it, we are something that is 180 degrees from what manufacturing and Bethlehem Steel did on the site. And you think about the history of the site and it's now gone through three complete iterations. This was an agricultural site before Bethlehem Steel, and then it had one hundred-plus years of incredible manufacturing industrial history, and then the site went dormant in 1995.

> And we come in to reinvigorate the site on a completely different mixed-use, entertainment-type facility and an integrated resort. So in no shape or form can we mask this as a replacement for an industrial site. It's just a new use.

Although the Sands created as many jobs as were lost at the very end when the plant's structural steel department shut down, it will never compare to employment on the site during the heyday of production, nor the hourly wages, benefits, and protections that steelworkers earned. A comparison of Las Vegas Sands Corp.'s global earnings to Bethlehem Steel's likewise reveals that the casino company's stunning profits surpass all of Bethlehem Steel's twentieth-century records while employing far fewer workers, even as Las Vegas Sands brings in only half of the Steel's peak revenues.[94] By many metrics these are fundamentally different economies.

While residents regularly draw on the past to make sense of the present, they are less eager to draw a different parallel between the two businesses—the "Honeymoon's Over" narrative that might suggest Las Vegas Sands, as a global corporation, could, like the Steel, ultimately abandon the city and evade its social commitments to less-mobile stakeholders. Jenny Fosco, an outspoken critic of developers' lack of historical reverence, reworked DeSalvio's narrative progression from the Moravians to the Sands to highlight a different connection:

> Bethlehem has had this big gorilla always telling it what to do. You had the Moravians, which were a closed sect for almost one hundred years. Then they sort of ran out of money and that's why they sold the farmland that became the Steel, the iron and steel, because they needed the money. So they open up and they sort of ran the town. Then you have railroads, canals, iron, steel, all with [nineteenth-century industrialist Asa] Packer coming in. They rule. Bethlehem Steel's just shy of one hundred years when it collapses. Now you have the casino. It's like another big gorilla. . . . I think the people of Bethlehem, if you will, and the greater area have always sort of just followed. You're part of the Moravians, you're part of the heavy industry or whatever. The Steel told you what to do. And now it's the casino.

A steelworker's daughter, Jenny rightly remembers that the story of the Steel is not entirely a positive one. The connections between the past cultural, economic, and geographic divisions with which this book opened and the ongoing tensions between Bethlehem's various ethnic groups today attests to the fact that historical continuity can have a negative underbelly. Narratively, as well as ritually and materially, Bethlehem's landscape is nonetheless a rich resource for residents to variously interpret what it means to live in a postindustrial community and experience economic change. While DeSalvio emphasized rupture and Jenny focused on ominous similarities between the eras, we have seen others push back on dominant discourses of forward-looking economic development plans through the positive meanings they draw from their work, historic preservation, their religious institutions, and their neighborhoods.

As its links to Macau and other international market-places attest, the experience of postindustrialism in Bethlehem is constantly changing. Freezing a place in amber and refusing to adapt to the ongoing process of deindustrialization has little practical potential. And yet, rather than "learn to love volatility," as champions of footloose capital mobility advise,[95] or "build" an acceptance of risk through architectural façades, the residents of Bethlehem and the Lehigh Valley suggest that historically sensitive redevelopment, supported by institutions that continue to recall a time when security, stability, and accountability were part of an agreement between corporations and the communities in which they are located, can be part of a global economy.

Conclusion

Postindustrial Planning and Possibility

BETHLEHEM MAY BE DEFINED by its unique histories, global connections, and political and economic influences, but the city's experience of postindustrial transition—and the ongoing implications for its citizens—finds echoes in many other locales. In the first decades of the twenty-first century, casino gambling was at the center of debates about urban futures across the United States. New York's voters, for example, approved an expansion of commercial casinos as a solution to fiscal woes in 2013. The Southern Tier, the central part of the state near the Pennsylvania border that had once employed thousands at industrial plants including General Electric, IBM, and the Endicott-Johnson shoe company, initially had been a target for investment, but state gaming commissioners excluded the region from its first round of recommendations for three casino licenses in 2014. The very same day, the governor announced a ban in New York on hydraulic fracking, the lucrative but controversial process of natural gas extraction, due to public health concerns. As one local put it, "The casinos went down, fracking went down—come on; this place is dead in the water now." He implied that the corporate extraction of local resources—whether natural gas or gamblers' paychecks—was the only way to keep the region afloat. Ten months later the gaming commissioners reversed course and backed a license for the Southern Tier.[1]

To the east, Massachusetts had not long before become the fortieth state to embrace casino gambling via a 2011 law allowing three resorts and one slots facility. Several developers who showed early interest had their eyes on shuttered industrial sites. Global casino titan Wynn Resorts bid to build on a former Monsanto chemical plant along the Mystic River outside

Boston. Wynn lured Robert DeSalvio, the president of the Bethlehem casino, away from Las Vegas Sands in 2014 in hopes of replicating his success with ushering a brownfield project through the state licensing process. The decision proved fruitful, and after winning a license that fall, Wynn took the first steps to remediate the polluted land and open a $1.6 billion property by 2018.

Meanwhile, former manufacturing hub Detroit, home to three downtown casinos since 1999, found itself immersed in municipal bankruptcy in 2013. A judge ruled that the city could retain access to the casinos' tax revenue given that the roughly $180 million in annual income represented one of the city's most stable sources of money. It was critical to keeping the city operable and funding its pension obligations. With the city's immediate needs met, Detroit was permitted to back out of a previous deal that had pledged these funds as collateral against paying other debts. In other words, the casino revenues had been implicated in the descent into bankruptcy in the first place.[2]

Atlantic City, which had since the 1970s bet on gambling as the key to urban revitalization, faced a different crisis. Four of Atlantic City's twelve casinos closed in 2014, including the $2.4 billion Revel resort that had opened just two years earlier. The closures left more than 8,000 casino employees out of work, numbers reminiscent of factory shutdowns and downsizings a generation earlier. Much like the Bethlehem steelworkers two decades before, Atlantic City workers who transferred to casino properties in neighboring states found that they lost workplace seniority or had to spend days off commuting back to their families in New Jersey.[3] New Jersey legislators proposed that the best solution for this blow to the economy might be to build more casinos in the northern part of the state to draw back the New Yorkers that were going to Bethlehem instead.

What all of these examples make clear is that the postindustrial legalization of casino gambling has fostered close, and in many cases dependent, relationships between state and municipal governments and casino corporations such that the ability to fund basic social services and economic growth is contingent upon the gaming industry's profitability.[4] Pennsylvania, which has reaped more than $1.3 billion in tax revenues from casinos in recent years, more money than any other U.S. gaming jurisdiction, emerged as a model for other states crafting legislation.[5] Many states that joined the fray, such as Ohio, Maryland, and Massachusetts, had grown tired of their citizens gambling (and, in effect, paying taxes) across state borders, preferring that they lose their money at home instead. An increasingly saturated market, however, meant casinos would start to cannibalize each other's profits as the pool of gamblers spread thin. As a result, Pennsylvania's gaming revenue plateaued by 2012, and legislators began to look for new sources of income. Much as dealers often switch jobs to "chase tips" at newer or trendier casinos, state lawmakers proposed expanding, as New Jersey had, into online gambling or allowing satellite locations of the casinos it had already licensed.

The close relationship between corporate growth and municipal services is not a new one, as Bethlehem's history can attest. But what does it portend for postindustrial redevelopment if revitalizing communities with private investment is contingent on their residents' ongoing sacrifices in the forms of declining wages, weakened job security, and gambling losses? The privatization of social protections and their vulnerability to incongruous funding priorities point toward broader trends that define the rise of "casino capitalism" far beyond the gaming industry. In this era of neoliberal economic reforms, individual risk-taking is valued over institutional safety nets. This is as much the case in government policies that cut welfare benefits and undermine collective bargaining as it is in the finance and technology sectors. In the world of big business, by the late 1990s, the paradigm of a social contract between industry and community had been replaced by the ubiquitous language of "corporate social responsibility," or CSR. Such CSR programs—in the gaming industry and elsewhere—emphasize charitable giving, workplace diversity, and commitments to environmental sustainability. Critics, however, argue that CSR is ultimately a form of corporate risk management, a flexible system of self-regulation designed to preempt more prescriptive or binding state-based calls for corporate contributions to public welfare.[6]

In this context of precariousness, harnessing corporate profit for social benefit has become one of the primary challenges that today's cities face. The interventions that policymakers, developers, and citizens make in the postindustrial landscape, I have argued, is crucial to this effort to "ground" liquid capital. It may seem optimistic to hope that the tools of urban planning can be used to reinvigorate connections between social accountability and economic profit. After all, casino-led development projects make clear that global capital maintains significant clout when pitting the needs of far-flung shareholders against calls for more localized understandings of "corporate community." The casino licensing process and debate in Bethlehem showed how little power residents had to block a casino in their city given that the Pennsylvania law had been written to deny a voter referendum. While Las Vegas Sands did not face a legal barrier to winning a state gaming license, the corporation nonetheless sought what is in CSR circles called a "social license," the assurance that community members would accept and facilitate, or at least not impede, its opening.[7] Indeed, many residents understood the Sands Casino's architectural allusions to the Steel's industrial history, its charitable donations to various local organizations, and even its first president's affable personality, to be part of an appeasement process to "get a foot in the door." One historic preservationist reflected the views of many critics when she referred to this asymmetrical relationship as the city's "Faustian bargain with legalized gambling and for-profit interests."[8] But even among the staunchest opponents, these gestures seemed to make the best of a done deal.

In an odder twist on how we think of casinos' social commitments, the Sands Casino has emerged as an unlikely and inadvertent lifeline where other urban protections have failed. Many immigrant bus riders make a living by selling their free-play vouchers and have no homes besides the bus waiting area.[9] An elderly bus rider who immigrated to New York from China, but was unable to work after a construction job injury, explained how a few times when he was seriously ill he had waited for someone in the Bethlehem casino to call an ambulance. Unable to speak English, it was the best and most efficient way he could think of to get medical treatment. "If you have money," he said, "a casino would lead you to death. But if you have no money, a casino could save your life."[10] This fundamental distortion of the social safety net presages great risk, even as it creates small openings for creative reworking of the free-market systems and entrepreneurial values that dominate economic and political discourse. Without attention to structural cracks and inequalities of the kind that class and ethnic tensions in Bethlehem reveal, these disparities will eventually bring any holdovers of social stability tumbling down.

Understanding postindustrialism as a period of continuous flux, rather than a clear-cut and inevitable stage in the forward march of market evolutions, thus opens up any number of outcomes—benefits as well as injuries. In contrast to thinking of deindustrialization as a clean break with a past economy and way of life, the experiences in Bethlehem, in all of their variety, make a strong case that the postindustrial landscape is neither a wasteland to be summarily discarded nor a blank slate for building pristine new futures. The closure of the Bethlehem plant was for many steelworkers, city officials, and other residents a defining moment and breaking point that foreclosed possibilities of once-stable futures. But lived from day to day, postindustrialism reflects an ongoing process marked by complicated, and at times paradoxical, continuities that also challenge well-worn categories of "before" and "after."

In casino dealers' assessments of the "line work" they perform, and in Bethlehem's transforming immigrant communities, for example, presumed historical divisions between manufacturing and service work and between local and global economies dissolve. Assumptions that so-called rational corporate actions exist outside of moral frameworks, or that economic and cultural displacement are distinct experiences become untenable when one dives into the swirls of concern over the casino licensing process or the Catholic church closures. Bethlehem has been a continuous global market*place* since the eighteenth century, a context in which abstract financial transactions always take on site-specific meanings and implications.

Asserting that a community's past commitments are still relevant and active has practical implications for economic development in our cities today. Residents, politicians, and developers regularly use the postindustrial landscape and the pasts embedded in it as both a resource and a weapon to make sense of and shape these ongoing transitions. For example, when the Sands Casino Bethlehem security guards voted to unionize in 2011 as Local 777 of the Law Enforcement Employees Benevolent Association, they shadowed the history of hard-fought labor struggles on the Steel site during the twentieth century. But union membership in communities across the United States has become a defensive position rather than a secure one.[11] After the guards accused Las Vegas Sands of unfairly blocking their attempts to negotiate a contract, Sands' attorneys likewise drew on the history of the casino site. Sands argued that the new organizing effort was directly and improperly affiliated with a non-guard union, USW Local 2599—the group that had represented the Bethlehem steelworkers. In making its case to the National Labor Relations Board (NLRB), Sands cited pictures on social media showing one of the guards, a former steelworker, wearing a Local 2599 shirt to visit his newborn grandchild at the hospital. Sands pointed to union materials that referred to the land on which the casino sits as "hallowed ground" as proof of the organizing effort's continuity with the steelworkers' labor activities.[12] Although the NLRB dismissed this "evidence" and determined that Sands' refusal to bargain with the workers was illegal, that decision was in many ways beside the point. Armed with ample legal funds to entangle the new local in a prolonged NLRB process, Sands' actions reflected a corporate tactic with its own long legacy; it was a way to delay union recognition and contract negotiation.[13]

Meanwhile, aside from Sands' commitment to keeping the blast furnaces from falling down while the casino is in operation, there are no written agreements with the city concerning the company's pledged reuse of other structures on the Steel site.[14] Looming competition from casinos in neighboring states, new and more attractive tax incentives offered to developers in nearby Allentown, and Las Vegas Sands' stated willingness to sell the Bethlehem business for the right price, have had Mayor Callahan and his successors moving to address the rest of the Steel site with urgency.[15] The mayor said the city "need[ed] to take advantage of this window of opportunity, so to speak," to develop the rest of the former brownfield so that it will be "not as reliant solely on gaming for its success." The uncertain economic climate supports opportunistic market logics, even as longer-term stability and heritage preservation remain the desired community goals. As slot attendant Julia Krause told me, "If something happens with the casino, things go bad, I think it's going to be another problem. But right now things are looking good."

Accountable Development and Casino Urbanism

In the face of all this economic, political, and social insecurity, what the future holds for Bethlehem and cities like it is not a foregone conclusion.

More than a process of zoning approvals and engineering, planning will be key to fixing capital in place and ensuring that long-term protections will be a part of economic growth. Other communities faced with such uncertainty have begun to formalize their "social licenses" with wealthy developers. As urban real estate became more attractive to investors in the late 1990s, for example, a new type of legally binding contract called a "community benefits agreement" (CBA) emerged to ensure that local residents would gain from economic growth. A CBA consists of a set of commitments a private developer makes directly to community members in order to win their support and smooth a path through regulatory approvals. Common stipulations go beyond vague expectations of tax revenue and jobs to include specific promises such as living wages, local hiring quotas, affordable housing, environmental remediation, or funds for community programs.[16] Part of what has been called a "new accountable development movement," CBA negotiations and their inclusion of resident voices stand in contrast to the top-down approaches that characterized urban renewal in vulnerable communities across the United States at mid-century, including the sanctioned displacement of the Northampton Heights neighborhood so that Bethlehem Steel could build a new furnace.

However, CBAs remain relatively rare. A few dozen have been enacted across the United States for a range of projects that include mixed-use urban development and stadium construction.[17] Two casinos, the SugarHouse Casino in Philadelphia and MGM in Prince George's County, Maryland, have entered into such agreements in recent years. While Sands' charitable donations to organizations in the Lehigh Valley fluctuate from year to year, SugarHouse, for example, has committed $1 million annually to community programs within a designated area around the property. Other stipulations in the two agreements include making efforts to hire local residents and use local vendors, maintaining public access to the riverfront, renovating vacant community buildings, specifying employee health benefits, and instituting workforce training programs.[18]

While the durability of these accountable development tools remains uncertain, they attempt to reinsert an active mechanism of citizen participation in and control over urban economic development. Massachusetts introduced a distinct but related process in its gaming law to get promises of community benefit in writing. Casino developers seeking state licenses were required to sign "host community agreements" with the cities in which they proposed to locate before the state commission would consider their applications. In contrast to what happened in Pennsylvania, the host communities then had to pass voter referendums affirming their residents' support. Voters overwhelmingly approved the proposals of Las Vegas-based corporations Wynn and MGM to build casinos in Everett and Springfield, respectively—bids that were ultimately successful—but a series of surprises followed with the defeats of voter referendums in West Springfield (Hard Rock), Palmer (Mohegan Sun), East Boston (Suffolk Downs), and Milford (Foxwoods). By the end of the licensing process, only a handful of applicants remained.[19]

The Massachusetts gaming commission included another curious requirement in the casino licensing process that challenged typical pro-growth boosterism. Among 211 questions on the licensing application, potential operators were asked to: "Describe the design features that will allow other uses of the buildings in the gaming establishment complex in the event that the applicant decides to cease gaming operations in the facility at some future date." Applicants, faced with a question asking them to undermine their own business pitches, expressed firm beliefs that such a time would never come. "We view this question as more theoretical in nature," MGM replied, despite the fact that not long after, Atlantic City would struggle to come up with ways to reuse four newly vacant casino resorts. Applicants described alternative uses such as convention space, destination retail and dining, or a satellite university campus.[20] Regardless of the practicality of any of the responses, the question was notable in that it briefly turned attention away from the short-term fix of gambling revenues and toward long-term planning.

As casino executives are increasingly asked to think and act like urban planners, the Massachusetts experiment actively promotes integrating redevelopment projects into existing urban cores. In many ways, the plans dreamed up for the postindustrial Bethlehem Steel site had reflected such an ideal from the start. Gated off from the community for a century before it closed, the acres of vacant land in the heart of the city presented local officials, corporate executives, and residents an opportunity to reconnect the brownfield to the surrounding neighborhoods. Early plans proposed "forging a future" via cultural amenities, various entertainment facilities, and loft-style condominiums, but it was ultimately casino gambling that proved able to foot the bill. By 2012 delegations from cities in Massachusetts that sought to attract casino capital to confront their own economic slumps were making pilgrimages to Bethlehem to seek advice.[21]

Developers, pressured by policymakers and residents to come up with visions that extend beyond casino walls, have increasingly put forth plans for projects that incorporate the broader postindustrial landscape and include community amenities. MGM Springfield's fifty-four page host community agreement, for example, contains a number of stipulations that actively connect the casino to the city's downtown, an area that had struggled to recover from tornado damage a few years earlier as well as the sustained effects of deindustrialization, demographic transformations, and class inequality. To win a gaming license, MGM agreed, among other commitments, to sponsor Springfield's sports teams, improve transportation and sewer systems, reuse and incorporate certain historic buildings into its design, and build a childcare center and public outdoor ice rink.[22] Although MGM, like Las Vegas Sands, reaps billions of dollars in profits from properties around the world, for Springfield this reflected a new local infrastructure—material and social—that could be both inclusive and durable.

Despite claims that globalization has made localities irrelevant, the emergent casino urbanism is anchored in market-places. It is not inconsequential that a community's success in securing a CBA or similar type of agreement for equitable development depends on the ability to leverage those aspects of the postindustrial economy that cannot be outsourced, namely the value attached to particular geographic locations. Communities that successfully challenge the structures of economic growth that indiscriminately support private profit can tip the balance back toward place-based social accountability and public good. At the least, there is an opportunity to move beyond an oppositional, and often ineffective, "not-in-my-backyard" model of spatial resistance toward a process of negotiation in which place is valued in multiple ways for a diverse set of interests.[23]

Alas, this vision of citizen engagement by which one might redistribute the advantages of urban development faces a number of significant challenges. In cities still reeling from the ongoing effects of deindustrialization and the accompanying loss of jobs and tax bases, nearly any promise of economic development seems too good to pass up. Whether it is a casino, fracking, a prison, or a landfill, even the most damaging or unsustainable industries offer a lifeline—even if a short one—for sinking economies. The deep pockets that private corporations have to remediate brownfields, purchase large parcels of vacant land, and make other interventions that are out of reach of municipal or state governments entrench conciliatory relationships in which money still calls the shots. Contracts asking corporations to hire local residents or contribute to community development funds often include ambiguous language requiring "good faith" or "commercially reasonable" efforts that can be difficult to enforce. Even with a written agreement, many communities are reluctant to appear "anti-business" and confront a developer that seems to be keeping the local economy afloat, regardless of whether jobs created or charitable donations live up to expectations.[24]

Finally, casino urbanism prompts the question: do we want for-profit developers acting as master planners for our cities? Public funding to cities has been declining for decades. In a competitive corporate environment, decisions about how much to invest in a community, including social programs or public infrastructure, are invariably subject to bottom-line calculations. Building a reputation as a "good corporate citizen" is not purely an ethical commitment; it offers a return on investment in terms of smoothing paths toward zoning approvals or quelling dissent that could detract from business. Planning interventions that present no direct upside from the for-profit perspective will remain difficult to attain. These are likely to include projects that might benefit low-income or otherwise disenfranchised residents, such as truly affordable housing, general job training and support, or investments in early childhood education. Whether accountable development agreements can become standard enough practice to effectively serve the needs of both capital and community over the long term thus remains an open question.

Looking Forward and Back

In the absence of or alongside formal CBAs and other accountable development agreements, residents also find ways to push back and demand recognition in their everyday interactions with the built environment. A manufacturing economy on the scale of the Steel is not coming back to Bethlehem, but neither is the ubiquitous vision of the postindustrial American city as a middle-class playground, a white-collar office park, or a neon-lit gambling destination a predestined outcome for urban development projects. Rather than wait for private developers to call all the shots for how the land in South Bethlehem should be used, residents have taken proactive steps to have their voices heard by building upon the openings that a landscape in flux provides.

The Sands' reconfiguration of the South Side as a gateway to the city for gamblers and tourists has refocused the attention of politicians, residents, and other developers toward long-neglected neighborhoods. Across from the casino on the Greenway, for example, the city built a park for skateboarders in 2010 in response to a decade-long grassroots campaign. The Bethlehem Skateplaza proved wildly popular in bringing together area youth of all backgrounds. The thirty-year-old small business owner who spearheaded the effort explained to me the plaza's deeper significance: "Now [the kids] don't have a reason just to kind of say, 'What's the local government ever done for me?' There's something there that they use on a daily basis that was built for them." The Skateplaza later added public restrooms, an amenity that the Sands' bus patrons have eagerly taken advantage of as well. The fresh interest in the South Side as a promising site for economic development has created other new spaces for overlooked residents to voice their concerns and desires. Despite the fact that Bethlehem has for decades had a large and growing Latino population, there had only been two Latinos on the seven-member city council, one in the 1960s and one in the early 2000s. That changed in 2015 when two Bethlehem citizens of Latino descent were elected, signaling the growing recognition that the city's immigrant neighborhoods face both specific challenges and unique opportunities.[25]

Other resident interventions into the postindustrial landscape draw explicitly on the city's industrial heritage to guard against being overpowered or silenced by new development. In the summer of 2015, the Hoover-Mason Trestle, an elevated rail line that had carried cars full of raw material from the ore yard and coke works to be converted into molten iron in the blast furnaces, reopened as a linear park modeled after New York's trendy High Line. Former steelworkers who previewed the new landscaped pathway looked out from the heights of the furnaces for the first time since the fires went cold twenty years earlier. The park represented a $15 million investment funded by the tax increment financing (TIF) district on the Steel site that captures the increased property taxes resulting from redevelopment. The Hoover-Mason Trestle begins at the Stock House Visitor Center across from ArtsQuest and is designed to connect pedestrians all the way to the casino. When the new park opened, however, it stopped prematurely, waiting for Las Vegas Sands to first move ahead with lagging redevelopment plans for the adjacent No. 2 Machine Shop.

In the meantime, a group of community organizations calling itself the Bethlehem Heritage Coalition successfully asserted its interest in telling the history of the site by helping to research and write content for an audio tour and series of interpretive panels along the elevated walkway. Coalition members included the Steelworkers' Archives, Historic Bethlehem Museums and Sites (formerly the Historic Bethlehem Partnership), and other groups that had previously been described as being unable to play in the same "sandbox."[26] The story they came together to author recounts the history of Bethlehem Steel and its buildings, the steelmaking process, and the South Side neighborhoods. It weighs noticeably toward the perspective of steelworkers who toiled in dangerous conditions and fought for union protections. A panel at the east end of the trestle describes how the city, concerned about the economic impact of the plant's closure, "initiated a revitalization effort," based on commercial, arts, and entertainment development, "while citizens of Bethlehem and former steelworkers fought to preserve the structures." Although the phrasing implies that growth politics and residents' attachments to historic buildings were end goals at odds, the interpretation concludes that Bethlehem today has found a "balance" between the two.

The legacy of "historic renewal" in Bethlehem suggests that, more than a balance of oppositional forces, preservation and development have long been part of the same process. As such, the effect of the Hoover-Mason Trestle is a powerful statement on postindustrial connection. Its original function linked different parts of the plant and facilitated steel production; today it connects major sites of new economic development—the arts center and the casino. The trestle promises to bring gamblers and other visitors to attractions outside the Sands' walls, spreading the benefit of new activity.

It also materially bridges Bethlehem's past, present, and future through a mix of old and new structures. The sleek pedestrian path passes rusted ore cars and a boarded up shanty. The signatures that welders drew with molten metal into the steel supports are a visible testament to steelworkers' enduring presence. Perhaps most importantly, the Hoover-Mason Trestle and its interpretive program connected developers and the city with previously fragmented community groups and local residents who felt they had been left out of other plans for the Steel site that focused only on profit potential. "We saw this opportunity to mobilize, and that we were going to be much, much stronger as a collective than we were as individual institutions," a member of the Bethlehem Heritage Coalition explained. The success of this collaboration reinvigorated ideals of citizen engagement and influence in development decisions that—even when referred to as public-private partnerships—are most often controlled by capital interests.

The power of the landscape's bridging function is that it can simultaneously elucidate a distance spanned and define a close connection. On the one hand, some things appear not to have changed. The path of creative destruction that capital forges through both the built environment and the market landscape has shaped life in Bethlehem at least since the Moravians arrived in 1741. Bethlehem's dependence on heavy manufacturing in the twentieth century may have been replaced by today's growing healthcare, education, distribution, and service sectors, but this twenty-first century economy shares much in common with those decades before World War II when non-union laborers competed with other ethnicities for jobs that lacked worker protections, dependable benefits, or living wages.[27] Whether economic development is led by Bethlehem Steel or Las Vegas Sands, corporate ownership and control over the land has long translated into a powerful ability to shape the city's fiscal policies, social structures, and demographic trends. Amid the ongoing transformations that characterize the postindustrial period as one of uncertainty, we might argue that not all continuities of place have been lost.

Portions of the Federal Writers' Project's 1939 guidebook to the region, for example, could slip seamlessly into the present. On the effects of the Steel's capital on the urban landscape, its authors wrote: "The communal plans of [Bethlehem's] founders have given way to individual and corporate ownership on a scale undreamed."[28] It is no far stretch to layer this assessment onto the twenty-first-century casino landscape and the privatized future it portends. When all that is old in Bethlehem seems relevant again, it suggests the new economy may not be so new.

At the same time, the links expressed in the 1939 guide make clear a troubling trajectory toward increased capital mobility delinked from place-based commitments—always idealized but now enabled in more ways than before. I have shown that in everyday experience, residents regularly invoke favorable memories of the past to make sense of these volatile transitions and cling to heritage preservation as a durable protection against social or economic up-endings. But for all the narrative connections one might make by comparing dealing blackjack to working with one's hands or referencing the hard work ethic of one's Hungarian ancestors, the reality is that many people in Bethlehem and in other postindustrial communities are worse off than a generation before. Income inequality in the United States has risen sharply since the 1970s. The proportion of wealth held by the top percentiles of American earners has shown significant increases, driven largely by huge wage increases among corporate executives. Meanwhile, lower- and middle-income households have seen their earnings stagnate or fall, and many have taken on debilitating debt as a result. For those caught in what scholars call the "precarity trap," this has led to increased anxiety, isolation, and antagonism toward others.[29] Those dreams of upward economic and social mobility once realized by so many postwar steelworkers have transformed into a game of chance with much lower odds of advancement.

Bethlehem's community has been fractured since its beginnings, and capital needs have long taken precedence over social ones—even if at times they seemed better aligned. But residents make clear that they have never lost hope for an alternative. Diverse responses to economic change, when brought together, can strengthen the reach of collective resistance to imbalances of power through a process of active placemaking. Like the ore bridge or the Hoover-Mason Trestle, the postindustrial landscape is a connector amid divisive and uneven development agendas. The buildings, memories, and ruins that comprise this landscape are best preserved not as architectural specimens or archival treasures—though many of them are. They should be valued for their more mundane characteristics as everyday touchstones for collective identity and durable checks against the short-term goals of for-profit development. When plans for urban revitalization are attuned to the local histories, cultures, and contingencies that shape places in complex ways, it becomes more difficult to treat citizens as generic consumers. Efforts to engage diverse communities will, by necessity, be more sensitive to the economic and social inequalities that inform daily, lived experiences. As more voices emerge to assert shifting expectations as to who should benefit from urban development projects in the long term, there is reason to hope for, as immigrant resident Javier Parker said, a better "history to look forward to." The postindustrial city could be another site of global capital extraction, or it could anchor dreams of a more equitable future.

Appendix: Note on Methods

My route to this project began as a personal one. My grandfather took a job as a mechanical engineer at the Steel in 1961. He and my grandmother lived in a home near the company's Homer Research Laboratories from 1963, when the Bethlehem Steel Corporation gave them permission to buy a parcel of land for which it had first refusal rights, until they moved to a retirement home in 1994, when I was eleven. Bethlehem—or "Christmas City, U.S.A."—was my family's holiday destination each December. My grandfather retired from Bethlehem Steel in 1977 when he qualified for his pension at age sixty-five. It was just before the corporation went steadily downhill. My mother and her two siblings went to high school in Bethlehem but left for college and, like many children of their generation, never moved back.

For me, returning to Bethlehem as an adult with no remaining family in town meant rediscovering the city as a not-quite-outsider. Over the course of my research, I lived full-time in Bethlehem for two summers (a combined six months in 2011 and 2012), and made frequent shorter trips, especially between 2009 and 2013. During this time, I recorded sixty-four formal interviews with seventy-six people (some were interviewed in pairs or, in one case, a group of three) who lived currently, or at some point in their lives, in Bethlehem or the Lehigh Valley. I began my research by contacting a high school friend of my aunt's whose mother still lived in town and proceeded with a series of cold calls to residents who held community leadership positions or had been vocal in public forums. I approached people at various community events where I conducted participant observation, including city council meetings, parades and festivals, and historical group meetings. My discussion of casino work derived in particular from contacts I made through the local community college's dealer training program. Over the course of the project I depended heavily on snowball sampling from my contacts' social networks.

I spoke with a broad cross section of the community in terms of age, class, gender, ethnicity, and professional background, although the fact that I conducted all interviews in English necessarily precluded some interactions. I depended on contacts who bridged the Spanish-speaking population to relate the concerns of those residents to whom I did not have immediate access. My efforts to speak with Chinese casino patrons were less successful given the language barriers. With some exceptions, I, in the end, relied on journalists and interpreters to convey their voices. My experience of being unable to communicate with the Chinese-speaking population at the casino to a small degree gave me affective access to how their minority status was at odds with the local community outside the casino walls.

The interviews I recorded lasted from twenty minutes to more than six hours; most were between one and two hours. I came with specific areas of interest in mind, asking about memories of the Steel and thoughts about the casino, but rather than begin with a set agenda or falsely assume I held more authority over my informants' experiences than they did themselves, I built my research questions from where these interlocutors guided me. For example, when I began the project I was unaware of the recent consolidation of the five national Catholic parishes in South Bethlehem, but I quickly learned that this event and its ongoing impact captured the emotional connection many residents felt to their former neighborhoods and the relationship between the closures and broader demographic and economic changes. In addition to formal interviews and dozens of informal conversations, I went on various walking and driving tours in the community. Some of these were run by community organizations. In other cases, I accepted personal offers from residents to show me parts of the city (and their own pasts), further elucidating for me the ways in which the landscape is used as a cultural tool to make sense of life experiences.

My archival research included burying myself in local sources at Lehigh University, the Moravian Archives, the Bethlehem Area Public Library, and Historic Bethlehem Partnership, as well as the Clarke & Rapuano papers at Cornell University, which include documentation of several postwar Bethlehem development projects. Although the archival encounter is often considered distinct from the ethnographic one, I found that the two experiences regularly merged. Some informants brought old photographs, newspaper clippings, or community bulletins to our interviews. In other cases, discovering which materials a local archive decided to save and how they were catalogued was as revealing of contemporary concerns and community relationships as it was of the pasts they documented. The Moravian Archives, for example, held shelves of (until I arrived) unopened file boxes of boardroom materials from the final years of the Bethlehem Steel Corporation's existence simply because they otherwise would have been thrown away. Although the materials do not fit the Archives' focus on the Moravians, its directors are reluctant to give up the materials to non-local or non-professional control.

On other occasions, the archive proved a useful site for meeting residents and learning their perspectives on the value their community's past holds in informing its future. One summer afternoon, I found myself sharing the usually empty space in the locked "Bethlehem Room" at the local public library. A woman and her two boys kept a respectful distance as they paged through old city directories. (Later, at a city council meeting, I learned they were seeking information on former commercial uses of a home in their neighborhood so they could launch a zoning challenge.) The mother walked by as I photographed a program celebrating the centennial of South Bethlehem's now-dissolved Italian Catholic Church. "That's my church!" she instantly exclaimed, telling me how her family had gone there for generations, how she grew up and was married there, and how its last priest had dug up his brother in the local cemetery and taken him to Italy with him when he retired. Although the church had been closed at that point for four years, and she had not attended since she moved across the river to a more prosperous neighborhood, her excitement over the centennial program and the discussion it launched embodied the historical consciousness I found so prevalent in the Bethlehem community.

My interdisciplinary approach speaks to multiple audiences. Some readers may have preferred that I documented individual biographies rather than represent worldviews with pseudonyms. Others may find local historical details distracting for making sense of broad trends in contemporary urban life—although I hope I have persuaded them otherwise. I contend that my mixed approach in understanding how economic transition is variously understood and experienced both over time and today makes a case that ethnographic and archival methods, when combined, are uniquely attuned to the blurred pasts, presents, and futures of this postindustrial moment. Together they reveal more about the urban condition than either practice could on its own.

I likewise present a model for studying small cities to understand the American urban landscape writ large. As the many voices in this book make obvious, redevelopment projects have multiple stakeholders. Although I have argued that Bethlehem is no less "global" than Chicago or New York, there is a unique opportunity in a city of 75,000 people to engage with a breadth of community members in ways that may only be possible on a neighborhood or interest-group scale in a larger metropolis. Moreover, although larger cities in the Rust Belt also have lost industrial plants and union jobs, these landscapes of loss and betrayal often are located in peripheral areas both in terms of geography and political attention. In a small city where the closure of a single factory can mean a gaping hole in the local tax base and hundreds of acres of vacant land immediately adjacent to downtown businesses and neighborhoods, its impacts have daily and material visibility both in city politics and in city life. No two postindustrial cities face the same challenges or have the same resources—economic, cultural, or political—to address them. I nonetheless hope that the approach I have taken to understand the Bethlehem community's direct engagement with interpreting and shaping the postindustrial landscape offers a comprehensive model for researching the localized impacts of economic change and adapting targeted interventions to other municipalities.

Notes

Introduction

1. The writers' attention to the plant and its labor force is also reflective of the project's Works Progress Administration funding. Federal Writers' Project (PA), *Northampton County Guide* (Bethlehem, PA: Times Publishing Co., 1939), 7, 75, 146.

2. David Venditta and Ardith Hilliard, eds., *Forging America: The Story of Bethlehem Steel*, 2nd ed. (Bethlehem, PA: The Morning Call, 2010), 45, 91; Bethlehem Steel Corporation, *1955 Annual Report* (Bethlehem, PA: The Corporation, 1956), 17. The city's population in 1940 was 58,490. U.S. Census Bureau, *Sixteenth Census of the United States: 1940: Population*, vol. 1: *Number of Inhabitants* (Washington, DC: Government Printing Office, 1942), 908.

3. See Lizabeth Cohen, *Making a New Deal: Industrial Workers in Chicago, 1919–1939* (Cambridge: Cambridge University Press, 1990); Joshua Freeman, "Delivering the Goods: Industrial Unionism during World War II," *Labor History* 19, no. 4 (1978): 570–593.

4. Kathryn Marie Dudley, *End of the Line: Lost Jobs, New Lives in Postindustrial America* (Chicago: University of Chicago Press, 1994), 177.

5. The casino industry uses the term "gaming" to stress the entertainment value of gambling. I use this softened term when it is in the context of the industry's interests.

6. I use the term "place" to refer to lived space, that is, space made culturally, socially, and/or economically meaningful in the ways people variously experience, talk about, remember, or use it. Places may have permeable boundaries, can change over time, and may hold different meanings for different individuals or groups of people. See Dolores Hayden, *The Power of Place: Urban Landscapes as Public History* (Cambridge, MA: MIT Press, 1995); Henri Lefebvre, *The Production of Space*, trans. Donald Nicholson-Smith (Oxford: Blackwell, 1991); John Agnew, "Space and Place," in *The SAGE Handbook of Geographical Knowledge*, ed. John Agnew and David Livingstone (London: Sage, 2011), 316–330.

7. Matt Assad, "Sands Opening Weekend Tops the Rest," *Morning Call*, May 27, 2009.

8. Daren Follweiler, "Museum 'Detective' Blows the Whistle on Bethlehem Steel," *Bethlehem Globe-Times*, April 21, 1985; Dennis Pearson, "The Normandie Whistle," 2009, http://www.eastlehighearn.com/Flame2.html. Video of the chain cutting and whistle blast can be found here: Bill Adams, "Sands Casino Resort Bethlehem Grand Opening," LehighValleyLive.com, video, 2:13, June 9, 2002, http://videos.lehighvalleylive.com/express-times/2009/06/sands_casino_resort_bethlehem.html.

9. See also Barbara Kirshenblatt-Gimblett, *Destination Culture: Tourism, Museums, and Heritage* (Berkeley: University of California Press, 1998).

10. Video of parts of the speech can be found here: Bill Adams, "Former Bethlehem Steelworker," LehighValleyLive.com, video, 1:59, June 9, 2009, http://videos.lehighvalleylive.com/express-times/2009/06/former_bethlehem_steel_worker.html.

11. Victor Turner famously adapted and extended Arnold van Gennep's 1908 linear theory of rites of passage. Victor Turner, "Social Dramas and Stories about Them," *Critical Inquiry* 7, no. 1 (Autumn, 1980): 141–168.

12. Kevin Lynch, *What Time Is This Place?* (Cambridge, MA: MIT Press, 1972), 168–173.

13. See Judith Schachter Modell, *A Town without Steel: Envisioning Homestead* (Pittsburgh: University of Pittsburgh Press, 1998); Thomas Gerhard Fuechtmann, *Steeples and Stacks: Religion and Steel Crisis in Youngstown* (Cambridge: Cambridge University Press, 1989); William Serrin, *Homestead: The Glory and Tragedy of an American Steel Town* (New York: Times Books, 1992); Steven P. Dandaneau, *A Town Abandoned: Flint, Michigan Confronts Deindustrialization* (Albany: State University of New York Press, 1996); Gregory Pappas, *The Magic City: Unemployment in a Working-Class Community* (Ithaca, NY: Cornell University Press, 1989); June C. Nash, *From Tank Town to High Tech: The Clash of Community and Industrial Cycles* (Albany: State University of New York Press, 1989); John Strohmeyer, *Crisis in Bethlehem: Big Steel's Struggle to Survive* (Bethesda, MD: Adler & Adler, 1986).

14. For a reinterpretation of "deindustrialization" that emphasizes temporal and geographic diversity of experience, see Jefferson Cowie and Joseph Heathcott, eds., *Beyond the Ruins: The Meanings of Deindustrialization* (Ithaca, NY: ILR Press, 2003). For another assessment of limitations to the declension narrative, see Andrew R. Highsmith, "Decline and Renewal in North American Cities," *Journal of Urban History* 37, no. 4 (2011): 619–626.

15. Jill Schennum, "Bethlehem Steelworkers: Reshaping the Industrial Working Class" (PhD diss., City University of New York, 2011), 18–20. An exception to the shock model that conceptualizes deindustrialization as a drawn-out process is Jefferson Cowie, *Capital Moves: RCA's Seventy-Year Quest for Cheap Labor* (Ithaca, NY: Cornell University Press, 1999).

16. Daniel Bell, *The Coming of Post-industrial Society: A Venture in Social Forecasting* (New York: Basic Books, 1973).

17. Alan Mallach, ed., *Rebuilding America's Legacy Cities: New Directions for the Industrial Heartland* (New York: American Assembly, Columbia University, 2012); Brent D. Ryan, *Design After Decline: How America Rebuilds Shrinking Cities* (Phila-

delphia: University of Pennsylvania Press, 2012); Margaret Dewar, Christina Kelly, and Hunter Morrison, “Planning for Better, Smaller Places after Population Loss: Lessons from Youngstown and Flint,” in *The City After Abandonment*, ed. Margaret Dewar and June Manning Thomas (Philadelphia: University of Pennsylvania Press, 2013), 289–316.

18. U.S. Census Bureau, Tables 1 and 2, in *2010 Census of Population and Housing* (Washington, DC: Government Printing Office, 2012), Part 24 (Michigan), 45; Part 34 (New York), 14; Part 40 (Pennsylvania), 100; Table 56, in *1980 Census of Population* (Washington, DC: Government Printing Office, 1983), Part 40 (Pennsylvania), 16; Table 5, in *1960 Census of Population* (Washington, DC: Government Printing Office, 1963), Part 24 (Michigan), 11; Part 34 (New York), 9; Part 40 (Pennsylvania), 16. All documents at: http://www.census.gov/prod/www/decennial.html.

19. Alan Mallach, *In Philadelphia's Shadow: Small Cities in the Third Federal Reserve District* (Philadelphia: Federal Reserve Bank of Philadelphia, 2012), http://www.philadelphiafed.org/community-development/publications/special-reports/small-cities-in-third-federal-reserve-district.pdf.

20. David Harvey, *A Brief History of Neoliberalism* (Oxford: Oxford University Press, 2005); Christine Walley, *Exit Zero: Family and Class in Postindustrial Chicago* (Chicago: University of Chicago Press, 2013); Christopher Mele, “Casinos, Prisons, Incinerators, and Other Fragments of Neoliberal Urban Development,” *Social Science History* 35, no. 3 (Fall 2011): 423–452; Vincanne Adams, *Markets of Sorrow, Labors of Faith: New Orleans in the Wake of Katrina* (Durham, NC: Duke University Press, 2013).

21. “Sheldon Adelson,” Forbes.com, http://www.forbes.com/profile/sheldon-adelson/. In the three years after 2009, Adelson made more money than any other American. Steven Bertoni, “Comeback Billionaire: How Adelson Dominates Chinese Gambling and U.S. Politics,” *Forbes*, March 12, 2012, 1.

22. Connie Bruck, “The Brass Ring: A Multibillionaire's Relentless Quest for Global Influence,” *New Yorker*, June 30, 2008, 43; Gary Rivlin, “When 3rd Place on the Rich List Just Isn't Enough,” *New York Times*, January 17, 2008.

23. Matt Assad, “Bigger Things to Come?,” *Morning Call*, June 10, 2009.

24. Barry Bluestone and Bennett Harrison, *The Deindustrialization of America: Plant Closings, Community Abandonment, and the Dismantling of Basic Industry* (New York: Basic Books, 1982); Sharon Zukin, *Landscapes of Power: From Detroit to Disney World* (Berkeley: University of California Press, 1991).

25. Bernard J. Frieden and Lynne B. Sagalyn, *Downtown, Inc.: How America Rebuilds Cities* (Cambridge, MA: MIT Press, 1989); Dennis R. Judd and Susan S. Fainstein, eds., *The Tourist City* (New Haven, CT: Yale University Press, 1999); Rachel Weber, “What Makes a Good Economic Development Deal?,” in *Retooling for Growth: Building a 21st Century Economy in America's Older Industrial Areas*, ed. Richard M. McGahey and Jennifer S. Vey (Washington, DC: Brookings Institution Press, 2008), 277–298.

26. Anne Bonds, “Economic Development, Racialization, and Privilege: ‘Yes in My Backyard’ Prison Politics and the Reinvention of Madras, Oregon,” *Annals of*

the Association of American Geographers 103, no. 6 (2013): 1389–1405; Mele, "Casinos, Prisons, Incinerators, and Other Fragments of Neoliberal Urban Development," 423–452; Anna J. Willow and Sara Wylie, "Politics, Ecology, and the New Anthropology of Energy: Exploring the Emerging Frontiers of Hydraulic Fracking," *Journal of Political Ecology* 21 (2014): 222–348.

27. Samuel Zipp, *Manhattan Projects: The Rise and Fall of Urban Renewal in Cold War New York* (Oxford: Oxford University Press, 2010); Suleiman Osman, *The Invention of Brownstone Brooklyn: Gentrification and the Search for Authenticity in Postwar New York* (Oxford: Oxford University Press, 2011); Neil Smith, *The New Urban Frontier: Gentrification and the Revanchist City* (London: Routledge, 1996).

28. Andrew Hurley, *Environmental Inequalities: Class, Race, and Industrial Pollution in Gary, Indiana, 1945–1980* (Chapel Hill: University of North Carolina Press, 1995); Julie Sze, *Noxious New York: The Racial Politics of Urban Health and Environmental Justice* (Cambridge, MA: MIT Press, 2007).

29. Arnold Hirsch, *Making the Second Ghetto: Race and Housing in Chicago, 1940–1960* (New York: Cambridge University Press, 1986); Thomas J. Sugrue, *The Origins of the Urban Crisis: Race and Inequality in Postwar Detroit* (Princeton, NJ: Princeton University Press, 1996); William Julius Wilson, *The Truly Disadvantaged: The Inner City, the Underclass, and Public Policy* (Chicago: University of Chicago Press, 1987); Robert J. Sampson, *Great American City: Chicago and the Enduring Neighborhood Effect* (Chicago: University of Chicago Press, 2011); Jason R. Hackworth, *The Neoliberal City: Governance, Ideology, and Development in American Urbanism* (Ithaca, NY: Cornell University Press, 2007).

30. Susan Strange, *Casino Capitalism* (Oxford: B. Blackwell, 1986); Harvey, *A Brief History of Neoliberalism.*

31. Lefebvre notes that social space is "at once *actual* (given) and *potential* (locus of possibilities)." And it is "at once a collection of *materials* (objects, things) and an ensemble of *materiel* (tools—and the procedures necessary to make efficient use of tools and of things in general)." *The Production of Space*, 191.

32. See Alison Isenberg, *Downtown America: A History of the Place and the People Who Made It* (Chicago: University of Chicago Press, 2004), 255–311. Cities that adopted a raze-and-forget strategy during the waves of factory closures in the 1980s and 1990s include Kenosha, Wisconsin (see Dudley, *End of the Line*) and Homestead, Pennsylvania. In Michael Moore's 1989 film *Roger and Me*, Flint, Michigan's failed AutoWorld theme park looms as an icon of an industrial town's inability to adapt to the new economy. But other communities like Birmingham, Alabama, Milwaukee, Wisconsin, and Lowell, Massachusetts, have adopted heritage-based revitalization strategies with more enthusiasm and success. See also Kirk Savage on Pittsburgh: "Monuments of a Lost Cause: The Postindustrial Campaign to Commemorate Steel," in Cowie and Heathcott, *Beyond the Ruins*, 237–256.

1. Order in the Landscape

1. Katherine Carté Engel, *Religion and Profit: Moravians in Early America* (Philadelphia: University of Pennsylvania Press, 2009), 18–19, 24–26.

2. Ibid., 32–62; W. Ross Yates et al., *Bethlehem of Pennsylvania: The First One Hundred Years 1741–1841* (Bethlehem, PA: Bethlehem Book Committee, Chamber of Commerce, 1968).

3. "No. 4 Specification of all our Buildings and Lands on 31 May 1758," and "Distribution of the Brethren in Bethlehem in their Various Trades and other Occupations, January 16, 1759," trans. Katherine Carté Engel, *Bethlehem Digital History Project*, Bethlehem Area Public Library, Reeves Library, Moravian College and Theological Seminary, 2000, http://bdhp.moravian.edu/community_records/business/specs/bldgspecscover.html; http://bdhp.moravian.edu/community_records/business/trades/catalogoftrades1.html.

4. William J. Murtagh, *Moravian Architecture and Town Planning* (Chapel Hill: University of North Carolina Press, 1967), 37.

5. Bethlehem Area Chamber of Commerce, *Bethlehem of Pennsylvania: A Walking Tour* (Bethlehem, PA: Chamber of Commerce, 1981), 7.

6. "Description of Bethlehem; in the State of Pennsylvania. In a Letter to a Friend. Dated Philadelphia, Arch Street, June 22d, 1790," *Massachusetts Magazine*, June 1791, 365–366. On visitors to Bethlehem, see Engel, *Religion and Profit*, 62–68.

7. Yates et al., *Bethlehem of Pennsylvania: The First One Hundred Years*, 215; Joseph Mortimer Levering, *A History of Bethlehem, Pennsylvania, 1741–1892* (Bethlehem, PA: Times Publishing Company, 1903), 676–689.

8. W. Ross Yates et al., *Bethlehem of Pennsylvania: The Golden Years* (Bethlehem, PA: Bethlehem Book Committee, 1976), 13.

9. *Manufacturing and Mercantile Resources of the Lehigh Valley including Historical Sketches of the Prominent Towns* (Philadelphia: Industrial Publishing Company, 1881), 68.

10. The largest immigrant groups came, in this order, from: Hungary, Austria, the former Czechoslovakia, Germany, Italy, and the former Yugoslavia (particularly the region of Prekmurje, now part of Slovenia, whose immigrants are locally called Windish). Bethlehem, PA, Bureau of Planning and Development, *The People of Bethlehem: Community Renewal Program Report Number 2* (Bethlehem, PA: Bureau of Planning and Development, 1967), 27, 56.

11. "Conditions in City Not So Bad as They're Painted, Says Mayor," *Bethlehem Globe-Times*, November 15, 1927. Casino opponents in Bethlehem directed me to *Dare to be Brave*, a local history of Mayor Robert Pfeifle (1929–1937) that lionizes him for "cleaning up" Bethlehem in the 1930s, literally chasing pimps from town and vowing there would not be slots in Bethlehem while he was in office. The book's message may have been informed by the legalization of casinos in Atlantic City the year before it was published, but it became a strikingly prescient resource for local resistance to gambling in 2005 and 2006. Frank Orpe and Jean Pfeifle McQuade, *Dare to be Brave* (Center Square, PA: Alpha Publications, 1977), 46–47.

12. Bethlehem Steel Corporation, *1955 Annual Report* (Bethlehem, PA: The Corporation, 1956), 17.

13. Before moving north, Grace and his wife Marion (a native Bethlehemite whose father had been a South Bethlehem burgess) had a home in South Bethlehem, just east of Fountain Hill. National Register Application for South Bethlehem,

Historic Bethlehem, Inc. Papers, Box 1 Beth. Historic District Nom Spillman Farmer HB2010.02: Mt. Airy District folder, National Register of Historic Places submission materials, Historic Bethlehem Partnership Archives, Bethlehem, PA (hereafter cited as HBP); Roger D. Simon, "Bethlehem Social Elites, 'The Steel,' and the Saucon Valley Country Club," in *Backcountry Crucibles: The Lehigh Valley from Settlement to Steel*, ed. Jean R. Soderlund and Catherine S. Parzynski (Bethlehem, PA: Lehigh University Press, 2008), 316.

14. Stanley A. West, *The Mexican Aztec Society: A Mexican-American Voluntary Association in Diachronic Perspective* (New York: Arno Press, 1976), 95–96.

15. In his study of Gary, Indiana, a U.S. Steel town, Andrew Hurley notes steel production and pollution were linked to prosperity into the early 1960s. Andrew Hurley, *Environmental Inequalities: Class, Race, and Industrial Pollution in Gary, Indiana, 1945–1980* (Chapel Hill: University of North Carolina Press, 1995), 61, 70, 146.

16. On cleanliness as a "middle-class property aesthetic" and dust understood as both material and metaphor, see Richard J. Callahan Jr., *Work and Faith in the Kentucky Coal Fields: Subject to Dust* (Bloomington: Indiana University Press, 2009), 84, 122–123.

17. Mary Douglas, *Purity and Danger: An Analysis of Concepts of Pollution and Taboo* (London: Routledge & Kegan Paul, 1966), 36–41.

18. Joseph Schumpeter, *Capitalism, Socialism, and Democracy* (New York: Harper Perennial, [1942] 2008), 81–86. Douglas writes, "We must, therefore, ask how dirt, which is normally destructive, sometimes becomes creative." *Purity and Danger*, 160. Max Page similarly argues that physical construction and destruction in the landscape and built environment "shows how capitalism inscribed its economic and social processes into the physical landscape of the city, and then into the minds of city people." Max Page, *The Creative Destruction of Manhattan, 1900–1940* (Chicago: University of Chicago Press, 1999), 2.

19. John Strohmeyer, *Crisis in Bethlehem: Big Steel's Struggle to Survive* (Bethesda, MD: Adler & Adler, 1986), 19.

20. The city's churches similarly institutionalized social class in Bethlehem, as I discuss in Chapter 5. Saucon Valley's present-day sense of tradition, as expressed on the Club's website by its Board of Governors, continues to evoke a thinly veiled class and ethnic exceptionalism: "'The membership takes pride in its heritage and strongly reaffirms the objectives and traditions of our founders. The Club provides a refuge from the outside world, a very private Club where good manners, a high moral code, personal integrity, etiquette, and mutual respect are inherent in the membership; where rules are seldom invoked because common sense, common courtesy, and allegiance to the principles of our heritage govern members' behavior; and where members and their families can relax and enjoy recreation, fine dining, and the social compatibility of other members.' Saucon Valley Country Club is symbolic of an age in which family values and standards of excellence have prevailed and continue—a true American legacy." Saucon Valley Country Club, "History," http://www.sauconvalleycc.org/club/scripts/library/view_document.asp?NS=PUBLIC&APP=80&DN=HISTORY#.

21. The Steel Club also excluded home office personnel, institutionalizing a split between local plant staff and corporate managers. Simon, "Bethlehem Social Elites," 322.

22. Another legend has it that Grace resigned from Augusta National, arguably the most prestigious golf club in the United States, because of a dispute over a hole being par 4 when he thought it should be par 3.

23. For more on Bethlehem's Steel-ordered social divisions, see Strohmeyer, *Crisis in Bethlehem.* On the Saucon Valley Country Club, see Simon, "Bethlehem Social Elites," 315–328. On the role of place-based story telling in delineating social structures and understandings, see Keith H. Basso, *Wisdom Sits in Places: Landscape and Language among the Western Apache* (Albuquerque: University of New Mexico Press, 1996).

24. Bethlehem, PA, Fine Arts Commission, *Christmas City Fair* (Bethlehem, PA: Fine Arts Commission, 1972), 29.

25. Several buildings at Lehigh University are named after Steel executives. Lehigh's sports teams were traditionally known as the Engineers. The team names were changed to the Mountain Hawks in November 1995, the same month that Bethlehem Steel stopped making steel at the Bethlehem plant.

26. Affected residents and environmental groups charged that while local elected officials had not been consulted, the Pennsylvania Secretary of Highways, a former Bethlehem Steel engineer named Robert Bartlett, met with Steel executives in the company's offices in 1967 to determine the route of Interstate 78, and hired Clarke & Rapuano, a consulting firm that the Steel regularly engaged, to aid in project studies. While much of the land affected belonged to Bethlehem Steel, the route cut through a city park as well as private residences and businesses. Local officials and businesses, including the tire dealer that also founded the Lehigh Valley Industrial Park, rallied behind the interstate project and its potential to open up new corridors for development. Bethlehem's mayor in 1980 stated that rerouting the Steel's trucks, as the earlier construction of the I-378 spur route had, was a primary reason for his support. For a sampling of news coverage in the *Bethlehem Globe-Times*, see Claire Heckenberger, "L. Saucon Goes to Court on I-78," October 7, 1970, 25; Glenn Kranzley, "I-78 Debate Rages 7 Hours," July 22, 1971, 15; Glenn Kranzley, "Suit Filed to Halt All I-78 Planning," October 4, 1972, 1; "Area Officials to Determine Fate of I-78," February 5, 1980, 19.

27. Bethlehem, PA, Fine Arts Commission, *Christmas City Fair*, 29; Clarke and Rapuano, Inc. and Russell Vannest Black, *An Interim Report on the City of Bethlehem* (Bethlehem, PA: Bethlehem Redevelopment Authority, 1956), n.p.

28. See Jack Metzgar, *Striking Steel: Solidarity Remembered* (Philadelphia: Temple University Press, 2000); Strohmeyer, *Crisis in Bethlehem*, 64–77; Judith Stein, *Running Steel, Running America: Race, Economic Policy and the Decline of Liberalism* (Chapel Hill: University of North Carolina Press, 1998), 22–26; Kenneth Warren, *Bethlehem Steel: Builder and Arsenal of America* (Pittsburgh: University of Pittsburgh Press, 2008), 205. On local effects, see also Grover H. Stainbrook Jr. and Polly Beste, *Lehigh Valley Industrial Park: A 2002 Perspective, Parks I–VI* (Bethlehem, PA: Lehigh Valley Industrial Park, 2002), 6–7.

29. According to Mark Reutter, foreign imports were already on the rise and the strike only widened the gap; see *Making Steel: Sparrows Point and the Rise and Ruin of American Industrial Might* (Urbana: University of Illinois Press, 2005), 423–427.

30. Wendy Warren and Christian D. Berg, "Coke Ovens Go Cold: Hundreds of Workers Clock in for the Last Time Friday as Bethlehem Steel Closes Its Last Plant in the City," *Morning Call*, March 28, 1998.

31. Pension Benefit Guarantee Corporation, "PBGC to Protect Pensions of 95,000 at Bethlehem Steel," news release, December 16, 2002, http://www.pbgc.gov/news/press/releases/pr03–09.html; Jill Schennum, "Bethlehem Steelworkers: Reshaping the Industrial Working Class" (PhD diss., City University of New York, 2011), 215–217.

32. Schennum, "Bethlehem Steelworkers," 320–334. One of the few benefits to survive the bankruptcy was prescription coverage for $10 a month for many former union employees and spouses, a program that ArcelorMittal, the eventual buyer of most of Bethlehem Steel's assets, provides.

33. David Venditta and Ardith Hilliard, eds., *Forging America: The Story of Bethlehem Steel*, 2nd ed. (Bethlehem, PA: The Morning Call, 2010), 104–105; Strohmeyer, *Crisis in Bethlehem*.

34. American firms invested in BOF technology in earnest beginning in 1962. Bethlehem Steel's new Burns Harbor plant, built in 1962, became the only fully modernized plant with a BOF in the U.S. Bethlehem Steel also built BOFs at its older Sparrows Point and Lackawanna plants before Bethlehem. Stein, *Running Steel, Running America*, 215–217; Warren, *Bethlehem Steel*, 184–187.

35. Venditta and Hilliard, *Forging America*, 118; Warren, *Bethlehem Steel*, 216–217.

36. See Warren, *Bethlehem Steel;* Venditta and Hilliard, *Forging America;* Frank A. Behum Sr., *30 Years under the Beam: Bethlehem Steel Exposed, As Told by Those Who Worked There* (Savannah, GA: Continental Shelf Publishing, 2010); Reutter, *Making Steel;* Stein, *Running Steel, Running America* and *Pivotal Decade: How the United States Traded Factories for Finance in the Seventies* (New Haven, CT: Yale University Press, 2010). For a defense of labor, see John P. Hoerr, *And the Wolf Finally Came: The Decline of the American Steel Industry* (Pittsburgh: University of Pittsburgh Press, 1988); for a defense of management, see Paul Tiffany, *The Decline of American Steel: How Management, Labor, and Government Went Wrong* (New York: Oxford University Press, 1988).

37. See Metzgar, *Striking Steel*, 35.

38. Paul Wirth, "Worker Participation Program at Bethlehem Steel Falls Apart," *Morning Call*, March 31, 1989; *The Boiler House Herald*, n.d., author's collection. Earlier that month PFP received the Pennsylvania Governor's Award for Labor-Management Cooperation, perhaps a last-ditch effort by the state to encourage cooperation on the eve of contract negotiations. Pennsylvania Labor and Industry Secretary Harris Wofford mistakenly declared at the ceremony that Bethlehem Steel and its workers "are pioneering a new era in which cooperation

is replacing confrontation as the standard operating procedure." "Steel, USW Get Cooperation Award," *Morning Call*, March 3, 1989.

39. Behum, *30 Years under the Beam*, 114. On a similar experience among GM plant workers in Linden, New Jersey, see Ruth Milkman, *Farewell to the Factory: Auto Workers in the Late Twentieth Century* (Berkeley: University of California Press, 1997).

40. Bethlehem had about 1,000 black residents, mostly migrants from the South, by the late 1920s. Most left during the Depression. The number of black residents did not exceed 1,000 again until 1960, when it still comprised less than 2 percent of the city's population. In 2010, Bethlehem's population was 7 percent black. Bethlehem, PA, Bureau of Planning and Development, *The People of Bethlehem*, 31, 58, 60; Venditta and Hilliard, *Forging America*, 67, 82.

41. See also Chapter 5. On Latinos, particularly Puerto Ricans, in Bethlehem, see Peter J. Antonsen, *A History of the Puerto Rican Community in Bethlehem, PA 1944–1993* (Bethlehem, PA: Council of Spanish Speaking Organizations of the Lehigh Valley, 1997); Alan Sorensen, "Hispanics Share American Dream Forged in Heat of the Steel Mill," *Bethlehem Globe-Times*, January 15, 1984. On the consent decree, see Stein, *Running Steel, Running America*, 169–196.

42. Barry Bluestone and Bennett Harrison, *The Deindustrialization of America: Plant Closings, Community Abandonment, and the Dismantling of Basic Industry* (New York: Basic Books, 1982).

43. In *Business Week*'s 1958 rankings of the highest paid executives in the United States, nine of the top twelve were from Bethlehem Steel. "Executive Pay: Only Modest Gains in 1957," *Business Week*, May 24, 1958, 86–104. "Steel Research Lab Facility is Dedicated by A.B. Homer," *Morning Call*, October 9, 1961.

44. See also June C. Nash, *From Tank Town to High Tech: The Clash of Community and Industrial Cycles* (Albany: State University of New York Press, 1989); Norman Caulfield, *NAFTA and Labor in North America* (Urbana: University of Illinois Press, 2010).

45. Bluestone and Harrison, *Deindustrialization of America*, 49–81.

46. Claudia Goldin and Robert Margo, "The Great Compression: The Wage Structure in the United States at Mid-century," *Quarterly Journal of Economics* 107, no. 1 (1992): 1–34.

47. In 1973 the USW gave up the right to strike in exchange for guarantees in the rest of the contract; benefits continued to increase during the 1970s. According to Jack Metzgar, during the economic downturn in the 1980s, the Basic Steel Contract unraveled as unions increasingly made concessions that undercut former protections. Metzgar, *Striking Steel*, 92, 136–138.

48. Jefferson Cowie, *Capital Moves: RCA's Seventy-Year Quest for Cheap Labor* (Ithaca, NY: Cornell University Press, 1999). See also Caulfield, *NAFTA and Labor in North America*.

49. Despite sharp cuts to the TRA program under Reagan, it rebounded after 2002 when it combined with the trade adjustment program that was part of the North American Free Trade Agreement (NAFTA). The 1993 NAFTA ratification

eliminated tariffs and other trade barriers between Canada, the United States, and Mexico. It made imports and outsourcing cheaper alternatives for U.S. companies, codifying the then-established pattern of privileging capital mobility over spatially fixed commitments. Cowie, *Capital Moves*, esp. 146–147. See also David Harvey, *A Brief History of Neoliberalism* (Oxford: Oxford University Press, 2005), 92, 101–103; Caulfield, *NAFTA and Labor in North America*.

50. "Steel Research Lab Facility is Dedicated by A.B. Homer," *Morning Call*, October 9, 1961.

51. While other companies provided executives with this sort of help, Bethlehem Steel was the first big firm to similarly aid blue- and white-collar workers. John S. DeMott and Frederick Ungeheuer, "After the Mill Shut Down," *Time*, August 15, 1983, 52.

52. See Walter G. Strange, *Job Loss: A Psychosocial Study of Workers' Reactions to a Plant Closing in a Company Town in Southern Appalachia* (Washington, DC: National Technical Information Service, 1977); N.E. Amundson and W.A. Borgen, "Coping with Unemployment: What Helps and What Hinders," *Journal of Employment Counseling* 24 (1987): 97–106; Celia Ray Hayhoe, "Helping Families in Transition Due to Unemployment," *Journal of Human Behavior in the Social Environment* 13, no. 1 (2006): 63–73.

53. DeMott and Ungeheuer, "After the Mill Shut Down."

54. Katherine S. Newman, *Falling from Grace: Downward Mobility in the Age of Affluence* (Berkeley: University of California Press, 1999), esp. chapters 3 and 6; Joy L. Hart and Tracy E. K'Meyer, "Worker Memory and Narrative: Personal Stories of Deindustrialization in Louisville, Kentucky," and Steve May and Laura Morrison, "Making Sense of Restructuring: Narratives of Accommodation among Downsized Workers," in *Beyond the Ruins: The Meanings of Deindustrialization*, ed. Jefferson Cowie and Joseph Heathcott (Ithaca, NY: ILR Press, 2003), 259–304; Gregory Pappas, *The Magic City: Unemployment in a Working-Class Community* (Ithaca, NY: Cornell University Press, 1989), 54, 84; Schennum, "Bethlehem Steelworkers," 203–204, 268.

55. For a comparison with Youngstown, see Sean Safford, *Why the Garden Club Couldn't Save Youngstown: The Transformation of the Rust Belt* (Cambridge, MA: Harvard University Press, 2009). Even amid the deindustrialization literature of crisis and trauma among blue-collar laborers, there is evidence of a more ready adaptation to change. Ruth Milkman's study of General Motors assembly line workers in New Jersey shows that those who took lump-sum buyouts when the plant automated in the mid-1980s were happier and more financially stable than the workers who remained, having welcomed the chance for a fresh start after the monotony and tension with GM's management. Of course, these were the workers who left voluntarily, were generally younger than workers who stayed, and were entering a robust economy. Milkman, *Farewell to the Factory*.

56. U.S. Bureau of Labor Statistics; Alan Mallach, *In Philadelphia's Shadow: Small Cities in the Third Federal Reserve District* (Philadelphia: Federal Reserve Bank of Philadelphia, 2012), 36, http://www.philadelphiafed.org/community-development/publications/special-reports/small-cities-in-third-federal-reserve-district.pdf.

57. On Kenosha, see Kathryn Marie Dudley, *The End of the Line: Lost Jobs, New Lives in Postindustrial America* (Chicago: University of Chicago Press, 1994); on Youngstown, see Sherry Lee Linkon and John Russo, *Steeltown U.S.A.: Work and Memory in Youngstown* (Lawrence: University Press of Kansas, 2002); on Homestead, see Judith Schachter Modell, *A Town Without Steel: Envisioning Homestead* (Pittsburgh: University of Pittsburgh Press, 1998). Much of Bethlehem Steel's shuttered Lackawanna plant near Buffalo was similarly flattened. Bethlehem Steel drew up mixed-use redevelopment plans for the waterfront site in 1998, but their realization has been slow in coming. Johnstown, Pennsylvania's Lower Works were listed as a National Historic Landmark in 1989, but it took years for Bethlehem to unload the abandoned properties.

58. Bethlehem City Council Minutes, September 20, 2005, City of Bethlehem Council Agenda and Minutes Archive, http://www.bethlehem-pa.gov/citycouncil/meetings/archive/2005/minutes/2005-09-19.html.

59. Ken Kunsman, "Steel to Sell Vacant Lot for Technology Center," *Morning Call*, May 4, 1993.

60. Bethlehem Steel became a model for concurrent state DEP and federal EPA remediation approval in 1999. Christian D. Berg, "Bethlehem Works Gets Environmental Go-Ahead," *Morning Call*, June 19, 1999.

61. Matt Assad, "Commerce Center Plans are Unveiled: Steel's $600 Million South Bethlehem Project Could Lure 10,000 Jobs," *Morning Call*, January 14, 1999.

62. Bill White, "Steel Asking for Free Rein on Key Site," *Morning Call*, March 14, 1996. See also Hugh Bronstein, "Bethlehem City Hall Split Over Steel Tract Rezoning—Mayor Ken Smith is Optimistic, the Planning Staff is Pessimistic," *Morning Call*, April 4, 1996.

63. The remaining 1,600 acres of steel land were similarly rezoned in 2003.

64. See Nicholas Dagen Bloom, *Merchant of Illusion: James Rouse, America's Salesman of the Businessman's Utopia* (Columbus: Ohio State University Press, 2004); Bernard J. Frieden and Lynne B. Sagalyn, *Downtown, Inc.: How America Rebuilds Cities* (Cambridge, MA: MIT Press, 1989).

65. See Alison Isenberg, *Downtown America: A History of the Place and the People Who Made It* (Chicago: University of Chicago Press, 2004), 256–311.

66. See Cathy Stanton, *The Lowell Experiment: Public History in a Postindustrial City* (Amherst: University of Massachusetts Press, 2006); W. David Lewis, *Sloss Furnaces and the Rise of the Birmingham District: An Industrial Epic* (Tuscaloosa: University of Alabama Press, 1994), 457–473.

67. For example, art directors worked for a decade to open a contemporary art museum in a former textile mill and electronics plant in North Adams, Massachusetts, a plan realized as MASS MoCA in 1999. See Sharon Zukin, *The Cultures of Cities* (Cambridge, MA: Blackwell, 1995), 79–107; Stephen C. Sheppard, Kay Oehler, Blair Benjamin, and Ari Kessler, *Culture and Revitalization: The Economic Effects of MASS MoCA on Its Community* (North Adams, MA: Center for Creative Community Development, 2006). On the "tourist city" trend, see Dennis R. Judd and Susan S. Fainstein, eds., *The Tourist City* (New Haven, CT: Yale University Press, 1999); Dennis R. Judd, ed., *The Infrastructure of Play: Building the Tourist City*

(Armonk, NY: M. E. Sharpe, 2003); Frieden and Sagalyn, *Downtown, Inc.*; Howard Gillette, *Camden after the Fall: Decline and Renewal in a Postindustrial City* (Philadelphia: University of Pennsylvania Press, 2005); Jonathan Mark Souther, *New Orleans on Parade: Tourism and the Transformation of the Crescent City* (Baton Rouge: Louisiana State University Press, 2006).

68. Jennifer Brown, "Mayor Looks Beyond Decline to Future," *Sunday Patriot-News*, April 18, 1999, B7. See also Stephen J. McGovern, "Evolving Visions of Waterfront Development in Postindustrial Philadelphia: the Formative Role of Elite Ideologies," *Journal of Planning History* 7, no. 4 (November 2008): 295–326.

69. Amazingly, Birmingham officials in the late 1970s proposed turning the Sloss Furnaces into a theme park of just this sort—with visitors riding in ore cars and skip tubs. It was rejected as impractical. Lewis, *Sloss Furnaces*, 460–461. The idea was not entirely without precedent. In nearby Mauch Chunk (now Jim Thorpe), Pennsylvania, the Switchback Railway, a coalmining train, operated as a joy ride from the 1870s (when the steam locomotive made the train obsolete) until 1938. It was the model for the Switchback Railway roller coaster at Coney Island, which opened in 1884. William Brandt, "Why Let Coal Have All the Fun?," Pennsylvania Center for the Book—Literary and Cultural Heritage Map, Spring 2010, http://pabook.libraries.psu.edu/palitmap/Switchback.html.

70. Among a series of articles reporting potential developers over the course of several years, see Natalie Kostelni, "Works Details Revealed," *Morning Call*, July 15, 1999.

71. Bethlehem Steel Corporation's affiliation with the Smithsonian came in part from the company's government affairs connections to Senator Daniel Patrick Moynihan of New York. Moynihan, who was on the Smithsonian Board of Regents at the time, had a long relationship with the corporation based on its presence in New York City and Lackawanna.

72. See Sharon Ann Holt, "History Keeps Bethlehem Steel from Going off the Rails: Moving a Complex Community Process toward Success," *The Public Historian* 28, no. 2 (Spring 2006): 31–44.

73. In a TIF district, the increased tax revenues from higher assessments as a result of real-estate development are dedicated for a certain period of time to finance the debt issued to pay for the project or pay for related infrastructure. See Frieden and Sagalyn, *Downtown, Inc.*, 155–170.

74. See Dudley, *The End of the Line;* Daniel Bell, *The Coming of Post-Industrial Society: A Venture in Social Forecasting* (New York: Basic Books, 1973).

75. Alexandra Berzon, "Jury Is Still Out on Bethlehem's Bet: Sluggish Pace of Las Vegas Sands Casino Project at Historic Steel Plant Leads Pennsylvania City to Lower Expectations," *Wall Street Journal*, April 7, 2010.

2. Christmas City and Sin City Simply Do Not Go Together

1. Matt Assad, "Hotel and Casino Campaign Comes to Musikfest," *Morning Call*, August 7, 2005.

2. Early plans for the Marina Bay Sands in Singapore showed that casino as The Venetian Singapore as well, but under government pressure the theme was scaled back before it opened in 2010. A stripped down version of the Grand Canal remains. Kah-Wee Lee, "Taming Vice: How Machines and Architecture Changed the Culture of Gambling," *UNLV Gaming Podcast*, podcast audio, University of Nevada Center for Gaming Research, September 15, 2011, http://digitalscholarship.unlv.edu/gaming_podcasts/15.

3. See Alison Isenberg, *Downtown America: A History of the Place and the People Who Made It* (Chicago: University of Chicago Press, 2004), 311.

4. See Bryant Simon, *Boardwalk of Dreams: Atlantic City and the Fate of Urban America* (New York: Oxford University Press, 2004), 194–222.

5. Pennsylvania legalized pari-mutuel betting (on horse races) in 1959 and bingo in 1981. On state lotteries, see Charles T. Clotfelter and Philip J. Cook, *Selling Hope: State Lotteries in America* (Cambridge, MA: Harvard University Press, 1989). Legal scholar I. Nelson Rose calls the trend that New Hampshire sparked in 1963 the "third wave of legalized gambling" to distinguish it from colonial and post–Civil War gambling eras. One might ask whether Pennsylvania's trend-setting legalization of land-based commercial casinos reflects a "fourth wave" or a crest in the third. See I. Nelson Rose, "The Legalization and Control of Casino Gambling," *Fordham Urban Law Journal* 8, no. 2 (1980): 245–300; John Dombrink and William Norman Thompson, *The Last Resort: Success and Failure in Campaigns for Casinos* (Reno: University of Nevada Press, 1990), 9–12.

6. "Pennsylvania Lottery Annual Sales and Benefit Reports," Pennsylvania Lottery, last modified 2015, http://www.palottery.state.pa.us/About-PA-Lottery/Annual-Economic-Reports.aspx.

7. See Peter Collins, *Gambling and the Public Interest* (Westport, CT: Praeger, 2003); Robert Goodman, *The Luck Business: The Devastating Consequences and Broken Promises of America's Gambling Explosion* (New York: Free Press, 1995).

8. Tribal gaming is federally regulated by the Indian Gaming Regulatory Act of 1988. Under this act, states often receive funds from Tribal casinos with slots and other "Vegas-style" games via required compacts with sovereign tribes. See Jessica R. Cattelino, *High Stakes: Florida Seminole Gaming and Sovereignty* (Durham, NC: Duke University Press, 2008), 14–16, 168; American Gaming Association, *2014 By the Book*, http://www.gettoknowgaming.org/by-the-book.

9. Clotfelter and Cook, *Selling Hope*, 215–232.

10. Pocono bills failed in 1977 and 1983 by a 5 to 1 margin. Dombrink and Thompson, *The Last Resort*, 119–126.

11. Robert Zausner, "Riverboat Gambling Bobs Back Onto Agenda," *Philadelphia Inquirer*, August 5, 1993; Michael de Courcy Hinds, "Riverboat Casinos Seek a Home in Pennsylvania," *New York Times*, April 7, 1994; Sabina Dietrick, Robert A. Beauregard, and Cheryl Zarlenga Kerchic, "Riverboat Gambling, Tourism, and Economic Development," in *The Tourist City*, ed. Dennis R. Judd and Susan S. Fainstein (New Haven, CT: Yale University Press, 1999), 234–244.

12. For a critical take of the 2004 bill's backroom deal making and cronyism, see Matthew Teague, "Gaming the System," *Philadelphia Magazine*, June 2007,

http://phillymag.com/articles/gaming-the-system. Concerned citizens contested the constitutionality of the process, but the Supreme Court upheld most of the bill. See Pennsylvanians Against Gambling Expansion Fund, Inc. v. Commonwealth, 877 A.2d 383 (2005); Brian D. Kravetz, "Recent Decision: The Supreme Court of Pennsylvania Sustains the Constitutionality of the Gaming Act: Pennsylvanians Against Gambling Expansion Fund, Inc. v. Commonwealth," *Duquesne Law Review* 44 (Spring 2006): 551–573.

13. Pennsylvania Act 1 (Omnibus Amendments Act), 4 Pa. Cons. Stat. §1–21 (2010) (passed January 7, 2010), http://www.legis.state.pa.us/WU01/LI/LI/US/HTM/2010/0/0001.HTM.

14. The radius depends on type of casino and size of the city in which it is located. For Bethlehem, it is a twenty-mile radius. On this model of licensing, see Collins, *Gambling and the Public Interest*, 54, 105–107. Other states have looked at the structure of Pennsylvania's gaming law as a model. See Matt Assad, "Pa. Has Become National Leader in Casino Planning," *Morning Call*, June 11, 2013.

15. New Jersey casinos pay an additional "alternative investment tax" of 1.25 percent on gross revenues, making the effective tax rate 9.25 percent. Nevada casinos pay tax of 3.5 percent on the first $50,000 of revenue each month, plus 4.5 percent on the next $84,000, and 6.75 percent on revenue exceeding $134,000. Pennsylvania's gaming tax revenue is almost double Nevada's. After a peak of $1.44 billion in 2012, Pennsylvania's tax revenues declined to $1.35 billion by 2014. American Gaming Association, *2012 State of the States: The AGA Survey of Casino Entertainment* (Washington, DC: American Gaming Association, 2012), http://www.americangaming.org/sites/default/files/uploads/docs/sos/aga_sos_2012_web.pdf; Pennsylvania Gaming Control Board, "Combined Slots and Table Games Revenue in Pennsylvania Rises 4.4% in 2012," news release, January 16, 2013, http://gamingcontrolboard.pa.gov/?pr=498; Pennsylvania Gaming Control Board (PGCB), "Table Games Revenue for December Up More Than 15%," news release, January 15, 2015, http://gamingcontrolboard.pa.gov/?pr=602.

16. Pennsylvania Act 71 (Race Horse Development and Gaming Act), 4 Pa. Cons. Stat. §1101–1904 (2004) (passed July 3, 2004), http://www.legis.state.pa.us/WU01/LI/LI/US/HTM/2004/0/0071.HTM. The Pennsylvania Supreme Court later severed certain funding recipients from the law, including volunteer fire fighters and forest reserves.

17. The Senate Democratic Appropriations Committee of the Commonwealth of Pennsylvania commissioned a report from the Innovation Group in 2003 titled "Pennsylvania Slot Machine Facilities: Statewide Revenue Projection," which laid out the most profitable markets and informed the drafting of Act 71. In a Grand Jury report, one of the framers of the bill describes drawing circles on a map to represent the law's mileage preclusions for how far apart casinos needed to be, beginning with those designated for Philadelphia and Pittsburgh. It "made it extremely predictable where the non-stated casinos would pop up. We knew there would definitely be one in the Lehigh Valley. I couldn't tell you if it was Bethlehem or Allentown in 2003, but I knew—willing to bet the ranch there was going to be one there," he said. Thirty-first Statewide Investigating Grand Jury, "Grand Jury

Report No. 1," Court of Common Pleas, Allegheny County, Pennsylvania, May 19, 2011, 9–13, http://www.poconorecord.com/assets/pdf/PR1364524.PDF.

18. Commonwealth of Pennsylvania Gaming Control Board Order IN RE: Applications for Category 2 Slot Machine Licenses in a Revenue or Tourism Enhanced Location, February 1, 2007, 82, http://gamingcontrolboard.pa.gov/files/adjudications/Cat2_AL_OA.pdf (hereafter cited as PGCB Order). According to former Bethlehem casino president Robert DeSalvio, there are 17.5 million people within a seventy-five-mile radius.

19. Chuck Ayers and Matt Assad, "Slots Sought for Ex-Steel Land," *Morning Call*, September 16, 2004; Chuck Ayers, "Casino Owner Links with BethWorks to Build Slots Parlor on Steel Tract," *Morning Call*, December 16, 2004; Chuck Ayers and Matt Assad, "BethWorks Now Wins Bid for LVIP Land," *Morning Call*, February 12, 2005. Ownership of Sands Bethworks is 10 percent BethWorks Now and 90 percent Sands Pennsylvania, Inc. (which is 96 percent owned by Las Vegas Sands Corp.). As of 2015, the primary partners in BethWorks Now were Bethlehem resident and attorney/developer Michael Perrucci, New York attorney Richard Fischbein, and New York real-estate investors Barry Gosin and James Kuhn of Newmark Grubb Knight Frank. Newmark principal Jeffrey Gural had an initial stake as well. Pennsylvania Gaming Control Board, "Facility Ownership Interests as of 1–31–15," 2015, http://gamingcontrolboard.pa.gov/files/licensure/reports/Ownership_Interests.pdf.

20. 2006 Public Input Hearing Written Comments Archive (hereafter cited as PGCB 2006), Lehigh Valley General, 12–13, Pennsylvania Gaming Control Board, http://www.pgcb.state.pa.us/files/hearings/comments/LEHIGH_VALLEY_GENERAL.pdf; PGCB 2006, Sands Bethworks 3, 85–86, http://www.pgcb.state.pa.us/files/hearings/comments/SANDS_BETHWORKS_3.pdf.

21. Pennsylvanians Against Gambling Expansion Fund, Inc. v. Commonwealth, 877 A.2d 383 (2005). On the limits of municipal governments, see James J. Connolly, "Can They Do It? The Capacity of Small Rust-Belt Cities to Reinvent Themselves in a Global Economy," in *After the Factory: Reinventing America's Industrial Small Cities*, ed. James J. Connolly (Lanham, MD: Lexington Books, 2010), 8–9.

22. Bethlehem City Council Minutes, September 20, 2005, City of Bethlehem Council Agenda and Minutes Archive, http://www.bethlehem-pa.gov/city_council/agenda_minutes/archive/2005/minutes/2005-09-19.htm.

23. John R. Logan and Harvey L. Molotch, *Urban Fortunes: The Political Economy of Place* (Berkeley: University of California Press, 1987), 157.

24. According to Harry Trend, who became secretary of the Chamber of Commerce the same year that Melhado became president, by the late 1930s the Chamber's membership was roughly 250 members, about 100 of whom were connected to Bethlehem Steel. Trend said Melhado's wealth let him make the Chamber his "plaything." "In the Age of Steel: Oral Histories from Bethlehem, Pennsylvania—Harry K. Trend," interview by Roger D. Simon, 1975, Beyond Steel Archive, Lehigh University, Bethlehem, PA, http://digital.lib.lehigh.edu/beyondsteel/pdf/trend_72_50.pdf. See also Bethlehem City Council Minutes,

May 3, 2005, City of Bethlehem Council Agenda and Minute Archive, http://www.bethlehem-pa.gov/city_council/agenda_minutes/archive/2005/minutes/2005-05-03.htm; Samson D. Oppenheim, ed., *The American Jewish Year Book 5679: September 7, 1918 to September 24, 1919* (Philadelphia: The Jewish Publication Society of America, 1918), 259. The switch was in the ballroom of the Hotel Bethlehem, built by Bethlehem Steel fifteen years earlier to accommodate corporate guests. "Yule Decorations Turned on during Public Ceremony," *Bethlehem Globe-Times*, December 8, 1937; "V. K. Melhado Succumbs to Heart Attack," *Bethlehem Globe-Times*, August 2, 1938. Precedents for using Christmas lights to boost business include Wanamaker's department store in nearby Philadelphia, which had elaborately decorated its Grand Court since the 1910s, and Country Club Plaza in Kansas City, Missouri, which began lighting the exteriors of its retail buildings in 1925 to create a beacon for automobile traffic. On the increasingly close fit in the early twentieth century between Christmas shopping and Christian symbols, see Leigh Eric Schmidt, *Consumer Rites: The Buying and Selling of American Holidays* (Princeton, NJ: Princeton University Press, 1995), 159, 167; William S. Worley, *J. C. Nichols and the Shaping of Kansas City: Innovation in Planned Residential Communities* (Columbia: University of Missouri Press, 1990), xxii.

25. "V. K. Melhado Succumbs to Heart Attack."

26. "Steel Company Presents Star to This City," *Bethlehem Globe-Times*, December 16, 1939. The new Star was ninety-one feet tall.

27. David Venditta and Ardith Hilliard, eds., *Forging America: The Story of Bethlehem Steel*, 2nd ed. (Bethlehem, PA: The Morning Call, 2010), 67, 90–91.

28. "Yule Lights Affected by 'Blackout Rulings,'" *Bethlehem Globe-Times*, December 24, 1941; "Star Dimmed as Precaution," *Bethlehem Globe-Times*, December 10, 1941; "City's Yuletide Ushers in Bi-Centennial Celebration," *Bethlehem Globe-Times*, December 26, 1941.

29. Lorna Neil, *Christmas in Bethlehem* (Bethlehem, PA: Oaks Printing Company, 1983), n.p.; Charles Strum "Weekend Excursion: O Little Town of . . . You Know," *New York Times*, December 8, 2000.

30. Vangie Roby Sweitzer, *Christmas in Bethlehem: A Moravian Heritage* (Bethlehem, PA: Central Moravian Church, 2000), 82.

31. Nicole Radzievich, "Battle Looms for Bethlehem's Soul," *Morning Call*, August 23, 2005.

32. PGCB 2006, Sands Bethworks 2, 38, http://www.pgcb.state.pa.us/files/hearings/comments/SANDS_BETHWORKS_2.pdf.

33. Bethlehem City Council Minutes, July 5, 2005, City of Bethlehem Council Agenda and Minutes Archive, http://www.bethlehem-pa.gov/city_council/agenda_minutes/archive/2005/agenda/2005-07-05.htm. John Winthrop adapted his famous 1630 sermon, "A Model of Christian Charity" in which he talks of the "city on a hill," from Matthew 5:14–16: "Ye are the light of the world. A city set on a hill cannot be hid. Nor do men light a lamp and put it under a bushel, but on a stand, and it gives light to all in the house. Let your light so shine before men, that they may see your good works and give glory to your Father who is in heaven."

34. John C. Ogden, *An Excursion into Bethlehem & Nazareth, in Pennsylvania, in the Year 1799; with a Succinct History of the Society of United Brethren, Commonly Called Moravians* (Philadelphia: Charles Cist, 1800), 11; Isaac Weld Jr., *Travels through the States of North America and the Provinces of Upper and Lower Canada, during the Years 1795, 1796, and 1797*, 4th ed. (London: John Stockdale, 1800), 542. On the close ties between the Moravians' religious and capitalist endeavors, see Katherine Carté Engel, *Religion and Profit: Moravians in Early America* (Philadelphia: University of Pennsylvania Press, 2009).

35. Bethlehem City Council Minutes, May 3, 2005.

36. PGCB 2006, Sands Bethworks 5, 17–19, 22–29, http://www.pgcb.state.pa.us/files/hearings/comments/SANDS_BETHWORKS_5.pdf.

37. PGCB 2006, Sands Bethworks 3, 71–73.

38. Engel, *Religion and Profit*, 42; Elisabeth Sommer, "Gambling with God: The Use of the Lot by the Moravian Brethren in the Eighteenth Century," *Journal of the History of Ideas* 59, no. 2 (April 1998): 267–286. Some casino proponents did point to the hypocrisy of religious arguments given that churches today commonly host bingo games and raffles.

39. See Jonathan Z. Smith, *To Take Place: Toward Theory in Ritual* (Chicago: University of Chicago Press, 1987); David Chidester and Edward T. Linenthal, eds., *American Sacred Space* (Bloomington: Indiana University Press, 1995); Louis P. Nelson, ed., *American Sanctuary: Understanding Sacred Spaces* (Bloomington: Indiana University Press, 2006).

40. Bethlehem City Council Minutes, August 2, 2005, City of Bethlehem Council Agenda and Minutes Archive, http://www.bethlehem-pa.gov/city_council/agenda_minutes/archive/2005/agenda/2005-08-02.htm.

41. See Robert A. Orsi, "Introduction: Crossing the City Line," in *Gods of the City*, ed. Robert A. Orsi (Bloomington: Indiana University Press, 1999), 1–78; Richard J. Callahan Jr., *Work and Faith in the Kentucky Coal Fields* (Bloomington: Indiana University Press, 2009).

42. See Robert N. Bellah, "Civil Religion in America," *Daedalus* 96, no. 1 (Winter 1967): 1–21.

43. Venditta and Hilliard, *Forging America*, 47; Kenneth Warren, *Bethlehem Steel: Builder and Arsenal of America* (Pittsburgh: University of Pittsburgh Press, 2008), 106.

44. Venditta and Hilliard, *Forging America*, 114; Warren, *Bethlehem Steel*, 144–145.

45. Adam Clark, "New Name for Founders Way Favored," *Morning Call*, June 8, 2010. On connections between linguistic appropriation and cultural displacement, see Jared Farmer, *On Zion's Mount: Mormons, Indians, and the American Landscape* (Cambridge, MA: Harvard University Press, 2008). On meanings connected to place, see Yi-Fu Tuan, *Space and Place: The Perspective of Experience* (Minneapolis: University of Minnesota Press, 1977); Pierre Nora, "Between Memory and History: Les Lieux de Mémoire," *Representations* 26 (Spring 1989): 7–24.

46. PGCB 2006, Sands Bethworks 5, 46.

47. PGCB 2006, Sands Bethworks 1, 16–17, http://www.pgcb.state.pa.us/files/hearings/comments/SANDS_BETHWORKS_1.pdf.

48. Some argue that the wording on the postcards was unclear, leading some casino opponents to mistakenly send them in. According to the city council, emails in support also outnumbered those in opposition two to one. See Bethlehem City Council minutes, September 20, 2005. In conjunction with the Pennsylvania Gaming Control Board hearings, Sands Bethworks had 6,193 supporting comments and 838 opposing comments. See PGCB Order, February 1, 2007, 108.

49. Arguments cast purely as moral objections rarely succeed in gambling debates. See PGCB Order, February 1, 2007; Collins, *Gambling and the Public Interest*, 10, 51; Dombrink and Thompson, *The Last Resort*, 56, 76.

50. Venditta and Hilliard, *Forging America*, 40. On the historical rise of risk-taking in parallel with industrialization, see Jonathan Levy, *Freaks of Fortune: The Emerging World of Capitalism and Risk in America* (Cambridge, MA: Harvard University Press, 2012).

51. Andy Abboud, Vice President Government Relations & Community Development, Las Vegas Sands Corp., to Councilman Joseph F. Leeson, Jr., September 28, 2006, Bethlehem City Council Minutes, October 3, 2006, City of Bethlehem Council Agenda and Minutes Archive, http://www.bethlehem-pa.gov/city_council/agenda_minutes/archive/2006/minutes/2006-10-03.htm.

52. These figures are adjusted net income from the corporation's financial reports. Only five years later in 2011, net income was $1.64 billion, due in large part to growing operations in Asia.

53. "It must be noted that the General Assembly has, through the enactment of the Pennsylvania Race Horse Development and Gaming Act, already established the policy in this Commonwealth that gaming establishments as outlined in the Act will be licensed. . . . The Board will not and indeed cannot countermand the intent and will of the General Assembly by refusing to issue licenses based upon those who oppose the spirit of the validly enacted statute." PGCB Order, February 1, 2007, 91, 108–109, 111–112.

54. M. Christine Boyer, *The City of Collective Memory: Its Historical Imagery and Architectural Entertainments* (Cambridge, MA: MIT Press, 1994), 6.

55. Transcript, "Pennsylvania Gaming Control Board Suitability Hearing IN RE: Sands BethWorks Gaming, LLC," December 6, 2006, 128, www.pgcb.state.pa.us/files/hearings/transcripts/Sands_Bethworks_12-06-06.pdf.

56. Nucor is also among the companies blamed for putting the big steel manufacturers out of business by relying on nonunion labor. Las Vegas Sands Corp. "'Standing of the Steel' Ceremony Marks Latest Phase of Construction for Sands Bethworks," news release, February 22, 2008, http://www.pasands.com/pdf/Standing_of_the_Steel.pdf.

57. According to local historians, "Engineers could assemble a building for any use—exterior envelope, structural system, and materials—by picking and choosing from a number of approved designs that had advanced over time." Tim Noble and Shelby Weaver, "Bethlehem Steel Lehigh Plant Mill #2 Annex," registration form

for the National Register of Historic Places, March 22, 2004, 12–13, https://www.dot7.state.pa.us/ce_imagery/phmc_scans/H125923_2.PDF.

58. RTKL has historic ties to James Rouse projects including Charles Center in Baltimore. Walsh Bishop, formerly based in Minneapolis, specialized in casino design. The photo anecdote is according to former Bethlehem Sands president Robert DeSalvio.

59. Las Vegas Sands Corp., *Sands Bethworks* (N.p.: n.p., [2005?]), 12.

60. Transcript, "Pennsylvania Gaming Control Board Suitability Hearing," 44.

61. Ibid., 75.

62. Betsy Hunter Bradley, *The Works: The Industrial Architecture of the United States* (New York: Oxford University Press, 1999), 163.

63. Jolyon Drury, *Factories, Planning, Design and Modernisation* (London: Architectural Press; New York: Nichols, 1981), 7–8.

64. Las Vegas Sands Corp., *Sands Bethworks*, 12.

65. Robert Venturi, Denise Scott Brown, and Steven Izenour, *Learning from Las Vegas: The Forgotten Symbolism of Architectural Form* (Cambridge, MA: MIT Press, 1977).

66. See Paul Steelman, "Thoughts on Atlantic City, Las Vegas, and Several Other Casino Jurisdictions," interview by David Schwartz, *UNLV Gaming Podcast*, podcast audio, University of Nevada Center for Gaming Research, November 29, 2011, http://digitalscholarship.unlv.edu/gaming_podcasts/50/; Paul Steelman, "The Future of Casino Architecture," interview by David Schwartz, *UNLV Gaming Podcast*, podcast audio, University of Nevada Center for Gaming Research, December 20, 2011, http://digitalscholarship.unlv.edu/gaming_podcasts/49/.

67. Casino design literature generally recommends low ceilings to create a more intimate and enjoyable experience. Bill Friedman, *Designing Casinos to Dominate the Competition* (Reno: University of Nevada Press, 2000).

68. Jeffrey J. Sallaz, "Politics of Organizational Adornment: Lessons from Las Vegas and Beyond," *American Sociological Review* 77, no. 1 (2012): 113.

69. Transcript, "Pennsylvania Gaming Control Board Suitability Hearing," 41–47, 54–55, 61–79, 92, 118–121.

70. Ibid., 46.

71. As Boyer argues, this is part of a heritage-development trend that has "sweetened and distilled our spatial sensibility into the looks and feel of cherished times and places." Boyer, *The City of Collective Memory*, 423.

72. On the "culture of the hands" versus "culture of the mind" dichotomy in the context of deindustrialization, see Kathryn Marie Dudley, *The End of the Line: Lost Jobs, New Lives in Postindustrial America* (Chicago: University of Chicago Press, 1994).

73. See Connolly, "Can They Do It?," in *After the Factory*. See also Judd and Fainstein, *The Tourist City;* Frieden and Sagalyn, *Downtown, Inc.;* Urban Land Institute, *Developing Urban Entertainment Centers* (Washington, DC: ULI, 1998); Donald F. Norris, "If We Build It, They Will Come! Tourism-Based Economic

Development in Baltimore," in *The Infrastructure of Play: Building the Tourist City*, ed. Dennis R. Judd (Armonk, NY: M. E. Sharpe, 2003), 125–167.

74. Of thirteen small manufacturing cities in the region, the other two top-ranked "rebounding cities" are Lancaster, Pennsylvania, and Wilmington, Delaware. They also have benefited from heritage tourism and redevelopment of the industrial waterfront, respectively. Alan Mallach, *In Philadelphia's Shadow: Small Cities in the Third Federal Reserve District* (Philadelphia: Federal Reserve Bank of Philadelphia, 2012), http://www.philadelphiafed.org/community-development/publications/special-reports/small-cities-in-third-federal-reserve-district.pdf.

3. The Postindustrial Factory

1. Connie Bruck, "The Brass Ring: A Multibillionaire's Relentless Quest for Global Influence," *New Yorker*, June 30, 2008, 43.

2. Carrie M. Lane, *A Company of One: Insecurity, Independence, and the New World Order of White-Collar Unemployment* (Ithaca, NY: ILR Press, 2011), 45–61; Richard Nelson Bolles, *What Color Is Your Parachute?: A Practical Manual for Job-Hunters and Career-Changers*, rev. ed. (Berkeley, CA: Ten Speed Press, 2013) (first published in 1970, this book is updated annually); Barbara Sher and Barbara Smith, *I Could Do Anything if I Only Knew What It Was: How to Discover What You Really Want and How to Get It* (New York: Delacorte Press, 1994).

3. Previously, each individual shareholder of the casino corporation would have had to apply for a gaming license from the state of Nevada.

4. John Dombrink and William N. Thompson, *The Last Resort: Success and Failure in Campaigns for Casinos* (Reno: University of Nevada Press, 1990), 2, 33.

5. See Susan Strange, *Casino Capitalism* (Oxford: B. Blackwell, 1986); David Harvey, *A Brief History of Neoliberalism* (Oxford: Oxford University Press, 2005); Jane L. Collins and Victoria Mayer, *Both Hands Tied: Welfare Reform and the Race to the Bottom in the Low-wage Labor Market* (Chicago: University of Chicago Press, 2010); Jeffrey J. Sallaz, *The Labor of Luck: Casino Capitalism in the United States and South Africa* (Berkeley: University of California Press, 2009).

6. See Lane, *A Company of One*, 4; Jennifer M. Silva, *Coming Up Short: Working-Class Adulthood in an Age of Uncertainty* (Oxford: Oxford University Press, 2013), 145–146.

7. Jill Schennum, "Bethlehem Steelworkers: Reshaping the Industrial Working Class" (PhD diss., City University of New York, 2011), 202–207, 232. Schennum also notes that seniority, once a benefit, is now devalued as age becomes a liability rather than an asset. "Reshaping the Working Class: Bethlehem Steelworkers in Postindustrial Work" (paper presented at the annual meeting for the American Studies Association, Washington, DC, November 21–24, 2013).

8. Pennsylvania regulations require dealers to have a certificate from a state-approved dealer training program. In addition to passing an extensive background check, Pennsylvania requires dealers to have a letter of intent to hire from the casino and CPR certification to get a state license. At Northampton Community

College, Sands provided the tables and other equipment to train dealers and underwrote some start-up costs, but NCC runs the program independently.

9. Gregory Pappas, *The Magic City: Unemployment in a Working-Class Community* (Ithaca, NY: Cornell University Press, 1989), 62; John R. Logan and Harvey L. Molotch, *Urban Fortunes: The Political Economy of Place* (Berkeley: University of California Press, 1987), 40–43.

10. Pam Thoma, NCC Dealer Training School, e-mail message to author, June 20, 2012.

11. See also Silva, *Coming Up Short.*

12. Katherine S. Newman, *Falling from Grace: Downward Mobility in the Age of Affluence* (Berkeley: University of California Press, 1999); Alejandro Portes and Min Zhou, "The New Second Generation: Segmented Assimilation and Its Variants," *Annals of the American Academy of Political and Social Science* 530 (November 1993): 74–96.

13. Jack Metzgar, *Striking Steel: Solidarity Remembered* (Philadelphia: Temple University Press, 2000), 43, 135–136. Despite the number of paid holidays, which included United Nations Day from 1979 until 1983, many workers preferred to work holidays at double-time pay. In 1983, the United Steelworkers ratified its first concessionary contract, which included giving up United Nation's Day, the thirteen-week sabbatical, and one week of vacation.

14. Hal Rothman, *Neon Metropolis: How Las Vegas Started the Twenty-first Century* (New York: Routledge, 2002), 16–18.

15. The other nonunion operator is Stations Casino. Rothman, *Neon Metropolis,* 63–88; Arnold M. Knightly, "Workers' Paradise: Tips Can Help Companies Deal With Unions," *Las Vegas Business Press,* August 18, 2008; Mike Davis, "Class Struggle in Oz," in *The Grit Beneath the Glitter: Tales from the Real Las Vegas,* ed. Hal K. Rothman and Mike Davis (Berkeley: University of California Press, 2002), 183–184.

16. In 2015, aspects of the case were still ongoing: Venetian Casino Resort, LLC v. National Labor Relations Board, No. 12-1021 (D.C. Cir. 2015), http://law.justia.com/cases/federal/appellate-courts/cadc/12-1021/12-1021-2015-07-10.html. The MGM Grand was the first big casino to open nonunion in 1993 and similarly claimed its sidewalks as private property when Culinary Union members picketed in 1994. Ultimately, MGM Grand changed course to become a union property.

17. Steve Esack, "Free Speech Rally to Protest Sands Casino," *Morning Call,* November 16, 2012. Many community organizers only joined the free speech coalition after being assured anonymity. They feared losing charitable donations from Las Vegas Sands, what some activists called "hush money."

18. Nicole Radzievich, "No Labor, Anti-Casino Activities at SteelStacks," *Morning Call,* June 27, 2011; Lynn Olanoff, "Free Speech Concerns Still Linger at Bethlehem's SteelStacks," *Express-Times,* September 22, 2012.

19. See, for example, "Raises Won't Deter Union," *Las Vegas Review-Journal,* February 27, 2008. The industry as a whole took a similar approach in the 1960s and early 1970s. In addition to higher wages and benefits, dealers and others were given clearer work rules and grievance procedures. James P. Kraft, *Vegas at Odds:*

Labor Conflict in a Leisure Economy, 1960–1985 (Baltimore: Johns Hopkins University Press, 2010), 91–92.

20. Matt Assad, "Sands Ordered to Accept Guard Union," *Morning Call*, June 1, 2012; Matt Assad, "Sands Casino Guards Join New Force in Attempt to Unionize," *Morning Call*, October 10, 2015. Although most of Atlantic City's twelve casinos have union contracts in place, Pennsylvania, as a new gaming market, has yet to see the impact. Since opening, only a few of the eleven casinos have been unionized, beginning with their food and beverage workers and security guards.

21. Kraft, *Vegas at Odds*, 73–95; Sallaz, *The Labor of Luck*, 62, 215–216. According to Sallaz, the Culinary Union's success is tied to a contractual promise to *not* organize dealers or help other unions that try to do so (267n57). He notes several failed attempts to unionize Vegas dealers (288n31). In Atlantic City, dealers did not vote to unionize until 2007, three decades after the first casinos opened. Ellen Mutari and Deborah M. Figart, "Transformations in Casino Gaming and the Unionization of Atlantic City's Dealers," *Review of Radical Political Economics* 40, no. 3 (Summer 2008): 258–265.

22. In 2010 dealers at Wynn Las Vegas approved the resort's first contract, a ten-year deal, three years after they voted for union representation. The initial impetus for organizing was a new policy that split a portion of dealers' tips with their supervisors, although the contract did not reverse the policy. Chris Sierotylas, "Wynn Dealers Approve 10-Year Contract," *Las Vegas Review-Journal*, November 2, 2010. Dealers at Caesars Palace voted in favor of the union in 2007 and agreed on a contract in 2012. The dealers in Las Vegas were organized by the Transport Workers Union. The United Auto Workers Union has organized dealers in Atlantic City and elsewhere. Steve Green, "Caesars Palace, Union Finally Agree on Contract Terms for Dealers," *Vegas Inc.*, July 11, 2012.

23. Sands requires that dealers know blackjack and one other table game. NCC offers courses in: roulette, craps, baccarat and mini/midi baccarat, Pai Gow tiles, Pai Gow poker, and poker. The cost of two courses in 2012 at NCC was between $1,300 and $1,800. A dealer's license costs $350 and must be renewed every three years.

24. Ronda Kaysen, "The Casino the State Saved," *New York Times*, January 3, 2012; Emily Previti, "Revel's Original Estimate of 5,500 Full-time Employees Will Now Be 38 Percent Part-Timers," PressofAtlanticCity.com, February 15, 2012. According to Las Vegas Sands, 6 percent of all positions at the Bethlehem casino resort were part-time in 2013. Lynn Olanoff, "Sands Casino Bethlehem: We Must Add Amenities to Remain Competitive," *Express-Times*, October 15, 2013.

25. See also Ruth Milkman, *Farewell to the Factory: Auto Workers in the Late Twentieth Century* (Berkeley: University of California Press, 1997).

26. See also David Harvey, *The New Imperialism* (Oxford: Oxford University Press, 2003), 26–31. Natasha Dow Schüll argues that gambling regulations "function primarily to streamline and protect commercial gambling revenue, serving the interests of business and government rather than those of consumers." *Addiction by Design: Machine Gambling in Las Vegas* (Princeton, NJ: Princeton University Press, 2012), 298.

27. Sands announced plans in 2015 for a "stadium" of 150 hybrid gaming stations—personal electronic tables that play against a live dealer in the middle. The model decreases the dealer-to-player ratio. Matt Assad, "Sands Casino Plans Expansion," *Morning Call*, April 7, 2015. Initial forays into online gambling require patrons to be located within the state in which the activity is legal, as confirmed by geo-location technology. In New Jersey, part of the business model is to give online gamblers bonus credits they can only spend in the state's physical casinos.

28. Lynn Olanoff, "Sands Casino Resort Bethlehem Looking to Hire 100 Full-Time Dealers," *Express-Times*, August 7, 2014.

29. This contradicts some casino design experts who suggest low ceilings and greater intimacy are more attractive to gamblers. See Bill Friedman, *Designing Casinos to Dominate the Competition: The Friedman International Standards of Casino Design* (Reno, NV: Institute for the Study of Gambling and Commercial Gaming, 2000). Compared to casinos in Las Vegas or Atlantic City, Sands Bethlehem is still relatively small.

30. According to the LVS 10-K for the year ended December 31, 2014, 88 percent of Las Vegas Sands' $14,583,849,000 in net revenue came from Macau and Singapore, and just over 3 percent came from Bethlehem. http://www.sec.gov/Archives/edgar/data/1300514/000130051415000005/lvs-20141231x10k.htm.

31. Steven Bertoni, "Comeback Billionaire: How Adelson Dominates Chinese Gambling and U.S. Politics," *Forbes*, March 12, 2012, 1. By the end of 2014 LVS's market cap had dropped to $56 billion largely in response to government scrutiny of high rollers in Macau.

32. Arlie Russell Hochschild, *The Managed Heart: Commercialization of Human Feeling* (Berkeley: University of California Press, 1983). Later works that examine emotional labor in the service industry include: Robin Leidner, *Fast Food, Fast Talk: Service Work and the Routinization of Everyday Life* (Berkeley: University of California Press, 1993); Katherine S. Newman, *No Shame in My Game: The Working Poor in the Inner City* (New York: Knopf and the Russell Sage Foundation, 1999); Rachel Sherman, *Class Acts: Service and Inequality in Luxury Hotels* (Berkeley: University of California Press, 2007). Although emotional labor is often feminized, 58 percent of all workers at Sands Bethlehem in 2015 were men. Pennsylvania Gaming Control Board, *2014–2015 Gaming Diversity Report* (Harrisburg, PA: PGCB, 2015), 14, http://gamingcontrolboard.pa.gov/files/communications/2014-2015_Gaming_Diversity_Report.pdf.

33. Leidner, *Fast Food, Fast Talk;* Sallaz, *The Labor of Luck*, 11.

34. Michael Burawoy, *Manufacturing Consent: Changes in the Labor Process under Monopoly Capitalism* (Chicago: University of Chicago Press, 1979); Sallaz explores parallels to Burawoy in the casino industry's "service production regime" in *The Labor of Luck*. Sherman also applies Burawoy's theory to service work, but argues for the need to depart from the factory model in *Class Acts*.

35. See Kathryn Marie Dudley, *The End of the Line: Lost Jobs, New Lives in Postindustrial America* (Chicago: University of Chicago Press, 1994), 106–115.

36. See also Sallaz, *The Labor of Luck*.

37. Pennsylvania Gaming Control Board, "Gaming Application Instructions," last modified July 9, 2012, http://gamingcontrolboard.pa.gov/files/licensure/applications/Application_Instructions_Gaming.pdf. The thorough procedures are in some ways a ritual to give the industry a perception of probity. The licensing fees also create more revenue for regulators (i.e., the state). Peter Collins, *Gambling and the Public Interest* (Westport, CT: Praeger, 2003), 64–67.

38. See Chapter 6 and Jeffery E. Singer, "The Casino as Lifeline," *Lens* (blog), *New York Times*, August 23, 2013, http://lens.blogs.nytimes.com/2013/08/23/the-casino-as-lifeline/?hp&_r=0.

39. Schüll argues that slot machines are designed for efficiency and compares players to factory line workers. While in an "experience economy" consumer concerns lie close to corporate concerns, when one recognizes gamblers as workers, it becomes clear that the relationship is not symmetrical. *Addiction by Design*, 52–75.

40. For every dollar spent gambling in Bethlehem's casino, in aggregate only about 91 cents come back to the players (83 cents on the tables and 93 cents in the slots). Most people will lose larger amounts of money for the few who hit big wins. These holds are according to LVS's 10-K for the year ended December 31, 2014, http://www.sec.gov/Archives/edgar/data/1300514/000130051415000005/lvs-20141231x10k.htm.

41. Schüll convincingly shows how the gaming industry frames addiction as an individual disease to avoid its own implication in profiting from problem gamblers' losses and protect itself from litigation. Given that casinos gather extensive data on player habits, countries like Australia and Canada have "duty of care actions" that increasingly put the responsibility on industry to keep problem gamblers from self-destruction. *Addiction by Design*, 257–289. For another postindustrial example of this fissure between social responsibility and economic measures, see Karen Ho's ethnography of investment bankers, *Liquidated: An Ethnography of Wall Street* (Durham, NC: Duke University Press, 2009).

42. Marshall Berman writes of the modern experience: "Our past, whatever it was, was a past in the process of disintegration; we yearn to grasp it, but it is baseless and elusive; we look back for something solid to lean on, only to find ourselves embracing ghosts." *All That Is Solid Melts Into Air: The Experience of Modernity*, 2nd ed. (New York: Penguin Books, 1988), 333; see also Anna Tsing, *Friction: An Ethnography of Global Connection* (Princeton, NJ: Princeton University Press, 2004), 55–57.

43. See Jack Metzgar, *Striking Steel*, 132–133.

44. Shane Hamilton describes postindustrialism as reflecting this shift since the 1950s from production to distribution. He highlights the deregulation of the trucking industry in 1980, which led to slashed wages and a weakened union, as key to understanding the transition. *Trucking Country: The Road to America's Wal-Mart Country* (Princeton, NJ: Princeton University Press, 2008).

45. By 2013 the east end of the site hosted roughly 2,500 jobs, the same number employed by the Steel's depleted structural division just before it shut down in 1995. See Nicole Radzievich, "Has 'Road to Nowhere' Sparked Development?," *Morning*

Call, January 2, 2012; Radzievich, "Warehouse the Size of Nearly 34 Football Fields Proposed for Bethlehem," *Morning Call*, March 25, 2014.

46. Pennsylvania Gaming Control Board, "Pennsylvania Slot Machine Revenue Up Nearly 6% in December," news release, January 5, 2015, http://gamingcontrolboard.pa.gov/?pr=601; PGCB, "Table Games Revenue for December Up More Than 15%," news release, January 15, 2015, http://gamingcontrolboard.pa.gov/?pr=602.

47. Pennsylvanians were promised property tax relief, which many locals say they have not received. Bethlehem's local share of casino tax revenues goes into the city's general fund, and thus cannot be specifically traced for how it is spent. Much of Bethlehem's budgeting is focused on offsetting rising city pension costs.

48. As of 2015 the casino employed just over 2,300, with roughly 700 additional people employed by the adjacent restaurants, events center, and retail spaces. Las Vegas Sands' charitable donations in Bethlehem and the Lehigh Valley in fiscal year 2012–2013 totaled $528,419, but dropped to $242,536 the following year, the lowest since the casino opened. In 2014–2015 charitable donations jumped to $901,825. Olanoff, "Sands Casino Resort Bethlehem: We Must Add . . ."; Pennsylvania Gaming Control Board, *2014–2015 Gaming Diversity Report*, 14; PGCB, *2010–2011 Gaming Diversity Report* (Harrisburg, PA: PGCB, 2011), 13, http://gamingcontrolboard.pa.gov/files/communications/2010-2011_Gaming_Diversity_Report.pdf.

49. Randy Martin, *The Financialization of Daily Life* (Philadelphia: Temple University Press, 2002), 104, 149. Interestingly, for some compulsive gamblers, there is no expectation of winning the jackpot; simply entering "the zone" where they know they will eventually lose all their money adds enough predictability to volatile everyday experiences to have a calming effect. Schüll, *Addiction by Design*, 208.

50. On "accumulation by dispossession," see Harvey, *A Brief History of Neoliberalism*, 159–165.

51. See Kevin Lynch, *What Time Is This Place?* (Cambridge, MA: MIT Press, 1972), 168–173.

4. A Steel Site in Limbo

1. Cathy Stanton makes a related argument about the ritual space of Lowell National Historic Park in Massachusetts. She is particularly interested in the role of historical narrative, while I further explore the relation of ritual and narrative to the built environment. Cathy Stanton, *The Lowell Experiment: Public History in a Postindustrial City* (Amherst: University of Massachusetts Press, 2006), 168–184.

2. Setha Low, "Towards an Anthropological Theory of Space and Place," *Semiotica* 175 (2009): 21–37; Anna Tsing, *Friction: An Ethnography of Global Connection* (Princeton, NJ: Princeton University Press, 2004).

3. A photo of the portrait, painted in 2009 by Ben Marcune of Bethlehem, is available here: http://photos.lehighvalleylive.com/express-times/2009/10/callahan_portrait_mayor2jpg.html.

4. Randall Mason describes how a "memory infrastructure" can provide continuity and stability amid the chaos of urban development in the context of preservation efforts in early-twentieth-century New York. *The Once and Future New York: Historic Preservation and the Modern City* (Minneapolis: University of Minnesota Press, 2009), x, xxv.

5. Pennsylvania's Urban Redevelopment Law of 1945 defined blight, created municipal Redevelopment Authorities, and enabled slum clearance as a public good. The 1947 Pennsylvania case, *Belovsky v. Redevelopment Authority of Philadelphia*, provided further foundations for urban renewal and eminent domain, upholding private use or reuse as a public good. With a few notable exceptions, including Alison Isenberg's diversely sourced *Downtown America* and David Schuyler's study of Lancaster, Pennsylvania, urban renewal scholarship has emphasized the experience of large cities, even as 40 percent of the more than $13 billion of federal money spent on these programs between 1950 and 1974 went to municipalities with less than 100,000 people. Alison Isenberg, *Downtown America: A History of the Place and the People who Made It* (Chicago: University of Chicago Press, 2004); David Schuyler, *A City Transformed: Redevelopment, Race, and Suburbanization in Lancaster, Pennsylvania, 1940–1980* (University Park: Pennsylvania State University Press, 2002); U.S. Department of Housing and Urban Development, *1974 Statistical Yearbook of the U.S. Department of Housing and Urban Development* (Washington, DC: U.S. Government Printing Office, 1974), 20.

6. Federal grants accounted for $9.1 million. Bethlehem, PA, Redevelopment Authority, *1966 Annual Report* (Bethlehem, PA: Redevelopment Authority, 1966), n.p.

7. Clarke and Rapuano, Inc. and Russell Vannest Black, *An Interim Report on the City of Bethlehem* (Bethlehem, PA: Bethlehem Redevelopment Authority, 1956).

8. Winston-Salem's nonprofit preservation group Old Salem, Inc. began restoring Old Salem, the Moravians' southern colonial settlement, in 1950.

9. Clarke and Rapuano, Inc. and Black, *An Interim Report on the City of Bethlehem*, n.p.

10. City of Bethlehem, PA, *Bethlehem Historic District Design Guidelines* (Bethlehem, PA: City of Bethlehem, 1993), n.p.; "Bethlehem the City, Its First 50 Years," *Bethlehem Globe-Times*, July 15, 1967.

11. On "historic renewal," see: Historic Bethlehem, Inc., *Annual Report to the Membership of Historic Bethlehem, Inc.: Summary of Activities from June 1, 1959–May 31, 1960* (Bethlehem, PA: Historic Bethlehem, Inc., [1960?]), Historic Bethlehem, Inc. Papers, Historic Bethlehem Partnership Archives, Bethlehem, PA (hereafter cited as HBP); "Historic Preservation via Urban Renewal," *Journal of Housing* 19, no. 6 (August 10, 1962): 314–315.

12. Historic Bethlehem, Inc., "News Bulletin," January 28, 1963, HBP.

13. See also Max Page and Randall Mason, eds., *Giving Preservation a History: Histories of Historic Preservation in the United States* (New York: Routledge, 2004); Stephanie R. Ryberg, "Historic Preservation's Urban Renewal Roots: Preservation and Planning in Midcentury Philadelphia," *Journal of Urban History* 39, no. 2 (2012): 193–213.

14. "Mid-City Boundaries Set for Redevelopment Plan," *Bethlehem Globe-Times*, April 25, 1957.

15. "What's Going on in Bethlehem?," *New York Herald Tribune*, October 1, 1961.

16. J. Dennis Robinson, *Strawbery Banke: A Seaport Museum 400 Years in the Making* (Portsmouth, NH: Peter E. Randall, 2007), 193–251; Paige W. Roberts, "The Politics of Preservation: Historical Consciousness and Community Identity in Portsmouth, New Hampshire" (PhD diss., George Washington University, 2000), 127–159.

17. "Historic Preservation via Urban Renewal," *Journal of Housing* 19, no. 6 (August 10, 1962): 296–315; Margaret Carrol, ed., *Historic Preservation through Urban Renewal* (Washington, DC: Urban Renewal Administration, Housing and Home Finance Agency, 1963). The other six cities listed in the *Journal of Housing* were Providence; Monterey, CA; Little Rock, AR; Mobile, AL; York, PA; and San Juan, Puerto Rico. The URA publication lists, in addition, Philadelphia (Society Hill), New Haven, CT (Wooster Square), San Francisco (Western Addition), Washington, DC (Southwest), Norfolk, VA, and Wilmington, NC. URA notes that federal funds can be used to prepare or augment the historic site, but cannot be used to restore historic structures. Actual restoration had to be done through a state or local public agency or private group.

18. Clarke and Rapuano, Inc., *Center City Bethlehem: A Report on the Plan for the Central Business District* (New York: Clarke and Rapuano, 1969), 22.

19. Clarke and Rapuano, Inc., *Sun Inn: An Examination of Four Sites* (New York: Clarke and Rapuano, 1970), n.p. Box 61, Clarke and Rapuano Records, 1940–1993, Division of Rare and Manuscript Collections, Cornell University Library, Ithaca, NY.

20. This was compounded by the sudden death in 1976 of the project's primary booster, First Valley Bank President Reese Jones, on a fishing trip in Florida. ("Renewal Leader Dies on Fla. Trip," *Bethlehem Globe-Times*, March 22, 1976.) Opposition had been spearheaded by Citizens for Constructive Renewal, a small group led by Lehigh University professor David Amidon. On Lancaster, see Schuyler, *A City Transformed*, 83–119.

21. "Tourists Retrace Pathways of History in Glowing City," *Bethlehem Globe-Times*, December 24, 1966. By the late 1960s, the putz regularly attracted more than 10,000 visitors, with numbers trending upwards and thousands more going on bus tours of the lights and to other holiday attractions. In 1966 Bethlehem's Christmas lighting display included 15,000 lights, an eighty-foot tree on the Hill-to-Hill Bridge (constructed of ninety-seven smaller trees fastened to a wooden framework), and 465 small trees throughout the city. "Shining Star Welcomes Visitors," *Bethlehem Globe-Times*, December 24, 1966; "Community Putz Viewed by 13,201 in 18-Day Stand," *Bethlehem Globe-Times*, January 2, 1968; Dan Church, "Magic of City at Christmas Draws Visitors in Record Numbers," *Bethlehem Globe-Times*, December 24, 1976.

22. Richard Francaviglia, "Selling Heritage Landscapes," in *Preserving Cultural Landscapes in America*, ed. Arnold R. Alanen and Robert Z. Melnick (Baltimore:

Johns Hopkins University Press, 2000), 45; Catherine M. Cameron and John B. Gatewood, "The Authentic Interior: Questing *Gemeinschaft* in Post-Industrial Society," *Human Organization* 53, no. 1 (Spring 1994): 24.

23. Norman Larson, "Historic Group Preserves Heritage," *Bethlehem Globe-Times*, December 23, 1967. A report for HBI in 1968 noted that the Sun Inn could be "a vital connecting point between heritage and commerce" given its "hinge" location on two shopping streets. Christopher Tunnard and Geoffrey Baker, *Bethlehem Historic Center Design Proposals, Historic Bethlehem Incorporated* (New Haven, CT: Tunnard and Baker, 1968), 12, HBP.

24. See for example, Historic Bethlehem, Inc., newsletters, November 1970, Fall 1975, Fall 1976, HBP.

25. Other projects that used urban renewal funds include the new City Center completed on the North Side in the Moravian district in 1967, and the clearance of land to allow Lehigh University to expand on the South Side.

26. National Heritage Corporation, *Bethlehem's Historic Main Street* (West Chester, PA: National Heritage Corporation and Design Group 2, 1976). Landscape architects/city planning consultants Christopher Tunnard and Geoffrey Baker had offered HBI similar recommendations in 1968. Tunnard and Baker, *Bethlehem Historic Center Design Proposals*, 14.

27. Urban Land Institute, *Recommendations for the Revitalization of the Downtown Business District for the City of Bethlehem, PA.* (Washington, DC: The Institute, 1976), 11, 20, 29.

28. Lil Junas, *Historic Bethlehem, Pennsylvania: A Photographic Glimpse* (Bethlehem, PA: Taylor Printing Services, Inc. and Lehigh Litho, Inc., 1985), 6; Historic Bethlehem, Inc., newsletter, Winter 1981, HBP.

29. See Howard Gillette, *Camden after the Fall: Decline and Renewal in a Post-industrial City* (Philadelphia: University of Pennsylvania Press, 2005); Jonathan Mark Souther, *New Orleans on Parade: Tourism and the Transformation of the Crescent City* (Baton Rouge: Louisiana State University Press, 2006).

30. Ann Markusen and Anne Gadwa, *Creative Placemaking* (Washington, DC: National Endowment for the Arts, 2010); Richard Florida, *The Rise of the Creative Class: And How It's Transforming Work, Leisure, Community and Everyday Life* (New York: Basic Books, 2002).

31. On initial plans, see Matt Assad, "Razing to Pave Way for Steel's New Life," *Morning Call*, April 18, 2007.

32. Avery Gordon, *Ghostly Matters: Haunting and the Sociological Imagination* (Minneapolis: University of Minnesota Press, 2008), 93.

33. Gordon emphasizes phenomenological haunting, but does not emphasize the haunted landscape to any great extent. See also Sherry Lee Linkon and John Russo, *Steeltown, U.S.A.: Work and Memory in Youngstown* (Lawrence: University Press of Kansas, 2002), 14–18.

34. Shelby Weaver Splain, "South Bethlehem Downtown Historic District," registration form for the National Register of Historic Places, May 2005, 9, 17, https://www.dot7.state.pa.us/ce_imagery/phmc_scans/H111695_01H.PDF.

35. See Arnold Hirsch, *Making the Second Ghetto: Race and Housing in Chicago, 1940–1960* (New York: Cambridge University Press, 1983); Howard Gillette, *Be-*

tween Justice and Beauty: Race, Planning, and the Failure of Urban Policy in Washington, D.C. (Baltimore: Johns Hopkins University Press, 1995); Schuyler, *A City Transformed;* Robert O. Self, *American Babylon: Race and the Struggle for Postwar Oakland* (Princeton, NJ: Princeton University Press, 2003), 134–159.

36. Bethlehem, PA, Redevelopment Authority, *1966 Annual Report*, n.p. The second major intervention on the South Side involved the "blighting" of 230 homes near Packer Ave. and Butler St., the removal of which allowed for Lehigh University's expansion. Half of the $17.5 million in projected funds were designated to the five South Side renewal projects.

37. "City Acts Tonight on Redevelopment for Portion of Northampton Heights," *Bethlehem Globe-Times*, January 19, 1965; "City Heeds Federal Warning, Moves for Heights Renewal," *Bethlehem Globe-Times*, January 20, 1965.

38. Joint Planning Commission Lehigh-Northampton Counties, *Minority Housing Problems* (Joint Planning Commission: Lehigh Valley, PA, 1971), 33. The Steel's backstage role in the selection of this renewal site fits the broader pattern of business interests driving redevelopment projects. Robert M. Fogelson, *Downtown: Its Rise and Fall, 1880–1950* (New Haven, CT: Yale University Press, 2001), 365; John R. Logan and Harvey L. Molotch, *Urban Fortunes: The Political Economy of Place* (Berkeley: University of California Press, 1987); Bernard Frieden and Lynne Sagalyn, *Downtown, Inc.: How America Rebuilds Cities* (Cambridge, MA: MIT Press, 1989), 17–27.

39. The shift in public perception as reflected in the local newspaper is stark. Opposition to the plan to tear down the Heights was significantly quelled when the Steel announced its modernization plan: "We would like to emphasize that the modernization and expansion program as proposed here will serve to strengthen the competitive position of the Bethlehem plant, contribute to the general economic well-being of the Lehigh Valley area, and make more secure the jobs of our local employees." "Steel Will Build $30 Million Oxygen Unit in Northampton Hts. Renewal Project," *Bethlehem Globe-Times*, April 1, 1965.

40. Per request following his interview, Frank Podleiszek is not a pseudonym.

41. "Rooney Sides with Steel, Hints at Low Cost Housing," *Bethlehem Globe-Times*, April 3, 1965.

42. The 1965 Pennsylvania case, *Crawford v. Redevelopment Authority*, determined that isolated, unblighted properties did not prevent a Redevelopment Authority from designating a broader area as blighted.

43. On the relationship between "souvenirs" and nostalgia, see Susan Stewart, *On Longing: Narratives of the Miniature, the Gigantic, the Souvenir, the Collection* (Durham, NC: Duke University Press, 1993), 135–145.

44. Julia Hell and Andreas Schonle, eds., *Ruins of Modernity* (Durham, NC: Duke University Press, 2010), 6–7; Tim Edensor, *Industrial Ruins: Space, Aesthetics and Materiality* (Oxford: Berg, 2005).

45. On the multiple (and shifting) understandings of historic preservation, see Page and Mason, eds., *Giving Preservation a History;* Alanen and Melnick, *Preserving Cultural Landscapes in America.*

46. See Mason, *The Once and Future New York*, 243, 248–249. For a brief history of the evolution of historic preservation's incorporation into economic

development through adaptive reuse, particularly since the end of federal urban renewal in the 1970s, see Andrew Hurley, *Beyond Preservation: Using Public History to Revitalize Inner Cities* (Philadelphia: Temple University Press, 2010), 1–31.

47. Max Page makes a similar argument in his study of New York City in the first half of the twentieth century. *The Creative Destruction of Manhattan, 1900–1940* (Chicago: University of Chicago Press, 1999), 2, 252. See also Sharon Zukin, *Landscapes of Power: From Detroit to Disney World* (Berkeley: University of California Press, 1991).

48. The Wynn resort, for example, replaces its carpet every nine to twelve months and revamps its hotel rooms every six years to stay "fresh." Marilyn Spiegel, "Luxury at Wynn Las Vegas," interview by David Schwartz, *UNLV Gaming Podcast*, podcast audio, University of Nevada Center for Gaming Research, March 3, 2011, http://digitalscholarship.unlv.edu/gaming_podcasts/46/.

49. The sculptures by Sidney Waugh portray: management, employees, consumers, stockholders, suppliers, raw materials, steelmaking, shipbuilding, and fabrication. Illustrator Dean Cornwell painted the murals. On the Bethlehem Steel Corporation's art collection, some of which was auctioned during bankruptcy, see Geoff Gehman, "Image through Images: How Bethlehem Steel's Art Collection Followed the Rise and Fall of a Giant," *Morning Call*, December 14, 2003. For images of the Cornwell murals, see http://www.johnsonandgriffiths.com/#/deancornwell/.

50. The building's heating system was linked to the blast furnaces, meaning once they shut down in 1995, so did the climate control.

51. "Steel Offices Transformed for Yuletide," *Bethlehem Globe-Times*, December 24, 1964.

52. Susan Stewart (*On Longing*, 37–69) argues that "the miniature" represents contained order and control, a stability and predictability in this case betrayed by the Steel's demise.

53. In January 2014 a grand jury recommended in a scathing report that the former steel executive who headed the NMIH be removed due to gross mismanagement of funds and failure to achieve the museum's mission. Funds that once totaled $15 million had shrunk to available assets of $700,000. Following the report, the Board voted to cut costs, hire a new director, and come up with a revised plan to open a museum. Matt Assad, "Industrial Museum Officials: Grand Jury Dead Wrong," *Morning Call*, January 31, 2014.

54. See Hurley, *Beyond Preservation*, ix.

55. Barbara Kirshenblatt-Gimblett calls this the "reciprocity of disappearance and exhibition." Kirshenblatt-Gimblett, *Destination Culture: Tourism, Museums, and Heritage* (Berkeley: University of California Press, 1998), 56. See also Stanton, *The Lowell Experiment*, xiii. Many of the artifacts have since been removed. Matt Assad, "Changing Some Gears at the Bethlehem Steel Site," *Morning Call*, February 26, 2006.

56. Save Our Steel, www.saveoursteel.org (archived website: https://web.archive.org/web/20140904180645/http://www.saveoursteel.org/). Mason calls this function of preservation a "memory infrastructure." It creates places representing

stability and continuity as a counterweight to the chaos of the urban environment. *The Once and Future New York*, x.

57. Save Our Steel, www.saveoursteel.org.

58. Phillips Preiss Grygiel LLC, *Preservation Plan for the City of Bethlehem, Pennsylvania* (Hoboken, NJ: Phillips Preiss Grygiel LLC, 2011), http://www.bethlehem-pa.gov/dept/planning_Zoning_Permits/preservationplan/PreservationPlan2011.pdf. While twenty Steel buildings are listed in the plan as "historic resources," there is no ordinance preventing developers from tearing down the buildings. The potential to legally protect Steel buildings from demolition remains mired in uncertainty given a City agreement in 2000, under Bethlehem Steel's reign, that the structures could not be added to the National Register of Historic Places. According to the City, this agreement, designed to give developers maximum flexibility, survived the post-bankruptcy transfer of ownership to Sands Bethworks.

59. About half of Bethlehem Steel's central office staff, roughly 2,500 people, worked in Martin Tower and the adjoining office facilities. Initially, only American-made cars were allowed to park in its underground garage. David Venditta and Ardith Hilliard, eds., *Forging America: The Story of Bethlehem Steel*, 2nd ed. (Bethlehem, PA: The Morning Call, 2010), 124; Timothy M. Noble, "Martin Tower," registration form for the National Register of Historic Places, January 20, 2010, 3–4, 16–17, https://www.dot7.state.pa.us/ce_imagery/phmc_scans/H155517_01H.pdf; Peter B. Treiber and Elizabeth A. Kovach, *Inside Bethlehem Steel: The Final Quarter Century* (Bethlehem, PA: PT Photo Books, 2007), 110.

60. Initial plans for the plaza outside the main entrance, designed by landscape architects Clarke & Rapuano, included a giant H-beam emblem inlaid in black granite, surrounded by terrazzo pavers. While the steel frame of the tower rose quickly in 1969, its completion was delayed nearly two years. Among other interim modifications, the granite H-beam plaza feature was eliminated in favor of plain concrete in August 1970 and further scaled back by May 1972. Clarke & Rapuano plans, Boxes 129 and 130 (Martin Tower), Clarke and Rapuano Records, 1940–1993, Division of Rare and Manuscript Collections, Cornell University Library, Ithaca, NY. Clarke & Rapuano drew a "Christmas Tree Study" in April 1970 denoting where the trees, traditionally displayed at the South Side SGO Building, would be relocated. Ibid., Box 129.

61. "Ground Broken for Tower," *Bethlehem Globe-Times*, August 25, 1969.

62. Noble, "Martin Tower," 17–18.

63. The owner-developers of Martin Tower are Lewis Ronca of Bethlehem and Norton Herrick of New Jersey. The assessed value of the real estate dropped from $31.5 million in 1999 to $1.7 million in 2010. Matt Assad, "Martin Tower Falling—In Value," *Morning Call*, November 5, 2010.

64. Noble, "Martin Tower," 6–7. On the opportunity for critique of capitalist structures at an industrial heritage site, see Stanton, *The Lowell Experiment*.

65. See also Linkon and Russo, *Steeltown, U.S.A.*, 241–247.

66. Noble, "Martin Tower," 11–12. The plan from 2007 was available here: http://www.martinaia.com/section/planning/residential/image5.jpg. On plans in

2010, see Matt Assad and Steve Esack, "New $223 Million Plan for Martin Tower," *Morning Call*, September 23, 2010. After the National Register designation, the developers sought approval of a Tax Increment Financing district to divert tax money from the parcel to infrastructure development for the next twenty years, but the Bethlehem Area School District voted in opposition. In 2013 the developers asked the city council to remove Martin Tower from a list of protected buildings, although they said they had no plans to tear the building down. Late that year, Martin Tower and its fifty-three-acre campus were included in Bethlehem's new state-awarded tax incentive district, the City Revitalization and Improvement Zone. The CRIZ designation allows developers to offset construction costs with state and local taxes from new business tenants. Although new plans for a $175 million mixed-use development were expected in 2014, as of late 2015 nothing had surfaced, and the city council moved to rezone the area to increase flexibility and remove a requirement to reuse Martin Tower. See Randy Kraft, "New TIF Plan Proposed for Bethlehem's Martin Tower," WFMZ.com, April 17, 2013; Sara Satullo, "Bethlehem Wins Tax Zone Designation; Mayor Likens Award to 'CRIZmas Present,'" *Express-Times*, December 30, 2013; Nicole Radzievich, "Public Packs Bethlehem Meeting on Martin Tower's Future," *Morning Call*, October 6, 2015.

67. See also Steve Esack, "Point/Counterpoint: Martin Tower TIF," *Morning Call*, October 2, 2010.

68. The Power of Place project in Los Angeles, led by Dolores Hayden from 1984 to 1991, is an exemplar of this turning point in interpretation. The not-for-profit helped recover and commemorate everyday histories of women, the working class, and minorities through public art and preservation. Dolores Hayden, *The Power of Place: Urban Landscapes as Public History* (Cambridge, MA: MIT Press, 1995). See also Hurley, *Beyond Preservation*, 32–54.

69. See Hayden, *Power of Place*, 227–238; Hurley, *Beyond Preservation*, 146–177.

70. Mid-Atlantic Regional Center for the Humanities, "Designing Interpretation for the Bethlehem Steel Site . . . and Beyond: Report from the June 2007 Public Conference," September 11, 2007; Sharon Ann Holt, "History Keeps Bethlehem Steel from Going off the Rails: Moving a Complex Community Process toward Success," *The Public Historian* 28, no. 2 (Spring 2006): 31–44; Lehigh Valley Industrial Heritage Coalition, *Draft Strategic Plan*, December 1, 2008.

71. On a similar dynamic between "locals" and "outsiders" in an industrial town, see Stanton, *The Lowell Experiment*, 190–228.

72. It is only within the past several years that the interviews have been made readily accessible to the public. The "In the Age of Steel" oral histories are available in the Beyond Steel Archive, Lehigh University, Bethlehem, PA, http://digital.lib.lehigh.edu/beyondsteel/.

73. "Steelworkers' Archives Inc. By-Laws," [2011?], www.steelworkersarchives.com/bylaws.pdf, accessed February 14, 2012.

74. As in the other collections, the minimal representation of women and the absence of workers of color at the 2012 exhibit was striking and left some Latino Steel veterans, for example, feeling left out. Many local historical groups also felt left out of the city's new, permanent visitor center exhibit in the former Stock

House, which they saw as being commandeered by ArtsQuest. See Nicole Radzievich, "Bethlehem's New Visitors Center Faces Challenges," *Morning Call*, March 4, 2012. Note: Historic Bethlehem Partnership changed its name to Historic Bethlehem Museums and Sites in 2012.

75. Historic Bethlehem Partnership described the tour as covering "the concept of the development of South Bethlehem from the Moravian farms in the 1700s to the rise of the steel industry and now the renaissance, in essence the rebirth, of arts and culture." Nicole Radzievich, "ArtsQuest Center to Offer Look at Bethlehem's Varied Past," *Morning Call*, April 9, 2011.

76. Although Bernie said the tours were an hour, newspaper accounts in 2005 state they were thirty minutes. The tours may have been longer in other years. The fact that Bernie ran over time is not in doubt. Spencer Soper, "Ex-steelworkers Lead Tours through Their Memories," *Morning Call*, August 28, 2005.

77. See also Nate Jastrzemski, "Turf & Tours," *Bethlehem Press*, March 9, 2011.

78. See Stanton, *The Lowell Experiment*, 182–183.

79. Lester Clore to H-Labor discussion network, "Questions about Bethlehem Steel and Labor History," December 9, 2013, H-Net Humanities and Social Sciences OnLine, http://h-net.msu.edu/cgi-bin/logbrowse.pl?trx=lm&list=H-Labor.

80. On the performativity of heritage, see Kirshenblatt-Gimblett, *Destination Culture*.

5. Landscapes of Life and Loss

1. Ruth also described that morning to a student from Lehigh University on November 9, 2010. As of 2015, this university-sponsored series of filmed interviews on the churches had yet to be digitized for Lehigh's Beyond Steel Archive. Ruth shared her personal copy with me. Unless noted otherwise, as here with "I felt like I had to be there," quotes are from my own interview on July 11, 2012.

2. John C. Seitz, *No Closure: Catholic Practice and Boston's Parish Shutdowns* (Cambridge, MA: Harvard University Press, 2011), 65–66.

3. See also Thomas J. Sugrue, *The Origins of the Urban Crisis: Race and Inequality in Postwar Detroit* (Princeton, NJ: Princeton University Press, 2005); Lilia Fernandez, *Brown in the Windy City: Mexicans and Puerto Ricans in Postwar Chicago* (Chicago: University of Chicago Press, 2012), 11–12.

4. For complementary analyses of ethnicity, multiplicity, and narratives of the past and loss in Harlem, see Sandhya Shukla, "Harlem's Pasts in Its Present," in *Ethnographies of Neoliberalism*, ed. Carol J. Greenhouse (Philadelphia: University of Pennsylvania Press, 2010), 177–191; Robert A. Orsi, "The Religious Boundaries of an Inbetween People: Street *Feste* and the Problem of the Dark-Skinned Other in Italian Harlem, 1920–1990," *American Quarterly* 44, no. 3 (September 1992): 313–347.

5. Bethlehem, PA, Bureau of Planning and Development, *The People of Bethlehem: Community Renewal Program Report Number 2* (Bethlehem, PA: Bureau of Planning and Development, 1967), 56.

6. "Conditions in City Not So Bad as They're Painted, Says Mayor," *Bethlehem Globe-Times*, November 15, 1927; Frank Orpe and Jean Pfeifle McQuade, *Dare to Be Brave* (Center Square, PA: Alpha Publications, 1977), 46–47; "In the Age of Steel: Oral Histories from Bethlehem, Pennsylvania—Joseph K. Mangan," interview by Dan Ponzol, 1976, Beyond Steel Archive, Lehigh University, Bethlehem, PA, http://digital.lib.lehigh.edu/beyondsteel/pdf/mangan_141.pdf.

7. U.S. Bureau of the Census, *Religious Bodies: 1926*, vol. 1 (Washington, DC: U.S. Government Printing Office, 1930), 356, 375. The eleven churches comprised a sixth of the sixty churches in the community, but 35 percent (12,076) of total church members. The density of the parishes is significant given the city's founding as a Protestant religious settlement.

8. See also John T. McGreevy, *Parish Boundaries: The Catholic Encounter with Race in the Twentieth-Century Urban North* (Chicago: University of Chicago Press, 1996); Lizabeth Cohen, *Making a New Deal: Industrial Workers in Chicago, 1919–1939* (Cambridge: Cambridge University Press, 1990); Robert A. Orsi, *The Madonna of 115th Street: Faith and Community in Italian Harlem, 1880–1950* (New Haven, CT: Yale University Press, 2002).

9. Bethlehem Bureau of Planning and Development, *The People of Bethlehem*, 55; Andrew G. Krause, "St. John Capistrano Church, 1903–2003 History," in *St. John Capistrano Roman Catholic Church, Bethlehem, Pennsylvania, 1903–2003 Centennial* (Bethlehem, PA: n.p., 2003), n.p.

10. I learned about the windows by speaking with a former parishioner. See also Dolly Rayner, "History of the Parish" in *St. Joseph's Roman Catholic Church 75th Jubilee: October 15, 1989* (Bethlehem, PA: St. Joseph's Roman Catholic Church, 1989), 23–25.

11. See also Thomas A. Tweed, *Our Lady of the Exile: Diasporic Religion at a Cuban Catholic Shrine in Miami* (New York: Oxford University Press, 1997), 93.

12. Orsi, *The Madonna of 115th Street*, xlv–xlix; McGreevy, *Parish Boundaries.*

13. Stanley West, in his dissertation citing an unpublished manuscript from 1967, affirms that the Steel Corporation deducted workers' church dues from their pay as a way to influence various ethnic groups via their clergy. Stanley A. West, *The Mexican Aztec Society: A Mexican-American Voluntary Association in Diachronic Perspective* (New York: Arno Press, 1976), 94–95.

14. On similar relationships between the U.S. Steel Corporation and churches in Gary, Indiana, and Duluth, Minnesota, in the early twentieth century, see James Welborn Lewis, *The Protestant Experience in Gary, Indiana, 1906–1975: At Home in the City* (Knoxville: University of Tennessee Press, 1992), 38, 78, 82; Arnold R. Alanen, *Morgan Park: Duluth, U.S. Steel, and the Forging of a Company Town* (Minneapolis: University of Minnesota Press, 2007), 168–172.

15. "In the Age of Steel: Oral Histories from Bethlehem, Pennsylvania—Joseph K. Mangan," 9; Roderick J. McIntosh, "Growing Up in the Shadow of 'The Steel,'" *Archaeology*, November/December 1999, 54–56.

16. David Venditta and Ardith Hilliard, eds., *Forging America: The Story of Bethlehem Steel*, 2nd ed. (Bethlehem, PA: The Morning Call, 2010), 42. On the transi-

tion from ethnic enclaves to a shared working-class identity in the 1920s and 1930s, see Cohen, *Making a New Deal.*

17. Nicole Radzievich, "Fledgling Labor Movement Recalled in Bethlehem," *Morning Call*, August 31, 2012. See also "State Constabulary in South Bethlehem," *Bethlehem Globe-Times*, February 26, 1910, 1; "Strike Situation in South Bethlehem," *Bethlehem Globe-Times*, February 28, 1910, 1; "The Local Strike Situation," *Bethlehem Globe-Times*, March 2, 1910, 1; "Funerals—Joseph Szambo," *Bethlehem Globe-Times*, March 2, 1910, 1, cited in Krause, "St. John Capistrano Church, 1903–2003 History."

18. Matthew Frye Jacobson, *Whiteness of a Different Color: European Immigrants and the Alchemy of Race* (Cambridge, MA: Harvard University Press, 1998); David R. Roedinger, *Working towards Whiteness: How America's Immigrants Became White, The Strange Journey from Ellis Island to the Suburbs* (New York: Basic Books, 2005); McGreevy, *Parish Boundaries*, 78–84; Cohen, *Making a New Deal.*

19. See also Gerald Gamm, *Urban Exodus: Why the Jews Left Boston and the Catholics Stayed* (Cambridge, MA: Harvard University Press, 1999), 20–21, 129–140.

20. Krause, "St. John Capistrano Church, 1903–2003 History."

21. Saints Cyril and Methodius School consolidated into a Catholic school on the North Side, but that school, Seton Academy, closed because of low enrollment in 2013.

22. See, for example, Peter L. Berger, *The Sacred Canopy: Elements of a Sociological Theory of Religion* (Garden City, NY: Doubleday, 1967).

23. See also Richard J. Callahan Jr., *Work and Faith in the Kentucky Coal Fields* (Bloomington: Indiana University Press, 2009).

24. Robert A. Orsi, "Introduction: Crossing the City Line," in *Gods of the City*, ed. Robert A. Orsi (Bloomington: Indiana University Press, 1999), 1–78.

25. McGreevy notes that psychologists also have likened parishioners' grief at being forced out of old ethnic neighborhoods to the loss of a family member. *Parish Boundaries*, 104.

26. A new rite of consecration in 1978, *Dedication of a Church and Altar*, codified this Vatican II shift from materialism to symbolism. Closing manuals inculcated detachment by asserting a symbolic and metaphorical rather than literal presence in parish things. Seitz, *No Closure*, 119–127, 133–140. On the pre–Vatican II emphasis on the buildings' and altars' immobility and rootedness, see also Gamm, *Urban Exodus*, 129–132. On the auctioning of objects from closed parishes in Pittsburgh, see also Paula M. Kane, "Getting beyond Gothic: Challenges for Contemporary Catholic Church Architecture," in *American Sanctuary: Understanding Sacred Spaces*, ed. Louis P. Nelson (Bloomington: Indiana University Press, 2006), 128–135.

27. Most of the parishioners in South Bethlehem's closed parishes were raised in the Catholic Church pre-Vatican II, when the structures themselves and many objects inside *were* considered sacred.

28. Kane, "Getting beyond Gothic," 133.

29. The Archdiocese of Boston, for example, issued a 168-page Closing Manual to priests as it prepared to shut down more than eighty parishes in 2004. The detailed recommendations for preparing the last mass emphasize rituals of continuity, including processions to new parishes, and assurances that the Church community is larger than the physical buildings. Priests were encouraged to be sensitive to parishioners' grief and tailor the last masses to their congregations' needs. Archdiocese of Boston, *Parish Closing Manual: "Rebuild My Church," Version 1.0* (Boston: Archdiocese of Boston, 2004), www.boston.com/news/special/parishes/Closing_Manual.pdf. For an analysis of the Boston manual, see Seitz, *No Closure*, 133–140. In Bethlehem, a prepared statement read before the last mass assured parishioners that, "While today marks an end of something beautiful we are called to place ourselves once again into God the Father's loving hands in total trust that he has something wonderful in store for us." Memorandum to St. John Capistrano Church, Bethlehem, PA, July 2008, private collection.

30. Robert Orsi urges taking informants' relationships with saints and other sacred figures as seriously as those with other humans, a "materialization of the moral life in Catholic culture." He writes, "It is impossible to exaggerate the importance of the figure of the guardian angel to mid-twentieth-century Catholic children's imaginations and spirituality. . . . Angels were said to be children's most dependable, loyal, and loving companions and protectors." Robert A. Orsi, *Between Heaven and Earth: The Religious Worlds People Make and the Scholars Who Study Them* (Princeton, NJ: Princeton University Press, 2005), 2, 73–109. (On guardian angels, see 103–106.)

31. On the cultural role of improvised and adaptive rituals, including establishing personal and collective continuity between childhood and old age, see Barbara Myerhoff, *Number Our Days* (New York: Simon and Schuster, 1978), 10, 108–109.

32. Interview with Lehigh University on November 9, 2010.

33. There is little overlap within the parish among Latinos who attend Spanish mass and residents of European ancestry who go to English mass. On a similar dynamic in Chicago, see William Julius Wilson and Richard P. Taub, *There Goes the Neighborhood: Racial, Ethnic, and Class Tensions in Four Chicago Neighborhoods and Their Meaning for America* (New York: Knopf, 2006), 71–74.

34. Paul Schuster Taylor, *Mexican Labor in the United States: Bethlehem, Pennsylvania* (Berkeley: University of California Press, 1931), 3; "The Time for Mexican Laborers Has Arrived [Ya Empieza la Epoca de Trabajo para los Braceros Mexicanos]," *La Prensa* (San Antonio), April 4, 1923, http://hsp.org/sites/default/files/april41923laprensa.pdf; "Mexicans Awaken the Jealousy of Pennsylvania Workers [Los Trabajadores Mexicanos Despiertanel Celo de los Obreros de Pensilvania]," trans. Andrew Coval, *La Prensa* (San Antonio), April 12, 1923, http://hsp.org/sites/default/files/april121923laprensa.pdf. Other industrial companies similarly recruited Mexicans; they were considered "white" for immigration purposes at this time. The railroads first recruited Mexicans to Chicago in 1916, followed in the 1920s by the steel and meatpacking industries. Fernandez, *Brown in the Windy City*, 63; Michael Innis-Jiménez, *Steel Barrio: The Great Mexican Migration to South Chi-*

cago, 1915–1940 (New York: New York University Press, 2013), 19–50; Alanen, *Morgan Park*, 122–123.

35. "Mexicans Awaken the Jealousy of Pennsylvania Workers."

36. According to Steel executives at the time, Mexicans were regarded as "better, more dependable workers than the Negroes." Taylor, *Mexican Labor in the United States*, 13.

37. There were 790 Mexicans on payroll in May 1923 after their initial recruitment; by May 1924 there were 232. Taylor, *Mexican Labor in the United States*, 3, 11–12; West, *The Mexican Aztec Society*, 98–135; "In the Age of Steel: Oral Histories from Bethlehem, Pennsylvania—Reuben E. Lopez Sr.," interview by Dennis Monnelly, 1975, Beyond Steel Archive, Lehigh University, Bethlehem, PA, 8–9, http://digital.lib.lehigh.edu/beyondsteel/pdf/lopez_152.pdf.; Peter J. Antonsen, *A History of the Puerto Rican Community in Bethlehem, Pa. 1944–1993* (Bethlehem, PA: Council of Spanish Speaking Organizations of the Lehigh Valley, 1997), 49–52.

38. In the 1950s an average of 41,212 Puerto Ricans migrated to the United States each year, peaking in 1953 at 69,124. The 1948 state-sponsored program Operation Bootstrap influenced migration, especially to New York. In addition to supporting industrialization on the island, the Puerto Rican and U.S. governments encouraged migration to ease high unemployment and reduce population on the island. During this time Mexicans were being deported, leading up to Operation Wetback in 1954. Between 1945 and 1964, 750,000 Puerto Ricans left their homeland, one-third of the Puerto Rican population. See Mérida Rúa, *A Grounded Identidad: Making New Lives in Chicago's Puerto Rican Neighborhoods* (New York: Oxford University Press, 2012), 3–6, 35–38; Fernandez, *Brown in the Windy City*, 34–36, 49–50, 54; Antonsen, *A History of the Puerto Rican Community*, 22.

A 1963 government report counts Bethlehem among thirty cities in the United States with the highest populations of Puerto Ricans. Commonwealth of Puerto Rico, Migration Division, Department of Labor, *Progress in Puerto Rico, Puerto Rican Migration: A Summary in Facts & Figures* (New York: Commonwealth of Puerto Rico Migration Division, Department of Labor, 1963), 15, 18, Box 3, file 3–6, Sergia P. Montz Papers, 1949–1998, Bethlehem Area Public Library, Bethlehem, PA (hereafter cited as BAPL).

39. Alan Sorensen, "Hispanics Share American Dream Forged in Heat of the Steel Mill," *Bethlehem Globe-Times*, January 15, 1984.

40. Antonsen, *A History of the Puerto Rican Community*, 48; Judith Stein, *Running Steel, Running America: Race, Economic Policy, and the Decline of Liberalism* (Chapel Hill: University of North Carolina Press, 1998), 169–196.

41. Bethlehem Bureau of Planning and Development, *The People of Bethlehem*, 60. There were over 2,100 Puerto Ricans in Bethlehem in 1966. *The People of Bethlehem* report makes the comparison to European immigrant neighborhoods clear: "The Puerto Ricans are following a pattern established by earlier ethnic groups. They have located in the less expensive rental units of the South Side, and have formed their sub-community around a church. Indications are that great strides are already being made be this group in living conditions, home ownership, and education of their children. It appears that participation of this

group in the city's general cultural life is proceeding, and assimilation may take less than the two generations previously required by other nationality groups." *The People of Bethlehem*, 30.

42. The organization's original name was the Council of Hispanic Organizations. See Antonsen, *A History of the Puerto Rican Community*, 51–53.

43. *CensusCD 1970*, *CensusCD 1980*, *CensusCD 1990*, *CensusCD 2000*, online database (E. Brunswick, NJ: GeoLytics, [2006?]); *U.S. Census, 2010*, http://www.census.gov/. According to Puerto Rican community leader Sergia Montz's calculations, by 1970 there were 7,400 Spanish-speaking residents, 6,200 from Puerto Rico. U.S. Census numbers are significantly lower, suggesting under-counting. See Box 1, file 1-35, Sergia P. Montz Papers, BAPL.

44. The Puerto Rican government's Migration Division also funded trips for Chicago police officers to the island. Fernandez, *Brown in the Windy City*, 72, 162.

45. Wes Willoughby, "Puerto Rican Story-4: Auto Troubles Biggest of All; Betting, Narcotics No Problem," *Bethlehem Globe-Times*, July 10, 1958; Wes Willoughby, "Puerto Rican Story-6: Spanish Speaking Services Ease Assimilation Problems," *Bethlehem Globe-Times*, July 12, 1958.

46. Rita McInerney, "Officials from Puerto Rico See Strides in Assimilation Here," *Bethlehem Globe-Times*, June 7, 1961, Box 1, file 1-5, Sergia P. Montz Papers, BAPL.

47. Robert Orsi notes that the "moral boundaries" of urban communities and urban selves are interconnected. Italian Americans in East Harlem similarly used the language of being forced out by Puerto Ricans while, in reality, they could finally afford to leave and were complicit in the community's decline. Orsi, "The Religious Boundaries of an Inbetween People," 329, 337.

48. Wes Willoughby, "Puerto Rican Story-1: Labor Rates Make City Major Center of Influx," *Bethlehem Globe-Times*, July 7, 1958.

49. The year 1970 marked a conflagration of tensions between Bethlehem's white police force and Puerto Rican youth in the city. Five Puerto Rican teenagers who shouted obscenities at the police were arrested and beaten in a lesson of "respect" following a September high school football game. Two months later police arrested twenty-one black and Puerto Rican youths following a brawl at a South Side bar. *Bethlehem Globe-Times* editor John Strohmeyer won a Pulitzer in 1972 for a series of editorials accusing the city of racial discrimination. All charges against the youths ultimately were dropped, but no disciplinary action against police was taken. The head of the human resources commission that investigated the first incident was forced to resign. See John Strohmeyer, "Remove Stigma," *Bethlehem Globe-Times*, January 18, 1971, and "Whitewash," *Bethlehem Globe-Times*, January 21, 1971. Police officer John Stein also resigned after the Ale House brawl over his disillusionment with the police department. John A. Stein, "Bethlehem Cop Tells of Agony on the Job," *Bethlehem Globe-Times*, January 14, 1971, and "Ex-Cop Tells Why He Quit," *Bethlehem Globe-Times*, January 15, 1971; "Statement by Dietz," *Bethlehem Globe-Times*, January 20, 1971.

50. Census data from 1970 to 2000 shows that while average incomes in Bethlehem have risen slightly (after adjusting for inflation), these figures on the South

Side have steadily decreased. For example (in 2010 dollars), average family income in the city increased from $69,629 in 1970 to $73,203 in 2000. In the five census tracts that make up South Bethlehem, average family income decreased from $55,951 to $45,880. Social Explorer Tables, Census 1970–2000, U.S. Census Bureau and Social Explorer.

51. Housing values in the five South Bethlehem census tracts, converted to 2000 dollars, increased 41.7 percent between 1970 and 2000 (to a median of $63,732), while housing values for the same period increased 52.7 percent in Bethlehem as a whole (to a median of $97,000). These rates were still higher than for the state (29.4 percent) and nation (25.8 percent). Social Explorer Tables, Census 1970 and 2000, U.S. Census Bureau and Social Explorer.

52. In 2013, 73 percent of Bethlehem's Latinos were from Puerto Rico compared to 82 percent twenty years before. One in five Latinos come from places other than Puerto Rico or Mexico. Social Explorer Tables, American Community Survey 2013 (Five-Year Estimates), "T15: Hispanic or Latino Origin by Specific Origin," and Census 1990, "T14: Detailed Hispanic Origin," U.S. Census Bureau and Social Explorer.

53. On a similar dynamic in Chicago, see Fernandez, *Brown in the Windy City*, 60, 86.

54. See Robert M. Fogelson, *Downtown: Its Rise and Fall, 1880–1950* (New Haven, CT: Yale University Press, 2001), 346–380; Robert A. Beauregard, *Voices of Decline: The Postwar Fate of U.S. Cities* (Oxford: B. Blackwell, 1993), 84–90, 135–154. A 1956 report on Puerto Ricans in Bethlehem by local Puerto Rican activist Sergia Montz outlines the structural impediments to good housing, but concludes by encouraging Puerto Ricans to learn English and adjust to "the American way of life." Sergia Montz, "A Report on the Puerto Rican Population in Bethlehem," June 1956, Box 1, file 1-37, Sergia P. Montz Papers, BAPL. See also a paper by Clarence Senior, chief of the Migration Division, Department of Labor, Commonwealth of Puerto Rico, read at the National Tuberculosis Association Annual Convention in Atlantic City: "Migrants: People—Not Problems," May 20, 1954, Box 3, file 3-6, Sergia P. Montz Papers, BAPL. See also Wilson and Taub, *There Goes the Neighborhood*, 28–29.

55. The same people who make such generalizations can also point to examples of Latino homeowners who maintain their properties well. See also Judith Goode and Jo Anne Schneider, *Reshaping Ethnic and Racial Relations in Philadelphia: Immigrants in a Divided City* (Philadelphia: Temple University Press, 1994), 229–232; Sugrue, *Origins of the Urban Crisis;* Fernandez, *Brown in the Windy City.*

56. Wilson and Taub cite strikingly similar language of "pride" in their study of Chicago neighborhoods in transition. White ethnics believed they worked hard for what they had and, as one informant said, "take pride in their property, take pride in their schools, just have that work ethic, that pride in the neighborhood." *There Goes the Neighborhood*, 33, 36–37, 59–60. Arnold Alanen describes a similar situation and changing landscape by the 1950s in the steel town of Duluth, Minnesota. Alanen, *Morgan Park*, 278–288.

57. Michael G. Kammen, *Digging Up the Dead: A History of Notable American Reburials* (Chicago: University of Chicago Press, 2010), x, 20; Rachel Buff, *Immigration and the Political Economy of Home: West Indian Brooklyn and American Indian Minneapolis, 1945–1992* (Berkeley: University of California Press, 2001), 2–5.

58. See, for example, "25 Tombstones Toppled at St. Michael's Cemetery," *Bethlehem Globe-Times*, September 24, 1973; "Vandals Strike Again at South Side Cemetery," *Morning Call*, August 18, 1987.

59. In addition to economic and cultural tensions, many Puerto Ricans are politically divided in debates about Puerto Rican statehood. On intraethnic tensions among Puerto Ricans, see Arlene M. Dávila, *Barrio Dreams: Puerto Ricans, Latinos, and the Neoliberal City* (Berkeley: University of California Press, 2004), 79–82.

60. The North Side is 14 percent Latino. U.S. Census 2010.

61. Alan Mallach, *In Philadelphia's Shadow: Small Cities in the Third Federal Reserve District* (Philadelphia: Federal Reserve Bank of Philadelphia, 2012), 32, http://www.philadelphiafed.org/community-development/publications/special-reports/small-cities-in-third-federal-reserve-district.pdf.

62. Social Explorer Tables, ACS 2013 (Five-Year Estimates), "T126: Poverty Status in 2013 (Hispanic or Latino)," and "T127: Poverty Status in 2013 (White Alone, Not Hispanic or Latino)," Social Explorer and U.S. Census Bureau. In Puerto Rico, the poverty rate is 45 percent. ACS 2013 (Five-Year Estimates), "B17001: Poverty Status in the Past 12 Months by Sex by Age [Puerto Rico]," Social Explorer and U.S. Census Bureau.

63. The theory of "segmented assimilation" argues that some new immigrants will assimilate not through upward mobility, but into the American-born underclass. Alejandro Portes and Min Zhou, "The New Second Generation: Segmented Assimilation and Its Variants," *Annals of the American Academy of Political and Social Science* 530 (November 1993): 74–96. Inversely, Jill Schennum notes how some former Bethlehem steelworkers who face economic hardships are hesitant to seek needed social services, for fear that they will be lumped in with the racialized "undeserving poor." Jill Schennum, "Bethlehem Steelworkers: Reshaping the Industrial Working Class" (PhD diss., City University of New York, 2011), 203–204.

64. The overall unemployment rates in Pennsylvania and nationally were 9.0 percent and 9.7 percent, respectively. Social Explorer Tables, ACS 2013 (Five-Year Estimates), "T47: Unemployment Rate for the Population 16 Years and Over (Hispanic or Latino)" and "T48: Unemployment Rate for the Population 16 Years and Over (White Alone, Not Hispanic or Latino)," Social Explorer and U.S. Census Bureau.

65. The classic study on the value of kinship ties among the American poor is Carol B. Stack, *All Our Kin: Strategies for Survival in a Black Community* (New York: Harper & Row, 1975). Matthew Desmond has challenged Stack's model by documenting more circumstantial "disposable ties" among strangers that likewise help the poor through financial hardship. The fact that many Latinos arrive in Bethlehem because they already know someone there suggests kinship ties remain salient, though one can assume both types of ties are present in the community.

Matthew Desmond, "Disposable Ties and the Urban Poor," *American Journal of Sociology* 117, no. 5 (March 2012): 1295–1335.

66. See Brent D. Ryan, *Design after Decline: How America Rebuilds Shrinking Cities* (Philadelphia: University of Pennsylvania Press, 2012).

67. Shukla, "Harlem's Past in Its Present," 178–179. See also Dávila, *Barrio Dreams*, 107, 112–115, 208; Rúa, *A Grounded Identidad*, 74–75.

68. Efforts by store owners in cities across the United States to revitalize businesses during the Depression by changing their façades presents an interesting historical parallel to the use of "face lifts" for economic development. See Alison Isenberg, *Downtown America: A History of the Place and the People Who Made It* (Chicago: University of Chicago Press, 2004), 143–152. The City of Bethlehem began using federal Community Development Block Grant money toward loans for façade fix-ups in 1993. The city program was augmented in 2005 to fix façades and address exterior code violations on four blocks along the South Side's Fourth Street business corridor, newly dubbed "Four Blocks International" for its "ethnic flair." See Nicole Radzievich, "South Side Project Makes Progress," *Morning Call*, May 23, 2007.

69. See Wilson and Taub, *There Goes the Neighborhood*, 161, 181–182.

70. Anita Amigo, "Week Was Beautiful and Good," *Bethlehem Globe-Times*, August 27, 1975, Box 1, file 1-23, Sergia P. Montz Papers, BAPL.

71. "Puerto Rican Parade, Sunday, June 29, 1975, 1:30 PM," Box 1, file 1-23, Sergia P. Montz Papers, BAPL.

72. Sergia Montz, "Saludos de la Comunidad Puertorriqueña a Bethlehem/ Greetings from the Puerto Rican Community to Bethlehem," June 29, 1975, Box 1, file 1-23, Sergia P. Montz Papers, BAPL.

73. Lilia Fernandez notes that tensions in Chicago between white ethnics and Latinos were not only racial, but generational, as elderly white residents "left behind" in neighborhoods that became Latino were confronted with a significantly younger new population of Mexicans and Puerto Ricans. *Brown in the Windy City*, 161, 217.

74. "Puerto Rican Pride in Bethlehem," June 26, 2010, http://www.topix.com /forum/city/bethlehem-pa/TKO5H4GLBTEOI8OQ7.

75. On Puerto Ricans' "perplexing" status of being U.S. citizens whom whites nonetheless perceive as foreign, see Fernandez, *Brown in the Windy City*, 153, 267–268.

76. On the profit potential in courting Latino populations, the marketing of ethnicity to broad publics, and the disciplining of ethnic organizations to fit the structures of mainstream cultural institutions, see Dávila, *Barrio Dreams*, 62, 119–126, 176–177.

77. The second Puerto Rican flag raising partly reflected a rift between two local Latino organizations. For attendance estimates, see Pamela Sroka-Holzmann, "Latin Americans Celebrate Three King Day Tradition at Bethlehem's ArtsQuest," *Express-Times*, January 6, 2013.

78. Dávila (*Barrio Dreams*, 165–175) similarly describes tensions over a Mexican parade in New York that is run by a professional multicultural events marketing

firm rather than by Mexicans in the community who feel they should control their own celebration.

6. What Happens in Bethlehem Depends on Macau

1. The statue was commissioned from Sun Jiabin, one of China's premier sculptors. The artist's most famous work is a 1978 marble statue in Beijing's Tiananmen Square of Mao Zedong, China's communist revolutionary who banned gambling in Mainland China.

2. See James Fallows, "Macau's Big Gamble," *The Atlantic*, September 2007, http://www.theatlantic.com/magazine/archive/2007/09/macau-s-big-gamble/306131/; Evan Osnos, "The God of Gamblers: Why Las Vegas is Moving to Macau," *New Yorker*, April 9, 2012, 46. In 2013, high rollers contributed about two-thirds of Macau's casino revenues, although middle-class spending was growing at a more rapid pace. Vinicy Chan, "Gamblers Betting $1.6 Million a Visit Aid Macau Casinos," *Bloomberg*, May 29, 2013. http://www.bloomberg.com/news/2013-05-28/gamblers-betting-1-6-million-a-visit-aid-macau-casinos.html.

3. While most of the Macau visitors are day-trippers, casino companies are increasingly investing in nongaming amenities to encourage longer stays. The Las Vegas Sands' Cotai Central development will offer 6,400 hotel rooms at completion. Together with its four other Asian properties, Sands in 2015 had close to 12,000 hotel rooms in Asia (with almost 4,000 more expected to be added by the end of 2016), far exceeding its 7,100 rooms in Las Vegas and 300 rooms in Bethlehem. Las Vegas Sands Corp. Form 10-K for the fiscal year ended December 31, 2014, http://www.sec.gov/Archives/edgar/data/1300514/000130051415000005/lvs-20141231x10k.htm.

4. No claim is made to the exclusive right to use the word "Cotai." See U.S. Patent and Trademark Office, Trademark Electronic Search System, "Cotai Strip," serial numbers: 85215493, 4623297, and 78588080.

5. Hoa Nguyen, "Minibaccarat Gaining Popularity in Atlantic City Despite Nationwide Card-Shuffling Scandals," *Press of Atlantic City*, October 2, 2012; Kelvin Chan, "Macau's Game of Choice—Baccarat," *Las Vegas Review-Journal*, June 13, 2013. At Sands Bethlehem, "mini baccarat" refers to a lower limit game in which only the dealer flips the cards and the cards are reused. The "midi baccarat" tables described here, where players flip and bend the cards, which are then disposed of, have a minimum wager of $50 at Sands Bethlehem.

6. In 2010 the percentage of Chinese residents in Bethlehem had reached 0.82 percent (2.9 percent of the total population was Asian) and was trending up. Social Explorer and U.S. Census, 1970–2010.

7. See Thomas Friedman, *The World Is Flat: A Brief History of the Twenty-first Century* (New York: Farrar, Straus and Giroux, 2005). Zygmunt Bauman also sees the possibility for segregation and deprivation in these processes, what David Harvey calls "space-time compression" that has intensified since the early 1970s. Zygmunt Bauman, *Globalization: The Human Consequences* (New York: Columbia

University Press, 1998); David Harvey, *The Condition of Postmodernity: An Enquiry into the Origins of Cultural Change* (Cambridge, MA: Blackwell, 1990).

8. Anna Tsing, *Friction: An Ethnography of Global Connection* (Princeton, NJ: Princeton University Press, 2004); Frederick Cooper, "What is the Concept of Globalization Good For? An African Historian's Perspective," *African Affairs* 100, no. 399 (2001): 189–213; Karen Ho, *Liquidated: An Ethnography of Wall Street* (Durham, NC: Duke University Press, 2008).

9. See Tsing, *Friction*, 126–127.

10. In 1857, the Church's American Northern and Southern Provinces became largely independent. The Southern Province is headquartered in Winston-Salem, North Carolina, founded by the Moravians in 1752.

11. Katherine Carté Engel, *Religion and Profit: Moravians in Early America* (Philadelphia: University of Pennsylvania Press, 2009), 99–110.

12. Ibid., 154–160.

13. Like many other religious institutions, the Moravian Church also remains involved in real-estate development and investment. In Bethlehem, corporate entities Moravian Development Corp. and the Bethlehem Area Moravians, Inc. handle the local church's not-for-profit holdings, including four apartment complexes for seniors and the mentally disabled, a retirement community, and a Moravian College dorm. A subsidiary called Zinzendorf Corporation controls for-profit development, including the lease for a gas station.

14. The two larger companies were Standard Oil and U.S. Steel. David Venditta and Ardith Hilliard, eds., *Forging America: The Story of Bethlehem Steel*, 2nd ed. (Bethlehem, Pa.: The Morning Call, 2010), 45.

15. "Mexicans Awaken the Jealousy of Pennsylvania Workers [Los Trabajadores Mexicanos Despiertanel Celo de los Obreros de Pensilvania]," trans. Andrew Coval, *La Prensa* (San Antonio), April 12, 1923, http://hsp.org/sites/default/files/april121923laprensa.pdf.

16. Kenneth Warren documents some, but not all, of these ore mine holdings in *Bethlehem Steel: Builder and Arsenal of America* (Pittsburgh: University of Pittsburgh Press, 2008). Bethlehem Steel contracted with Swedish mines in the 1910s. The Chilean mines, acquired in 1913, became particularly profitable during the 1920s and through most of the twentieth century. (Warren, 62–63, 97–99, 112, 119, 155–156.) The corporation expressed early interest in Venezuelan mines and purchased exploitation rights in 1933, but it did not develop the Venezuelan mines until World War II. They became the largest overseas source of ore for Bethlehem Steel by the early 1950s, with Chile and Canada also accounting for half the total supply at that point (146, 156). Bethlehem Steel looked to Africa after World War II and owned an interest in a Liberian mine from 1953 to 1984 (155, 251). According to Bethlehem Steel's corporate records, it explored South African mines from 1952 to 1961. Brazilian holdings dated to 1942 (though Warren dates these to the 1970s). Mexican mining dated to 1919. (Bethlehem Steel Corporation, *History*, vols. 1–3, *Real Estate*, October 19, 1970, Box: BSC Corporate Summaries, Bethlehem Steel Corporation Records, Moravian Archives, Bethlehem, PA.) Bethlehem Steel sold many of its interests in

foreign mines in the 1980s. The corporation also had subsidiaries in Malaysia and Italy, among other nations.

17. John Strohmeyer notes in his book on Bethlehem Steel that "profits from international operations, headquartered in a tax haven such as the Bahamas, could be recycled into other international investments; no taxes needed to be paid until the profits were returned to the home office." The Nassau operations were active from 1951 to 1961. According to Strohmeyer, no public announcement was ever made of the Nassau expansion, and it was never mentioned in annual reports. The offices acted as go-betweens for Bethlehem Steel's numerous subsidiaries, buying and selling ore without ever seeing the raw material, for example, to take advantage of tax incentives. *Crisis in Bethlehem: Big Steel's Struggle to Survive* (Pittsburgh: University of Pittsburgh Press, 1986), 54–59.

18. Bethlehem Steel Corporation, *History*, vols. 1–3, *Real Estate.*

19. Venditta and Hilliard, *Forging America*, 127. Others attribute this statement to David Roderick, CEO of U.S. Steel. The origin of the iconic declaration is in some ways besides the point given its ability to stand in for descriptions of a particular corporate vision and shift in market logic.

20. Bethlehem Steel Corporation, "1999–2001 Financial/Liquidity Plan (April 21, 1999 confidential draft)," 1999, section G, p. A-1, File 1-2-2-262B: BD meeting April 28, 1999 Part II, Box: B/D Background Material 1999, Bethlehem Steel Corporation Records, Moravian Archives, Bethlehem, PA.

21. Ho, *Liquidated*, 122–168.

22. James L. Rowe Jr., "Bethlehem's Loss: Uncertain Estimate; Did Bethlehem Lose $477 Million?," *Washington Post*, December 27, 1977; "Worst Three-Month Loss Ever," *Time*, November 7, 1977.

23. Raymond Bonner, "Bethlehem Steel 4th-Quarter Loss Huge," *New York Times*, January 27, 1983.

24. Jerry Landauer, "New York Port Agency's $30 Million Saving on Steel Work Prompts Antitrust Inquiry," *Wall Street Journal*, July 16, 1969; Venditta and Hilliard, *Forging America*, 57–58. See also, David Bensman and Roberta Lynch, *Rusted Dreams: Hard Times in a Steel Community* (New York: McGraw-Hill, 1987), 83–87; Steven High, *Industrial Sunset: The Making of North America's Rust Belt, 1969–1984* (Toronto: University of Toronto Press, 2003), 136–137, 168.

25. Thanks to Christopher Kramaric for his insight on the foundational steel columns, or "trees," for the towers produced in Coatesville. After the destruction of the towers on September 11, 2001, these trees, rooted several stories into the ground, were all that remained standing. In their ruined state, they again became nationalist symbols.

26. Dan Hartzell, "Steel for South Side Hotel May Not Be From Bethlehem," *Morning Call*, June 3, 1992; Stephen Posivak Jr., "Letter to the Editor: Why Foreign Steel at New Motel?," *Morning Call*, June 9, 1992; Hartzell, "Union Supporters Picket Opening of Bethlehem South Side Hotel," *Morning Call*, November 19, 1992.

27. ArcelorMittal was the result of Mittal's takeover of Arcelor in 2006. Mittal had been founded in India, was headquartered in the Netherlands, and was managed from London (by one of the richest men in the world, Lakshmi Mittal). Ar-

celor was the result of a merger between steel companies in Spain, France, and Luxembourg. ArcelorMittal's North American headquarters are in Chicago. See also Ho, *Liquidated*, 306–309.

28. Bethlehem, its counties, and its adjacent cities together receive under the state's gaming law a "host fee" or "local share" each year of either $10 million or 2 percent of the casino's gross revenue, whichever is greater. The local share of the Sands revenues for the 2014–2015 fiscal year totaled $19,997,732 for the region, of which $9,835,639 went to the City of Bethlehem. Pennsylvania Gaming Control Board, *Annual Report, 2014–2015* (Harrisburg, PA: Pennsylvania Gaming Control Board, 2014), 21, http://gamingcontrolboard.pa.gov/files/communications/2014-2015_PGCB_Annual_Report_min.pdf. Sands employed 2,363 people in 2015. Approximately 350 worked in the outlet mall, 225 in casino restaurants not owned by Sands, and 40 at the events center. When ArtsQuest SteelStacks is included, Sands says 3,000 jobs can be attributed to the casino's development. In FY 2012–2013 Sands Bethlehem gave $528,419 in charitable donations; this dropped to $242,536 the next year, but increased to $901,825 in FY 2014–2105. Lynn Olanoff, "Sands Casino Resort Bethlehem: We Must Add Amenities to Remain Competitive," *Express-Times*, October 15, 2013; Pennsylvania Gaming Control Board, *2014–2015 Gaming Diversity Report* (Harrisburg, PA: Pennsylvania Gaming Control Board, 2015), 14, http://gamingcontrolboard.pa.gov/files/communications/2014-2015_Gaming_Diversity_Report.pdf.

29. David Harvey, *The New Imperialism* (Oxford: Oxford University Press, 2003), 27, 86, 103–105.

30. See Steven Gregory, *The Devil behind the Mirror: Globalization and Politics in the Dominican Republic* (Berkeley: University of California Press, 2007), 4–10, 209–216, 244–245; Cooper, "What is the Concept of Globalization Good For?," 207.

31. See Fallows, "Macau's Big Gamble"; Osnos, "The God of Gamblers."

32. Kah-Wee Lee, "Regulating design in Singapore: a survey of the Government Land Sales (GLS) Programme," *Environment and Planning C: Government and Policy* 28, no. 1 (2010): 160.

33. Design accounted for 30 percent of the evaluation. Other criteria were tourism appeal and contribution (40 percent), level of development investment (20 percent), and the developer's strength and track record (10 percent). Ibid., 161.

34. Las Vegas Sands does not own The Parisian casino in Las Vegas, which also features an Eiffel Tower. At least two other new projects in Macau also reference French opulence; France is a popular destination for newly wealthy Chinese citizens. Kelvin Chan, "Casino Capital Macau Bets Glitzy Wave of New Resorts Will Bring More Gamblers, Families," *U.S. News*, May 26, 2015.

35. Paul Steelman, "Thoughts on Atlantic City, Las Vegas, and Several Other Casino Jurisdictions," interview by David Schwartz, *UNLV Gaming Podcast*, podcast audio, University of Nevada Center for Gaming Research, November 29, 2011, http://digitalscholarship.unlv.edu/gaming_podcasts/50/; Paul Steelman, "The Future of Casino Architecture," interview by David Schwartz, *UNLV Gaming Podcast*, podcast audio, University of Nevada Center for Gaming Research, December 20, 2011, http://digitalscholarship.unlv.edu/gaming_podcasts/49/.

36. The plans include a replica Great Wall of China, faux terra cotta warriors, and a panda exhibit. Genting Group has casinos in Malaysia, the Philippines, the United Kingdom, and New York. It is also Sands' only competitor in Singapore. Richard N. Velotta, "Asian-Themed Megaresort Planned for old Stardust Site," VegasInc.com, March 4, 2013, http://www.vegasinc.com/news/2013/mar/04/old-stardust-site-sold-new-strip-casino/.

37. Matt Assad, "Sands Casino Plans Expansion," *Morning Call*, April 7, 2015.

38. Macau taxes casino revenues at 39 percent. According to World Bank data, Macau had the fastest growing economy in the world. Kate O'Keefe, "Macau Funding Infrastructure Renewal with Casino Winnings," *Wall Street Journal*, September 25, 2013.

39. Michael Grimes, "Melco Crown 'Rewarded' with Labour Quota," *Macau Business Daily*, September 8, 2013.

40. Unemployment in Macau in 2015 had been roughly flat at 2 percent since 2012. Government of Macao Special Administrative Region Statistics and Census Service, *Population Estimate 2014* (Macao, March 2015), http://www.dsec.gov.mo/Statistic.aspx?NodeGuid=3c3f3a28-9661-4a5f-b876-83d8b3eade28#P20471; "Labour Force Participation Rate, Unemployment Rate and Underemployment Rate, http://www.dsec.gov.mo/PredefinedReport.aspx?ReportID=5; Vinicy Chan, "Macau Labor Shortage Seen as Hurdle for Casino Expansion," Bloomberg.com, May 22, 2012, http://www.bloomberg.com/news/2012-05-21/macau-labor-shortage-seen-as-hurdle-for-casino-expansion.html. In the last quarter of 2014, dealers in Macau earned an average of $2,250 per month; in 2011 Macau dealers took home $2,000 per month, compared to $1,900 in Las Vegas and $1,800 in Singapore. Government of Macao Special Administrative Region Statistics and Census Service, *Survey on Manpower Needs and Wages—Gaming Sector, 4th Quarter 2014* (Macao: March, 2015), http://www.dsec.gov.mo/Statistic.aspx?NodeGuid=6289ca07-25cc-450b-8499-4e34765c1769#P20488; "Casino Dealers Unhappy with Bonuses," Marketing-Interactive.com, March 3, 2011, http://www.marketing-interactive.com/news/24959.

41. Shawn A. Turner, "LV Sands Bets on Global Development," *Hotel News Now*, June 1, 2012. The casino industry's efforts to find a path of least resistance mimic other "vice" industries such as tobacco, which has turned its attention to marketing cigarettes in the developing world where there are fewer regulations and more opportunities to profit. Natasha Dow Schüll, *Addiction by Design: Machine Gambling in Las Vegas* (Princeton, NJ: Princeton University Press, 2012), 300–310; Allan M. Brandt, *The Cigarette Century: The Rise, Fall, and Deadly Persistence of the Product that Defined America* (New York: Basic Books, 2007), 449–492.

42. Tom Burridge, "Spain's Dilemmas over 'Eurovegas' Mega Casino Plans," *BBC News*, March 20, 2012; Giles Tremlett, "'EuroVegas' to Rise in Madrid as Sheldon Adelson Signs Casino Deal," *Guardian*, September 10, 2012; Sharon Smyth and Charles Penty, "Las Vegas Sands Picks Alcoron for 'EuroVegas' Casino in Spain," *Bloomberg Businessweek*, February 8, 2013; Michael Grimes, "Mañana—Spanish Govt Stalls on Adelson's Smoking Plea," *Macau Business Daily*, August 13, 2013.

43. Tobias Buck, "Sheldon Adelson Cancels $30bn Eurovegas Project in Spain," *Financial Times*, December 13, 2013.

44. Lynn Olanoff, "Las Vegas Sands Corp. Confirms Possible Bethlehem Casino Sale," *Express-Times*, January 23, 2013; Matt Assad, "Sands Bethlehem Casino to Be Sold to Tropicana?," *Morning Call*, April 9, 2014.

45. Ron Sylvester, "Sheldon Adelson: 'Las Vegas Is a Core Asset. I'm Never Going to Sell It,'" *Las Vegas Sun News*, April 26, 2012.

46. See Tsing, *Friction*, 68, 74.

47. Carol Smith, "Honeymoon's Over: Sands Must Complete Project," *Bethlehem Press*, March 10, 2010.

48. DeSalvio's comment came during the October 2009 town hall forum at Northampton Community College. For Las Vegas Sands Corp., answering to shareholders in effect means answering to Sheldon Adelson, who with his family holds a 52 percent stake in the company. Among "risk factors" listed in the company's financial filings is the fact that, "The interests of Mr. Adelson may conflict with your interests." See, for example, Las Vegas Sands Corp. Form 10-K for the fiscal year ended December 31, 2012, 23, http://www.sec.gov/Archives/edgar/data/1300514/000119312513087854/d448401d10k.htm.

49. Matt Assad, "Bethlehem Sands Casino Not for Sale," *Morning Call*, May 2, 2014. Steven Gregory describes a similar dynamic when the original owner of a Megaport project in the Dominican Republic sold the port to another multinational firm that was no longer bound to promises made during negotiations. *The Devil behind the Mirror*, 235.

50. Matt Assad, "New Bethlehem Sands Casino Exec Plans Major Expansion," *Morning Call*, October 4, 2014; Nicole Radzievich, "Sands Plans for Future at Former Steel Plant," *Morning Call*, June 9, 2015.

51. Matt Assad, "Like Bethlehem Steel before It, Sands Casino is Remaking South Side," *Morning Call*, October 8, 2013; Assad, "Sands Casino Leads the State in Buying Liquor," *Morning Call*, November 2, 2013.

52. See Matthew Frye Jacobson, *Barbarian Virtues: The United States Encounters Foreign Peoples at Home and Abroad, 1876–1917* (New York: Hill and Wang, 2000), 26–38, 70–72; Matthew Guterl and Christine Skwiot, "Atlantic and Pacific Crossings: Race, Empire, and 'the Labor Problem' in the Late Nineteenth Century," *Radical History Review* 91 (Winter 2005): 40–61.

53. Many casino properties in Las Vegas and elsewhere cater to Chinese gamblers through feng shui and other design choices. The Encore resort in Vegas eliminated floor numbers 40–49 because four is an unlucky number in Chinese tradition. MGM Grand removed the signature lion statue at its entrance when Chinese gamblers, who found it inauspicious to walk through the mouth of a lion, took their business elsewhere. Qing Han, "Chinese Culture and Casino Customer Service" (Professional paper, University of Nevada, Las Vegas, 2011), 8, 11–12, http://digitalscholarship.unlv.edu/thesesdissertations/1148.

54. Other American casinos similarly court the Asian population. See Thomas Ott, "Horseshoe Casino Cleveland Makes Special Effort to Cater to Asian American Gamblers," *Plain Dealer*, October 18, 2012.

55. Kristin McCabe, "Chinese Immigrants in the United States," Migration Policy Institute, January 2012, http://www.migrationinformation.org/USFocus/display.cfm?id=876#3.

56. Sociologist Min Zhou argues that erosion in the Chinese welfare state, which under communist rule included food rations and state housing, coupled with more open networks of migration, capital, and employment, have diminished incentives (and state-enforced admonitions) to stay in one place. Min Zhou, *Contemporary Chinese America: Immigration, Ethnicity, and Community Transformation* (Philadelphia: Temple University Press, 2009), 38.

57. In FY 2012 almost 82,000 people born in China immigrated to the United States, the most from any nation other than Mexico, for a total of more than 714,000 people over ten years. McCabe, "Chinese Immigrants in the United States"; U.S. Department of Homeland Security, *Yearbook of Immigration Statistics: 2012* (Washington, DC: U.S. Department of Homeland Security, Office of Immigration Statistics, 2013), 12, http://www.dhs.gov/sites/default/files/publications/immigration-statistics/yearbook/2012/ois_yb_2012.pdf.

58. White House, "We Can't Wait: President Obama Takes Actions to Increase Travel and Tourism in the United States," news release, January 19, 2012, http://www.whitehouse.gov/the-press-office/2012/01/19/we-can-t-wait-president-obama-takes-actions-increase-travel-and-tourism-; U.S. Department of State, "State Department Processes One Millionth Visa in China for Fiscal Year 2012," news release, July 12, 2012, http://www.state.gov/r/pa/prs/ps/2012/07/194940.htm.

59. U.S. Department of Homeland Security, *Yearbook: 2012*, 67; *Yearbook of Immigration Statistics: 2013* (Washington, DC: U.S. Department of Homeland Security, Office of Immigration Statistics, 2014), 67, http://www.dhs.gov/sites/default/files/publications/immigration-statistics/yearbook/2013/ois_yb_2013.pdf. Figures are based on I-94 visa admissions. Figures calculated for Chinese citizens include Mainland China, Macau, and Hong Kong, but not Taiwan, which has a longer history of U.S. immigration during the Mainland's communist rule. Among a variety of types of visitor visas, the most common types are B1 business visas and B2 tourist visas, typically allowing six-month stays. A limited number of H1B and H2B work visas typically allow stays of three years and one year, respectively. They can sometimes be extended to allow respective stays of six and three years.

60. Associated Press, "Crash Highlights Gambling's Role in Chinese Culture," *Washington Times*, March 16, 2011.

61. "Second Chinatowns" in Flushing and Fresh Meadows, Queens, and in Sunset Park, Brooklyn, typically comprise upwardly mobile or second-generation immigrants. (Buses also come from the heavily Asian neighborhood of Elmhurst, Queens.) Less than 15 percent of New York's Chinese residents live within "Old Chinatown's" borders in Manhattan. Zhou, *Contemporary Chinese America*, 6–7, 57–61, 103–104, 222.

62. Matt Assad and Pamela Lehman, "Asians at Sands Bethlehem Casino 'Ride Bus to Live,'" *Morning Call*, March 29, 2014.

63. Robert DeSalvio, "Sands Bethlehem Operations," PowerPoint presentation, September 2011, files.shareholder.com/downloads/ABEA-242MDE/0x0x501796/5bfe65ea-7d36-4f77-b061-87d6cbdf9e0a/7_-_Bethlehem.pdf.

64. Yeong-Ung Yang, *Bus-kkun* (2015), video, 4:29, http://m.newsfund.media.daum.net/episode/533.

65. Zhou, *Contemporary Chinese America*, 187, 196; Peter Kwong, *The New Chinatown* (New York: Hill and Wang, 1987), 65–66.

66. Kwong, *The New Chinatown*, 69–70. A similar paradox exists in the simultaneous perceptions of Chinese Americans as "model minorities" who show significant socioeconomic and educational gains, especially in the second generation, and "perpetual outsiders" who must constantly prove their Americanness. Zhou, *Contemporary Chinese America*, 221–235. Other riders are desperate and hopelessly addicted to riding the bus. Assad and Lehman, "Asians at Sands Bethlehem Casino 'Ride Bus to Live.' "

67. Zhou, *Contemporary Chinese America*, 99–122.

68. Associated Press, "Crash Highlights Gambling's Role in Chinese Culture."

69. Jeffery E. Singer, "The Casino as Lifeline," *Lens* (blog), *New York Times*, August 23, 2013, http://lens.blogs.nytimes.com/2013/08/23/the-casino-as-lifeline/?_r=0; Assad and Lehman, "Asians at Sands Bethlehem Casino 'Ride Bus to Live' "; Matt Assad, "Sands Casino Bus-Hoppers Beat Odds Using Free Money," *Morning Call*, March 30, 2014.

70. Assad and Lehman, "Asians at Sands Bethlehem Casino 'Ride Bus to Live."

71. For an example of a customer service model that explains many Chinese gambling particularities but fails to address dealers' interests, see Qing Han, "Chinese Culture and Casino Customer Service," 20–23.

72. See Min Zhou, *Contemporary Chinese America*, 20, 221–235.

73. Erika Lee, *At America's Gates: Chinese Immigration during the Exclusion Era, 1882–1943* (Chapel Hill: University of North Carolina Press, 2003); Jacobson, *Barbarian Virtues*, 75–81.

74. See Nayan Shah, *Contagious Divides: Epidemics and Race in San Francisco's Chinatown* (Berkeley: University of California Press, 2001), 17–76; Lee, *At America's Gates*, 81–84.

75. The spatialization of discrimination against the Chinese in America has a long history. See Shah, *Contagious Divides;* Mary Ting Yi Liu, "Race and Disease in Urban Geography," *Reviews in American History* 30, no. 3 (September 2002): 453–462.

76. The proportion of Asian dealers at Sands is significantly higher than at other Pennsylvania casinos. Assad, "Like Bethlehem Steel before It"; Pennsylvania Gaming Control Board, *2014–2015 Gaming Diversity Report*, 14.

77. South Bethlehem is made up of Census Tracts 109–113. In Census Tract 113, which comprises the neighborhoods across from the casino, the Chinese population tripled between 2000 and 2010 to 136 people, but then declined slightly. South Bethlehem's Asian population also includes significant numbers of Indian and Pakistani residents. There was no large change in the Korean population, which

constitutes less than 0.5 percent of the South Bethlehem population. Social Explorer Tables, Census 2000 and 2010, and American Community Survey 2009 (Five-Year Estimates) and 2013 (Five-Year Estimates), "T16: Asian by Specific Origin," U.S. Census Bureau and Social Explorer.

78. Jane Jacobs, *The Death and Life of Great American Cities* (New York: Random House, 1961; reprint, New York: Vintage Books, 1992), 29–54. Bethlehem's block watches are not officially affiliated with the national Neighborhood Watch program sponsored since 1972 by the National Sheriff's Association, but they follow the same model of citizen partnership with the police. "Our History," USAonWatch, last modified 2012, http://www.usaonwatch.org/about/history.aspx.

79. Mary Douglas, *Risk and Blame: Essays in Cultural Theory* (London: Routledge, 1992); Deborah Lupton, *Risk* (London: Routledge, 1999), 36–57.

80. Mike Davis, *City of Quartz: Excavating the Future in Los Angeles* (London: Verso, 1990), 223–240. See also M. Christine Boyer, *The City of Collective Memory: Its Historical Imagery and Architectural Entertainments* (Cambridge, MA: MIT Press, 1994), 412. Crime prevention strategies of "defensible space" and "crime prevention through environmental design," or CPTED, date to the 1970s. These are physical strategies for mitigating risk, often by denying access of undesirables—who are frequently identified via preconceived notions of race, ethnicity, gender, age, socioeconomic status, or appearance—to certain spaces via urban design. See Oscar Newman, *Defensible Space: Crime Prevention through Urban Design* (New York: Macmillan, 1972); C. Ray Jeffery, *Crime Prevention through Environmental Design*, 2nd ed. (Beverly Hills, CA: Sage Publications, 1977).

81. On the desire for, and barriers to, cultural and racial diversity in public spaces, see Setha Low, Dana Taplin, and Suzanne Scheld, *Rethinking Urban Parks: Public Space and Cultural Diversity* (Austin: University of Texas Press, 2005), 60–62, 195–201.

82. Lynn Olanoff, "Bethlehem Businesses Fed Up with Sands Casino Resort Bethlehem Loiterers," *Express-Times*, August 2, 2012; Assad, "Asians at Sands Bethlehem Casino 'Ride Bus to Live' "; Singer, "The Casino as Lifeline."

83. See Shah, *Contagious Divides;* Teresa P. R. Caldeira, *City of Walls: Crime, Segregation, and Citizenship in São Paulo* (Berkeley: University of California Press, 2000), 19–40, 77–79.

84. Olanoff, "Bethlehem Businesses Fed Up."

85. The Touchstone Theater in South Bethlehem began a two-year, community-based project in 2014 to produce two plays and auxiliary events "inspired by the sudden influx of Chinese population in Bethlehem, PA" and "examining the 'East meets West' exchange happening in our own back yard." "Journey from the East," 2015, http://www.touchstone.org/who-we-are/building-community/current-projects/.

86. See also Caldeira, *City of Walls*, 298, 309–335.

87. According to local Sands President Robert DeSalvio in 2013, 90 percent of casino employees lived within a ten-mile radius. Pennsylvania Gaming Control Board, *2014–2015 Gaming Diversity Report*, 14.

88. Assad and Lehman, "Asians at Sands Bethlehem Casino 'Ride Bus to Live.' "

89. *Bethlehem: The Christmas City* (Easton, PA: Lou Reda Productions, 2011), film.

90. See Jefferson Cowie and Nick Salvatore, "The Long Exception: Rethinking the Place of the New Deal in American History," *International Labor and Working-Class History* 74, no. 1 (Fall 2008): 3–32; Jonathan Levy, *Freaks of Fortune: The Emerging World of Capitalism and Risk in America* (Cambridge, MA: Harvard University Press, 2012), 316.

91. Douglas, *Risk and Blame*, 15.

92. See Christine J. Walley, *Exit Zero: Family and Class in Postindustrial Chicago* (Chicago: University of Chicago Press, 2013), 91.

93. Douglas, *Risk and Blame*, 34.

94. Bethlehem Steel Corporation (1904–2000) and Las Vegas Sands Corp. annual reports.

95. Nassim Nicholas Taleb, "Learning to Love Volatility," *Wall Street Journal*, November 16, 2012.

Conclusion

1. Jesse McKinley, "Shock in Southern Tier of New York as Hopes of Gambling and Fracking Both Die," *New York Times*, December 18, 2014; Charles V. Bagli and Marc Santora, "Panel Backs Casino for Southern Tier Area of New York State," *New York Times*, October 14, 2015.

2. Mary Williams Walsh, "Detroit's Casino-Tax Dollars Become Big Issue in Bankruptcy Case," *New York Times*, September 23, 2013; Karen Pierog and Joseph Lichterman, "Analysis: Gambling Revenue at Heart of Detroit's Dilemmas, New and Old," *Reuters*, January 20, 2014.

3. Amy Rosenberg, "Former A. C. Casino Workers Reshuffle Their Lives," *Philadelphia Inquirer*, March 2, 2015.

4. Tribal gaming represents a distinct model, but one that also sustains government services. Tribes that run casinos are sovereign, and revenue from gaming goes to tribal budgets that fund new facilities, social services, cultural programming, and in some cases regular per capita dividend payments to members. Although Tribal casinos are exempt from most taxes, states and municipalities work out revenue-sharing agreements with tribes to capture some of the profits. Jessica Cattelino, *High Stakes: Florida Seminole Gaming and Sovereignty* (Durham, NC: Duke University Press, 2008), 62, 103–105, 134–137, 154–155, 168.

5. Pennsylvania tax revenues reached a peak of $1.44 billion in 2012, then declined slightly through 2015. Pennsylvania Gaming Control Board, "Both Casino Slots and Table Games Revenues Increase in Pennsylvania during the 2014/2015 Fiscal Year," news release, July 16, 2015, http://gamingcontrolboard.pa.gov/?pr=626.

6. Ronen Shamir, "Socially Responsible Private Regulation: World-Culture or World-Capitalism?," *Law and Society Review* 45, no. 2 (2011): 313–336; Marina Welker, *Enacting the Corporation: An American Mining Firm in Post-authoritarian*

Indonesia (Berkeley: University of California Press, 2014), 13–14. See also Geoff Freeman to American Gaming Association SmartBrief email list, "AGA Breaking News—New Community Impact Video," December 9, 2013.

7. Welker, *Enacting the Corporation*, 56.

8. Sharon Ann Holt, "History Keeps Bethlehem Steel from Going off the Rails: Moving a Complex Community Process toward Success," *The Public Historian* 28, no. 2 (Spring 2006): 32.

9. Jeffery E. Singer, "The Casino as Lifeline," *Lens* (blog), *New York Times*, August 23, 2013, http://lens.blogs.nytimes.com/2013/08/23/the-casino-as-lifeline/?hp&_r=0; Matt Assad and Pamela Lehman, "Asians at Sands Bethlehem Casino 'Ride Bus to Live,'" *Morning Call*, March 29, 2014.

10. Yeong-Ung Yang, *Bus-kkun* (2015), video, 4:29, http://m.newsfund.media.daum.net/episode/533; Yang, "Bus-kkun," yeongungyang.com, 2015.

11. Steven Henry Lopez, *Reorganizing the Rust Belt: An Inside Study of the American Labor Movement* (Berkeley: University of California Press, 2004), 52–61.

12. National Labor Relations Board, Final Brief, Case Nos. 12-1240, 12-1311: Sands Bethworks Gaming, LLC v. National Labor Relations Board (D.C. Cir. December 14, 2012), 56, http://apps.nlrb.gov/link/document.aspx/09031d4580ecdb59.

13. Lopez, *Reorganizing the Rust Belt*, 182–183. In 2015 the security guards decided to change their affiliation to the Security Police Fire Professionals of America (SPFPA) precisely because they feared LEEBA did not have the legal budget to sustain the fight. This meant starting the unionization process from scratch. Matt Assad, "Sands Casino Guards Join New Force in Attempt to Unionize," *Morning Call*, October 10, 2015.

14. Lynn Olanoff, "Bethlehem Steel Corp. Blast Furnaces Are Now Center Stage in City's Redevelopment," *Express Times*, June 27, 2011; Olanoff, "Sands Casino Resort Bethlehem Hits Five-Year Mark with Few Complaints," *Express Times*, May 18, 2014.

15. In 2013 Bethlehem won a competitive designation from the state for a City Revitalization and Improvement Zone (CRIZ) that offers tax incentives for developers to invest in certain city projects, including the redevelopment of Martin Tower and the No. 2 Machine Shop. But in the first two years of the CRIZ it had failed to attract significant investment. Many felt it could not compete with the more powerful Neighborhood Improvement Zone (NIZ) designated by the state in 2009 around a new hockey arena in downtown Allentown. Lynn Olanoff, "Bethlehem's CRIZ Not Living Up to 'Shovel-Ready' Billing; Officials Explain Why," *Express Times*, April 20, 2015.

16. Julian Gross, Greg LeRoy, and Madeline Janis-Aparicio, *Community Benefits Agreements: Making Development Projects Accountable* (Washington, DC: Good Jobs First and California Partnership for Working Families, 2005); Colleen Cain, "Negotiating with the Growth Machine: Community Benefits Agreements and Value-Conscious Growth," *Sociological Forum* 29, no. 4 (2014): 937–958; Virginia Parks and Dorian Warren, "The Politics and Practice of Economic Justice: Community Benefits Agreements as Tactic of the New Accountable Development Movement," *Journal of Community Practice* 17 (2009): 88–106.

17. Cain, "Negotiating with the Growth Machine," 942.

18. The MGM "CBA" was negotiated with the county government rather than directly with local citizens. "Community Benefit Agreement between Prince George's County and MGM National Harbor, LLC," June 9, 2014, http://www.princegeorgescountymd.gov/sites/ExecutiveBranch/News/Documents/CBA-between-PGC-MGMNationalHarbor-062172014_2.pdf; "Community Benefits Agreement Relating to the SugarHouse Casino, a Development of HSP Gaming, L.P, a Delaware Limited Partnership," November 20, 2008, http://penntreatyssd.com/wp-content/uploads/2015/01/Executed-CBA-and-SSD-Documents.pdf.

19. "A Look at Current Casino Proposals in Mass.," *Boston Globe*, December 1, 2013, http://www.boston.com/news/local/massachusetts/2013/12/01/look-current-casino-proposals-mass/oKNrOoZhwXPZ1ydyitRH5J/story.html.

20. Blue Tarp reDevelopment, LLC, "RFA-2 Application for a Category 1 or Category 2 Gaming License," December 27, 2013; and Mohegan Sun Massachusetts, LLC, "RFA-2 Application," December 31, 2013, 181, Massachusetts Gaming Commission, http://massgaming.com/licensing/resort-casino-phase-2-applications-2/; https://www.dropbox.com/sh/5whx4tt0izzncz9/AACbZkma7r61YX8cLGOG-nM2a/MGM%20Application.pdf; https://www.dropbox.com/s/o46km3l1avrngcp/Mohegan%20Application.pdf.

21. "Highlights of Allentown-Bethlehem, PA Visit," *City2City Pioneer Valley* (blog), December 6, 2012, http://www.city2cityspringfield.org/blog/highlights-of-allentown-bethlehem-pa-visit/; Matt Camera, "New Bedford City Council Plans Road Trip to Bethlehem Casino," *SouthCoastToday.com* (New Bedford, MA), November 15, 2013, http://www.southcoasttoday.com/apps/pbcs.dll/article?AID=/20131115/NEWS/311150322.

22. "Host Community Agreement by and between City of Springfield, Massachusetts, and Blue Tarp reDevelopment, LLC," May 14, 2013, http://massgaming.com/wp-content/uploads/Springfield-Host-Community-Agreement.pdf.

23. Cain, "Negotiating with the Growth Machine," 943, 949; Gross et al., *Community Benefits Agreements.*

24. Rachel Weber, "Do Better Contracts Make Better Economic Development Incentives?," *Journal of the American Planning Association* 68, no. 1 (Winter 2002): 43–55.

25. Lynn Olanoff, "Bethlehem in Line to Get First Two Latino Council Members in 10 Years," *Express Times*, May 26, 2015.

26. Members of the Bethlehem Heritage Coalition included Lehigh University's South Side Initiative, Historic Bethlehem Museums and Sites, the Steelworkers' Archives, the South Bethlehem Historical Society, the National Museum of Industrial History, and the Delaware and Lehigh National Heritage Corridor/National Canal Museum.

27. See Jefferson Cowie and Nick Salvatore, "The Long Exception: Rethinking the Place of the New Deal in American History," *International Labor and Working-Class History* 74, no. 1 (Fall 2008): 3–32.

28. Federal Writers' Project (PA), *Northampton County Guide* (Bethlehem, PA: Times Publishing Co., 1939), 148.

29. Christine J. Walley, *Exit Zero: Family and Class in Postindustrial Chicago* (Chicago: University of Chicago Press, 2013), 153–158; Guy Standing, *The Precariat: The New Dangerous Class* (London: Bloomsbury Academic, 2011), 19–25, 48–49; Jennifer M. Silva, *Coming Up Short: Working-Class Adulthood in an Age of Uncertainty* (Oxford: Oxford University Press, 2013); Thomas Piketty, *Capital in the Twenty-first Century*, trans. Arthur Goldhammer (Cambridge, MA: Harvard University Press, 2014), 291–303.

Acknowledgments

First and foremost, my thanks go to the many past and present residents of Bethlehem and the Lehigh Valley with whom I spoke, especially those who spent the time to meet for formal interviews. Though many of you are not identified by your real names in the book, I hope you recognize the insights you have offered. Your generosity made this project possible and has documented an important moment of community transition, even if some of my conclusions may be different from your own.

For their research assistance, thanks go to Lanie Graf and Paul Peucker, formerly and currently at the Moravian Archives; Amy Frey, formerly at Historic Bethlehem Museums and Sites; Julia Maserjian at Lehigh University's Digital Scholarship Center; Tracy Samuelson at the City of Bethlehem Bureau of Planning and Zoning; and the members of the South Bethlehem Historical Society and the Steelworkers' Archives. I also thank staff at the Bethlehem Area Public Library and the Northampton Community College Dealer Training School. I am grateful to Tina Bradford, Jenna Lay, Bobbie Thayer, Julie Rohe, and Cara Crumbliss for helping me with housing while I did my research, and to my aunt Joy Shipman for her early local connections and excellent memory.

For reading and listening to pieces of the manuscript along the way and sharing their insights into the Bethlehem community, I thank Howard Gillette, Seth Moglen, and Jill Schennum. Kai Erikson, Mérida Rúa, and Dolores Hayden saw and encouraged this project from its earliest stages. Jean-Christophe Agnew and Kathryn Lofton helped usher it towards its potential. And Kathryn Dudley had faith in the value of this research even when I had moments of doubt myself. Her work and dedication have been models for my own.

I have benefited immensely from the feedback of other colleagues. Many thanks go to the Yale American Studies Program; Alison Kanosky, Rebecca Jacobs, Andy Horowitz, Sierra Bell, and the other members of the Ethnography and Oral History Working Group at Yale; the Newberry Library Urban History Dissertation Group; the Chicago History Museum Urban History Seminars; and numerous conference audiences and commentators. My undergraduate students may not realize how much their fresh insights during our seminars helped me think through this book's revisions.

My editor, Andrew Kinney, and two anonymous readers were integral to shaping this book into its final form with their generous comments and thoughtful critiques. Thank you also to Katrina Vassallo and Scarlett Wilkes at Harvard University Press, and to John Donohue and Elliot Bratton at Westchester Publishing Services. I thank Stephen Fan and the Lyman Allyn Art Museum for including me in their *Sub-Urbanisms* exhibit and symposium in 2014 and for allowing me to reuse portions of my essay from the exhibit catalogue here, in Chapter 6. Certain themes presented in this book grew out of an earlier article in the *Journal of Planning History* in 2013. The John Morton Blum Fellowship and the Mellon Foundation Integrated Humanities Postdoctoral Fellowship at Yale provided support along the way. Ben Meader was a pleasure to work with on my maps.

Finally, I thank my family for their invaluable encouragement. They have lived by example the importance of community engagement. My grandparents Jack and Jule Shipman did not live to see this project take shape, but the trips to visit them in Bethlehem are very much at its origins. My grandparents Bob and Jane Taft supported my education from the beginning and would have been proud to see my ongoing endeavor reach this accomplishment. I thank my parents, Roger and Laurel Taft, for their enthusiasm and unfaltering confidence in the path I've taken from my childhood to today. And I thank my husband, Jason Kang, for his patience and unwavering support for a work that was just beginning when we met. I look forward to reliving, sharing, and anticipating many more pasts, presents, and futures together.

Index